Bourdieu's Theory of Social

Bourdieu's theory of social fields is one of his key contributions to social sciences and humanities. However, it has never been subjected to genuine critical examination. This book fills that gap and offers a clear and wide-ranging introduction to the theory. It includes a critical discussion of its methodology and relevance in different subject areas in the social sciences and humanities.

Part I, 'theoretical investigations', offers a theoretical account of the theory, while also identifying some of its limitations and discussing several strategies to overcome them. Part II, 'Education, culture and organization', presents the theory at work and highlights its advantages and disadvantages. The focus in Part III, devoted to 'the State and public policy', is on the formation and evolution of the State and public policy in different contexts. The chapters show the usefulness of field theory in describing, explaining and understanding the functioning of the State at different stages in its historical trajectory, including its recent redefinition with the advent of the neoliberal age. A final chapter outlines a postcolonial use of the theory of fields.

Prior to his death in 2015, **Mathieu Hilgers** was Associate Professor at Université Libre de Bruxelles (Anthropology), Associate Member at Harvard University (African Studies) and Visiting Fellow at Goldsmiths, University of London (Sociology). His research focused on the relationship between urbanization, capitalism and state building and discusses theory on globalization, social class and neoliberalism. He published more than 45 papers in scientific journals and books some of which specifically discuss the work of Bourdieu. His most recent book is *Une Ethnographie à l'échelle de la ville* (Paris, Karthala, 2009).

Eric Mangez is Professor of Sociology at the University of Louvain (UCL), Belgium, where he teaches sociological theory, research method and political sociology. He has published several papers and books that exploit Bourdieu's field theory. He is author of *Réformer les contenus d'enseignement. Une sociologie du curriculum* (Paris, PUF, 2008), and co-editor of the *World Yearbook of Education 2014*.

Routledge Advances in Sociology

Bourdieu's Theory of Social Fields

Concepts and applications

Edited by
Mathieu Hilgers and Eric Mangez

LONDON AND NEW YORK

First edition published 2015
by Routledge
2 Park Square, Milton Park, Abingdon, Oxfordshire OX14 4RN

and by Routledge
711 Third Avenue, New York, NY 10017

First issued in paperback 2014

Routledge is an imprint of the Taylor and Francis Group, an informa business

British Library Cataloguing in Publication Data
A catalogue record for this book is available from the British Library

Library of Congress Cataloging in Publication Data
Bourdieu's theory of social fields : concepts and applications / edited by
Mathieu Hilgers and Eric Mangez.
     pages cm. – (Routledge advances in sociology)
     1. Bourdieu, Pierre, 1930-2002. 2. Sociology–France–History. 3.
Sociology–Methodology. I. Hilgers, Mathieu, 1979- II. Mangez, Eric.
   HM477.F8B68 2014
   301.0944–dc23
                  2014000798

ISBN 978-1-138-77765-1 (hbk)
ISBN 978-1-138-92104-7 (pbk)
ISBN 978-1-315-77249-3 (ebk)

Typeset in Times New Roman
by Taylor & Francis Books

Contents

List of illustrations

Figures

Boxes

List of contributors

Géraldine André is a research fellow at the National Funds for Scientific Research at the University of Liège. She has published articles in international journals and a monograph on educational guidance, school choices and social inheritance. Her most recent book is *L'Orientation scolaire* (Presses Universitaire de France, 2012).

Vincent Dubois is Professor at the University of Strasbourg, France, member of the Institute for Political Studies and of the SAGE research unit (UMR CNRS 7363). His research fields include cultural sociology and policy, language policy, poverty and welfare and more generally sociological approach to public policy. In addition to more than 70 scholarly articles, he has published eight books, including *The Bureaucrat and the Poor* (Ashgate, 2010), *The Sociology of Wind Bands* (Ashgate, 2013, with Méon and Pierru), *Culture as a Vocation* (forthcoming, Routledge).

Julien Duval is a research fellow at the CNRS. He is a member of the CREST. Field theory is central to his work. He is the author of two important books published in Bourdieu's collection, *Critique de la raison journalistique. Les transformations de la presse économique en France* (Paris, Le Seuil, 'Liber', 2004), and *Le Mythe du 'trou de la Sécu'* (Paris, Raisons d'agir, 2007).

Forest Gregg is a graduate student at the University of Chicago.

Prior to his death in 2015, **Mathieu Hilgers** was Associate Professor at Université Libre de Bruxelles (Anthropology), Associate Member at Harvard University (African Studies) and Visiting Fellow at Goldsmiths, University of London (Sociology). His research focused on the relationship between urbanization, capitalism and state building and discusses theory on globalization, social class and neoliberalism. He published more than 45 papers in scientific journals and books some of which specifically discuss the work of Bourdieu. His most recent book is *Une Ethnographie à l'échelle de la ville* (Paris, Karthala, 2009).

Bernard Lahire is full Professor of Sociology at the Ecole Normale Supérieure de Lyon. Bernard Lahire is well known for his critical development of

Bourdieu's sociology. He has published several papers and books to develop a dispositionalist and contextualist approach. His empirical works focuse on education, culture, literature and art. He has published 19 other books, the most recent of which in English was The Plural Actor (Cambridge, Polity Press, 2011). He was awarded the CNRS silver medal 2012 for the human and social sciences.

Georges Liénard is Emeritus Professor of Sociology at the University of Louvain. He is currently Visiting Professor and Associate Researcher at the CIRTES-UCL. His expertise includes sociology of education, culture, work and inequalities. He was active in Bourdieu's research group while writing his own PhD, published together with Emile Servais in 1978 and entitled *Capital culturel et inégalités sociales: morales de classes et destinées sociale.*

Eric Mangez is Professor of Sociology at the University of Louvain (UCL), Belgium, where he teaches sociological theory, research method and political sociology. He has published several papers and books that exploit Bourdieu's field theory. He is author of *Réformer les contenus d'enseignement. Une sociologie du curriculum* (Paris, PUF, 2008), and co-editor of the *World Yearbook of Education 2014.*

John Levi Martin received a PhD in Sociology from the University of California at Berkeley, where he was recently a Professor, after being a Professor at the University of Wisconsin at Madison and an Assistant Professor at Rutgers – The State University of New Jersey at New Brunswick. He is now a Professor at the University of Chicago, where he enjoys teaching classical theory. He has published several well-known articles dedicated to field theory and won the theory section award from the American Sociological Association in 2010 and in 2012 for his two lastest books, *Social Structures* (Princeton University Press, 2009), and *The Explanation of Social Action* (Oxford University Press, 2011).

Thomas Medvetz is Assistant Professer at UC San Diego. His research on think tanks, the American conservative movement and the public role of intellectuals has appeared in journals such as *Actes de Recherche en Sciences Sociales*, the *Annual Review of Sociology, Politics & Society*, and *Qualitative Sociology*. His first book, *Think Tanks in America* was published by University of Chicago Press in 2012.

Louis Pinto is Emeritus Director of Research at the CNRS. He worked under the direction of Bourdieu and has published numerous important studies on Bourdieu and ten books, many of which use field theory to grasp and analyse their object, notably *La Vocation et le métier de philosophe. Pour une sociologie de la philosophie dans la France contemporaine* (Paris, Seuil, 2007), and *La Théorie souveraine. Les philosophes français et la sociologie au 20ème siècle* (Paris, éd. du Cerf, collection Passages, 2009).

Gisele Sapiro is one of Bourdieu's former students and is the Director of the Centre de sociologie européenne founded by Bourdieu. She is Director of Research at the CNRS, and director of study at the École des Hautes Études en Sciences Sociales (EHESS). She has published more than 80 articles in international journals, and six books. She has notably edited a book devoted to the work of Pierre Bourdieu with Louis Pinto. Her most recent book is *La Responsabilité de l'écrivain. Littérature, droit et morale en France, XIXe–XXIe siècles* (Paris, Seuil, 2011).

Loïc Wacquant is Professor of Sociology at the University of California, Berkeley, and Researcher at the Centre européen de sociologie et de science politique, Paris. His research spans urban relegation, ethnoracial domination, the penal state, incarnation, and social theory and the politics of reason. His books have been translated in some 20 languages and include the trilogy *Urban Outcasts: A Comparative Sociology of Advanced Marginality* (2008), *Punishing the Poor: The Neoliberal Government of Social Insecurity* (2009), and *Deadly Symbiosis: Race and the Rise of the Penal State* (2014). He has recently completed the new expanded edition of his book with Pierre Bourdieu, *An Invitation to Reflexive Sociology* (2014). For more information, see loicwacquant.net

Acknowledgements

Some of the chapters in this volume were first presented at the workshop 'Utiliser la théorie des champs pour comprendre le monde social – Journée d'étude autour du travail de Pierre Bourdieu', organized by Mathieu Hilgers in March 2009, at UCLouvain (Belgium) with the support of the Fonds de la Recherche Scientifique (FNRS, Fund for Scientific Research) and the Department of Sociology and Anthropology. A number of people who are not represented as authors nonetheless contributed to the conference in a significant ways. They include especially Pierre-Joseph Laurent and Luc van Campenhoudt. The book has been published with the support of the FNRS and the Institute for the Analysis of Change in Contemporary and Historical Societies (Iacchos) at UCLouvain. The editors of the book would like to thank these institutions for their support, and Richard Nice for his translation into English of some chapters originally written in French, Loic Wacquant for his suggestions and all the contributors for their participation.

Introduction to Pierre Bourdieu's theory of social fields

Mathieu Hilgers and Eric Mangez

> Thinking in terms of fields requires a conversion of one's entire usual vision of the social world, a vision interested only in those things which are visible … In fact, just as the Newtonian theory of gravitation could be developed only by breaking away from Cartesian realism, which refused to recognize any mode of physical action other than impact, direct contact, in the same way, the notion of the field presupposes that one break away from the realist representation which leads one to reduce the effect of the milieu to the effect of the direct action that takes place in any interaction. It is the structure of the relations constitutive of the space of the field which determines the forms that can be assumed by the visible relations of interaction and the very content of the experience that agents may have of them.
>
> (Bourdieu, 1982: 41; Bourdieu 1990c: 192)

This work aims to introduce the reader to Pierre Bourdieu's theory of fields, to evaluate it critically and, through case studies, to test its implementation in the analysis of new objects. While the use of Bourdieu's concept of the habitus has given rise to countless discussions, the literature strangely remains more silent on the theory of fields, although it lies at the heart of his work. A series published by Éditions du Seuil, started and initially edited by Bourdieu, includes a number of monographs that apply the theory of fields;[1] some journals have devoted whole issues to explicitly mobilizing the theory in order to study specific areas, and a growing number of works make use of it. However, critical discussions that seek to give an account of this theory both in general terms and in particular areas remain rare. The aim of this work is to fill that gap. One of the hypotheses put forward in this book is that the theory of fields constitutes an adequate tool for explaining and understanding the social world but that its use must be rigorously circumscribed and correspond to certain methodological principles.

The book is in three parts. The first is made up of contributions that present, analyse and discuss the theoretical and epistemological foundations of Bourdieu's theory of fields. The second consists of research papers that critically mobilize this theory to study education, journalism, cinema, literature and culture. The third is devoted to the analysis of the state, power and the bureaucratic field. Some reflections are developed in the afterword to put theory of social fields at work in the postcolonial age.

To make this book easier to read for those who are less familiar with Bourdieu's theory, this Introduction offers a presentation of the theory and develops some points of discussion with regard to it. To do so, we start by reconstituting the epistemological background from which it arises in order to emphasize its primary specificity: *social reality is conceived as fundamentally relational* – it is therefore the relationships among the elements, and not the elements themselves, that must be at the heart of the analysis. Once these epistemological bases have been established, we present the theory of fields, particularly emphasizing the process of the emergence and autonomization of fields and then discussing the place it gives to reproduction and social change. Finally we present a method for implementing this theory, point to some problems that arise when one tries to use it, and briefly present the various chapters.

The epistemological basis of field theory[2]

Bourdieu developed the main arguments of his theory of fields at a very early stage. Three important articles set out the first principles: 'Champ intellectuel et projet créateur' (1966), 'Genèse et structure du champ religieux' (1971a) and 'Une interprétation de la théorie de la religion selon Max Weber' (1971b). In these works, devoted to distinct objects, Bourdieu shows how the differentiation of the domains of human activity that accompanies the process of modernization of societies leads to the creation of social spaces with a specific legitimacy and functioning.

When Bourdieu was developing his theory, the concept of the field was already in common use in other disciplines. Physics, mathematics and psychology had devised field theories with various degrees of systematicity. While the theory of fields developed in sociology by Bourdieu was constructed in a relatively autonomous fashion, it nonetheless shares a common epistemology with them.[3] It seems useful to outline briefly this common epistemological background.

There is an abundant literature on the origin of the concept of the field, the various field theories in physics and the associated philosophy of nature (see for example Hesse 1961). In classical theories of physics, space and time were conceived as the forms within which the world – of which matter is the substance – is actualized. Through all its changes in appearance, matter remained fundamentally unaltered: 'Matter was imagined to be a substance involved in every change, and it was thought that every piece of matter could be measured as a quantity, and that its characteristic expression as a substance was the Law of Conservation of Matter which asserts that matter remains constant in amount throughout every change' (Weyl 1920: 1). Here, matter is the principle of change and form is the principle of determination that permits change. According to Cassirer, modern field theory displaced the old substance theory: 'The field itself can no longer be understood as a merely additive whole, as an aggregate of parts. The field is not a thing-concept but a relation-concept; it is not composed of pieces but is a system, a totality of lines of force' (Cassirer 2000: 92). In mathematics, too, 'the relational structure as such, not the absolute property of the elements, constitutes the real object of mathematical investigation' (Cassirer 1923: 93). The true 'elements' of mathematical calculation are, in this sense, not so much magnitudes as relationships. For Cassirer, it is precisely this shift from a substantialist mode of thought to relational thinking that characterizes modern science. Only the set of relationships on which a system is based, and which is to be found in each particular configuration, truly gives access to the object. From this standpoint, it is not so much the properties of an object or a configuration as the network of (cor)relations that is woven between them and other neighbouring formations that is the focus of analysis. Thus field theory rejects an absolute space-time, which, by definition, would have to refer to an individual object, in favour of a relational space-time that no longer designates an individual but a system of relations (cf. Ghins 1990: 16–28).

Jean-Claude Passeron points out that Bourdieu and he took over the concept of the field from *Gestalt* theory, in particular the work of Kurt Lewin (Passeron 2003: 42–43). The concept of the psychological field developed by Lewin (1935) shares only the background of a relational epistemology with the concept of the 'physical field'. Knowing the individual from 'observation of his behaviour, one can deduce the properties of the field around him, and, conversely, knowing the properties of the field around the individual, one can deduce his properties from observation of his behaviour' (Faucheux 1959: 7). Thus, 'a certain distribution of forces determines the behaviour of an individual possessing particular properties' (Faucheux 1959: 6). The structure of the relations between the individual and the environment is central – the former is a function of the latter and vice versa. The behaviour thus depends on the configuration of the psychological field at a given moment.

One of Lewin's objectives is to construct a psychology that breaks away from Aristotelian substantialism, in which 'the environment plays a part only in so far as it may give rise to "disturbances", forced modifications of the processes which follow from the nature of the object concerned' (Lewin 1935: 29). The vectors that define the movements of an object are completely determined by the object itself; they do not depend on the object's relation to the environment and they inherently belong to the object, regardless of its setting, at all times. By contrast, in modern science, the dynamics of a phenomenon are no longer analysed as immanent to the object but as consubstantial with the relational space in which it takes place. The vectors that determine the dynamics of a phenomenon can therefore themselves only be described in terms of 'concrete totalities' encompassing both the object and the situation.

Gestalt therapists still work with a methodology inspired by field theory. Malcolm Parlett (1991) sets out five principles at the heart of field theory. The principle of 'organization', derived from Lewin, asserts that the meaning of an individual fact depends on the total situation and more particularly on its position in the 'field'. The principle of 'contemporaneity' postulates that a situation 'at a given time' includes 'the past-as-remembered-now' and 'the future-as anticipated-now', and that these are part of the 'field' in the present. The principle of 'singularity' assumes that 'circumstances are never quite the same, and each of several persons ... has a different perspective'. The principle of 'changing process' refers to the fact that 'experience is always provisional rather than permanent: nothing is fixed and static in an absolute way'. The field is constructed and reconstructed moment by moment. Finally, the principle of 'possible relevance' asserts that no part of the total field can be excluded in advance as inherently irrelevant; everything in the 'field' is part of the total organization and is potentially meaningful.

What can we draw from this for our purpose? First, according to Lewin, field theory is here primarily a method rather than a theory: '[It] can hardly be called correct or incorrect in the same way as a theory in the usual sense of the term. Field theory is probably best characterized as a method: namely, a method of analysing causal relations and of building scientific constructs' (Lewin 1943: 45). Next, field theory, as described above, when used methodologically, implies, first, that 'the dynamics of the processes is always to be derived from the relations of the concrete individual to the concrete situation' (Lewin 1935: 41); second, that the structural properties of the totality of a dynamics, in the social field as in the physical field, are different from the structural properties of the parts of the dynamics, and that these structural properties are characterized by the relations among the parts rather than by the parts themselves (Lewin 1949: 280–81);[4] and consequently, third, that a 'social event' depends on the whole social field rather than some selected elements. It is indeed a property of fields that they are 'systems of relations independent of the populations defined by those relations' (Bourdieu and Wacquant 1992: 82). Finally, with regard to the physical field, it can be said that to speak of a field 'is to give primacy to this system of objective relations over the particles themselves' (Bourdieu and Wacquant 1992: 82). Social agents are of course not particles, mechanically pushed and pulled by external forces: 'They are, rather, bearers of capitals and, depending on their trajectory and on the position they occupy in the field by virtue of their endowment (volume and structure) in capital, they have a propensity to orient themselves actively either towards the conservation of the distribution of capital or towards the subversion of that distribution' (Bourdieu and Wacquant 1992: 108–9).

There is no need to pursue further the comparison of the different field theories; moreover, this work has already been done in some research (Martin 2003) and is taken further in Martin and Gregg's contribution to this book (Chapter 1). Field theory in sociology naturally has a number of features specific to the discipline (the aim of superseding dualisms, the importance of the history of the field, etc.), but what characterizes field theories, regardless of the discipline, and therefore constitutes their common epistemological background, is that they reject the existence of an absolute (social or physical) space and consequently of individual objects or agents existing independently of a set of relations. Space, whether social or physical, is relational. The field implies the existence of an indivisible dynamics between a totality and the elements that constitute it (Passeron 2003: 41). It does not designate an entity but a system of relations. The effectiveness of the principles underlying the theoretical method of analysis in terms of field therefore stems from the fact that they express the general characteristics of the mechanisms of interdependence (Lewin 1949: 284). The field is the analytical space defined by the interdependence of the entities that compose a structure of positions among which there are power relations.

From field theory to the theory of social fields

The epistemological basis of field theory is transversal to Bourdieu's work: the social world is a relational space. However, in Bourdieu's work the notion of the field is not only meant to imply a relational form of epistemology, but also serves to designate distinct sub-spaces within the global space. There are various fields within the social world, and each field is a relational space of its own, dedicated to a specific type of activity. In this sense, as Lahire has pointed out, Bourdieu's theory of fields sets itself in a long line of reflection on 'the historical differentiation of social activities or functions and the social division of labour' (Lahire 1999: 26; see also his contribution to this volume, Chapter 2). The theory of fields explicitly refers to Durkheim as regards the historical constitution and autonomization of fields, to Marx for the interpretation of the effects of this autonomization, and to Weber for the construction of the autonomy of a field and its internal struggles.

In the course of this process, various domains, occupations and groups are led to codify their functioning. More precisely, for Bourdieu a field is a relatively autonomous domain of activity that responds to rules of functioning and institutions that are specific to it and which define the relations among the agents. Each field has its specific rules: the political field has to maintain a close relationship with the individuals external to the field, because political agents derive their legitimacy from the representation of the citizens (Bourdieu 2000b); the scientific field is marked by a competition among agents so specialized that only they are able to judge the scientific value of the works of their competitors (Bourdieu 1976); the economic field is distinguished by the fact that 'within it the sanctions are especially brutal and behaviours can overtly be directed towards the maximization of individual material profit' (Bourdieu 1997d: 57), and so on. However, beneath the substantial variations that distinguish each of the fields and the specific rules of their functioning, it is possible to bring to light the invariants that shape and structure them.

Indeed, Bourdieu went on to apply, develop and refine his theory, bringing it to bear on a wide range of domains that seemingly had nothing in common except the fact of being specialized: religion (Bourdieu 1971a, 1971c; Bourdieu and de Saint Martin 1982); education (Bourdieu and de Saint Martin 1987a, 1987b; Bourdieu 1989); science (Bourdieu 1975a, 1976, 1978, 1984a,

1995, 1997a, 2001b); symbolic goods (Bourdieu 1971c, 1972a, 1977a); culture (Bourdieu 1979a, 1991a, 1992); the economy (Bourdieu 1990a, 1997d, 2000a); haute couture (Bourdieu 1975b, with Delsaut); the state (Bourdieu 1989, 1990a, 1994, 1997c); law (Bourdieu 1986); politics (Bourdieu 1981, 1990a, 1996b, 2000c); journalism (Bourdieu 1996e); power (Bourdieu 1990a, 1994), etc. As he criss-crossed between studies devoted to particular domains and more general formulations, his theory of fields was constantly refined to become a fruitful and effective sociological theory. To present the main lines of this theory, this second section will now focus on: 1 the genesis and impact of field autonomy; 2 the field of power and its relations to specific fields; 3 homologies of position between fields; and 4 the social field and the habitus.

The genesis and impact of field autonomy

What happens when a domain of activity wins its (relative) autonomy from social, political and economic constraints? The autonomization of spheres of activities, functions and groups generates elites responsible for the legitimate interpretation of practices and representations in specific areas of activity. These elites rationalize an implicit system of schemes of action, systematizing it in the form of explicit norms. This autonomization is marked by the emergence of a type of capital (for example, in the religious field it is religious capital, i.e. a specific form of accumulated symbolic capital), whose main holders constitute the elites of the field. All specific capital in a field, whether religious, artistic, political or scientific, is in reality a capital of recognition. As soon as the rules that define the legitimate activity in a field are modified, so too is the distribution of recognition. The struggle in a field is thus a struggle to impose a definition of legitimate recognition, in which victory leads to more or less monopolistic control of the definition of the forms of legitimacy prevailing in the field. The history of the field is the history of the internal and external struggles that animate it, the history of the distribution of the specific capital and the variation of this capital. The field is temporalized along with them.

   The progressive autonomy of a domain of activity transforms the relationships among the individuals who are linked to the activity in question. Increasingly, their practices and productions are evaluated according to criteria internal to the domain of activity. The creation of authorities and mechanisms for selection and consecration that are partly immune to external influences is an indicator of this autonomy. The growing autonomy of the intellectual field leads to the emergence of autonomous intellectuals, that of the artistic field leads to the emergence of the figure of the artist, etc. The example of the religious field, the focus of Bourdieu's first articles, is illustrative. According to him the expansion of monotheism is linked to the emergence of a tightly organized body of priests, whose autonomy facilitated the systematization and moralization of beliefs. This autonomy is seen in the emergence and legitimation of a religious esotericism, autarkic references, knowledge and practices only accessible to those who occupy certain positions in the religious field. Through its knowledge and practices, a corps of specialists is consolidated and proceeds to monopolize a rare, socially recognized knowledge of which it is the exclusive holder. It thereby becomes the repository of 'the specific competence necessary for the production or reproduction of a deliberately organized corpus of knowledge', whose authority is reinforced by 'the objective dispossession of those who are excluded from it', who are thereby constituted as the profane laity (Bourdieu 1971a: 304; Bourdieu 1991b: 9).

In becoming more autonomous, the functioning of a field also increases the closure effects. The greater its autonomy, the more the field is produced by and produces agents who master and possess an area of specific competence. The more it functions in accordance with the interests inherent in the type of activity that characterizes it, 'the greater the separation from the laity' (Bourdieu 2000c: 58) and the more specific become the capital, the competences and the 'sense of the game'. This closure is an index of the autonomy of the field. It is for the politician to speak of politics, for writers to speak of literature, and so on. As the field closes in on itself, the practical mastery of the specific heritage of its history, objectified and celebrated in past works by the guardians of legitimate knowledge, is also autonomized and increasingly constitutes a minimum entry tariff that every new entrant must pay. The autonomization of a domain of activity generates the *doxa*, an *illusio* that forms the prereflexive belief of the agents of the field, i.e. a set of presuppositions that implies adherence to a domain of activity and implicitly defines the conditions of membership.

The more autonomous a field, the more it produces an autonomous and specific language, representations and practices, and the more the perception of realities is subject to the logic specific to the field. The autonomization of the criteria (aesthetic, religious, scientific, etc.) that govern production, and the importance of these criteria in building a structure of relations specific to a domain of activity, leads the agents who are active within it to perceive the real on the basis of the principles shared in this field. In other words, as autonomy increases, the refraction effect grows and the agents tend to divert, translate and interpret external phenomena in terms of the stakes, logics and beliefs specific to the field and the positions they occupy within it. The agents of the field then tend to perceive the world – inside and outside the field – through a prism constructed within the field.[5]

The study of the genesis of fields provides an articulated set of theoretical propositions that make it possible to identify the features marking the emergence of a new domain of activity, notably, the appearance of a specialized elite, the rationalization and constitution of specific knowledge (a specific language), the creation of authorities providing recognition and consecration, the setting of a tariff for entry into the field, transformation of the schemes of perception, growing refraction.

8 *Mathieu Hilgers and Eric Mangez*

The field of power and its relation to specific fields

The autonomy of fields is relative. Each field is subject to two opposing principles of hierarchization – 'an external or heteronomous principle of hierarchization that applies to the field the hierarchy prevailing in the field of power, and an internal or autonomous principle that hierarchizes in accordance with the values specific to the field' (Mounier 2001: 71). The 'field of power' is thus a key concept for understanding the structure of specific fields. In contrast to other fields, whose content can in a sense be grasped intuitively, the field of power has a more abstract character. It is not linked to a specific activity; it is 'the space of relations of force between agents or between institutions having in common the possession of the capital necessary to occupy dominant positions in the different fields' (Bourdieu 1992: 300; Bourdieu 1996a: 215). Within the field of power two fractions compete with one another: an economic fraction and a cultural fraction. The economic fraction (usually situated at the top right-hand side of Bourdieu's schematization of the social structure) is the dominant fraction of the dominant class, while the cultural fraction (situated at the top left-hand side of the schema) is the dominated fraction of the dominant class (see Figure I.1). The field of power is thus structured by the opposition between cultural capital (dominated) and economic capital (dominating).

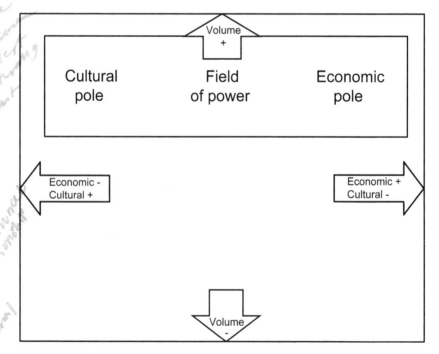

Figure I.1 The field of power
Source: Adapted from Bourdieu 1992:178

Every specific field is likely to be affected by the field of power, generating within its own structure two opposing poles that correspond structurally, albeit indirectly and in a more or less refracted and unrecognizable manner, to the tensions between the competing poles of the field of power (Figure I.2, adapted from Bourdieu 1992: 178; see also Bourdieu 1983: 329). The literary or artistic field, for example, will generate 'an autonomous pole (e.g. 'art for art's sake') and a heteronomous pole 'favourable to those who dominate the field economically and politically (e.g. "bourgeois art")' (Bourdieu 1983: 321).' Hence in the literary field, new avant-gardist products are opposed to mass products, just as the pole of 'high culture' is opposed to another pole producing commercial cultural goods in the artistic field. Following the same logic, in the field of science, fundamental research (knowledge produced for the sake of knowledge) is opposed to more applied or oriented forms of knowledge production (Bourdieu 1995). In education, one can also note an opposition between those who conceive education as an autonomous domain primarily concerned with cultural matters, and those who emphasize education in relation to external concerns such as economic prosperity and competitiveness (see André and Hilgers in this volume, Chapter 4; see also Mangez and Hilgers 2012; Mangez 2008). All such oppositions are the refracted and more or less misrecognizable manifestations of the tensions within the field of power.

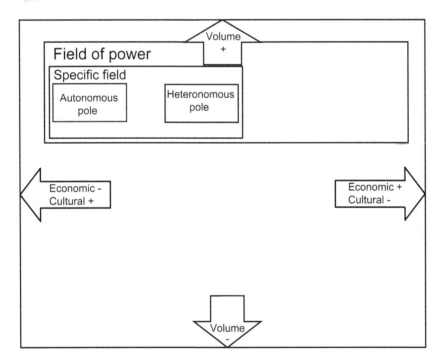

Figure I.2 The field of power and its relation to specific fields
Source: Adapted from Bourdieu 1983: 329; and Bourdieu 1992: 178

Each specific field is therefore a social space structured – vertically – by a criterion of volume of resources (dominated/dominant) and – horizontally – by a criterion of structure of resources (an autonomous pole, where specific or 'spiritual' capital predominates/a heteronomous pole, where 'temporal' capital predominates). In addition, each field is structured, in accordance with an internal principle of hierarchization, by the history of its internal struggles and it is therefore also marked by other specific dividing lines.

The more autonomous a field, the less sensitive it is to the external principle of hierarchy, and vice versa. This is particularly clear when one considers, for example, the shift from a totalitarian system towards democracy with regard to the transformation of the hierarchies that shape legitimacy in science and art, as Sapiro puts it in this volume (Chapter 5), or when one studies the relations between economic journalism and the market (see Duval in this volume, Chapter 6). Transformations of the equilibria in the domains of power thus have more or less direct effects on the internal dynamics of autonomous domains of activity. For example, in the overall structure of the capital effective in the field of power, the growth in the relative value of economic capital that characterizes our neoliberal societies tends to reduce the autonomy of the fields (Mangez and Hilgers 2012). The growing domination of the economic field over the educational field or the literary field is transforming the role, place and power of the agents active in these fields by consolidating the relative value of economic capital and weakening that of cultural capital (Mangez 2008). The erosion of the relative autonomy of the literary field vis-à-vis the economic field has the effect of consolidating the position of the values that are most guaranteed in commercial terms ('bestsellers') at the expense of subversive agents (Bourdieu 1992; Sapiro 2003); and this, quite logically, affects their subversive strategies.

Positions and position-takings

A field is a structure of relative positions within which the actors and groups think, act and take positions. These relative positions are defined by the volume and structure of their capital. In their position-takings, persons and groups – sometimes unconsciously – pursue interests linked to their relative positions in the field, which may consist in preserving or transforming the position they occupy and the resources associated with it. The position of an actor or a group depends not only on the way in which it manages to renew itself but also on the ways in which all the other actors in the field evolve or seek to evolve (Vandenberghe 1999).

According to Bourdieu, 'If one takes seriously both the Durkheimian hypothesis of the social origin of schemes of thought, perception, appreciation and action and the fact of class divisions, one is necessarily driven to the hypothesis that a correspondence exists between social structures (strictly speaking, power structures) and mental structures' (Bourdieu 1971a: 300; Bourdieu 1991b: 5). There is a correspondence[6] between the objective divisions of the social world, social structures and the mental structures that agents mobilize in order to act in a world structured in this way (Bourdieu 1989: 7). Hence one can distinguish the symbolic order from the social order of the field. Symbolic structures order the field (and the social world) by classifying and categorizing it at the level of meaning: how do people think, how do they order the world cognitively within the field, what are their position-takings? Social structures, on the other hand, order the world by classifying and categorizing it according to the objective resources, positions and trajectories of individuals and groups.

Examining the structures of positions will often lead one to identify actors relatively well established in the field, who therefore have a certain interest in the maintenance of the established order or the modification of this order within limits that enable them to strengthen their domination. Conversely, newcomers will tend to implement strategies aimed at subverting the symbolic order; otherwise they will tend to undergo a form of symbolic violence that leads them to recognize the legitimacy of a symbolic order that is unfavourable to them. The chances that established actors will succeed in preserving the order are, however, greater than the probability of subversion. The more legitimate an agent, the more her peers consume her products, and the more they consume her products, the more legitimate she becomes. The accumulation of this symbolic capital makes it possible to secure a more or less complete monopoly over the definition of the forms of legitimacy prevailing in the field. The stabilization of a hegemonic version of legitimacy helps to fix the distribution of positions in the space of relations that constitutes a field. The field is thus subject to a generalized Matthew effect[7] – which is why the theory of social fields may appear a theory of reproduction.

It would, however, be reductive and mistaken to see in the theory of fields only a theory of reproduction. In reality, the theory of fields makes it possible to understand and explain the phenomena of reproduction while also giving a central place to change and movement within a field (Boyer 2003). In fact, fields are marked by struggles that constantly modify their internal power balances. The question of change within fields is therefore crucial.[8]

Bourdieu's theory comprises, for example, a theory of cultural change (Gartman 2002)[9] which offers important insights for understanding the dynamics of fields. It explains how innovative cultural goods are usually first produced by an avant-garde situated at the lower level (bottom) of the autonomous pole (position A in Figure I.3) of their field (whether the literary field, the scientific field, the field of art, or any other 'cultural' field). They attempt to produce 'pure' products (art for art's sake, knowledge for the sake of knowledge), they seek recognition by their peers and try to distinguish themselves from the more established senior figures of their field who are situated higher up (consecrated avant-garde) at the autonomous pole of the field (position B). As the avant-garde gain access to symbolic recognition, they and their products move up (from A to B, i.e. consecration) in the direction of the more consecrated avant-garde. From there on, successful producers are then eventually likely to 'sell out' and be attracted by the more heteronomous pole of the field. Hence they move laterally (from B to C: selling out) towards heteronomous interests. Such a move is all the more likely as the economic elite always seeks new cultural products to secure and renew its distinction from the masses. Products that are used and consumed by the dominant economic interests are, however, eventually likely to become mass products because the masses tend to imitate them (from C to D: massification).

It is important to underline that the products' characteristics and their utilization will vary as they move along this inverted U-curve (from A to B, from B to C, from C to D). As cultural goods move from one social space to another, they are reconstituted or reinterpreted to suit the requirements and the 'logic' of that space: translation from one social space to another is necessarily accompanied by a translation of meaning, form and shape. The products produced on the left-hand side (pole A or B), which are originally meant to be consumed by the producers' peers (restricted audience), are constructed according to the internal rules of the field, and that gives them specific characteristics. Once attracted towards the right-hand side (pole C), their meaning, purpose and conditions of fabrication evolve. Indeed, they are then meant to support external interests: hence their shape and form is defined accordingly (rather than according to the internal requirements of the field).

This theory of cultural change does not exhaust the range of possible dynamics. Every field is subject to contingency and is, moreover, capable of functioning in accordance with logics that are specific to it. Nonetheless, all fields are structured and historicized. Because they each have a 'structural history' (Bourdieu 1989: 265–328; Bourdieu 1996c: 188–229), they are subject to homologous transformative logics, seen particularly in the positions taken by the agents of the field. As has been seen by following the path of the inverted U-curve, these position-takings vary according to the agents' positions within the fields.

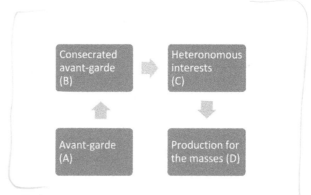

Figure I.3 Bourdieu's theory of cultural change and the 'inverted U-curve'
Source: Inspired by Gartman 2002: 259

Homologies of position

The relations among fields and those between fields and the overall social space constitute another key to the analysis of change. This is why the relations among fields, and the specific dynamics they imply, merit specific, detailed analyses. One of the key aspects of this question is the structural homology among fields. Fields are spaces of oppositions and they are related through the homology of their structures (Bourdieu 1971a: 319; Bourdieu 1991b: 22). More precisely, Bourdieu hypothesizes that there are structural affinities between individuals occupying homologous positions in different fields or in the social structure. Hence actors situated in a given position within a given field are likely to be sympathetic to – and 'close to' – actors who occupy a homologous position in another field or in the general social structure: when acting in different specific fields, those who occupy a homologous position (for example, a dominant position), will tend to be related to one another by an invisible homology of position. This stems from the fact that 'the homology of positions (...) encourage[s] a *practical recognition* of interests' (Bourdieu 1988b: 110; Bourdieu 1991d: 97), the actors being linked to one another through 'the invariant, or indeed universal, content of the relationship between the dominant and the dominated' (Bourdieu 1984c: 10; Bourdieu 1985: 737).

A distinction must be made between homologies of position among dominant positions and homologies of position among dominated positions. By definition, the former *mainly* link economically dominant actors who as such have an interest in the consolidation of the established order. Thus, for example, the annual meetings of the World Economic Forum in Davos bring together economic and political actors who occupy dominant positions in a range of fields and sub-fields. However, the fact that dominant actors, united by a homology of position, have an interest in maintaining and consolidating established order, and therefore in reproducing the space of relative positions, does not necessarily mean that they are opposed to change. In reality, as Bourdieu and Boltanski observed as early as 1976, one of the means used by the dominant actors to consolidate and reproduce their position consists in developing a discourse that presents change as an imperative that is incumbent upon all: we must change our ways, be ready to make sacrifices to meet the challenges that face us, the demands of competitiveness, the new economic challengers, etc. (Bourdieu and Boltanski 1976).

The change in question is 'heteronomous': it is presented as a necessity imposed 'from outside'. It therefore differs radically from the theory of cultural change mentioned earlier, which made autonomy the key to and source of change in the field. The discourse on the necessity of change propagated by the economically dominant actors functions in reality as a means of weakening the relative autonomy of the specific fields. Heteronomizing the specific fields amounts to placing them at the service of external economic (and political) ends. It can be seen at the present time that the situation of economic and financial crisis is reinforcing even more the relative power of the dominant economic actors, allies in the field of power, and tends to subordinate cultural capital (and therefore the activity of the specific fields) to 'external' criteria. The situation is deleterious to the autonomy of the specific fields. All these fields are put under pressure, they are subjected to external evaluations and 'accountability', required to furnish indicators proving their utility and efficiency. Heteronomous criteria play an increasing role in the specific fields and help to normalize 'new' practices: marketing has entered the political field, entrepreneurialism into the social field, performance measurement into the field of education, etc. Change is omnipresent but it is change oriented towards external control of the specific fields and conservation of the established order.

Faced with this dominant discourse, the position taken by intellectuals, who are objectively situated in an ambivalent position, dominant in the social space but dominated in the field of power, is crucial. Either they introduce into their own field this imperative of permanent change, of a race to modernize, and so become the (possibly unwitting) accomplices of the dominant economic actors; or they perceive this discourse as a means of domination serving the interests of the dominant and strive to analyse and expose it. In this second scenario, an alliance between those dominated in the field of power and those dominated in the social space can then be constructed on the basis of their homology of position.

The homology of positions that relates dominated actors to one another is indeed a key mechanism that may support a different, more subversive, process of change. Most often, when Bourdieu identifies and analyses homologies of position between dominated positions, it is the alliance between those dominated in the field of power and those dominated in the social space or other specific fields that interests him. This is indeed how he outlines what one could call a sociology of Marx's sociology, observing that the sociological reason why Marx could develop a theory tending to serve the objective interests – and hence transform the position – of the agents 'most completely dispossessed of the economic and cultural means of production' was that he and they occupied homologous positions: as a producer of cultural goods Marx was dominated among the dominant within the field of power while they occupied a dominated position within the field of class relations (Bourdieu 1984c: 9; Bourdieu 1985: 736).[10]

The World Social Forum and the various anti-globalization protest movements typically seek to forge alliances based on a homology of dominated positions. The counter-summit to the 2003 G8 meeting in Évian, for example, modelled on the 1999 Seattle protests, brought together on the one hand 'occupationally and socially precarious' actors (unemployed or low-skilled) and, on the other hand, a significant proportion drawn from more favourably positioned socio-occupational categories, culturally dominant but economically dominated, among which 'the most strongly represented were the higher intellectual occupations (teaching and research, 34%), the higher scientific or technical occupations (12%), the health and social work professions (6%) and, more generally, intermediate public-sector occupations (primary and secondary teachers and associated categories)' (Fillieule *et al.* 2004: 25). The homology between dominated positions, in contrast to that between dominant positions, unites actors who have an interest in changing the established order. The complicity that can be constructed between those dominated in the field of power and those dominated in the social space then constitutes a factor of change oriented towards emancipation since it can lead the former to provide the latter with 'a view of the social world that breaks with the dominant view' (Bourdieu 1984c: 9; Bourdieu 1985: 736). The struggles by the dominated among the dominant within the field of power can thus 'advance ... at least formal recognition of the interests of the dominated' (Bourdieu 1997b: 124; Bourdieu 2000c: 103). In some cases, this may simply lead the dominated to try to preserve 'the rights they have won' against the demands for change formulated by the economically dominant actors. A situation can thus develop in which the dominant actors implement conservation strategies that involve the demand for change, while the dominated actors implement subversion strategies that involve the demand for the maintenance of their threatened rights (Bourdieu 1998a).

Thus the theory of fields foregrounds certain types of solidarity that are objectively linked to the homologous positions that individuals occupy in differentiated domains.[11] It remains limited as regards the understanding of solidarities that go beyond this homology of position but which nonetheless bring individuals and groups together around common struggles (such as the gay, feminist or antiracist movements), even if, in some cases, it can be observed that, independently of the variations of positions, the individuals share a common experience of relative exclusion and relegation. In other cases, as with the ecologist movements, the solidarities linked to the logics of fields prove insufficient to account for the dynamics at work. Thus, contrary to some unwarranted generalizations, it is important to note that even if it can serve as a basis for a more general reflection, the theory of fields constitutes an analysis whose scope is limited to bringing to light the particular logics of specific domains.[12]

Bourdieu shows that homologies between dominant positions can engender alliances favourable to the conservation and consolidation of the relations of domination (which sometimes use discourse on the necessity of change as a means), in contrast to homologies between dominated positions, which generate alliances among actors who are objectively interested in the transformation of the structures of established positions (even if they sometimes defend the maintenance of rights that have been won). These two types of homologies and alliances among actors must also be examined in terms of the habitus that they link. From this standpoint, what fundamentally distinguishes these two types of homologies lies in the fact that homologies between dominant positions tend to link actors with similar habitus, who are thereby more likely to 'understand' one another and come to 'spontaneous agreements', whereas homologies among dominated positions, when they include those of actors dominated within the field of power, are more likely to bring together actors whose habitus are 'divergent and, at least potentially, antagonistic' (Bourdieu 1984a: 233; Bourdieu 1988a: 180). The description above of the participants in the Évian 'counter-summit' is a good illustration of this.

The articulation of the concept of the habitus with the concept of the field gives rise to a complex theory that makes it possible both to identify the conditions favourable to change and understand why the process of change in the service of the preservation of the structures of positions is sociologically more probable than change oriented towards transforming them. It can then be better understood why alliances between dominated positions, potential motors of change oriented towards social transformation, are sociologically more fragile and less durable than the alliances among dominant actors that are generally at the heart of conservative revolutions. Bringing to light the importance of the relationship between field and habitus enables us to offer some clarifications as regards the relationship between the structure of the relative positions that compose the social space of a domain of autonomized activity and the system of incorporated dispositions generating schemes of perception, appreciation, thought and action of each agent who occupies it.

Field and habitus

The relationship between field and habitus is the product of the meeting of two histories, always incomplete and different. It is the encounter of a reified history – inscribed and objectified in things and structures, in the form of a field, the structure of a relational and differential space – and an embodied history, the incorporation of the division of the objective structures in the form of a habitus, a practice-generating system structured by this inter-nalization (Bourdieu 1982: 37–38; Bourdieu 1990c: 91). From it stems a complicity that is 'the basis of quasi-magical participation between these two realizations of history … In the relationship between habitus and field, between the feel for the game and the game itself … the stakes of the game are generated' (Bourdieu 1997b: 170; Bourdieu 2000c: 151); they are non-thetic stakes that present themselves with the self-evidence of the naturaliza-tion effect of the field. Depending on the degree of penetration of the objective structures of the field into the shaping of the habitus, this relationship is more or less well adjusted. The habitus will correspond more or less well to certain positions in the field.

Practical reality is made up of constant misalignments and multiple uncer-tainties, which generate the history and the dynamics of the field. However, Bourdieu himself often focused, at least at the theoretical level, on the case of perfect congruence (Vandenberghe 1999), one that would be characterized by perfect adjustment between the positions, the dispositions, the subjective aspirations and the objective situations encountered by all the actors. In reality, the situation of perfect congruence (and hence identical reproduction) corresponds to a purely theoretical state, highly improbable in practice. Moreover the knowledge, the language, the authorities, the positions and oppositions that develop in the genesis of a field are never fixed once and for all; their definition and redefinition are constantly contested by the participation of the agents in the functioning of the field. This dynamic of misalignments has to be analysed by clarifying the relationship between the field and the habitus.

Phenomena of hysteresis are one of the possible forms of mismatch between the cognitive structures and the objective structures that originally corresponded to them. In the course of his socialization, the agent internalizes, according to his milieu and trajectory, the objective rules that govern the social world (and in particular the functioning of a field). The closer the correspondence between the habitus and the objective rules, the more the potentialities of the habitus have a favourable space to emerge. In a field or beyond it, the greater this coincidence, the more the agents are at ease with the rule, so that they can keep in line with its demands, play regularly with the rule and thus distinguish themselves by an excellence that is opposed to the conformity of individuals limited to pure and simple execution of the rules. Conversely, the less congruence there is, the less the agents manage to 'fall into line with rules that are made against them' (Bourdieu 1980a: 185 n.18; Bourdieu 1990b: 298 n.12). The 'Don Quixote effect' (Bourdieu 1979a: 122; Bourdieu 1984b: 109) perfectly illustrates this phenomenon of hysteresis: with the nostalgia for a vanished order in which it coincided perfectly with the world, a habitus corresponding to a past state of the social order perpetuates dispositions that now run 'in neutral' (Hilgers 2007).

Every habitus is subject in one way or another to more or less strong effects of hysteresis, i.e. a 'negative secondary reinforcement' (Bourdieu 1972b: 260; Bourdieu 1977e: 78), when, struggling to adapt themselves, practices deviate too far from their space of legitimacy, in other words, from the objective structures within which they are most legitimate. Because the structures of a given environment shape the habitus and are subsequently transformed, while the habitus partially rigidifies, it is necessarily subject to more or less great hysteresis effects. Within a field, hysteresis can thus explain the difficulty some agents have in grasping the import of historical crises – the discrepancy between their capacity to perceive objective opportunities and the effective manifestation of these opportunities (see for example Bourdieu 1979b: 15). The rigidity of cognitive structures is reinforced by ageing and by the fact that agents tend not to expose themselves to situations that call into question the information they have accumulated in the course of their existence (Bourdieu 1987).

Just as some agents lag behind change in the social world, so others run ahead of it and anticipate structures or oppositions that exist only latently. The champions of subversion, of whom the figure of the messiah, or the *nomothete*, such as Flaubert in literature (Bourdieu 1991a), or Manet in painting (Bourdieu 2013) i.e. the producers of new norms within a field, are the strongest incarnation. The subversive, the innovator, 'can mobilize groups or classes' or even the dominated fractions within a field 'who recognize his language because they recognize themselves in it' and because it actualizes a meaning that already existed there in latent or implicit form (Bourdieu 1971a). Sometimes, the individual or group that brings about subversion in a field activates a series of schemes that make it possible to conceive another representation of the world, other logics of interests, other games and other stakes. In other words they are key components in the emergence of symbolic revolution. Crisis situations favour the emergence of prophetic or radical discourses because they throw up configurations and conditions of reception that make an alternative discourse audible. In these extreme moments, the struggle can then be a battle to transfer specific capital from one position to another.

Because agents are rarely socialized in one single universe, they often have a 'cleft habitus' (Bourdieu 1997b: 79; Bourdieu 2000c: 64), in other words they have several repertoires of dispositions that they activate according to the circumstances (Hilgers 2009; Lahire 2010), and whose contradictions may induce reflexivity. Depending on their capacity to activate these dispositions, on the circumstances and on the position they occupy in the field, these cleavages may lead them to occupy positions marked by a more or less strong hysteresis or a more or less strong nomothesis.

After this presentation of the main lines of Bourdieu's theory of fields, we turn to the issue of its implementation.

Implementing the theory of social fields: the visible and the invisible

'The real is relational', Bourdieu often said (e.g. 1992: 97), pastiching Hegel – but can these relations (between positions, between products, between positions and productions) be grasped if they are not directly observable? How can one identify the effect of the interrelations if they only rarely produce simple causalities? How do we observe the unobservable and empirically ground the analysis in indicators? To put it another way, how do we proceed in concrete terms to make the theory operational?

A number of difficulties can be overcome by applying the following principle: we have to study the field through its effects, and from its effects we infer its specific properties. Since these effects are moreover rarely the product of a simple causality, at each stage in the process we must not only consider the properties of the objects and actors but also relate and interpret our empirical observations in terms of the networks of relations within which they are set. It should be noted that multiple correspondence analysis, much used by Bourdieu, is a powerful tool here because it makes it possible to produce data that can be handled relationally (Bourdieu 1992: 72; Bourdieu 1996a: 96). It more readily exposes the interrelations while avoiding the substantialist fallacy which assigns explanatory factors to variables.

Multiple correspondence analysis is a technique that makes it possible to treat a group of variables as a set without establishing relationships *a priori*

(Legros 1989). It differs from traditional approaches inasmuch as the variables all have the same status: 'there is therefore no question of considering that certain variables are dependent or independent, i.e. explanatory or to be explained' (Legros 1989: 137). Using this approach one can break with the illusion of the constancy of variables and better identify the meaning that the indicators take on in the relationship, but also 'the meaning they receive from it' (Bourdieu 1979a: 17).

It makes it possible to construct graphic representations that project onto the same plane, simultaneously, relationships that are generally represented in a succession of cross-referenced tables (Legros 1989: 16). These representations are constructed in such a way that the positions that the agents, groups or institutions within them occupy 'on paper' form a representation of their relative positions in the social space. To avoid errors in interpretation of such figures, however, it is important to understand the relationships among the points in this space by relating them to the scalar product of their coordinates. With the aid of social topology, one can then analyse relative positions and objective relationships between positions 'occupied in the distributions of resources which are or can become active, effective' (Bourdieu 1987: 152).

To put the theory of fields to work we can distinguish three main stages (cf. Bourdieu 1992), which must then be articulated together.

Evaluating the degree of autonomy of the field

First stage: locate the position of the field in question in the overall social space and in relation to the other fields, in order to evaluate its degree of relative autonomy with respect to external interests and to neighbouring fields (in particular the field of power, the economic sphere and the political sphere). How does one proceed? How is the relative autonomy of a field to be measured? It can be estimated by identifying the 'nature' of the constraints on the various actors in the field and examining whether these arise from the field itself – in other words, whether they result from rules specific to the particular activity that prevails there, or whether they derive from the imperatives of another field, i.e. are the agents in field X subject to constraints stemming from field Y or Z? More concretely, in the field of literature, for example (Sapiro 2003, and Chapter 5 in this book), are writers subject to strong political or economic constraints? When such constraints are exerted on the producers or consumers in a field, one needs to show – in accordance with a logic that remains centred on the effects of the field – how they affect the 'internal' characteristics of the goods produced and consumed and the forms and conditions in which they are produced and consumed. So the characteristics of the products and the conditions of their production and consumption are understood in terms of the set of relations in which they are involved, and the substantialist fallacy is avoided.

In a general way, one can also evaluate the relative autonomy of the field by examining whether and to what extent species of capital and resources derived from other fields have value and can legitimately be used and produce effects there. A deficit of autonomy can be detected when capital and resources from other fields have some legitimacy and produce an effect on the structure of positions in the field in question. The more autonomous a field is, the more potent its specific capital.

The question of autonomy raises different issues in different fields. In a democratic context, the autonomization of the political field with respect to social demands and 'external' social interests is liable to produce effects that run counter to its representative function (Bourdieu 2000c). By contrast, in the scientific field, the increasing autonomy of the field and the reflexive awareness that the agents of the field have of external pressures and demands are conducive to the development of the field (Bourdieu 1997a). Just as the problematic of relative autonomy varies between fields, so too, within a given field, the actors are not all subject to the same constraints. Depending on their position and the volume and structure of their capital, they are more or less constrained and capable of acting in compliance with the autonomy of the field.[13]

Describing the symbolic order

Having established the degree of autonomy of the field, the next step is to analyse the activity that constitutes the specificity of the domain in question. The aim is to grasp the particularity of the field – its specific capital, its specific rules and the symbolic order of its specific productions. One has to situate its productions relative to one another, identifying the connections and oppositions among them (schools, movements, polemics and battles). In this way one can map the symbolic structure of the field.

In a field, symbolic ordering consists in a declarative activity in which agents participate through statements, practices, labelling, naming, interrelating (of actors, actions, qualities, 'seminal works', means, objects, values, etc.). Symbolic orderings constitute efforts at constructing reality (Bourdieu 1977c). One of the axioms of the theory of fields is that naming and classifying operations always play a partisan role in the unending struggle to impose the legitimate definition of the symbolic order. Sociological analysis has to keep its distance from these terms, which are implicitly or explicitly weapons in the struggle. The sociologist cannot make use of them as analytical terms without himself becoming involved in the symbolic struggle, which is not his role, and above all because they mask the processes through which classifications and categorizations are generated in the domain in question. To describe the symbolic structure of a field, one has to detach oneself from the emic categories and make them the object of analysis.

The efforts deployed to produce and transform the symbolic order of the field (in a conservative or subversive direction) are based on a structure that they themselves structure and which can be brought to light by means of an internal analysis, by establishing the whole set of relationships among the elements of this symbolic order and identifying the relations among these elements.[14] Once again it is the relational dimension – and not the supposed substantial characteristics of the products and actors – that lies at the centre of the analysis.

Reconstituting the structure of positions

In the struggle for the definition of the legitimate symbolic structures, individuals and groups have unequal means at their disposal, linked to their positions. The third stage in implementing the field approach has to concentrate on objectifying the structures of relative positions. Who are the main (individual or collective) actors engaged in the work of production, distribution and consumption? What is the organizing principle of the structure of positions that links, opposes, distinguishes and hierarchizes them? The approach of external analysis goes beyond internal analysis of the specific products of the field and gives priority to study of the positions and trajectories of the agents in the social structure, in the given field, and possibly in other fields.[15] As in the other stages of the analysis, examination of the structures of positions has to include a diachronic perspective (the trajectories and the changes in the structure and volume of the resources of the various actors).

The first requirement is to describe the structure of the objective relations among the positions occupied by the competing agents or institutions in the field, in particular the relative positions and resources of the producers and also the relative positions and resources of producers and consumers. These multiple oppositions which structure the field are played out against a background of shared beliefs and interests that cause them to exist and give them meaning. Objectifying a space of positions presupposes that one relates each individual to a system of coordinates that enable him/her to be situated objectively in a space structured by various dimensions. Each dimension must correspond to a type of resource (capital) effective within the field. Indicators (material and immaterial properties) adapted to the particularities of the field in question must be devised, to make it possible to objectify the resources of the agents in the field.

Articulating the symbolic and the social

We have now presented three major stages in implementing the theory of social fields. They make it possible to produce information that is essential for analysing a social universe from this relational standpoint. The heart of the analysis consists, however, in dynamically articulating the empirical elements yielded by these three stages of work. The latter should not be seen as successive operations but rather as levels that are superimposed and feed into each other to produce the analysis. None of these levels of analysis is sufficient in itself – they have to be interrelated. The internal and external levels of the analysis are articulated dialectically. The symbolic order of the field has a complex relationship with the structures of objective positions. It results from a social order at the same time as it prefigures it in a dynamic of permanent transformation.

The examination, in relational terms, of the positions that the agents (especially the producers and the receivers) occupy relative to one another, the resources they have or aspire to have, and the trajectories that have brought them there, is what enables one to grasp the specific interests that they (partly unconsciously) pursue. It is then possible to *understand*, in all the senses that Bourdieu gives to this term (Bourdieu 1993d: 903–35; Bourdieu 1999: 607–26), the meaning of their production (or their reception/consumption). This meaning is not to be sought exclusively within the products specific to the field but rather in the structure of social relations in which the agents are immersed.

Open questions and concluding remarks

The stages of work suggested here are useful as soon as one studies (and defines fields as) domains of specific activity. In its conventional interpretation, Bourdieu's sociology of fields is used to account for the social organization of a domain of activity that has become increasingly autonomous (Bourdieu 1968, 1971a, 1991a). The three stages of work that have been outlined should be seen in this perspective.

However, when one tries to put this theory to work some difficulties arise and have led to several critical discussions that are analysed from many standpoints in this book. The first is perhaps the status of the theory itself. Should we regard it as a nomological theory or as a strictly methodological one? Is it strictly methodological, arguing that we should think the real relationally, that an object cannot be defined by its intrinsic properties alone and that it has to be re-placed in the structure of relations in which it is embedded? Or is it nomological, postulating that the real is relational, being concerned with the functioning of relatively autonomized domains of specific activity and highlighting their 'social laws'? No definitive answer can be derived from the Bourdieusian *corpus*. Some authors see it only as a method (Pinto 2000) or 'a *pense-bête*, a memory jogger', as Bourdieu (1992: 228) himself put it, whereas others reflect on its ontological scope (Moessinger 1994; Gautier 2012). These two tropes subsume many of the discussions that concern the theory. One group appears more concerned by ontological matters, the other by methodological aspects. To illustrate this dissent, we will briefly deal with two questions generally faced when trying to put the theory of fields to work. The first – is all action in a field guided by a principle of maximization of utility? – will be developed in relation with the nomological aspect. The second – what is a field and how are its limits to be defined? – will be associated with the methodological dimension of the theory.[16]

In a field, on the basis of their dispositions towards the future and the volume and structure of their capital, agents develop strategies (with or without strategic intentions) oriented towards the conservation or increase of their assets. Thus, even when no conscious rationality is in play, in objective terms, given the dispositions of the agent, action seems to be the product of a maximizing tendency, as if the structures of practice were informed by an immanent teleological principle leading the agent to act optimally, without necessarily being aware of it, to 'achieve the objectives inscribed in the logic of a particular field, at the lowest cost' (Bourdieu 1980a: 85; Bourdieu 1990b: 50). Here, Bourdieu's statement clearly lies beyond purely methodological questions. It also concerns the nomological aspect of the theory, i.e. the ambition of bringing to light the *laws* of functioning of the social (Bourdieu 1980b: 113; Bourdieu 1993c: 72). However, this postulate of the interest inherent in practice is problematic.

According to Bourdieu, when an individual lets his social nature follow its inclinations in a field where the objective rules are congruent with his dispositions, without even trying to do so he produces acts that correspond to the course that rational action would recommend. His acts have the appearance of rational actions without necessarily being guided by rationality. They are simply *reasonable*, Bourdieu tells us. Paradoxically, reasonable action is not based on reason; it springs from the practical sense. The common mistake made by economists is to confuse this practical sense with the rationality of the agent. However, even if this action does not spring from logical rationality, it is always guided by a logic of maximization of (not necessarily economic) utility. Without being linked by a logical calculation, practical logics always seem subordinated to an axiomatic of interest.

Bourdieu gives an excellent example of the over-interpretations to which this axiomatic can lead (or what an ironist would call the 'scholastic fallacy') in his analysis of the scientific field: 'There is no scientific choice ... that does not constitute, in one or other of its aspects, a social strategy of investment aimed at maximizing the specific profit, inseparably political and scientific, provided by the field' (Bourdieu 1976: 91; Bourdieu 1991c: 9–10). However, not all agents are driven by the same *libido sciendi* to the point of objectively (and deliberately or not) organizing each of their acts in relation to a potential profit. Even in the hyper-competitive neoliberal context of contemporary research, experience shows that the scientific choices of all agents do not systematically imply a principle of maximization (Hilgers 2013). This is even more true when one considers the agent as a consumer rather than as a producer.[17] Thus, the axiomatic of interest, even when 'reasonable' rather than rational, does not seem capable of accounting for all the practices of an agent.

A social field is indeed governed by investment in the game (*illusio*) and the 'feel for the game' that is played in the domain of activity that specifies it, but this investment varies from one individual to another. Internalization of the objective rules leads one to acquire dispositions (the sense of the rules, play, stakes) specific to the field in question, but the dispositions actualized in this structure of positions also result from individual trajectory and capital. A 'cleft habitus' (Bourdieu 1997b: 79; Bourdieu 2000c: 64) may lead agents to make a hybrid investment in a domain of activity rather than (consciously or not) seek to maximize social, symbolic, cultural or economic utility. The efficacy of dispositions and of the different species of capital depends on how far they correspond to the dominant tendencies of the field.

By contrast, if one regards this axiomatic of interest as a methodological decision taken in order to analyse the logic of a field, one can simply assert that all choices (here, scientific ones) are made in a space of relations within which they constitute, *nolens volens*, an objective investment whose pertinence can be interpreted in terms of the profit of recognition that they secure. In other words, this way of perceiving action is deliberately constructed for the purposes of analysis, it effects a reduction, a simplification, an abstraction of empirical reality which makes it possible to apprehend the reality but which does not aim to describe its principle. The answer to the question of the axiomatic of interest is thus quite different depending on whether one considers the theory of fields as methodological or nomological.

In this Introduction we have deliberately tried to consider the theory of social fields from a methodological point of view and to delimit its application. This presupposes that one methodologically and empirically define what a field is. However, how can one draw the boundaries of fields if they interpenetrate, if each field contains sub-fields that themselves contain others, and if at the same time 'a field does not have parts, components [since] every subfield has its own logic, rules and regularities, and each stage in the division of a field ... entails a genuine qualitative leap' (Bourdieu and Wacquant 1992: 104)? Bourdieu himself sometimes applied the term 'field' to social universes much broader than domains of specialized activity, sometimes to much more restricted social universes. Sometimes it seems that the social space in its totality can be analysed as a field: 'The position of a given agent in the social space can ... be defined by the position he occupies in the different fields ... One can ... construct a simplified model of the social field as a whole, a model which allows one to plot each agent's position in all possible spaces' (Bourdieu 1984c: 3; Bourdieu 1985: 724). Sometimes Bourdieu refers to the field of the social classes (Bourdieu 1984b). By contrast, in other cases, the concept is applied to much more limited social spaces. The family, for example, is considered as a field (Bourdieu 1993b), i.e. both as 'a field of forces, whose necessity is imposed on agents who are engaged in it, and as a field of struggles within which agents confront each other, with differentiated means and ends according to their position in the structure of the field of forces, thus contributing to conserving or transforming its structure' (Bourdieu 1994: 55; Bourdieu 1998c: 32). So it is not surprising that those most familiar with the theory, such as former disciple Nathalie Heinich, have a particularly broad interpretation of the idea of the field.[18] The question of the limits appears even more complicated and less decidable if one explicitly adopts a nomological point of view which aims to define a field *per se*.

If, however, one opts for a pragmatic approach, the theory of fields appears to be a *model* in the sense defined in *The Craft of Sociology*: a 'system of relations among selected, abstracted, and simplified properties which is deliberately constructed for purposes of description, exposition and prediction and which is therefore kept under full control', but which 'in no way leads to the principle of the reality that it mimics' (Bourdieu *et al.* 1972: 75; Bourdieu *et al.* 1991: 52). In the project to forge an analytical approach to grasping a specific domain of activities relationally the notion of the limits of the field can constitute a useful epistemic tool but it has to be theoretically constructed in conjunction with empirical research. When he seeks to define what a field is, Bourdieu states that 'we may think of a field as a space within which a field effect is exercised, so that what happens to any object that traverses this space cannot be explained solely by the intrinsic properties of the object in question' (Bourdieu and Wacquant 1992: 100). This definition may be considered tautological. This problem commonly arises in work based on a relational epistemology (Martin 2003). It stems from the fact that a field only exists and can only be analysed through its effects. So how can we define the limits of a field?

By articulating the three stages that we have described to analyse specific social universes, one can 'assess how concretely they are constituted, where they stop, who gets in and who does not, and whether at all they form a field' (Bourdieu and Wacquant 1992: 101). The question of the boundaries is then raised and resolved pragmatically 'in the field itself and therefore admits of no *a priori* answer' (Bourdieu and Wacquant 1992: 100). The boundaries can be observed where the field effects cease. They are apparent in the social space through the inefficacy of the rules or capital that are specific to it. In some cases, the boundaries are extremely codified, in others they are porous, but they are always fought over, because 'to define boundaries, defend them and control entries is to defend the established order in the field' (Bourdieu 1992: 369; Bourdieu 1996a: 225). When one bears in mind the three stages of work and their articulation – evaluating the degree of autonomy, describing the symbolic orders, reconstituting the structure of positions – it is easier to understand the answer that Bourdieu gives to Wacquant on the question of the boundaries of the field: 'In empirical work, it is one and the same thing to determine what the field is, where its limits lie, etc., and to determine what species of capital are active within it, in what limits, and so on ... In order to construct the field, one must identify the forms of specific capital that operate within it, and to construct the forms of specific capital one must know the specific logic of the field' (Bourdieu and Wacquant 1992: 98, 108). It is necessary to articulate the internal and external analyses and avoid what has been called the substantialist fallacy.

The theory of social fields is a methodology but while this methodology appears useful to highlight the laws of the social, some problems arise that are not limited to strictly methodological issues. The question of the status of the theory remains open and more fundamentally the theory could be useful for different purposes. Bourdieu's theory is not a fixed theory. It can even be said that it remained provisional, since its author died before he could complete his project.[19] Today the theory is 'in the public domain'; it belongs to the common heritage of social sciences, with all the latitudes that this permits. This being so, rather than limit ourselves to an orthodox hermeneutics that seeks in the comparison of texts the resolution of their contradictions, rather than seeing these contradictions as limitations, we have opted to consider them as the mark of the provisional character of the theory and to seek to establish its fruitfulness from a pragmatic point of view. In other words, our aim has been to establish an effective way to work with Bourdieu's theory of fields and this is also the clear aim of the following chapters of the book.

The book is in three parts. Part I, 'theoretical investigations', offers a theoretical account of the theory, while also identifying some of its limitations and discussing several strategies to overcome them. Part II, 'education, culture and organization', presents case studies focusing on educational and cultural institutions. They show the theory at work and identify how field theory can make us see things differently while also noting what it does not allow us to see. The focus in Part III, devoted to 'the State and public policy', is on the formation and evolution of the State in different contexts. The chapters show the usefulness of field theory in describing, explaining and understanding the functioning of the State at different stages in its historical trajectory, including its recent redefinition with the advent of the neoliberal age. The afterword discussed the theory from a postcolonial angle.

In Chapter 1 John Levi Martin and Forest Gregg deepen the epistemological background that we have outlined in this Introduction. They trace the history of field theory from German philosophy and psychology and physical theories. Martin and Gregg show that while this genealogy was largely extinguished within American social theory somewhere in the 1970s, as it was dying out in the United States, Pierre Bourdieu was resurrecting field theory in France. Their chapter emphasizes certain aspects where Bourdieu made important advances that will be necessary for any similar field-theoretic approach. They also discuss the potentially problematic or confusing aspects of Bourdieu's own work – in particular, the relation between social space and particular fields; the relation between capital and field position; and the relation of vectors to extra-field positions or outcomes.

In Chapter 2, Lahire develops a very clear and rich critique of the concept of the field which highlights the relevance of the concept while also providing analytical tools to overcome some of its limitations. In particular, the chapter develops and enriches Grignon and Passeron's well-known critique of Bourdieu's lack of consideration for the productive capacity of the dominated segments of the social world (1989). Indeed, one of the limitations of the concept of the field lies in its tendency to consider consumers, the users (including the middle class) as forming a social space structured by the same principles as those that structure and divide the elites. The chapter offers several insights as to how to overcome these limitations by refining the theory. Lahire points out that the concept of field (like those of 'world' or 'game') is linked to a long tradition of sociological and anthropological reflections on the social differentiation of activities or functions. From this starting point, he develops propositions for a critical extension of Bourdieu's work. Not only does the emergence of autonomized domains of activity presuppose that there have been societies 'without fields' but, moreover, in differentiated societies Lahire argues, not every action context is a field. For Lahire, in analysing a field, in the historical sense of the concept, one must above all avoid slipping into a reductive explanation of practices or productions (works, discourses, etc.) in terms of the field. He develops a critique of the reductionist abuse of the theory which especially applies to 'secondary fields' that offer low rewards, are barely institutionalized or professionalized, and which he calls 'games'. Contrasting 'fields' with 'games', Lahire points out the difficulties related to transferring the general theory of the 'field' in order to describe and analyse the functioning of an autonomized domain of specific activities. Finally, he considers the positive or negative effects of the autonomization of these multiple social microcosms and the progressive self-enclosure to which it can lead.

Chapter 3, by Louis Pinto, aims to clarify the notion of the field. Pinto argues that Bourdieu's theory of fields attempts to overcome certain oppositions that formed social sciences. The posture appears 'Leibnizian' and develops an original 'rationalist empiricism' to reduce the gap between theory and experience. This relational thinking combines a typically Leibnizian ethic of treatment of opposing paths (objectivism and subjectivism, structure and history, interest and disinterestedness) with a use of Marx, Durkheim and Weber to show the interest of 'situating oneself at the geometric vantage point in the various perspectives from which one can see, at the same time, both what can and what cannot be perceived from each of these separate points of view' (Bourdieu 1991b: 2). Moreover contrary to many prejudicies and as we have shown from a different perspective in this introduction, this chaper shows that field theory makes it possible to develop a rigourous structural conception of social change.

Part II sets Bourdieu's theory to work in various domains of activity: education, literature, journalism, cinema and public policy. Chapter 4 by André and Hilgers puts field methodology back into research in education that is one of the central domaine of reseach of Bourdieu. This chapter shows the importance to bring back the notion of field to grasp some dynamics recently analyzed by sociology of education. In the early 1990s, new research highlighted the growing instability and many uncertainties of teachers' judgement, characterized by the pluralization of its systems of reference, and many researchers turned away from Bourdieu (André 2012). However, this chapter shows that even in a context of plurality and uncertainties, field theory remains extremely useful in shedding light on the sociological foundations of teachers' judgement. Indeed, in spite of many changes, this judgement remains profoundly linked to structural influences such as the position of their school in the school field. In order to identify schools' positions in a local field, André and Hilgers suggest establishing their economic capital and their cultural capital. Identifying a school's position presupposes that concepts used to describe the positions of individual agents be transposed to collective agents. By constructing the positions of three schools in a local field they establish the impact of position in the field on teachers' judgement and on the positions they take in the educational and vocational orientation of their pupils.

Chapter 5 is devoted to an analysis of the literary field another central domain of research for Bourdieu. According to Pierre Bourdieu's analysis, the emergence of the literary field results from an historical process by which literary activity became autonomous from different types of external constraints. Sapiro gives a provisional account of these types of constraints, focusing on the French case. She suggests classifying national literary fields according to their dependence on the state or on the market. In authoritarian regimes, the state is an instrument of control put at the service of an ideological system in favour of the ruling class which in turn determines the supply of cultural goods. The liberalization of the book market has favoured the relative liberation of literary field from state control. However, the market also has constraints of its own, which implies, notably for literature, the risk of standardization and a widening of the gap between professionalized author of best-sellers and innovative writers.

In Chapter 6 Duval shows the benefits provided by the field approach when studying economic journalism and the cinema. First, the notion of the field is useful in facilitating a shift away from common-sense representations and providing a point of entry into structural and scientific representations of social phenomena. The model is a fruitful instrument in the task of refining analysis of relations between political power, the economy and the press. The notion of the field serves to outline a general view of a social realm. A second advantage lies in it requiring the researcher to investigate questions systematically and to elaborate an ambitious analytical framework. This framework challenges the dominant explanation produced by economic models and involves questions that highlight numerous aspects of the realm studied. Third, it fosters a comparative approach and brings to light some specification of the universe studied. Comparison of the journalistic, literary and cinematic fields shows that these domains can never be totally autonomous and that the structure and efficacy of a field vary according to its national embeddedness. In other words, the author demonstrates concretely how to use the notion of the field as a tool for research which aims to combine empirical and theoretical perspectives to further the understanding of economic journalism and the cinema.

Part III focuses on the State and public policy. The field of power is at the centre of Chapter 7 by Mangez and Liénard. More precisely, they examine the problematic of the relative autonomy of fields in the Belgian context, focusing on the relationship between the field of power and different specific fields. Does the concept of the field still function in the same way (and as effectively) when translated into a context other than that of French society?

Is it equally pertinent in all contexts marked by a form of differentiation of spheres of activity? Studying the Belgian context leads them to consider not only the process of functional differentiation that gives rise to fields but also a process of cultural fragmentation from which emerge what Belgian and Dutch intellectuals habitually call the 'pillars'.

In Chapter 8, Dubois advocates a more systematic use of the theory of fields in policy analysis. Policy analysis has constructed its own concepts to describe groups and relations within the policy process. The latter include notions such as 'policy networks' or 'policy communities', 'iron triangles', 'advocacy coalitions', 'issue networks', 'epistemic communities'. Yet Bourdieu's field sociology remains seldom applied in this subject. The theory of fields can nevertheless prove particularly useful in avoiding normative bias or the analytical limitations of ad hoc policy analysis categories. It is very helpful in objectifying the specific positions and systems of relations in which decisions and policies are made. Dubois shows that it can also contribute to the understanding of both concrete relations and the more abstract relationship between this specific field (the policy field, *stricto sensu*) and other social fields: first, those directly concerned with a particular policy (for instance the arts field vis-à-vis cultural policy); second, those involved at different levels of policy making (e.g. the scientific field providing expertise to shed light on a problem or used by policy makers in a legitimization strategy). It shows how this theory could be incorporated into policy analysis, which has been constructed as a specific academic subject in sociological research and theory. It offers examples taken from Bourdieu's work (on the state, housing policy and the 'field of power'), and from recent research (on cultural and social policies, for instance).

In Chapter 9 Medvetz focuses on the growing breed of 'think tanks' which he understands as a useful case for thinking about power in organizations. The chapter extends the scholarly discussion about the relationship between organizations, power and fields by identifying four ways of thinking about organizational power from a standpoint informed by field theory. Medvetz compares the analytical advantages of considering a) think tanks as inhabitants of a larger field, b) think tanks as a field itself, c) think tanks and power of sporning multiple fields, d) think tanks as a boundary organisation that creates and maintains symbolic and legitimate instituational separations and notably spaces between fields. Medvetz analyse the benefits and pitfalls of four approaches rooted in one particular analytical perspective.

In *The Weight of the World* and related essays, Pierre Bourdieu proposed conceiving the state as a 'splintered space' of forces competing for control over the definition and distribution of public goods, and which he call the 'bureaucratic field'. In Chapter 10, Wacquant argues that the bureaucratic field is traversed by a double struggle. The first pits the 'higher state nobility' of policy makers against the 'lower state nobility' of executants attached to the traditional missions of government. The second sets the 'left hand' against the 'right hand' of the state. The left hand in charge of 'social functions' –

public education, health, housing, welfare and labour law while the right hand, is charged with enforcing the new economic discipline via budget cuts, fiscal incentives and economic deregulation. Wacquant shows that Bourdieu concept of bureaucratic field constitutes a valuable tool to grasp and analyze these struggles at the heart of the neoliberal state and a powerful analytical key to develop a tick sociological specification of neoliberalism.

At the end of the book, we put forward a view from another angle on the theory of fields, considering it from the subaltern point of view of societies described as little or non-differentiated. Examining Bourdieu's theory from this point of view opens up three new areas of questioning. The first concerns the functioning of the theory in contexts that are not characterized by unification of the cultural market, the second discusses the links between social differentiation and capitalism, and the third considers how the theory of fields can shed light on the process of globalization.

Notes

1 Notable examples are the works of Christin 1997; Geay 1999; Bourdieu 2000c; Lebaron 2000; Boschetti 2001; Lenoir 2003; Duval 2004; Mary 2006; Pinto 2007; Tissot 2007; Durand 2008; Garcia-Parpet 2009, etc.
2 This section draws freely on extracts from texts written in collaboration with Yves Patte for a book on field theory, which never came to completion. Some passages, some quotations and the structure of some paragraphs in this history have been previously published in Patte (2006). We take the liberty of reproducing them, with his agreement, since they were several times discussed among us and written collectively. As acknowledged in the first note in Patte (2006), part of that article was to appear in a work then being co-written with Mathieu Hilgers.
3 As Martin (2003) points out, Bourdieu explicitly compared social fields with electro-magnetic fields but later criticized those who make such comparisons.
4 This point is debatable, since Bourdieu sometimes considers that a field has no parts, that the sub-fields are relatively autonomous domains, and that a move from a field to a sub-field is a qualitative leap. Nonetheless, even when considering that a field is a whole, one can say that these elements have relationships; the dominant fraction of the dominated class or the dominated fraction of the dominant class, the group of the producers, the group of the consumers and the group of the distributors are interrelated, so that they can be regarded as non-independent parts of a totality.
5 One of the difficulties of this thesis is that it refers to a quasi-pure situation. Indeed, as some contributors to this volume show, in the empirical world people often belong to different more or less institutionalized fields, and their perception can rarely be reduced to one field.
6 Such correspondence is never direct, it is not a simple reflection (see for example Bourdieu 1999: 1101).
7 'For whosoever hath, to him shall be given, and he shall have more abundance: but whosoever hath not, from him shall be taken away even that he hath.' Matthew 13:12.
8 In envisaging the theory of social fields as a theory of social change rather than as a theory strictly limited to reproduction, we pursue here the critique of a vast literature that reduces Bourdieu's work to a crude determinism; we have previously examined the relationship between habitus, freedom and reflexivity (Hilgers 2006, 2009).

9 Gartman offers one of the most illuminating presentations and applications of Bourdieu's theory of cultural change. 'Cultural innovations follow the path of an inverted U-curve. They start at the bottom of the restricted subfield among unknown avant-garde artists, rise to the top of the subfield as works of the consecrated avant-garde, and then migrate laterally to the top of the large-scale subfield as bourgeois art, until imitation by the petty bourgeoisie lowers them to the status of commercial art' (Gartman 2002: 259).

10 According to Bourdieu, the problem with Marx is that he did not objectify what his scientific production owed to his specific position.

11 Postulating the existence of these objective solidarities, Bourdieu argues for a 'corporatism of the universal' (Bourdieu 1992: 543–58; Bourdieu 1996a: 337–48) that would facilitate the production of a 'collective intellectual' capable of resisting the ravages of neoliberalism (Bourdieu 2001a). The homology of the structure of fields is thus potentially the bearer of effects capable of extending beyond the domain of activity itself.

12 The relational epistemology that underlies this theory has an explanatory potential that goes far beyond the domains of autonomized activities. It has sometimes led to uses that confuse 'context' and 'field'.

13 The figure of Mallarmé, for example, is emblematic of the autonomy of the modern poetic field. Benefiting from a literary tradition to which he could implicitly refer and with which he could play without fearing hermeticism, freed from the need to be accessible to the outsider but subject to the sense of the forms and formalities of the literary field (Durand 2008), his production, eventually sanctified by school textbooks, was not subject to economic considerations, although he did not have the financial autonomy to break free of all constraints (unlike Flaubert, who had a secure private income and no children to provide for).

14 One element 'is more important than' some other element; a given element 'serves' a finality; one event 'is preliminary to' another event; an actor 'has' some characteristic and quality; a given action 'is' legitimate or illegitimate; a given product or attitude is presented as 'outstanding' or 'sacred' as opposed to 'ordinary', 'vulgar' or 'profane' products and attitudes, etc.

15 The more or less clear correspondences between the structure of the positions specific to the field and the relative positions of the actors in the field within the overall social structure constitute, moreover, a possible indicator of the degree of relative autonomy of the field in question vis-à-vis the field of power. A strong correspondence between a part of the overall social space (e.g. the fractions of the upper classes combining high economic capital with high cultural capital) and a specific sub-space within a field (e.g. judges within the legal field; Bourdieu 1986) will be the objective index of a low autonomy of the field in question with respect to the structure of the social classes.

16 Needless to say, the opposite would have been possible: the axiomatic of interest could be approached as a methodological question while the limits of the field could be seen as an ontological problem.

17 Lahire in this book shows that the question of reception remains at this stage relatively unexplored in Bourdieu's theory.

18 'Of all the concepts that make up the Bourdieusian "toolbox", the idea of the "field" is perhaps the most universalizable, because its very definition makes it a constituent foundation of all human activity: everyone is capable of being set in a context, in a history, in relation to specific stakes, which make it a collective phenomenon without, however, belonging to a framework as general as "society"' (Heinich 2007: 134).

19 'This chapter, which aims to draw out of the historical analyses of the literary field presented above some propositions which are valid for the whole set of fields of cultural production, tends to leave aside the specific logic of each of the specialized

fields (religious, political, juridical, philosophical, scientific) that I have analysed elsewhere, and which will be the subject of a future work' (Bourdieu 1992: 298–99; Bourdieu 1996a: 380). See notably the posthumous manuscript 'Sur Manet: Une révolution symbolique' (Bourdieu 2013).

References

André, G. 2012. *L'orientation scolaire. Héritages sociaux et jugements professoraux.* Paris: PUF.

Boschetti, A. 2001. *La Poésie partout. Apollinaire, Homme-époque (1898–1918).* Paris: Seuil.

Bourdieu, P. 1966. 'Champ intellectuel et projet créateur'. *Les Temps modernes*, 246, 865–906 (translated as 1968).

——1968. 'Intellectual Field and Creative Project'. *Social Science Information*, 8(2), 89–119.

——1971a. 'Genèse et structure du champ religieux'. *Revue française de sociologie*, 12 (3), 295–334 (translated as 1991b).

——1971b. 'Une interprétation de la théorie de la religion selon Max Weber'. *Archives européennes de sociologie*, 12(1), 3–21.

——1971c. 'Le marché des biens symboliques'. *L'Année sociologique*, 22, 49–126.

——1972a. 'Éléments pour une théorie de la production, de la circulation et de la consommation des biens symboliques'. *Revue de l'Institut de Sociologie*, 45(4), 751–60.

——1972b. *Esquisse d'une théorie de la pratique.* Mouton: Paris (translated as 1977e).

——1975a. 'Méthode scientifique et hiérarchie des objets'. *Actes de la Recherche en Science Sociales*, 2/3, 4–6.

——, with Delsaut, Y. 1975b. 'Le couturier et sa griffe: contribution à une théorie de la magie'. *Actes de la recherche en sciences sociales*, 1, 7–36.

——1976. 'Le champ scientifique'. *Actes de la Recherche en Science Sociales*. 2/3, 88–104 (translated as 1991c).

——1977a. 'La production de la croyance: contribution à une économie des biens symboliques'. *Actes de la Recherche en Science Sociales*, 13, 3–43 (translated as 1993a).

——1977b. *Algérie 60. Structures économiques et structures temporelles.* Paris: Éditions de Minuit (translated as 1979b).

——1977c. 'Sur le pouvoir symbolique'. *Annales E.S.C.*, 32(3), 405–11 (translated as 1977d).

——1977d. 'Symbolic Power'. In D. Gleeson (ed.), *Identity and Structure: Issues in the Sociology of Education.* Driffield: Nafferton Books, 112–19.

——1977e. *Outline of a Theory of Practice.* Cambridge: Cambridge University Press.

——1978. 'Sur l'objectivation participante'. *Actes de la recherche en sciences sociales*, 2/3, 67–94.

——1979a. *La Distinction. Critique sociale du jugement de gout.* Paris: Éditions de Minuit (translated as 1984b).

——1979b. *Algeria 1960.* Cambridge: Cambridge University Press; Paris: Éditions de la Maison des Sciences de l'Homme.

——1980a. *Le sens pratique.* Paris: Éditions de Minuit (translated as 1990b).

——1980b. *Questions de sociologie.* Paris: Éditions de Minuit (translated as 1993c).

——1981. 'La représentation politique. Éléments pour une théorie du champ politique'. *Actes de la recherche en sciences sociales*, 36/37, 3–24.

——1982. *Leçon sur la leçon*. Paris: Editions de Minuit (translated as 'A Lecture on the Lecture' in 1990c, 177–98).

——1983. 'The Field of Cultural Production, or: The Economic World Reversed'. *Poetics*, 12(4/5), 311–56.

——1984a. *Homo Academicus*. Paris: Éditions de Minuit (translated as 1988a).

——1984b. *Distinction: A Social Critique of the Judgement of Taste*. London: Routledge; Cambridge, MA: Harvard University Press.

——1984c. 'Espace social et genèse des classes'. *Actes de la recherche en sciences sociales*, 52–53, 3–12 (translated as 1985).

——1985. 'The Social Space and the Genesis of Groups'. *Theory and Society*, 14(6), 723–44.

——1986. 'La force du droit. Eléments pour une sociologie du champ juridique'. *Actes de la recherche en sciences sociales*, 64, 5–19.

——1987. *Choses dites*. Paris: Éditions de Minuit.

——1988a. *Homo Academicus*. Cambridge: Polity Press; Stanford, CA: Stanford University Press.

——1988b. *L'ontologie politique de Martin Heidegger*. Paris: Éditions de Minuit (translated as 1991d).

——1989. *La Noblesse d'État. Grandes écoles et esprit de corps*. Paris: Éditions de Minuit (translated as 1996c).

——1990a. 'Droit et passe-droit. Le champ des pouvoirs territoriaux et la mise en œuvre des règlements'. *Actes de la recherche en sciences sociales*, 81–82, 86–96.

——1990b. *The Logic of Practice*. Cambridge: Polity Press.

——1990c. *In Other Words: Essays Towards a Reflexive Sociology*. Stanford: Stanford University Press; Cambridge: Polity.

——1991a. 'Le champ littéraire'. *Actes de la recherche en sciences sociales*, 89, 3–46.

——1991b. 'Genesis and Structure of the Religious Field'. *Comparative Social Research*, 13, 1–44.

——1991c. 'The Peculiar History of Scientific Reason'. *Sociological Forum* 6(1), 3–26.

——1991d. *The Political Ontology of Martin Heidegger*. Stanford: Stanford University Press; Cambridge: Polity.

——1992. *Les Règles de l'art. Genèse et structure du champ littéraire*. Paris: Seuil (translated as 1996a).

——1993a. 'The Production of Belief: Contribution to an Economy of Symbolic Goods'. In R. Johnson (ed.) *The Field of Cultural Production*. Cambridge: Polity Press; New York: Columbia University Press, 74–111.

——1993b. 'A propos de la famille comme catégorie réalisée'. *Actes de la recherche en sciences sociales*, 100, 32–36 (translated as 1996d).

——1993c. *Sociology in Question*. London: Sage Publications.

——(ed.) 1993d. *La Misère du monde*. Paris: Éditions du Seuil (translated as 1999).

——1994. *Raisons pratiques. Sur la théorie de l'action*. Paris: Seuil (translated as 1998c)

——1995. 'La cause de la science'. *Actes de la recherche en sciences sociales*, 106–7, 3–10.

——1996a. *The Rules of Art: Genesis and Structure of the Literary Field*. Cambridge: Polity; Stanford: Stanford University Press.

——1996b. 'Champ politique, champ des sciences sociales, champ journalistique'. *Cahiers de recherche*, 15 (Lyon: GRS).

——1996c. *The State Nobility: Elite Schools in the Field of Power*. Cambridge: Polity; Stanford: Stanford University Press.

——1996d. 'On the Family as a Realized Category'. *Theory, Culture & Society*, 13(1), 19–26.

——1996e. *Sur la télévision. Suivi de l'Emprise du journalisme.* Paris: Liber-Raisons d'agir.

——1997a. *Les Usages sociaux de la science: Pour une sociologie clinique du champ scientifique.* Paris: INRA.

——1997b. *Méditations pascaliennes.* Paris: Seuil (translated as 2000c).

——1997c. 'De la maison du roi à la raison d'État. Un modèle de la genèse du champ bureaucratique'. *Actes de la recherche en sciences sociales*, 118, 55–68 (translated as 2004a).

——1997d. 'Le champ économique'. *Actes de la recherche en sciences sociales*, 119, 48–66.

——1998a. *Contre-feux.* Paris: Éditions Raison d'agir (translated as 1998b).

——1998b. *Acts of Resistance: Against the New Myths of Our Time.* Cambridge: Polity.

——1998c. *Practical Reason: On the Theory of Action.* Cambridge: Polity; Stanford: Stanford University Press.

——(ed.) 1999. *The Weight of the World: Social Suffering in Contemporary Society.* Cambridge: Polity Press.

——2000a. *Les Structures sociales de l'économie.* Paris: Seuil (translated as 2003).

——2000b. *Pascalian Meditations.* Cambridge: Polity; Stanford: Stanford University Press.

——2000c. *Propos sur le champ politique.* Lyon: Presse Universitaire de Lyon.

——2001a. *Langage et pouvoir symbolique.* Paris: Fayard.

——2001b. *Science de la science et réflexivité.* Paris: Éditions Raisons d'agir (translated as 2004b).

——2003. *The Social Structures of the Economy.* Cambridge: Polity Press.

——2004a. 'From the King's House to the Reason of State: A Model of the Genesis of the Bureaucratic Field'. *Constellations*, 11(1), 16–36.

——2004b. *Science of Science and Reflexivity.* Cambridge: Polity Press.

——2013. *Sur Manet: Une révolution symbolique.* Paris: Seuil/Raisons d'agir.

Bourdieu, P. and Boltanski, L. 1976. 'La production de l'idéologie dominante. *Actes de la recherche en sciences sociales*, 2(2/3), 3–73.

Bourdieu, P., Chamboredon, J.-C. and Passeron, J.-C. 1972. *Le Métier de sociologue: préalables épistemologiques.* Paris: Mouton (translated as 1991).

——1991. *The Craft of Sociology: Epistemological Preliminaries.* New York: Walter de Gruyter.

Bourdieu, P. and de Saint Martin, M. 1982. 'La sainte famille. L'épiscopat français dans le champ du pouvoir'. *Actes de la recherche en sciences sociales*, 44–45, 2–53.

——1987a. 'Agrégation et ségrégation. Le champ des grandes écoles et le champ du pouvoir'. *Actes de la recherche en sciences sociales*, 69, 2–50.

——1987b. 'Variations et invariants. Éléments pour une histoire structurale du champ des grandes écoles'. *Actes de la recherche en sciences sociales*, 70, 3–30.

Bourdieu, P. and Wacquant, L.J.D. 1992. *An Invitation to Reflexive Sociology.* Chicago: University of Chicago Press; Cambridge: Polity Press.

Boyer, R. 2003. 'L'Anthropologie économique de Pierre Bourdieu'. *Actes de la recherche en sciences sociales*, 150, 65–78.

Cassirer, E. 1923. *Substance and Function and Einstein's Theory of Relativity.* Chicago and London: Open Court Publishing Co.

——2000. *The Logic of the Cultural Sciences: Five Studies.* New Haven: Yale University Press.

Christin, O. 1997. *La Paix de religion. L'autonomisation de la raison politique au XVIe siècle.* Paris: Éditions du Seuil.

Durand, G. 2008. *Du sens des formes au sens des formalités.* Paris: Éditions du Seuil.

Duval, J. 2004. *Critique de la raison journalistique. Les transformations de la presse economique en France.* Paris: Éditions du Seuil.

Faucheux, C. 1959. Introduction to K. Lewin, Psychologie dynamique. Les relations humaines. Paris: PUF (French translation of Lewin 1935).

Fillieule O., Blanchard, Ph., Agrikoliansky, E., Bandler, M., Passy, F., Sommier, I. 2004. 'L'Altermondialisation en réseaux. Trajectoires militantes, multipositionnalité et formes de l'engagement: les participants du contre-sommet du G8 d'Evian'. *Politix*, 17(68), 13–48. doi: 10.3406/polix.2004.1992.

Garcia-Parpet, M.-F. 2009. *Le Marché de l'excellence. Les grands crus à l'épreuve de la mondialisation.* Paris: Seuil.

Gartman, D. 1991. 'Culture as Class Symbolization or Mass Reification? A Critique of Bourdieu's *Distinction*'. *American Journal of Sociology*, 97(2), 421–47.

——2002. 'Bourdieu's Theory of Cultural Change: Explication, Application, Critique'. *Sociological Theory*, 20(2), 255–77.

Gautier, C. 2012. *La force du social: enquête philosophique sur la sociologie des pratiques de Pierre Bourdieu.* Paris: Cerf.

Geay, B. 1999. *Profession: Instituteurs. Mémoire politique et actions syndicale.* Paris: Seuil.

Ghins, M. 1990. *L'Inertie et l'espace absolu de Newton à Einstein.* Brussels: Académie royale de Belgique.

Grignon, C. and Passeron, J.C. 1989. *Le Savant et le Populaire, Misérabilisme et populisme en sociologie et en littérature.* Paris: Gallimard/Le Seuil.

Heinich, N. 2007. *Pourquoi Bourdieu.* Paris: Gallimard.

Hesse, M. 1961. *Forces and Fields: The Concept of Action at a Distance in the History of Physics.* London: Thomas Nelson & Sons Ltd.

Hilgers, M. 2006. *Liberté et habitus chez Pierre Bourdieu.* EspacesTemps.net. www. espacestemps.net/document2064.html.

——2007. 'Hysteresis', in *ABCédaire Pierre Bourdieu.* Paris: Sil Maris-Vrin, 87–89

—— 2009. 'Habitus, Freedom and Reflexivity'. *Theory and Psychology*, 19(6), 728–55.

——2013 'Embodying Neoliberalism. Thoughts and responses to critics'. *Social Anthropology*, 21(1), 75–89.

Lahire, B. 1999. 'Champ, hors-champ, contrechamp'. In B. Lahire (ed.) *Le Travail sociologique de Pierre Bourdieu, dette et critique.* Paris: La Découverte, 23–57.

——2010. *The Plural Actor.* Cambridge: Polity Press.

Lebaron, F. 2000. *La croyance économique. Les économistes entre science et politique.* Paris: Seuil.

Legros, E. 1989. *L'Analyse des correspondances. Démarches et réflexions critiques.* Louvain-la-Neuve: CIACO.

Lenoir, R. 2003. *Généalogie de la morale familiale.* Paris: Seuil.

Lewin, K. 1935. *A Dynamic Theory of Personality.* New York and London: McGraw-Hill.

——1943. 'Defining the "Field at a Given Time"'. In K. Lewin, *Field Theory in Social Science. Selected Theoretical Papers.* Westport, CT: Greenwood Press.

——1949. 'Cassirer's Philosophy of Science and the Social Sciences'. In P.A. Schilpp (ed.) *The Philosophy of Ernst Cassirer.* Illinois: Library of Living Philosophers.

Mangez, E. 2008. *Réformer les contenus d'enseignement. Une sociologie du curriculum.* Paris: PUF.

Mangez, E. and Hilgers, M. 2012. 'The Field of Knowledge and the Policy Field in Education: PISA and the Production of Knowledge for Policy'. *European Educational Research Journal*, 11(2), 189–205.

Martin, J.L. 2003. 'What is Field Theory?' *American Journal of Sociology*, 109(1), 1–49.

Mary, P. 2006. *La Nouvelle Vague et le cinéma d'auteur. Socio-analyse d'une révolution artistique.* Paris: Seuil.

Moessinger, P. 1994. 'Tentative de clarification de la théorie de Bourdieu'. *Archives Européennes de Sociologie*, 35, 323–33.

Mounier, P. 2001. *Pierre Bourdieu, une introduction.* Paris: Agora.

Parlett, M. 1991. 'Reflections on Field Theory'. *The British Gestalt Journal*, 1, 68–91.

Passeron, J.-C. 2003. 'Mort d'un ami, disparition d'un penseur'. In P. Encrevé and R.-M. Lagrave (eds) *Travailler avec Bourdieu.* Paris: Flammarion, 17–90.

Patte, Y. 2006. 'Sur le concept de "champ". L'approche "more geometrico" d'un débat public, la prostitution en Belgique'. *Sociologie et sociétés*, 38(1), 235–61.

Pinto, L. 2000. *Pierre Bourdieu et la théorie du monde social.* Paris: Éditions du Seuil.

——2007. *La vocation et le métier de philosophe. Pour une sociologie de la philosophie dans la France contemporaine.* Paris: Éditions du Seuil.

Sapiro, G. 2003. 'The Literary Field Between the State and the Market'. *Poetics*, 31(5), 441–64.

Tissot, S. 2007. *L'État et les quartiers. Genèse d'une catégorie de l'action publique.* Paris: Seuil.

Vandenberghe, F. 1999. '"The Real is Relational": An Epistemological Analysis of Pierre Bourdieu's Generative Structuralism'. *Sociological Theory*, 17(1), 32–67.

Weyl, H. 1920. *Space-Time-Matter.* London: Methuen.

Part I
Theoretical investigations

1 Was Bourdieu a field theorist?[1]

John Levi Martin and Forest Gregg

Introduction

Field theory was introduced into the psychological social sciences in the mid-twentieth century by German psychologists and philosophers (after the war, mainly expatriates to the United States). Influenced by physics, these thinkers borrowed the distinctive features of physical field theories for application to the human realm. While this genealogy was largely extinguished within American social theory somewhere in the 1970s, as it was dying out in the United States, Pierre Bourdieu was resurrecting field theory in France, making it the heart of his own explanatory apparatus. His renown has led many current students of the social sciences to conflate field theory and Bourdieu's own writings, making it impossible even to ask whether Bourdieu was indeed a rigorous field theorist, let alone to see in what directions his ideas have contributed to the project of field theory.

In this chapter, we first outline the fundamental characteristics of field theory in the natural sciences. We then briefly discuss how this was adapted by the Gestalt theorists for the case of human behaviour. We then argue that Bourdieu was indeed a rigorous field theorist. Assuming that the outlines of Bourdieu's own work are familiar enough to our readers, we do not document Bourdieu's use of core field theoretic principles, but instead concentrate on where we believe he made important advances that will be necessary for any similar field theoretic approach. We finally discuss what we believe are the potentially problematic or confusing aspects of Bourdieu's own work considered in field theoretic terms. These are: 1 the relation between social space and particular fields; 2 the relation between capital and field position; and 3 the relation of vectors to extra-field positions or outcomes.

Essences of field theory

Some characteristics of field theory

Field theory, as an approach, developed first and most fully in the physical sciences through various attempts to comprehend how one thing could affect another without some substantive medium. While there are a number of different fields, and theories of each have varied over the course of their development, the best model of intellectually rigorous field theory would be classical (non-relativistic) electro-magnetism, though the important features here are found in similar systems. (Newtonian gravitation has much in common with field theory, but only Einstein's general relativity actually technically gave it a field theoretic form; Hesse 1970: 226.)

Field theories really took the basic form of the fluid mechanics developed in the eighteenth century, in which equations linked a 'flow' or potential for transmitted force to spatial coordinates, but applied this form to situations where no fluid could be found; examples are motion induced by gravity, electricity, or magnetism (Hesse 1970: 181; Rummel 1975: 26; also cf. Köhler 1947: 127). An examination of classical electro-magnetism suggests that field theory may be said to have the following characteristics:

- It purports to explain changes in the states of some elements (e.g. a static field induces motion in a charged particle) but need not appeal to changes in states of other elements (that is, 'causes').
- These changes in state involve an interaction between the field and the existing states of the elements (e.g. a particle of positive charge moves one way and one of negative charge another) (see Maxwell 1954 [1891]: 68; Koffka 1935: 42; Köhler 1947: 300).
- The elements have particular attributes which make them susceptible to the field effect (particles differ in the degree and direction of charge).
- The field without the elements is only a potential for the creation of force, without any existent force (Hesse 1970: 196).
- The field itself is organized and differential (Koffka 1935: 117). At any position the field is a vector of potential force and these vectors are neither randomly nor discontinuously distributed.

It is worth pointing out how utterly at odds such a conception is with the conventional understanding of causality in the social sciences. According to this conception, elements have attributes, mutually exclusive attributes often being considered instances of a 'variable'. Some of an element's variables are imagined to be linked together mechanically, such that a change in one variable must produce a change in another. While the mechanism may yet be obscure, social scientists recognize causality when a change in state in one variable of an element produced by external manipulation *impels* a change in state in another variable of that element. Causality follows a mental image of external impulsion taken from classical mechanics (basically the conception of Hobbes, though more Rube Goldberg than Minnesota Fats), but recasts this in terms of variables, as opposed to substances (see Abbott 1988).

In contrast, a rigorous field theoretic approach allows for one element's state to change without requiring that it be due to a change in state in another element (let alone a *different* change in the state in the same element).

Such a field theoretic approach was introduced into the social and behavioural sciences by the Gestalt psychologists. We go on to review the central emphasis of the Gestalt school, and then how the members formulated field theory.

The development of field theory

The non-independence of percepts

The Gestalt idea is generally attributed to Christian Ehrenfels, who had studied with Alexius Meinong at Graz. Ehrenfels (1988 [1890]: 112) pointed out not only that there are qualities that can only exist as a whole (for example, a timbre or a melody), but that we are not aware of any conscious activity whereby we generate this quality through synthesis. While acknowledging Ehrenfels's priority, the motive force in establishing an empirical school of psychology was really Max Wertheimer, who had attended lectures by Ehrenfels (Heider 1983: 44).

However, Wertheimer had also been influenced by Carl Stumpf, who had sketched the lines for the sort of phenomenology that was to turn into Gestalt psychology. Responding to the debate over the position of the 'cultural sciences' (*Geisteswissenschaften*; Dilthey 1988 [1883]: 78, 91, 97, 125, 131), Stumpf argued that more fundamental than either of the two commonly identified branches of sciences (natural and cultural) was phenomenology, a science of the structure of the phenomena with which each of these begin. (Stumpf's student Husserl was later to emphasize one version of such a phenomenological study as a form of 'pure psychology'.)[2] This phenomenology demonstrates that our world is not the world of the Cartesians. First, in contrast to the pure, isotropic and homogenous space of geometry, the space we live in has certain relations built into it (at any time, some things 'are' to the left, say), and it has unevenesses in it (and indeed, our vision has boundaries) (Stumpf 1907: 72, 9). These are characteristics of the objects we confront, not things we put into them.

Stumpf thus proposed not only an ideal phenomenology that retained the distinction between the pure visions of the natural sciences and our actual experienced world, but a version of psychology attuned to philosophical questions (as opposed to the narrower professionalism of the American model). Both these principles – an embracing of immediate experience and an engagement with philosophical questions – marked the approach of Stumpf's students who were to found the Gestalt school: in addition to Wertheimer, Wolfgang Köhler and Kurt Koffka (Smith 1988: 12, 45; Neisser 2002: 4; Ash 1998: 118, 120, 124).[3]

What Wertheimer did was to seize upon one key aspect of this idea as the basis for experimental research. Both Stumpf and Ehrenfels had pointed to the importance of our capacity to hear harmonics – relations – as unities. The way to understand our actual, empirical, phenomenological experience would be to investigate how we captured such whole forms ('Gestalts') as unified objects of experience (and not as aggregates or syntheses). In other words, Stumpf's phenomenology was inseparable from two other pre-sciences that he proposed, a science of structure and a science-of-relations, for the objects that we perceive – or at least their character as quality-bearing objects – are themselves structures, and structures are sets of relations.

A phenomenology of relations

These planks were of great utility for psychologists attempting to account for the non-independence of perceptual elements, which did not square with the dominant mechanistic explanation of sight. According to this latter view, photons stimulate retinal cells which lead to neurons firing which lead to a copy of the visual field reproduced in some portion of the brain. This field is then processed according to some mental template, leading to a distinction between the psychology of perception and the psychology of judgement.

Wertheimer (1922: 48, v) called this the 'mosaic or bundle thesis' of perception and consciousness: that all higher-order elements were the sum of elemental contents constructed according to mere 'and' summation. Connections between elements were generally ascribed to 'association', a type of relation that was indifferent to the content of the elements (cf. Cassirer 1923 [1910]: 285). Those who began from this assumption had a difficult time explaining cases in which our perception of one thing (e.g. distance) is affected by something else in the visual field: they were forced to argue that these were illusions of *judgement*. Wertheimer, in contrast, began from an assumption that what we perceive is a totality of relations that far from being arbitrary expressed the nature of the concrete laws of their formal structure (Wertheimer 1922: 53). While the 'mosaic thesis' assumed that the unit percepts were primary, and the larger structures derivative of some act of mental formulation, Wertheimer argued that the whole was primary, and its structural principles as objective as anything else.

It is not, of course, invariably the case that there is such a complicity between mental and environmental structures; indeed, we can subjectively experience and scientifically study the transition whereby we bring our mental structure into alignment with the environment, a process which Köhler (1925 [1917]: 17, 99, 173ff, 190, 198; also Köhler 1938: 31) called 'insight', 'a complete solution with reference to the whole lay-out of the field'. In contrast to behaviourist theories which predicted a continuous transition between random and useful behaviour, Köhler argued that it was easy to see the discontinuity in behaviour exactly at the point in which the subject (person or animal) manages to encompass the problem as a whole, and carries out actions with steps that, taken in isolation, contribute nothing to the solution.[4] This was a reasonable and relatively rigorous extrapolation from Gestalt studies of perception. In contrast to the mosaic thesis which imagines the perceptual field is always composed of 'parts', a Gestalt exists when any sub-set of the overall field must be understood as a *position* in reference to the set of other positions (Metzger 1986 [1975]: 160). So, too, Köhler argued, when the animal 'gets it', we can understand any action only in terms of a position in a sequence that, as a whole and only then, provides a solution.

Gestalts and fields

Thus Gestalt theorists had argued that one could not understand how an organism sensed the environment without attention to the field of perception as a whole.[5] Thus one reason for the transition to field theory was that the Gestalt psychologists were most interested in the field of perception (that is, the perceptual field), and they argued that there were tension relations between different parts of this field. Any one percept (bit of perception) was likely to have its meaning only in relation to others. Köhler recalled that his goal was to determine 'why percepts at a distance have an effect on one another. This is only possible, we assumed (and we followed Faraday in doing so), if the individual percept has a field and if the "field", which surrounds the percept, does not merely reveal the presence of this percept but also presents its specific properties' (cited in Mey 1972: 13ff; for a discussion of the relation of Gestalt theory to field theory, see Mohr n.d., forthcoming).

The non-independence of parts, then, was the key insight that led Gestalt psychology to see the perceptual field *as* a field, as opposed to an indifferent Cartesian space. The visual field is organized into wholes from the earliest stages of our perceptual experience. As Köhler (1947: 118, cf. 259) wrote in his classic introduction to Gestalt psychology, 'As to the statement that sensory experience is a mosaic of purely local facts in the sense that each point of a sensory field depends exclusively upon its local stimulus, I must repeat that no grounds have ever been given for this radical assumption. Rather it seems to be the expression of an a priori belief about what ought to be the nature of things, experience to the contrary notwithstanding'.

However, field theory was implied by three other considerations. One was an epistemological conviction of the importance of mutual self-organization of systems, the sorts of ideas that we would now associate with Luhmann (1995). We seem to take for granted, Köhler (1929: 107, 145) wrote, that 'the processes of nature, if they are left to their own "blind" play, will never produce anything like order'. In contrast, Köhler (1929: 112, 121) proposed that seemingly independent elements are interdependent in ways that give rise to an overall set of dynamics. Thus the field emerges from the constant reciprocal adjustments of elements in relation to one another. This, Köhler argued, was in contrast to the dominant explanatory principles in which any form of change or regularity involved external *impulsion*, which he termed the 'machine theory'. This machine theory with its emphasis on external constraint might be well and good for the case of water in a pipe, but consider a drop in the ocean, along with other drops: each one moves according to the resultant vector of forces coming from its interaction with all other drops.[6]

This technically implies a field theory, for we have a set of positions such that at any point and time, there is one resulting force at any position that can be described as a vector. 'All the resultant forces together form one texture of stresses' (Köhler 1929: 134, 139).

Köhler's illustrations of physical systems (such as water molecules) were not thrown out carelessly; he had a fundamentally unified understanding of the relationship between fields and Gestalts that spanned the smallest physical systems and the most distinctly human phenomenological experiences. In a controversial (1920) work, he had made a careful argument for the existence of Gestalts in physical systems, using as his key example the way in which a variable amount of electric charge would be identically distributed across the surface of a conductor of a particular shape. (That is, the density distribution would be the same no matter what the magnitude of total charge.) This occurred because, argued Köhler, two aspects explained the final distribution of charge; one, the topography of the conductor, but the other, the dynamic laws of interaction which were one form of a general class of dynamics that led to self-organizing stability (or instability), depending on initial conditions.

The vectors that described the movement of charged particles were, thought Köhler, not different in nature from those that were experienced in the phenomenological world. To make this mapping, Köhler carefully considered the simplest phenomenological vector known to him, that which occurs when a lighter and a darker area of the visual field abut one another. We know that there is an interaction here (indeed, you are likely to see a 'border' in the form of a distinct and dark line between such areas), and Köhler argued that this was best understood as arising from the differential in potential across the two areas. There must, he argued, be some area in the brain in which two similar areas also abutted, also with some sort of potential difference.

The final verdict is still out on some of these issues, but Köhler was overly optimistic in his assumptions as to the simplicity of his neurological model. However, while it seems that differences in the visual fields do not map as neatly onto differentials between locations in the visual cortex as he thought, the overall logic remains sound. For, just as Köhler argued, neurons fire precisely because of an electrochemical potential building up along an axon. Further, as he emphasized, neurons are unshielded cables, meaning that it is not that a pulse travels 'inside' the neuron, but that one travels inside while the inverse charge proceeds on the outside.[7] This suggests that brain processes (unlike computer processes) are physically interdependent and themselves have field-like properties. Other scientists basically bracketed this not because Köhler's argument was wrong (the logic is fine as far as it goes, although there actually is a fair amount of insulating shielding of at least motor-system neurons), but because it was too complex to think about. Our default model of the brain in the social sciences still falsely assumes neurons as perfectly insulated wires.

In sum, one could be brought to a field theory from elementary considerations of neurology as well as from general epistemic considerations, but

Köhler also argued that the phenomenology of primate behaviour pointed us towards a field theoretic exploration of behaviour. Most famously, in his early work with apes, Köhler (1925 [1917]: 14, 89, 180, 182; also Köhler 1938: 95) had described their movement in some cases using a metaphor of traversing one of the 'lines of force' that Faraday saw emerging from magnets. One example was the inability of an animal near a desired object to move away in order to take a successful indirect path around an intervening obstacle, this inability increasing the closer the animal came to the object, such that an animal beginning on an insightful, indirect path might be drawn helplessly to the object if he came too near it, and would end up abandoning the successful initial plan. In such cases, the animal's action would be better explained by proposing that the object had a gravity-like pull than by attempting to explain the animal responding to differential stimuli from the environment.

Such phenomena are to be seen in humans as well as apes. Köhler gives the hypothetical example of a kindly boss trying to upbraid an underling. 'You may see him walking up and down before the other, as a magnetic needle swings in the field of force ... ' The boss can say the *nice* things while looking into the other's eyes. 'Social forces are not opposed to that; on the contrary, they operate precisely in that direction. But try to look into another's eyes, i.e., toward what we experience ... as the center of the other man's personality, and tell him what obligates you to be less friendly ... !' (Köhler 1929: 254). 'Just as this man feels his intentions bending around and his words avoiding the socially decisive step, his visible behavior appears to us as persistently deflected from the main direction, which is toward the other, and especially the visible center of his personality, i.e., his eyes' (Köhler 1929: 255).

In sum, we may see field phenomena as observers, and resulting descriptions of the behaviour of the ape or the boss that invokes the fields of force anchored by certain objects (the bananas, the eyes of the underling) will be parsimonious and generative of predictions, but this external observer-based invocation of field theory has its direct counterpart in the lived experience of actors. The forces are not merely convenient ways of summarizing complex data (as they are in physics), but are (as Durkheim continually emphasized) felt by each of us. When one feels a fright, said Köhler (1929: 381, 390), along with the fright there arises 'a vehement impulse to move away from the locus of that event'. 'In dynamics such a tendency toward increasing the distance between two things or events is called a field of force'.[8]

In sum, the field theory developed by the Gestalt theorists, in addition to fulfilling the general requirements of any field theory, had three characteristic dualities. The first was that the emphasis on the non-independence of elements was coupled with an equally strong emphasis on the generation of overall order through local dynamics. The second was that the topographic representation of the motion of actors mapped on to regularities in the phenomenological experience of actors, for the vectors that characterize the field are potentials for the subjective states of wilful actors. The third is that the relational nature of these vectors means that the same experiences that tell us the qualities of objects, tell us about our own position (Köhler 1947: 297; this was more emphasized by the ecological psychologist J.J. Gibson 1986 [1979]; cf. Mannheim 1940: 212ff).

All of these dualities are characteristic of Bourdieu's approach, and indeed are key to its field theoretic status. Perhaps for this reason, they have been the focus of criticism, as unfamiliarity with a rigorous field theory has frequently led to confusion as would-be critics imagined that Bourdieu's account must be deterministic in some way, or involve a two-stage engine whereby objective and subjective 'causes' politely take their turn. Rather than these being slippages in Bourdieu's logic, they stem from the inherent characteristics of any field theory. The reason for these parallels with the Gestalt school, we argue, is not direct influence, but the inner logic of a coherent field theoretic approach.

From Köhler to sociology

Köhler's ideas were quite influential in psychology for a time, but they entered into the social sciences as well. The most important transmission was in the work of Köhler's friend and colleague Kurt Koffka, who tried to defend and extend Köhler's field theory. A second important route came in the United States, as the psychologist Edward Tolman attempted to smuggle ideas of purposiveness and meaningful wholes from Gestalt theory into American behaviourism; Tolman (1954) went on to contribute a field theory of psychology for the Parsons and Shils volume *Toward a General Theory of Action.*

In addition, there were a few uses of field theory in German social sciences, the first (of which we are aware) being Karl Brandt's (1952) use in economics (though also see Geiger 1949: 51ff).[9] Friedrich Fürstenberg (1969 [1962]) then applied field theory to occupational stratification in an illuminating and enlightening way, anticipating many of the key arguments later made by Bourdieu.

However, it was Lewin, a colleague of Köhler and Wertheimer at the Psychological Institute (see Marrow 1969: 13), who put field theory on the map in social psychology. While Lewin (1951: 240) claimed to find his inspiration for his conception of field in Einstein, his definition of a field as 'a totality of coexisting facts which are conceived of as mutually dependent' is clearly derived from the Gestalt emphasis on totality, and the analytic direction of 'the way from above to below'. Lewin also continued Köhler's emphasis on a coherent phenomenological grounding of behaviour in the qualitative experience of the organism, as well as the ontological complicity of the mind and the world.

Lewin's own attempts to push field theory in a new direction were less successful scientifically than they were professionally – because he enjoyed making topological diagrams of every particular argument he wanted to make, and Americans took more kindly to pictures than abstractions (and we must not deny Lewin's own interpersonal charisma), his idiosyncratic and somewhat flatter version of field theory became the focus of attention in sociology, while Köhler turned his thoughts more to philosophy than sociology. Thus there was little sustained attempt to develop a rigorous field theory of behaviour (with the exception of the ecological psychologists; pursuing this would take us too far afield).

Bourdieu

Bourdieu and his predecessors

While Bourdieu in his early work made references to Lewin (see Swartz 1997: 123 n.15) and takes an epigraph from him in (Bourdieu 1996b [1992]: 177, also 181), he generally did not highlight the connections of his approach to other field theorists (e.g. Bourdieu 1985b); when asked (Bourdieu and Wacquant 1992: 97), he seemed to prefer to emphasize (with perfectly good reason) the joint influence on both himself and Lewin of Cassirer. It is quite likely that Bourdieu's exposure to other Gestalt theorists came indirectly (most certainly through Merleau-Ponty, who was closely in dialogue with the results of the Gestalt psychologists, but also via Sartre, who used some of Lewin's ideas in his work on the emotions and also in *Being and Nothingness*[10]). The homomorphism of Bourdieu's work with that of the Gestalt/field theorists is indicative not of borrowing, but of the internal consistency of the approach.

Because the reader is likely to be able to see that Bourdieu's field theory not only satisfies but highlights the particular aspects we have noted as fundamental to any field theory,[11] and to note the parallels to the work of Köhler, rather than focus on an exhaustive documentation of this, here we wish to emphasize Bourdieu's distinct contribution to field theory. Thus we are not interested in the temporal process whereby Bourdieu's ideas developed, but rather how his most decisive interventions contribute to the wider project of field theory. Further, we emphasize that such a project requires rational reconstruction as opposed to fundamentalism in our understanding of Bourdieu's writings – we are not only permitted but required to surgically remove other aspects of his work before concentrating on his field theory, and indeed to establish the inner consistency of this theory if necessary even against Bourdieu himself.

Our argument is not the weak one that Bourdieu 'was a field theorist' (and certainly not that he was merely 'another' field theorist), nor even that he revived a slumbering tradition, but that he was responsible for key breakthroughs that are necessary for any further progress in the field theoretic tradition. Most importantly, Bourdieu's emphasis on the habitus, far from being an idiosyncratic addition, turns out to be a necessary component of a social field theory, and solves the gravest problem with the Gestalt theory, namely its reliance on naïve realism. The Gestalt theorists, Köhler in particular, went from the (defensible) major premise that the phenomenological world of experience is as real as worlds get to the (more problematic) argument that we could in any and all case(s) barring psychosis treat the qualities of someone's experience as 'in' the things experienced. Such naïve realism is fine as far as it goes, but it doesn't go very far in the social sciences, where we are used to antithetical qualitative experience (one man's mead is another man's poison[12]). It is one thing to say that to the hungry rat, the cheese beckons because the cheese *is* good, but does the cello piece by Xennakis beckon for the same reason?

Bourdieu emphasized that a plausible theory of practice had to have a component in which we become the sort-of-beast that we are; that is, that we develop that particular set of responses and dispositions to the world that allow the world's properties to be meaningful *to us* (Bourdieu 1969 [1966]: 182). (A more complete discussion of the relation of habit and habitus to field theory will be found in Martin 2011.) In classical magnetism, the process whereby a substance is made to generate the field effect is known as 'hysteresis' and Bourdieu understood the importance of its place in any social field theory. It is perhaps significant that this sort of developmental account is now being proposed (quite independently) in ecological psychology for the same reasons (Chemero 2009).

Second, from his relatively early work (Bourdieu 1977 [1972]) to later (e.g. Bourdieu 1996b [1992]: 10), Bourdieu argued that it is no mixed metaphor to consider a field both a field of forces and a field of struggle that has game-like aspects to it. Although one might argue that Köhler's understanding of dynamics already implied this notion of the game, Bourdieu made what is almost certainly the correct linkage of this abstract question to the nature of human social action, namely that the dynamics involve expectations, expectations that may be violated, as social contestation is often a poorly policed game.

Finally, as Bourdieu has often emphasized, his use of correspondence analysis as a core analytic technique is certainly rigorously related to a relational perspective (Bourdieu *et al.* 1991 [1968]: 254; 1988 [1984]: 23f; Bourdieu and Wacquant 1992: 96) and most probably it has physical field theoretic interpretations that have an analogous interpretation for the application to social science.

However, Bourdieu's field theoretic approach has some potential problems. Note that here we do not consider as problematic all those aspects of Bourdieu's work that are not tightly coupled to the field theoretic aspects (for Bourdieu's theory is not only a field theoretic one). Rather, we point to aspects of Bourdieu's field theory that, understood *as* field theory, raise certain issues. We will tend to use as our main illustration Bourdieu's analysis of the literary field, which is perhaps his most orthodox application of core field theoretic principles (see Bourdieu 1996b [1992]: 9 where he ties the field in physics to the phenomenological field and, quite true to Köhler, notes that the motion is due not only to the forces in the field but also the objects' initial inertia[13]).

Space and homology

One potential area of confusion pertains to the relation between the different fields and the underlying social space. In a rigorous field theoretic treatment, space can be treated in one of two ways. It can be the empty and neutral positions of Newtonian/Cartesian space, in which case fields are things that can occur *in* space (with their vectors pointing to positions in this space), or it can be the warped space of Einstein, meaning that it is inseparable from fields. Bourdieu usually seems to go in the first direction: his space is one that is generally proposed as an analytic simplification (a bird's-eye view), yet one that maps onto fields with their different dimensionality and different sets of positions. However, at other times Bourdieu treats the space as itself having the same properties as a field (as in Bourdieu 1985a: 724), and speaks of an overall 'social field' (later, e.g. Bourdieu 1996a [1989], the 'field of power' seems to fulfil a similar function with similarly confusing results).[14]

Related to this issue is the question of the reasons for the homology between fields. We will here distinguish between two types of homology: substantive and formal. Two fields are substantively homologous if there is a mapping of a position in one to a position in the other based on transposable characteristics of the position (which includes likely characteristics of occupants). Thus we may speak of a homology in the field of dance to the field of music if certain dance and certain music is 'light' and 'pretty' while other dance and other music is 'difficult' and 'intellectual'. So too we might speak of a homology if the same distribution of persons is found across the fields (thus in both fields, say, elementary school teachers are together and separated from clerical workers). The simplest substantive homology occurs when the dimensions of social space are recognizable in the positions that actors take in the field.

We would say that two fields are formally homologous when we can identify similar formal principles across the fields, although the positions, the persons, or the types of persons are not similarly distributed in the two fields. For example, the field of calligraphy and the field of grass track motorcycle racing may be formally homologous in that the key differentiation pits (in this imaginary example) purists against challengers, but there are no substantive similarities across positions (thus in one field the purists may be older while in the other they are younger, in one field the purists may be more educated while in the other less so, and so on).

There are good reasons to expect both sorts of homologies. Regarding the former, we must acknowledge that the processes that pertain to the formation of habitus tend to be early and hence associated with a fundamental position in social space. After all, we are not raised in the field of photography, but in a lower middle-class provincial neighbourhood, say. Field experience may indeed alter habitus, but associations between varieties of habitus and field position are more likely to arise by those of different habitus having different reactions to the field effect than by the habitus internalizing different field trajectories.[15]

Thus given that fields recruit from the same social space (Bourdieu 1984 [1979]), and given that aspects of habitus that are predictably related to position in social space are also relevant for field dynamics, we would certainly expect some sort of non-independence across position in fields. However, Bourdieu clearly believes that this sort of gross substantive homology is necessarily limited.

For one, Bourdieu emphasizes that all fields have their own autonomous lawfulness (Bourdieu 1969 [1966]: 161ff; Bourdieu 1990: 389; Bourdieu 1993: 72). There may indeed be transposable aspects of position in social space, but these must be translated into the specific logic of each field in order for them to become operative. Although this vision of autonomy is logically compatible with complete homology, it does not seem that Bourdieu would accept this conclusion. It is true that eggheads are eggheads (and meatheads are meatheads) when they listen to music, and also when they dine, and also when they read books, and so on, and so we might expect them to sort themselves out in similar fashion across fields. However, if even in intricate and involuted worlds like those of music composition, philosophy or haute couture, we were only to find the usual suspects in the same positions but wearing different hats, no one would seriously embark on a field theoretic account.

There may also be good reason for formal homologies, at least in certain types of fields. Perhaps the single most fundamental formal homology would have to do with one's total amount of capital – in every field, some are on top, some on the bottom; some dominant, some dominated. Such homologies then could lead to some sort of shared experience and perhaps explain sympathetic relations across fields or to social space in general – even though the lower-upper class may be more like the upper-middle class in economic terms, in experiential terms they may feel more like the lower-middle class given their experience of being relatively dominated in their social world (cf. Abbott 2001: 183ff). This could account for Bourdieu's argument not only that the dominated fraction of a cultural field has an inclination to *speak* to those dominated overall (Bourdieu 1985a: 735–36), but that there is a more fundamental mapping between certain cultural fields and 'the field of power or the social field in its entirety' (Bourdieu 1996b [1992]: 205, also see 164, 250; also see Bourdieu 1993: 143ff).

We may proceed further on these lines and propose a general second dimension. Consider a 'well-defined field' with only a single axis of internal stratification in which a dominant position means nothing other than the capacity to consecrate others (and to have been so consecrated)[16]. Others will struggle not only to attain the capital of this field, but to adapt the rules so that whatever capital they are most likely to be able to attain is most likely to be *the* capital of the field. Adopting Sartre's formula, we might say that a field is a game whose game is in question.

This suggests a differentiation between heterodoxy and orthodoxy, which, perhaps crossed with a second dimension of total volume of capital, could be found across fields. Indeed, this is one aspect of the homology that Bourdieu often discusses. Yet there is a second formal homology which is somewhat different. We might imagine that in many fields we find a core differentiation that pertains to the degree of commitment to the inherent logic of the field and a correlative dispersion of strategies and trajectories (e.g., Bourdieu [1992] 1996: 161). Some buy in to the 'illusio' without reservation and pursue the stakes of the field with total commitment, only looking for the approval of those who are approved of by other insiders (what Lang and Lang [1988] and Lena [2010] call 'recognition'). In contrast to these 'buy ins' are the 'sell-outs' – those who, even if they too are susceptible to the special magic of the field, still seek a 'renown' in Lang and Lang's terms that is bought through whoring their goods to outsiders. Although this might be a form of heterodoxy, it is not the same as the heterodoxy that is compatible with purity. Indeed, we might imagine the orthodox being challenged by the impure popularizers on the one hand, and the young Turks on the other. Hence an autonomous orientation appears as pure and a heteronomous as impure, which would suggest a stable formal division ... were it not for the fact that there can be fierce debate as to what the inner principles of the field actually *are* (an important point to which we return below).

Bourdieu makes few global statements about homology, but he seems to shift among these three types of homology (one substantive, two formal) depending on the case, and perhaps gives more of an impression of an over-arching logic of homology than is warranted. (His key method of correspon-dence analysis does not uniquely identify dimensions; these are interpretations proposed by the analyst. Homology is then in many ways an assumption, not a finding.) Further, we have the sense that were a committed Lévi-Straussian to attempt to work out the binary oppositions underlying Bourdieu's own thought, she would determine that Bourdieu tends to associate the opposition of purity:impurity with culture:economy and, at least in cultural fields, with endogenous:exogenous and hence autonomous:heteronomous.[17]

That is, Bourdieu not only tended to assume (especially in Wacquant 1993: 24) the overriding importance of the division within the ruling class pointed to by Marx and Engels (1976 [1845]) between the active rulers (on the one hand) and the ideologues who make up the illusions of the class (on the other), but its ubiquitous microcosmic analogues, precisely because the fields he tended to find interesting were those in which these dynamics were at play. Thus it may seem that at least in cultural fields, there is a homology with social space because of the separation between endogenously generated repu-tation as opposed to exogenously generated renown. One would not, of course, expect this homology to appear in the same form in the field of finan-cial physics, or that of venture capital, or perhaps even that of top 40 pop music.

So the confidence with which those inspired by Bourdieu go about looking for a distinction between autonomy and heteronomy may be an overly optimistic one – for in most cases, this is not a formal characteristic of fields but an evaluative overlay at best, and an ideological obfuscation at worst. While perhaps winners do not always get to write all the history books and make the losers those who 'started the war,' still, the inner principles of today's field is likely to be determined by tomorrow's configuration of positions. That the *eigengesetzlichkeit* of a field is nothing other than the consecration of contingency, however, in no way forbids a science of regularities.

This issue of homology is related to the question of whether there is some inherent difficulty in what to consider as 'a' field. Most field theorists dismiss this as an irrelevancy stemming from an incomplete grasp of the nature of field theory: fields are not defined nominalistically, by the analyst forcing a cookie cutter on the material, but rather are defined by the real, experienced, mutual orientation of sets of actors. However, if one makes a claim as to the general existence of a homology to social space, where one draws the boundaries may make quite a difference. There may indeed be (as Bourdieu shows) a homology between social space and the choice of various activities, including sports to play, not only for amateurs, but even for professionals. But there is no single 'field of sport' in the sense of a set of professionals or aficionados pursuing a single stakes as there might be in the field of gymnastics.[18]

Were there such a global field – that is, not only might gymnastics might appeal to those with one capital composition and rugby to those with a different one, but there would be meaningful trajectories from gymnastics to rugby and vice versa as all were oriented to the same prizes – we might expect the same sort of homology to social space that one sees in terms of choices of sports to watch or participate in. Absent such a field, it is not clear how we should establish homology to social space *within* the actual fields. Would the field of professional gymnastics be homologous to the sub-portion of social space from which those attracted to gymnastics tend to come? Would it still be a microcosm for the larger space? Or would it merely have similar axes, and thus possess analogy but not homology?

Again, if one considers 'wrestling' in entire, one might well find that there are obdurate social distinctions between those who only follow college wrestling and those who only follow (contemporary) 'professional' wrestling, let alone *lucha libre* or midget professional wrestling within this. But as even those few college wrestlers who go on to post-college professional careers in martial arts do so not under the WWF but under some other aegis, it seems implausible to bundle these as 'a' field. And if we separate them, it seems unlike that within either college or professional wrestling one could replicate the *Rules of Art* and establish a close homology between field position and position in social space.

It seems very likely that the only solution to this problem will be a de-emphasis on the study 'of' fields as entities in favour of an exploration of fundamental field theoretical *processes*. This conclusion is supported by our consideration of a second possible problem with Bourdieu's analysis.

Capital and position

This pertains to the status of 'capital'. It is not entirely clear whether in the strictest sense there is any need for capital as a distinct theoretic term, if one also has field position. To make this point, we must clarify our language. We may see two analytic choices regarding the usage of the word 'capital,' the first being whether capital is by definition strictly correlative to a specific field or not, and the second being whether capital is inherently a relation (as is 'being to the left of'), or whether it is a non-relational resource (that is, something like 'mass,' that might be used to *establish* relations such as 'heavier than' but is independent of other entities). Of the four resulting combinations, one strikes us as the most consistent with field theory, which is a relational and field-specific definition of capital; contrapositively it seems quite unlikely that anyone would use the idea of capital to denote field-independent resources.

The question, then, is whether there is reason to allow 'capital' to cover either field-specific resources or generalized relational advantages. Along the lines of the first option, one might propose that anything that facilitates the pursuit of the goal of a field should be considered a 'capital,' perhaps especially if it has a tendency towards its own cumulation. This can happen even for a non-relationally defined resource – for example, upper body strength makes it easier to do the exercises that build upper body strength, even if one is the only human alive. Indeed, we believe that in casual employment of Bourdieu's terminology there is often this substitution of resource for capital.

Yet we believe that this interpretation is not only anathema to Bourdieu's project, but inconsistent with field theoretic principles. Regarding the first, it seems clear that Bourdieu used 'capital' in what we must consider a Marxist/ scientific, and not a bourgeois/ideological, way (we will defend this seemingly archaic terminology). That is, for Marx, capital is relationally defined; a heap of wood, a set of machines, fuel, and so on, are not capital; they only become so as part of the relation that involves private appropriation and expropriation. When we explain the profit made by the furniture company as a natural result of 'the capital,' we mystically imagine that the wood and machines have a tendency to rush about and turn themselves into money. One might as well begin one's understanding of economics by waiting for elves to help out the shoemaker at night. Rather, it is because of the particular social relations associated with wage labor that the surplus time accumulates in one area of the production relation in the form of profit.

So, too, to consider capital non-relational would be to risk fetishizing and naturalizing that very endogenous product of field-situated struggle that we seek to explain ('Why, he is the poet laureate because of his very high *word/ smithing capital*!'). In other words, to make capital into resource is to remove it from the explanatory power of the field, and to do that is necessarily to also fix the *stakes* of the field – to make this in effect exogenous. But the conception of the goal of action in the field as endogenously defined is, we hold, another of the key aspects of Bourdieu's work that constituted a coherent advance in his field theory over that of his predecessors.

Now this does not mean that it cannot be possible to maintain that there is a relational definition of capital that is not fully-field dependent (our other possibility), in the sense that we might see capital-relations outside of a field. But if our previous reasoning is correct, this could only indicate a stage or site of the organization of relations that falls short of a true field. There can be artistic capital before there is a coherent art field, but once there is a field, there can be no artistic capital not in relation to this field. Such anomalous situations of relational but not field-specific capital, then, are outside of the scope of field theory, and need currently be considered no longer.

In sum, it seems that capital must be understood as a field-specific constellation of relations. But in that case, it seems hard to imagine how there could be any capital other than field position. For example, an artist might indeed have high fine motor coordination, but if no one in the field of drawing believed that she was an accomplished draughtsman, it seems that it would be incorrect to say something like 'despite the fact that she has a low field position, she has high artistic capital', which confuses resource and capital, and places the capital outside the field's range of effective consecration. Accepting such a usage would be equivalent to making capital a *resource* as opposed to a *relation*. If we insist that the field is not simply the set of recognized positions but the distillation of all sets of relations that have implications for the production and experience of relations, it seems that capital is redundant with field position.[19]

But there is a second problem with 'capital' that leads us to draw back from an immediate resolution. And this is that 'capital' tends not only to bleed into *position*, but at other times, it seems to shade off into position's subjective counterpart, habitus (for an example where Bourdieu sees the two as fundamentally consubstantial, see Bourdieu 1993: 86). Indeed, it seems that in cases of 'bodily capital' (e.g. Desmond 2007; Martin and George 2006; Wacquant 2004), the two might even be coterminous – or at least, the habitus functions as capital in some fields.

Certainly, we could also defensibly retain 'capital' as the actor's theory of the field; that is, capital is how actors think of field position. However, this would still imply that we should prefer theoretical accounts that dispense with capital as an axis of stratification (much like Bourdieu's correspondence analyses, in which positions are defined wholly relationally, and 'capital' is only a rough interpretive overlay). More importantly, this would imply that it is not a pressing concern to identify particular species, sub-species and sub-varieties as different 'capitals' as if this taxonomic work had a strong theoretical implication.

We tend to believe that accepting this implication would be beneficial for field theoretic work. To abuse Marx's terminology, we may say that one of the unintended consequences of Bourdieu's theorizing has been a dramatic acceleration of the 'self-expansion of capital' – the incentive for researchers to demarcate new fields by sticking the explorer's flag in the virgin territory of an unclaimed form of capital.[20] Should each field theory prove successful, the likely resulting overcrowding would force us to admit ever more precise forms of capital (not only truck drivers' capital used in the field of trucking, nor even interstate truck drivers' capital used in the sub-field of interstate trucking, but tandem interstate container truck drivers' capital, and so on). Although a field theoretic account may indeed shed light on sociological questions pertaining to this or any other activity, and the specification of the stakes and organization of this field would prove necessary for this project, this does not mean that the mere naming of any field and its attendant capital can be considered an advance. Thus although a rich description of the phenomenologies of different realms of organization, as well as their inter-dependencies, is indeed a worthy task, absent an investigation of processes that are common (or vary interpretably) across cases, if not the arrangement of cases in an interpretable structure, a fractal and futile exploration of fractioning fractions that leads only to a Linnaean taxonomy is no advance.

Vectors and Positions

The final issue, one pertaining to the relation between vectors and position, is perhaps not a problem in Bourdieu, but the consistency of his approach for a field theory may not have been made clear. In a classic field, the vector associated at one position points (or so it seems) to a second position. At every position there is a single vector, and the force induced in an object is indifferent to the past. Some difficulties in assimilating Bourdieu's perspective might arise from the following: that the pulls and pushes Bourdieu describes have to do with practices and not positions; that Bourdieu emphasizes the importance of history; that Bourdieu indeed often considers trajectory itself a fundamental (usually third) dimension in his investigations.

Regarding the first, Bourdieu (1996b [1992]: 231) gives the formula 'the *space of* positions tends to govern the *space of position-takings*', (at other times, 'the space of positions' and 'the space of dispositions') which seems to imply the necessity for two dually linked spaces. However, we believe that Bourdieu's insight is more compatible with a simple field account than this makes clear. Bourdieu sometimes preferred catchy recombinations of basic words or roots, seemingly believing that the conjunction of dualities would induce enlightenment in the reader (as well as providing a new generation of jump rope rhymes for children of academics). However, it might be more accurate to say that what the space of position governs are the taking of *strategies* (practices that are objectively strategic) and that in field theoretic terms these are best understood as *directions*. Further, the wonderful thing about a field is that the fact that at one position there is a vector pointing in a certain direction in no way implies that an object (even one beginning at this position with no velocity) will proceed in that direction. The cascaded local interactions that lead to a field tend to produce continuously curving 'lines of

force' in all but the simplest (single point-mass) cases. Thus (as Faraday demonstrated) at any point the vector is a tangent to the curve of force. There is no reason for agents to think about their strategies in terms of the positions they 'point to', for our local sense of 'where to go' is not where we are likely to end up.

Second, Bourdieu emphasizes the importance of history, because it is only experience that, for one thing, makes some of us susceptible to the magnetism of a particular field by developing its particular 'libido' (for example, Wacquant's (2004) description of being drawn into the field of prizefighting), and experience that, to some extent, re-shapes our bodies. This is indeed a point of difference from most other field theoretic accounts, but as we have noted in our discussion of Bourdieu's use of the habitus, this seems a necessary emendation for the application of field theory for the social sciences.

Finally, we have noted some of the complexity that arises because Bourdieu treats trajectory as a dimension, but we must be sympathetic, because what Bourdieu is grappling with is something handled previously by Köhler (1938), and this is that a field is a field of *forces* – not momentums or velocities. Thus at any instant, two objects in the same position are indeed subject to the exact same force, but that does not mean that we will find them in the same position at another instance. We must take into account the initial velocities that bring the objects to this position. Thus when Bourdieu emphasizes that there is a strict duality between position and dispositions (Bourdieu 1996b [1992]: 265), he is being somewhat inexact. His use of a third dimension of trajectory is the proper reminder that positions are places where paths cross, which means, as Rosanne Barr noted, you meet the same people on your way down whom you met on the way up (so be nice to them the first time!).

Conclusion

Pierre Bourdieu's field theory is more than a set of metaphors, for field theory is a coherent explanatory approach, one particular form of relationalism that was developed by psychologist-philosophers and which made a few appearances in the social sciences. This field theory is consonant with field theories in the physical sciences, although that in itself might not be of importance, given that field theory in the social sciences, despite being compatible with various mathematical techniques, is itself not mathematized. Field theory in the social sciences therefore must be understood as a general explanatory framework. However, it is not circular, silly, pathological, or in flagrant contradiction with what we know about human beings, which is not something that can be said of all general explanatory approaches in the social sciences. Further, our field theory has an advantage in that our elements can give us reports regarding the experiential analogues to the forces used in analytic accounts.

Pierre Bourdieu's work, though not all field theoretic (as there are other aspects of his work and claims that we do not treat here) is an exemplary use of field theory in the social sciences. As such, his work necessarily shares fundamental explanatory principles with those of earlier field theorists, most importantly Wolfgang Köhler. However, Bourdieu's integration of habitus solves the problem of Köhler's reliance on naïve realism, which worked reasonably well for the Gestalt theorists' studies of vision but less well when it came to social action. Thus his work indicates the possibility of theoretical progress, and there is, one is happy to note, still room for additional progress within the field theoretic tradition.

Notes

1 We are extremely grateful for comments and criticism from Matt George, Mathieu Hilgers, Ben Merriman, and especially Loïc Wacquant.
2 Husserl made many of the same points as the Gestalt theorists in contradistinction to conventional psychology, most importantly that we must refrain from attempting to argue that what something 'is' is different from how it appears in the intuition, and a general criticism of what he called the 'modern nominalism' of *conceptualism*, confusing concepts of things with things themselves in experience. In contrast to most philosophies of consciousness, he also stressed the apt nature of our evolved system for developing ideas (Husserl 1970 [1900]: 204, 268). However, Husserl's anti-empirical take (see, e.g. Husserl 1997 [1927]) led him to stress a distantiation (bracketing) of experience that cut against the directions of the Gestalt school. (As Merleau-Ponty (1962: xiiff) said, Husserl objected to investigations that explored how we make use of our relation to the world – Husserl preferred just to be *'filled with wonder* at it'; cf. Köhler 1938: 45, cf. 68.) Or as Stumpf (1907: 35) said, Husserl only explored the genetic, and not the descriptive, tasks of a fundamental psychology. When Husserl's approach finally made its way into the social sciences via Schutz (1967 [1932]: xxxi), every connection to empiricism had been severed and phenomenology equated with 'the most rigorous philosophical reflection'.
3 Koffka, Köhler and Kurt Lewin all studied under Stumpf; Wertheimer did not but spent a number of years at Stumpf's Berlin institute (Heider 1983: 105; Ash 1998: 34, 105).
4 Köhler (1925 [1917]: 18, 206) also pointed out that the behaviourist tradition placed its rats in mazes in which, according to design, it was impossible to get a vantage point of the whole, a largely unnatural situation, though one compatible with the assumption that since the rat understands nothing, it is 'poor, exhausted chance' that 'has to do all the work that the animal is unable to do directly'.
5 While they adopted the idea of 'field' from the visual field, it is interesting to note that Maxwell (1954 [1891]: ix) also saw field theory as holistic – he commented that 'Faraday's methods resembled those in which we begin with the whole and arrive at the parts by analysis, while the ordinary mathematical methods were founded on the principle of beginning with the parts and building up the whole by synthesis'.
6 Further, the principle of 'terseness' (*Prägnanz*), used to explain why we parse the visual field into fewer simple structures (even if occluded or overlapping), seems to have been connected in Köhler's mind with an idea like that of surface tension. He wrote that 'in contrast to the indifferent mosaic of sensations assumed in older theory, this order of the field shows a strong "predilection" for certain general kinds of organization as against others, exactly as the formation of molecules and the working of surface forces in physics operates in certain definite directions' (Köhler 1929: 158).

7 'To be "the electropositive side" of such a physical system is no less a *gestalt property* in a definite electrochemical whole than to be "the dark side" is a *gestalt property* in a sensory pair' (Köhler 1929: 219).

8 This experienced impulse must, assumed Köhler, be dual to a neurological impulse in the brain and hence in the brain field we must also be having such a field of force.

9 Even earlier, Lundberg (1939: 103, 260, 311) had, drawing upon Gestalt theory, incorporated aspects of field theory into his system, but they were merely one minor part of a conglomerate theory that lacked simple coherence (though many aspects are still impressive today).

10 Lizardo (2010: 682 n.18) points out that Richard Nice's translation obscured Bourdieu's use of Lewin's idea of hodological space, a term also adopted by Sartre.

11 For example, in one terse summary of his commitment to a field theoretic approach, Bourdieu (1982, cited in Bourdieu and Wacquant 1992: 96 n.48; see also Bourdieu 1993: 21) says, 'To think in terms of field demands a conversion of the whole ordinary vision of the social world which fastens only on visible things [i.e. the individual and the group] … In fact, just as the Newtonian theory of gravitation could only be constructed against Cartesian realism which wanted to recognize no mode of action other than collision, direct contact, the notion of field presupposes a break with the realist representation which leads us to reduce the effect of the *environment* to the effect of direct action as actualized during an interaction'.

12 Or in terms of the 'conflict of the faculties' that are likely to polarize sociology departments between symbolic interactionists at one extreme and mathematical sociologists at the other, 'One man's Mead is another man's Poisson'. This is an old joke as well as a bad one, but in danger of becoming extinct because, due to the loss of knowledge of what mead was (and of its sometimes toxic nature), the phrase is changing to 'meat,' and there were no symbolic interactionists with the name 'Meat.'

13 Also see the wonderful comparison of actors to iron filings in Bourdieu 1996b [1992]: 58, also 19.

14 Then there are times in which fields are spaces; thus Bourdieu (1993: 72) writes that fields are 'structured spaces of positions … whose properties depend on their position within these spaces'. We do not address the idea of the 'field of power' here, as it seems to us to be an attempt to forcibly weld Bourdieu's field theory into a larger substantive theory by abusing terminology, somewhat akin to the confusing parsimony gained by considering Grand Central Station another 'rail line'.

15 There is also the question of whether there might be some fields that cannot be combined for reasons no one would predict – say, it turns out that because of the musculature and neural organization of the human body, one cannot successfully embody the capital necessary for both the field of painting and the field of lawn bowling, although print making and lawn bowling go quite well together.

16 Note that we consider that, by definition, dominance means the power of consecration of *persons* (and not the establishment or validation of rules); while in some cases there may indeed be rules or such not, these are strictly secondary both analytically and practically. In its most general form, 'rules' are the theories that the non-dominant form to account for consecration with the (partially justified) hope that one can go from such accounts to recipes. Of course, as Lieberson (1985) argues, the thing about ruling is that you get to write the rules that allow you to change the rules so that you get to keep on writing the rules. Thus college essays were introduced to allow elites to continue consecrating their own young; when others studied the resulting outcomes they came up with 'rules' that can be used in Princeton Review classes, but would not strictly binding on the decisions of elites (not that these are still in control of – or even recognizably present in – admissions organizations). In our merito-bureaucratic age, we must beware of taking the *a posteriori* results of consecration struggles as a priori rules.

17 Thus in the wonderful diagram of the space of the arts and social science faculties in *Homo Academicus* (Bourdieu 1988 [1984]: 276), tastefully placed as the final appendix, one cannot deny that the vertical dimension tends to correspond to age (and perhaps renown), while horizontal indeed reflects those of different types of universities. Yet the arrangement paralleling Bourdieu's other graphs seems strongly to suggest that those like Pierre Grappin (ex-resistance member, member of the Légion d'honneur, a Germanicist at Nanterre who seems most notable for his German–French dictionary) who possess high institutional power are akin to the uncouth nouveau riche, while those like Claude Lévi-Strauss (who after a dis-organized career as an exile received a chair at the Collège de France) not only have more intellectual renown, but correspond more to the 'autonomous' cultural pole. (Bourdieu himself sits exactly where young Turks are expected.)

18 Allowing a 'field of sport' simply because of its predictable homologous mapping to social space would imply just as well allowing an even more encompassing 'field of recreation' (say, in some areas of social space all sports are rejected in favor of other pursuits such as ham radio) and indeed a 'field of hedonic action' (why ignore those workaholics who prefer not to have any hobbies?) and eventually a 'field of everything.' This does not mean that at one point when 'sports' as such were being introduced there could not have been a relatively undifferentiated field of sport (see Defrance 2013).

19 More technically, we might imagine capital as a reduction of the multidimensional vector indicating field position to a scalar; thus for any field, we might imagine drawing a set of contours showing people of equal capital, as Bourdieu's charts of social space have a total capital volume as a dimension.

20 This is not meant as a dismissive dig, as one of us has participated in this sort of effort (Martin and George 2006). Further, we note that this is a somewhat tendentious translation of Marx, but as it has become widely accepted, we leave things at that.

References

Abbott, A. 1988. 'Transcending General Linear Reality'. *Sociological Theory*, 6, 160–85.
——2001. *Chaos of Disciplines*. Chicago: University of Chicago Press.
Ash, M. 1998. *Gestalt Psychology in German Culture 1890–1967*. Cambridge: Cambridge University Press.
Bourdieu, P. 1969 [1966]. 'Intellectual Field and Creative Project'. *Social Science Information*, 8, 189–119.
——1977 [1972]. *Outline of a Theory of Practice*. Cambridge: Cambridge University Press.
——1984 [1979]. *Distinction: A Social Critique of the Judgment of Taste*. Cambridge, MA: Harvard University Press.
——1985a. 'The Social Space and the Genesis of Groups'. *Theory and Society*, 14, 723–44.
——1985b. 'The Genesis of the Concepts of Habitus and of Field'. *Sociocriticism*, 2, 11–24.
——1988 [1984]. *Homo Academicus*. Stanford: Stanford University Press.
——1990. 'The Scholastic Point of View'. *Cultural Anthropology*, 5, 380–91.
——1993. *Sociology in Question*. London: Sage.
——1996a [1989]. *The State Nobility*. Stanford: Stanford University Press.
——1996b [1992]. *The Rules of Art*. Stanford: Stanford University Press.
Bourdieu, P., Chamboredon, J.-C. and Passeron, J.-C. 1991 [1968]. *The Craft of Sociology*. New York: Walter de Gruyter.

60   *John Levi Martin and Forest Gregg*

Bourdieu, P. and Wacquant, L.J.D. 1992. *An Invitation to Reflexive Sociology.* Chicago: University of Chicago Press; Cambridge: Polity Press.

Brandt, K. 1952. *Struktur der Wirtschaftsdynamik.* Frankfurt am Main: Verlag Fritz Knapp.

Cassirer, E. 1923 [1910]. *Substance and Function, and Einstein's Theory of Relativity.* Chicago: Open Court.

Chemero, A. 2009. *Radical Embodied Cognitive Science.* Cambridge, MA: The MIT Press.

Desmond, M. 2007. *On the Fireline.* Chicago: University of Chicago Press.

Defrance, J. 2013. 'The Making of a Field with Weak Autonomy: The Case of the Sports Field in France, 1895–1955.' Pp. 303–26 in *Bourdieu and Historical Analysis,* edited by Philip S. Gorski. Durham: Duke University Press.

Dilthey, W. 1988 [1883]. *Introduction to the Human Sciences.* Detroit, MI: Wayne State University Press.

Ehrenfels, C. 1988 [1890]. 'On "Gestalt Qualities"'. In B. Smith (ed.) *Foundations of Gestalt Theory.* Munich: Philosophia Verlag, 82–117.

Fürstenberg, F. 1969. *Das Aufstiegsproblem in der modernen Gesellschaft.* Stuttgart: Ferdinand Enke Verlag.

Geiger, T. 1949. *Die Klassengesellschaft im Schmelztiegel.* Köln: Verlag Gustav Kiepenheuer.

Gibson, J. 1986 [1979]. *The Ecological Approach to Visual Perception.* Hillsdale, NJ: Lawrence Erlbaum.

Heider, F. 1983. *The Life of a Psychologist.* Lawrence, KS: University of Kansas Press.

Hesse, M. 1970. *Forces and Fields: The Concept of Action at a Distance in the History of Physics.* Westport, CT: Greenwood Press.

Husserl, E. 1970 [1900]. *Logical Investigations,* vol. I, trans. J.N. Findlay. New York: Routledge and Kegan Paul.

——1997 [1927]. 'Phenomenology' (first draft of article written for *Encyclopaedia Britannica*), trans. Thomas Sheehan. In Thomas Sheehan and Richard E. Palmer (eds) *Psychological and Transcendental Phenomenology and the Confrontation with Heidegger (1927–1931).* Dordrecht: Kluwer Academic Publishers.

Koffka, K. 1935. *Principles of Gestalt Psychology.* New York: Harcourt, Brace and Co.

Köhler, W. 1925 [1917]. *The Mentality of Apes.* London: Routledge and Kegan Paul.

——1920. *Die physichen Gestalten in Ruhe und im stationären Zustand. Braunschweig.* Germany: Friedr. Vieweg und Sohn.

——1929. *Gestalt Psychology.* New York: Liveright.

——1938. *The Place of Values in a World of Fact.* New York: Liveright.

——1947. *Gestalt Psychology.* New York: Liveright.

Lang, G.E. and Lang, K. 1988. 'Recognition and Renown: The Survival of Artistic Reputation.' *American Journal of Sociology* 94: 79–109.

Lena, J. 2010. 'Recognition and Renown in Rap Music: Tracing Reputation through Aesthetic Conventions.' Paper presented at the annual meetings of the American Sociological Association (ASA). Atlanta, GA.

Lewin, K. 1951. *Field Theory in Social Science,* ed. Dorwin Cartwright. New York: Harper and Brothers.

Lieberson, S. 1985. *Making it Count.* Berkeley: University of California Press.

Lizardo, O. 2010. 'Beyond the Antinomies of Structure: Levi-Strauss, Giddens, Bourdieu and the Self'. *Theory and Society,* 39, 651–88.

Luhmann, N. 1995 [1984]. *Social Systems.* Stanford, CA: Stanford University Press.

Lundberg, G. 1939. *Foundations of Sociology.* New York: Macmillan.

Mannheim, K. 1940. *Man and Society in an Age of Reconstruction.* New York: Harcourt, Brace and World.

Marrow, A. 1969. *The Practical Theorist: The Life and Work of Kurt Lewin.* New York: Basic Books.

Martin, J. 2011. *The Explanation of Social Action.* Princeton, NJ: Princeton University Press.

Martin, J.L. and George, M. 2006. 'Theories of Sexual Stratification: Toward an Analytics of the Sexual Field and a Theory of Sexual Capital'. *Sociological Theory,* 24, 107–32.

Marx, K. and Engels F. [1845–1846] 1976. *The German Ideology.* Pp. 19-539 in *Collected Works,* Volume 5. New York: International Publishers.

Maxwell, J. 1954 [1891]. *A Treatise on Electricity and Magnetism.* New York: Dover.

Merleau-Ponty, M. 1962. *The Phenomenology of Perception.* London: Routledge and Kegan Paul.

Metzger, W. 1986 [1975]. 'Die Entdeckung der Prägnanztendenz'. In M. Stadler and H. Crabus (ed.) *Gestalt Psychologie.* Frankfurt: Verlag Waldermar Kramer, 145–81.

Mey, Harald. 1972 [1965]. *Field Theory: A Study of its Applications in the Social Sciences.* New York: St Martin's Press.

Mohr, J. n.d. 'Implicit Terrains: Meaning, Measurement, and Spatial Metaphors in Organizational Theory'. In M. Ventresca and J. Porac (ed.) *Constructing Industries and Markets.* New York: Elsevier, forthcoming.

Neisser, U. 2002. *Wolfgang Köhler 1887–1967: A Biographical Memoir.* Biographical Memoirs Series, Vol. 81. Washington, DC: National Academy Press.

Rummel, R. 1975. *Understanding Conflict and War. Volume I. The Dynamic Psychological Field.* New York: John Wiley and Sons.

Schutz, A. 1967 [1932]. *The Phenomenology of the Social World.* Evanston, IL: Northwestern University Press.

Smith, B. 1988. 'Gestalt Theory: An Essay in Philosophy'. In B. Smith (ed.) *Foundations of Gestalt Theory.* Munich: Philosophia Verlag, 11–81.

Spiegel, B. 1961. *Die Struktur Der Meinungsverteilung im Sozialen Feld: Das Psychologische Marktmodell.* Bern: Verlag Hans Huber.

Stumpf, C. 1907. *Zur Einteilung der Wissenschaften.* Berlin: Verlag der Königl. Akademie der Wissenschaften.

Swartz, D. 1997. *Culture and Power.* Chicago: University of Chicago Press.

Tolman, E. 1954. 'A Psychological Model'. In T. Parsons and E. Shils (ed.) *Toward a General Theory of Action.* Cambridge, MA: Harvard University Press, 277–361.

Wacquant, L. 1993. 'From Ruling Class to Field of Power: An Interview with Pierre Bourdieu on La noblesse d'État.' *Theory, Culture and Society* 10: 19–44.

Wacquant, L. 2004. *Body and Soul: Notebooks of an Apprentice Boxer.* New York: Oxford University Press.

Wertheimer, M. 1922. 'Untersuchungen zur Lehre von der Gestalt. I. Prinzipielle Bermerkungen'. *Psychologische Forschung,* 1, 47–58.

2 The limits of the field

Elements for a theory of the social differentiation of activities

Bernard Lahire

> Only in the work of science can one love what one destroys, continue the past while denying it, revere one's master by contradicting him.

> (Bachelard 1999: 252)

Preamble

One expeditious way of pre-emptively disqualifying all theoretical work of criticism is to describe it as 'scholastic'. When they pronounce such a verdict, those who have an interest in the maintenance of the existing theoretical order and the freezing of concepts to which they are emotionally and intellectually attached seek to discourage any innovative approach that would have the more or less long-term consequence of relegating them to the past and 'superseding' them. The critical reflection that I undertake here on the concept of the 'field' is neither more nor less theoretical than the work that Pierre Bourdieu himself undertook in dialogue with the sociology of Max Weber as he strove to construct his theory of fields (Bourdieu 1971). It springs from and is supported by empirical research from the past 20 years or so in various areas: education, culture and then literature.[1]

In discussing this theory by starting out from empirical questions, I hope to be able at the same time to help promote a way of discussing and using the concepts. The sociologist should not regard concepts as anything more than tools that are more or less useful depending on the task at hand. In everyday life, no one would think of using a screwdriver to drive in a nail – but many social science researchers unfortunately make such mistakes without realizing it.

The concept of the field (like those of 'world' or 'game', also considered in this discussion) belongs to a long tradition of sociological and anthropological reflection on the social differentiation of activities or functions. In the work of Marx, Durkheim, Weber or Simmel[2] one finds reflections on the evolution of societies that are marked by a centuries-long tendency to move, as Herbert Spencer put it, from the 'homogeneous' towards the 'heterogeneous'. Initially indistinct functions – economic, political, legal, religious, ethical, aesthetic, scientific, etc. – are progressively separated and sometimes even organized into specific social microcosms that have their own laws, their specific logic. In Durkheim's reflections on the division of labour, or Weber's on the 'spheres of activity' and their 'specific legality', one finds the same concern to understand the process of differentiation of activities and functions and the functioning of the microcosms that result from this differentiating process.

Before going further, I can summarize my argument in the form of a few propositions:

- Fields have a history and only have meaning in the framework of differentiated societies. Hence there are societies 'without fields' (just as there are societies 'without a State', 'without writing', 'without schools', etc.). The concept of the field is therefore not universally relevant independently of the historical nature of the social configurations that social actors form among themselves.
- Even in differentiated societies, not every relevant context of action is necessarily a field. Fields are universes specific to the dominant classes or the elites. They are 'fields of power' (as Bourdieu sometimes made clear). They are universes that organize permanent competitions for the appropriation of a specific capital – political, journalistic, religious, scientific, economic, artistic, literary capital, etc.
- This simple observation should lead researchers to develop reflection and research projects: 1 on social universes (institutions, more or less broad configurations of relations of interdependence or frameworks of interaction) that are not fields;[3] 2 on all the non-field areas (e.g. 'amateur' or leisure activities, with no more than local stakes which do not give rise to struggles of the same kind as in fields), where actors who otherwise may or may not belong to a field act and interact;[4] 3 on socially mixed sites of interaction among individuals belonging to a field and others who do not take part in the competition organized within the field but are simple supports or aids to the 'competitors'; or 4 on dominated areas (without major power stakes)[5] involving only dominated individuals and groups (where are the 'fields' of the working class, of housewives, or the homeless, etc.?).
- When one is indeed dealing with a field, in the historical sense of the concept (a social microcosm that has historically become differentiated from other existing microcosms and where struggles take place for the appropriation of a specific 'power'), one may often deplore the slippage towards a reductionist explanation of practices or productions (works, discourses, etc.) in terms of the field: everything is explained by its position in the field; the truth of every practice within the field is to be sought

entirely within the limits of the field and social actors are thus reduced to their being-as-member-of-the-field. From the scientific advance that consists in specifying the social determinants bearing on behaviours, there is a slippage to a confinement within the narrow bounds of the field. The researcher then forgets that life outside the field (before an actor enters it – in the family, at school, and in a whole series of other socialization frameworks – and parallel to it) is important for understanding what happens within the field.

- The critique of reductionist over-use of field theory is especially relevant in the case of a 'secondary field' – one yielding low profits, weakly institutionalized and barely professionalized – which I call a 'game' (making use of the word's relationship with 'work': paid work/play (disinterested leisure pursuits), main activity/secondary activity, serious activity/'pointless' activity, etc.). This is true of artistic universes that are often based, for a long period in the artists' lives, on a parallel remunerative 'day job'. The problem is of the same type that leads the researcher to distinguish between an enveloping, long, systematic socialization and a specialized, short, discontinuous one. To treat artists as beings solely defined by their artistic properties is an error of abstraction: one is generally not 'a writer' in the way that one is 'a surgeon' or 'a sociologist'. Consideration of spaces and times outside fields partially calls into question the notion of autonomy, to which one may prefer the term 'specificity'. What is at stake in the literary game is specific (and irreducible to the stakes of the philosophical or sociological fields) but never separable from what writers experience outside the game.

- Researchers' propensity to transfer the model of the 'field' in order to describe and analyse the functioning of a great number of universes has led them to neglect analysis of the specificities of each 'field'. As a result they have privileged analysis in terms of the sociology of power and not deployed a sociology of knowledge and practices that would have enabled them to 'enter into the flesh' (the 'content' and 'form') of particular practices and works (journalistic, philosophical, scientific, legal, literary, etc.).

- The long historical process of differentiation of domains of activities and functions can lead actors in the most differentiated societies to reflect on the positive or negative effects of the autonomization, and even the progressive self-enclosure, of the multiple social microcosms. However, the normative point of view on these phenomena is sometimes positive (especially when it is a matter of defending the autonomy of the universes of cultural and scientific production), sometimes negative (when one is criticizing the undesirable side-effects of the divide between 'experts' and 'lay persons' or deploring the indifference or contempt for ordinary problems shown by actors in the political and economic universes). These contradictions lead researchers to discriminate between the different types of social universes rather more than they normally do.

Expanding the sociological imagination and imposing empirical tasks

Good sociological concepts are those that expand the scientific imagination and, at the same time, impose new empirical tasks, acts of research that the sociologist would never have been led to perform without them. In terms of such a definition, the concept of the field can indisputably be a useful concept in sociological research once one moves beyond a purely decorative or rhetorical usage and avoids making it a vague equivalent of 'universe', 'domain' or 'world'. One may, however, decide that *some* of the properties that, according to Bourdieu, characterize fields are pertinent (e.g. relative autonomy, specificity of the stakes and rules of the game, interest or *illusio*, power relations, struggles, relations between dominant and dominated, etc.); one may also agree with *some* of the theoretical requirements for constructing these social microcosms (e.g. the implementation of a relational or structural mode of thought), without being convinced that these properties and requirements are specific to the historical configurations that such a concept designates, and without assuming that field theory exhausts the reality of social differentiation.

My aim will therefore be, first, to show that field theory is only one solution – among other possibilities – built up from various pre-existing theoretical traditions. Like any social science researcher, Bourdieu defined his concept of the field by combining several theoretical schemes belonging to different theoretical universes (notably Durkheim, Marx and Weber). What I aim to bring out is the idea that researchers can perfectly well take some of the same basic elements or components and with them construct concepts different from that of 'field' in order to understand different aspects of our highly differentiated societies. By unpacking the properties that appear to be interlinked and inseparable in 'field theory', one can gain a conceptual freedom of action and help to liberate the sociological imagination in its study of the plurality of social worlds. To move on from what Bourdieu says – rather than ignoring it – one has to ask oneself what it is that he specifically says (which he often presents as being universally pertinent) and what it is that he necessarily does not discuss and which we sometimes – unlike him – want to study.[6]

In a further part of my argument I thus point out certain lacunae in field theory, i.e. things that remain untouched after it has passed over them. I dwell here at rather greater length on the question of the necessary specification of this theory, taking the example of the 'literary game': the use of the concept of the 'game' to designate certain social universes that, like the literary universe, are only rarely inhabited as a 'primary occupation' but rather as secondary (and very rarely remunerative) universes by actors who permanently live a 'double life', seemed to me necessary.

This reflection is followed by a critical examination of how field theory neglects study of discourses, works or practices in favour of an analysis of the agents, their trajectories, their positions or their strategies, and the struggles that take place among them. Finally, the idea of the relative autonomy of fields, which leads Bourdieu into normative reflections on the 'good' and 'bad' autonomy of fields, gives rise to a series of questions aiming to shed light on the nature of the phenomena of autonomy that are involved.

A field of battles

It is both easy and difficult to summarize the essential properties of fields in a few words. While the task is made easier by the author himself, who several times discussed a concept that took a central place in his sociology from the 1980s,[7] it is also made harder by the small, almost imperceptible inflections it undergoes in each particular use.

The fundamental and relatively invariant elements of the definition of the field that can be extracted from the author's various books and articles on the question are the following:

- A field is a microcosm in the macrocosm of the encompassing (national) social space.
- Each field has its specific rules of the game and specific stakes, irreducible to the rules of the game and the stakes of other fields (what 'drives' a mathematician – and the way he is 'driven' – are quite unlike what 'drives' an industrialist or a fashion designer and the ways they are 'driven').
- A field is a 'system' or a structured 'space' of positions.
- This space is a space of struggles among the various agents occupying the various positions.
- The 'stake' of these struggles is the appropriation of the capital specific to the field (the monopoly of the legitimate specific capital) and/or the redefinition of this capital.
- Capital is unequally distributed within the field, so that there are dominant and dominated agents.
- The unequal distribution of capital determines the structure of the field, which is therefore defined by the state of historical power relations among the forces (agents and institutions) present in the field.
- The practices and strategies of the agents can be understood if one relates them to their positions in the field.
- Among the invariant strategies, one finds the opposition between strategies of conservation and strategies of subversion (of the existing state of the power relations). The former are more often those of the dominant and the latter those of the dominated (and more especially of the 'new entrants'). This opposition may take the form of a conflict between 'ancients' and 'moderns', 'orthodox' and 'heterodox', 'conservatives' and 'revolutionaries', etc.
- While engaged in struggle against one another, the agents of a field none-theless all have an interest in the existence of the field, and therefore maintain an 'objective complicity' beyond the struggles among them.
- The social interests are always specific to each field and therefore cannot be reduced to economic interest.

- To each field there corresponds a habitus (a system of incorporated dispositions) specific to the field (philological habitus, legal habitus, footballer's habitus, etc.). Only those who have incorporated the habitus specific to the field are able to play the game and to believe in (the importance of) the game.
- Each agent of the field is characterized by his/her social trajectory, habitus and position in the field.
- A field has a relative autonomy: the struggles that take place within it have a logic of their own, but the outcomes of the struggles (economic, social, political, etc.) outside the field also weigh heavily on the development of the internal power relations.

This list of properties should be regarded as provisional summary of the state of research in the area, based on a (limited but already significant) series of case studies, carried out more or less well and in varying degrees of detail,[8] which can serve to guide the researcher in his/her research. Unfortunately, one too often sees researchers speaking, without even thinking about it (but bowing to authority or the language of a 'school'), of 'fields' (of this or of that), presupposing before they even start that the universe they are talking about is organized like a field. Instead of applying a scientific reasoning of the type, 'Let us hypothesize that the universe in question is a field and then see whether it really is one, and in any case let us consider what kind of universe it is and what its relative specificities or singularities are', many researchers short-circuit this procedure and – putting the cart before the horse – largely assume the results of the research before even starting it.

The social differentiation of activities: a long sociological tradition

The theory of fields takes its place in a long tradition of sociological and anthropological reflections on the historical differentiation of activities or social functions and the social division of labour. From Spencer to Elias, through Marx, Durkheim, Weber or Simmel, this theme constantly recurs in the writings of theoreticians of the social world. Bourdieu explicitly places himself in this long theoretical sequence:

> The emergence of a field of power goes hand in hand with the emergence of a number of relatively autonomous fields, and thus with a differentiation of the social world (which we must take care not to confuse with a process of stratification, although it does lead to the establishment of social hierarchies). This process has previously been analysed by Durkheim, who, extending the work of Spencer, for whom the universe goes 'from the homogeneous toward the heterogeneous', sets against Bergson's 'unitarist vitalism' the evolution that leads from the 'primitive state of nondivision' in which the 'diverse functions' are already present but 'in a state of confusion' (religious life, for example, combining rites, morality,

law, art and even the beginnings of a science) to the 'progressive separation of all these diverse yet primitively blended functions': 'secular and
scientific thought became separated from mythical and religious thought;
art became separated from worship; morality and the law became separated from rites' (Durkheim 1983). Durkheim sees in this confusion of
different forms of activity an obstacle to the full realization of any one of
them: 'Primitively, all forms of activity, all functions are assembled together, as each other's prisoners: they are obstacles to each other; each
prevents the other from completely realizing its nature'. If Weber hardly
notes an advance away from primitive lack of differentiation, he does
show, at least for the economy, that the appearance of separate domains
is accompanied by the institution of a specific legality, manifested by a
constitutive *as such* (the economy as such, etc.).

(Bourdieu 1996a: 433, n.2)

By situating field theory in this way, Bourdieu shows that the concept of the
field is indeed an historical concept (bound up with particular socio-historical
contexts) and not a formal notion that one might use regardless of the terrain
in question. What the concept of the field designates is the product of a long
process of social differentiation of functions and domains of activity. As an
historical concept, the concept of the field therefore has historical and social
limits of validity. It can in particular be deduced from the quotation above
that societies have not always been organized in such ways that fields could
appear within them ('there are societies without fields') and one can take the
argument further by adding that not every relatively autonomous universe
within highly differentiated societies is necessarily a 'field'.[9]

Durkheim and the beginnings of field theory

It is clear that in formulating his theory of fields, Bourdieu derived a number
of interpretative schemes from Durkheim's reflections on the social division of
labour. First, Durkheim emphasizes that such a process of division of labour
is observable in all 'regions' of the social world and not exclusively in the
world of economic production (with its increasingly ramified occupational
and especially industrial branches). Even the political, cultural, administrative, legal and scientific domains undergo the same 'fragmentation'
(Durkheim 1997: 2).

Such a process of continuous evolution separates us from traditional
societies, characterized by their original 'state of indistinction and homogeneity', and in particular by the enveloping, embracing omnipresence of the
religious. In these societies 'everybody ... accepts and practises without argument the same religion; different sects and quarrels are unknown: they would
not be tolerated. At this time, religion includes everything, extends to everything. It embraces, although in a very confused state, besides religious beliefs
proper, ethics, law, the principles of political organization, and even science,

or at least what passes for it. It regulates even the minutiae of private life' (Durkheim 1997: 90).

This original relative indistinction of the economic, the political, the religious, the cognitive, etc., presents, moreover, a major problem for the analyst, in as much as the set of categories it has available to describe the social world ('the economy', 'politics', 'religion', 'ethics', 'culture', 'representation', 'system', etc.) is the product in language of the autonomization-differentiation of domains of social practices. The uncontrolled use of such categories leads in particular to all the economistic, politistic, etc. distortions. For example, apprehending the mythico-ritual reality of traditional societies on the basis of the notion of 'religion' can lead to a series of misunderstandings. One can be led to think that one is dealing with a particular, specific social practice, distinct from other practices, and with relatively autonomous discourses. However, as Jack Goody notes with reference to African societies, 'in African languages I find no equivalent for the western word "religion" (or indeed "ritual"), and more importantly the actors do not appear to look upon religious beliefs and practices in the same way that we, whether Muslim, Jew, Hindu, Buddhist, Christian or atheist, do – that is, as a distinct set' (Goody 1986: 4). If one wants to continue to speak of religion, it has to be made clear that one is talking about a total religion, which organizes and gives meaning to all practices and not a quite relative vision of the world (i.e. one vision of the world among others) to which one might choose to adhere or not. As Serge Gruzinski so well puts it, the 'idolatry' of the indigenous Mexicans 'is inseparable from a social tissue and ... far from occupying an external sphere, it constitutes a way of expressing, informing and playing out social relations' (Gruzinski 1993: 217). It is 'in no way a supplement that extends or amplifies the real or adds its ritual warranty to the most diverse manifestations of human activity' (Gruzinski 1993: 221). It is not a system for defining reality among other competing systems for defining reality, which might enable the actors to say: 'this is religious and that is not', 'this is the work of men, that is the work of the gods.'

What, though, in the social world, pushes towards differentiation? Durkheim provides an answer that seems, at first sight, somewhat formal and mechanistic: 'The division of labour', he writes, 'varies in direct proportion to the volume and density of societies and if it progresses in a continuous manner over the course of social development it is because societies become regularly more dense and generally more voluminous' (Durkheim 1997: 205). So it would be purely a question of morphology. In fact, however, bringing in characteristics of density and volume, he goes on to set up a more complex and original interpretative schema. To summarize Durkheim's position, one could say that increasing density and volume create a problem of social and symbolic space for the different individuals making up the social formation. If everyone 'ran' for a small number of common objectives, the great majority of the 'runners' would be frustrated, but if a series of specific, differentiated competitions is organized, everyone can run with a chance of not being too badly ranked. The social differentiation of functions is thus a way of lowering the general rate of frustration, by multiplying the possibilities of being socially recognized: 'The division of labour is therefore a result of the struggle for existence: but it is a gentle dénouement. Thanks to it, rivals are not obliged to eliminate one another, but can coexist side by side' (Durkheim 1997: 213). Bourdieu says nothing different when, supporting his argument with the works of an historian of law, with reference to medieval Italy, he writes: 'Gerschenkron shows that, as soon as jurists won their independence from princes, each one began to carve up the speciality so as to be a big fish in a little stream rather than a little fish in a big stream' (Bourdieu 1990: 39). Creating a sub-universe is a way of reducing the tensions that arose in large part from the fact that too many shared a different definition of the original activity.[10]

Each universe has its own stakes and its specific prestige, which explains how the soldier can seek military glory and remain indifferent to scientific renown (and conversely for the scientist – 'you can't make a philosopher compete for the prizes that interest a geographer'; Bourdieu 1980: 72; Bourdieu 1993):

> The soldier seeks military glory, the priest moral authority, the statesman power, the industrialist wealth, the scientist professional fame. Each one of them can therefore reach his goal without preventing others from reaching theirs. This is the case even when the functions are less remote from one another. The medical eye specialist does not compete with the one who cares for the mentally ill, the shoemaker does not compete with the hatter, the mason with the cabinet-maker, the physicist with the chemist, etc.
>
> (Durkheim 1997: 209–10)

When Durkheim evokes a first type of struggle or competition (the two terms *lutte* and *concurrence* are used) between relatively close functions, and especially between 'the brewer and the winegrower, the draper and the maker of silks, the poet and the musician', who 'often attempt mutually to supplant each other', he is pointing to struggles akin to those seen today between aspirants to the status of 'intellectual': while engaged in specific universes, philosophers and sociologists, among others, are nonetheless sometimes in competition for access to the status of 'public intellectual': 'As in this case [these functions] satisfy similar needs by different means, it is inevitable that they should seek, more or less, to encroach upon others' (Durkheim 1997: 210). Thus we see there phenomena close to those described in terms of relations (of competition, power and domination) between fields.

The second case of struggles mentioned by Durkheim corresponds well to the struggles internal to each field, which may eventually generate new subdivisions. The closer agents are to each other, the more intense the competition; the further apart they feel, the more a relative indifference reduces the tensions: 'As for those that discharge exactly the same function, they cannot prosper save to the detriment of their fellows. If therefore one represents these different functions in the form of a cluster of branches springing from a common root, the struggle is least between the extreme points, whilst it increases steadily as it approaches the centre' (Durkheim 1997: 210).

Max Weber: spheres of activity and registers of social action

In his presentation of Max Weber's *Sociology of Religion*, Jean-Pierre Grossein points out that Weber was 'opposed to all forms of reductionism', never ceasing to 'emphasize the autonomy of the different registers of social action', which 'each follow their own law': 'This idea is condensed in the concept of *Eigengesetzlichkeit*, "specific legality". It applies to all spheres, as is clearly shown by the "Intermediate Reflections" and it refers to "internal" or "immanent" logics' (Grossein, in Weber 1996: 122).

Indeed, Weber's approach to religions clearly addresses the question of the relative autonomy of the different ways of living religiously and the different religious conceptions – ways of life and conceptions that are never simple reflections of the material or symbolic interests of a class or group. External influences must, in some way, find their translation in specifically religious language and actions (Weber 1996: 335). It is the differentiation of registers of action that leads to the progressive awareness of logics or 'legalities' specific to each of them: 'The rationalization and conscious sublimation of man's relations to the various spheres of values, internal and external, as well as religious and secular, have then pressed towards making conscious *the internal and lawful autonomy* of the individual spheres; thereby letting them drift into those tensions which remain hidden to the original naïve relation with the external world' (Weber 1946: 328).

This then is the interpretative scheme of the 'internal', 'specific', 'immanent' logic used by Bourdieu to define fields. By becoming autonomous and differentiated (as a way of winning an identity of its own, by comparison), each sphere discovers, or rather produces, its own law: the 'business is business' of economic logic (which maintains that 'morality has no place in business') or the 'the law is the law' of the legal order then distinguish themselves from the 'religious ethic of brotherhood'.

However, what social realities does Max Weber have in mind when he speaks of 'registers of social action' or 'spheres of activity'? More precisely, is he thinking only of universes resembling those that Bourdieu designates as fields? A reading of the texts shows that it would be a mistake to reduce Weber's understanding of the process of differentiation and autonomization to such social configurations (Weber 1946). Certain spheres of activity apparently resemble what could be called fields (spheres of economic, political, religious, aesthetic or intellectual activities), but others are fairly clearly distinguished from them (domestic life, erotic-sexual activities, the ethical dimension of activities, etc.), but often even the former can be regarded more as registers of action or dimensions of social life than as activities set in relatively autonomized space-times. Indeed, Weber speaks as much of the 'social and psychological ties with the family, ... possession of worldly goods, ... political, economic, artistic and erotic activities' (Weber 1993: 166) as of 'spheres'. This last notion refers to a three-dimensional, self-enclosed space, while there are erotic, ethical, aesthetic, economic, etc., dimensions in practices that are not necessarily turned towards such specialized functions. Similarly, a universe like that of the family is a site where multiple functions (parental, erotic, ethical, aesthetic, economic, political, etc.) proceed.

All this should make one wonder whether the idea of the differentiation and autonomization of fields does not sometimes produce the illusion of the sharp separation of the different activities, when this separation, clearly observable at one level of analysis (that of the 'professional producers' attached to these different universes), may be less distinct at other levels (those of the circulation, application or appropriation of the products of these activities). While it seems clear, for example, that, from the point of view of their respective stakes, the economic, legal, philosophical or sporting fields generally 'drive' social different agents, in different and parallel space-times, the picture is more complex if one considers matters from another standpoint. Thus, in our contemporary societies, the economic universe is not a universe truly distinct from other universes. There are hardly any activities that now escape the logic of the attribution of economic values to their products, services, etc., and that of commercial exchange. The economic market is therefore a transversal reality with respect to all domains of activity, and economic logic (economic reasoning or calculation) is omnipresent, to one degree or another: even when a universe cultivates its specificity and autonomy to the highest degree (e.g. the educational, artistic or literary universes), at some time or other it always encounters this economic logic (even the 'purest' forms of educational training always find a translation – even if it is unfavourable – on the employment market, the 'purest' authors or artists sell their works, etc.). The same is true for the political or legal fields, which may, by their very nature, penetrate or cover all domains of social life (from private life to public professional or leisure activities, etc.). Are they then logics, functions or dimensions of social life, as much as separate universes or spheres? The variety of the vocabulary used is the sign both of an analytical difficulty and the existence of a multiplicity of instances in reality.[11] At all events, any attempt to reduce all social contexts to fields would be an unjustified generalization.

Not every pertinent context of activity is a field

We live in strongly differentiated societies – urbanized, differentiated state societies, as Norbert Elias (1991) wrote – and it is therefore crucial to grasp the phenomena of social differentiation, particularly with a view to taking account of social determinations more specific and more subtle than those linked to membership of groups or classes. But what are these differentiated social contexts? One thinks fairly spontaneously of the spheres of activity, social universes or institutions around which sociology has organized a large proportion of its domains of study: the family, the school, the occupational universe, the church, the association, the sports club, the world of art, politics, etc., but these different social universes are not equivalent.

For example, while the family framework (in all its observable forms) is, in modern societies, one of the most universal matrices of socialization, the church (in the present day) or the sports club not only constitute social universes frequented by only a fraction of the population, but are places where certain actors practise their main social activity (the priest, the sports trainer, the professional sportsman and -woman), whereas other agents are there only for a limited time and devote only a small part of their time and energy to them. Some social universes are therefore such that they divide the actors into full-time 'producers' – the 'professionals' – and 'consumer-spectators' or 'amateurs'. However, such a distinction has no sense as regards, for example, the familial world: one does not 'frequent' that world as a leisure activity; one does not 'practise' the activity of father, mother, spouse, son or daughter as an 'amateur', as against others who do it as 'professionals'; one does not present a 'family show' to 'spectators', etc.

It can be seen, simply by considering these examples, that one can be invested by the *illusio* specific to a social universe although this universe may not combine the set of properties that would make it possible to define it as a field.[12] The family is one such area, distinguished quite sharply from universes such as those formed by journalists, philosophers or politicians. Conversely, one can 'live' in a universe without being totally taken up by it, by the *illusio* specific to this universe, i.e. without entering into the competition, without deploying strategies to win the capital specific to it. One can participate in a universe as an amateur practitioner (as opposed to a professional practitioner), as a simple consumer (rather than a producer), or as a simple participant in its material organization, taking no direct part in the game that is played there. For example, an individual may train in a tennis club once a week for personal relaxation, without being ranked or seeking to be ranked, and therefore not haunted by the stakes of competition that exist among professional players. He may also watch tennis matches without himself playing tennis. Finally, he may be plunged almost materially into the heart of the game without being concerned with the stakes of the struggle and competition of the game, because he is one of those who prepare the grass at Wimbledon or clean the changing rooms at Roland Garros. In these instances, the forces that impact so powerfully on professional players (the protagonists in spectacles that can be watched, the central agents of the field who battle to win the maximum of specific capital) do not act on him.

It may be thought that I have used poor examples in comparing such activities. The correct approach would indeed be to find the pertinent field on which these different social actors are set, a field that exerts a force of attraction on them and mobilizes their energies. However, even moving in that direction (seeking to find the adequate field), one has to observe that some actors or some activities cannot readily be fitted into fields.

A large proportion of the individuals in our societies (the working classes, which are excluded from the start from the fields of power) prove to be 'off-field', lost in a vast 'social space' whose axes of structuration are the volume and structure of the capital possessed (essentially cultural and economic capital). Bourdieu himself admits this indirectly when he explains understanding the work of a celebrated author poses particular problems compared with interpreting the text of an interview with a 'simple layperson', 'notably the belonging of its author to a field' (Bourdieu 1996c: 392 n.25). If one wanted to pursue the metaphor of the spectacle, one might say that field theory devotes much energy to shedding light on the big scenes where stakes of power are played for, but little to understanding those who build the stages, assemble the scenery, clean the theatre, photocopy documents or type letters, etc. Ultimately a great majority of the actors in our societies are left off-field by an analysis in terms of field that privileges study of the 'major competitors' – in whichever type of domain the competition takes place – and their specific stakes.

Likewise, all the activities in which we engage only temporarily (amateur football or chess, occasional meetings and discussions with friends in a bar or in the street, etc.) cannot be assigned to particular fields, because these activities are not systematically organized as spaces of positions and struggles among the different agents occupying these positions. Field theory therefore shows little interest in the off-field life of the agents who battle within a field. It is, however, impossible to proceed as if journalists, footballers, philosophers or jurists could be reduced to their being-as-member-of-a-field.

Contrary, then, to what the most general formulae may suggest, everything (individual, institution, practice, situation or interaction) cannot be attached to a field. In fact, fields correspond fairly well, 1 to domains of professional (and/or public) activities, while excluding populations without a professional activity (and among them, a majority of women); and, more precisely still, 2 to prestigious professional and/or public activities, for which the notion of 'capital' has a meaning and which can therefore organize themselves as spaces of competition and struggle for the conquest of this specific capital (as opposed to subaltern occupations or activities: 'junior' managerial staff, service personnel, manual workers, etc.).

Whether one takes the political field, the journalistic field, the publishing field, the field of haute couture, the philosophical field, etc., it can be seen one is dealing both with actors who have prestigious professional activities, and with the observation of these actors on the basis solely of their professional activities, although they also have places in many other frameworks – social, private or public, long-term or ephemeral. It is from this point of view – which is remarkably revelatory, given the double exclusion of 'off-field time' and 'off-field actors' – that this sociology not only interests itself in the situation of those who are virtually 'born into the field' or 'born into the game', but sometimes unjustifiably generalizes this model of situation: 'The *illusio* is a kind of knowledge that is based on being born into the game, belonging to the game by birth: to say that I know the game in this way means that I have it in my veins, in my fingertips, that it plays within me, without me, as when my body responds to a feint before I even saw it' (Bourdieu 1989: 44).[13]

Another theorist interested in the plurality of social worlds, Anselm L. Strauss (1993: 212–15), did not evade the complexity that necessarily confronts any analyst on account of the diversity of types of world in our social formations. For Strauss, a social world is defined all at once by an activity, places, a technology, organizations and an internal division of labour. Like Bourdieu, he stresses the fact that if the boundaries of the worlds are fuzzy, this is due to the existence of perpetual internal disputes about the limits of the social world in question. Thus he described the struggles within the world of art or the world of medicine to determine who is (and who is not) a 'genuine' artist, who are the legitimate representatives of medicine and who are the 'charlatans', etc. These social worlds vary according to their function, their size, their lifespan, their origin, their historical trajectory, their relation to State power, their social composition, their geographical extent (some have only a local existence, others have a national or international dimension), their internal degree of hierarchization, the degree of commitment they demand, etc. While clearly more empiricist and less theoretically clear-cut than Bourdieu, Strauss nonetheless makes it possible to investigate worlds that are not fields and to discover, in relation to universes that can be studied in terms of field, aspects in which field theory is not interested.

Field theory therefore constitutes a way of responding to a series of scientific problems, but may itself be an obstacle to knowledge of the social world (especially, as will be seen, when it becomes the be-all and end-all of all contextualization of practices). This can first happen when it ignores the constant movements that the actors of a field make between the field in which they are producers, the fields in which they are simple consumer-spectators and the multiple situations that cannot be described as fields – thus reducing the actor to his/her being-as-member-of-a-field. It also happens when field theory neglects the situation of those who define themselves socially (and constitute themselves mentally) outside any activity in a particular field (as is the case, for example, of housewives, who have no professional or public activity,[14] and for a proportion of the retired, who are more or less summarily placed off-field[15]). Finally, it leaves us ill-equipped to understand actors outside fields, the 'foot soldiers'. For all these reasons, field theory (in fact one should always endeavour to speak of the theory of fields of power) cannot constitute a general and universal theory, but can be a regional theory of the social world.

A regional theory claiming universality

Many social science researchers would agree that practices can only be understood at the point of connection between an internalized past (whether referred to terms of culture, mentality, habits or dispositions) and the present social context in which the practice arises. However, for Bourdieu every context is necessarily a field and that is why he can put forward the following sociological equation: '[(habitus) (capital)] + field = practice' (Bourdieu 1984: 101). Similarly, he often insists on the conceptual interdependence of the terms *habitus* and *field*: 'Habitus is valid only in relation with field, capital is valid only in relation with field' (Bourdieu 1989); or again: 'To understand human practices in differentiated societies, one has to know about fields and, on the other hand, one has to take account of what I call habitus' (Bourdieu 1989). Yet, bearing in mind the previous reflections on fields, one can only be surprised at such an obligatory coupling, which, if strictly applied, would make it impossible to understand a host of actors and actions.

'Habitus' is – fortunately – *not* 'only valid in relation with field'. As a concept linked to a theory of socialization, the idea of the habitus aims to grasp what it is, in the social world, lives in the incorporated state. However, it was initially devised to understand practices in weakly differentiated universes (such as Kabyle society) that are societies without separate fields. Practices can indeed be well understood at the intersection of incorporated dispositions (which sometimes take the form of habitus).[16]

Bourdieu clearly situates his research programme and his concept of the field between the (too) large extents of 'long-range history' (*l'histoire de longue durée*) (the refuge, in his view, of all social philosophies) and the 'history of events' (*l'histoire événementielle*):

> If we are not to abandon the real universe of practices in its totality to chance or mystery, we must indeed seek in a structural history of the social spaces – field of power, artistic field, intellectual field or scientific field – in which the dispositions that make up 'great men' are engendered and realized, the means of filling the gap between the slow and imperceptible movements of the economic or demographic infrastructure and the surface agitation recorded by the day-to-day chronicles of political, literary or artistic history.
>
> (Bourdieu 1990: 190)

From such a standpoint (neither *histoire de longue durée* nor the micro-contexts of *l'histoire événementielle* or, elsewhere, of microsociology), it is clear that the objects of microsociology can appear to him as slight and insignificant. What, indeed, is the weight of a study of the interaction between a client and a cinema cashier (Goffman 1981) beside the study of the social strategies to conserve or subvert and the struggles for State power or scientific authority? Yet the example of such an interaction shows clearly that not everything can be understood through field theory. Some human activities – in which field would one place that kind of commercial interaction? – and some dimensions of human activities – here the phenomena of presupposition or expectation of the interpretative procedures applied by members of the same community – escape such an approach.

As soon as one is persuaded that the only relevant context (neither too 'macro' nor too 'micro') is that of the 'field', other theoretical constructions can be rejected on grounds of 'error', 'lesser complexity', or scientific 'regression'. Thus Bourdieu judges that the notion of the *art world* used by Howard S. Becker in the United States, 'marks a regression in relation to the theory of the field' (Bourdieu 1996c: 204). He can likewise declare, unambiguously, that 'the notion of the field of power is an immense progress', and that many researchers 'make enormous errors, even empirical ones, because they do not have this notion' (Bourdieu and Grenfell 1995: 8). Bourdieu would certainly have readily acknowledged that field theory is perfectible, but there is no doubt that for him it constituted the historically most accomplished scientific theory, the last link in a long chain of scientific theorizations of the facts of social differentiation.

From the historical field to the metaphor of the field of forces

Should one retain the historical character of the field or make it a concept of universal applicability? In other words, should one reserve the term 'field' to designate the relatively autonomous sub-universes historically constituted in the course of the social differentiation of functions and the social division of labour, or should one be able to use the concept to designate any kind of historical and social situation? If one takes the first option, then one is acknowledging that just as the State, social classes or the economic market have not always existed, so not everything is a field – there were social realities before there were fields and there may now be social contexts that cannot be analysed in terms of a field. It is this first option, both more rigorous in the use of definitions and more concerned to historicize concepts, that seems to me scientifically more productive, since it avoids rigidifying concepts into universal passwords.

When speaking of the family as a field, Bourdieu nonetheless seems to invite a metaphorical and less rigorous use of the term, which then designates no more than configurations within which there are power relations among agents with differentiated objective properties, interests, strategies, etc. He writes: '[while] the family, in order to exist and subsist, has to function as a *body*, it always tends to function as a *field*, with its physical, economic and, above all, symbolic power relations (linked for example to the volume and structure of the capital possessed by each member), its struggles for conservation and reproduction of these power relations … ' (Bourdieu 1996d: 22).

The fact that the family (like other universes or other less autonomized social situations), like any other social reality, should be studied through a relational mode of thought – Norbert Elias's notion of a configuration of relations of interdependence is also the product of such a scientific approach (Lahire 1995, 1999b) – and can also be seen, in part, as the site of power relations among individuals with differentiated social properties, does not mean that it can usefully be considered a field. It is a durable, relatively autonomous institution of socialization, yet not a 'field'.

As a relatively autonomous universe, which has its own logic of functioning, the family is a configuration of relations of interdependence which, in contrast to a field – and even if the adults of this universe belong to fields – most often constitutes the framework in which the child is born and discovers the social world, the framework that exercises a very strong – early, systematic, intense and extended – socializing force on him/her. From this point of view, the family does not constitute a space where one essentially observes the appropriation of a – mysterious – 'familial capital'.[17] The relations between parents and children or between spouses are in fact as much made up of solidarity, mutual help and cooperation as of struggle, and the different members of a family – parents and children in particular – have neither the same status nor the same role, with the former performing a more or less long-term function of protection, care and education of the latter.

Finally, unlike a field, the family is a form of collective life that does not specialize (or specify) its 'influence' on the actors involved in it. It is the non-specialized site where all the other social dimensions (economic, moral, political, religious, aesthetic, sport, food, etc.) that are distributed among differentiated fields are permanently managed or intervene without differentiation. That is why Durkheim could establish a clear difference between the family and the corporation:

> Undoubtedly, one difference will always exist between them, inasmuch as family members share in common their entire existence, whereas the members of a corporation share only their professional concerns. The family is a kind of complete society whose influence extends to economic activity as well as to that of religion, politics, and science, etc. Everything of any importance that we do, even outside the home, has repercussions upon it and sparks off an appropriate reaction. In one sense the corporation's sphere of influence is more limited.
>
> (Durkheim 1997 [1893]: xliv–xlv)[18]

The literary game versus the literary field

In the course of a recent study of writers, conducted in the spirit of a sociology of the practical conditions (economic, spatial and temporal) of literary activity, I was led to distance myself from the notion of the 'literary field' (Lahire 2006). The origins of this conceptual modification are linked to the critical remarks so far formulated on the failure of field theory to take account of time spent outside fields and the consequent reduction of social actors to 'being-as-member-of-the-field'. While this critique relates to all social actors in differentiated societies where individuals are generally led to frequent a variety of social contexts, it is even more crucial for actors such as writers, the majority of whom, for economic reasons, are only intermittently engaged in the literary universe.

Although it is symbolically highly prized and can generate intense personal vocations and investments, the literary universe is overall very little professionalized and brings very little financial reward. It therefore brings together individuals who in their very great majority belong, for economic reasons, to various other occupational universes. Generally forced to exercise a 'second job', participants in the literary universe are closer to 'players' – who regularly exit the game to 'earn their living' outside it – than full-time 'agents' of a field. It is particularly for this reason that I preferred to speak of the 'literary game' rather than a 'literary field'. The concept of the 'literary game' in fact designates a secondary field, very different in its functioning of parent fields – academic fields and scientific fields in particular – which have the economic means to convert the individuals involved in them into permanent agents and so lead to devote the greater part of their energy to their service.

In contrast to Bourdieu, who uses the metaphor of the game as a simple pedagogic means of explaining what a field is, one can sustain the metaphor of the 'literary game' and exploit its potentialities to differentiate types of universes that offer very different conditions of life to their respective participants. Because they proceed as if the literary universe were a field like others, the users of field theory have not taken note of the fact that reducing individuals to their status as 'agents of the literary field' is much more problematic than elsewhere, in as much as these individuals are distinguished by their frequent double lives, for reasons linked to the properties of the field in question. One of the scientific issues in this reformulation lies in the endeavour to *specify* field theory, since it seems to me useful to designate differently social universes that differ both in terms of their relations with the State and the market, and in terms of their relationship with their respective audiences or the conditions of their members.

A social universe unlike others

Literary writing is therefore an activity practised to a large extent by individuals who do not derive the bulk of their incomes from doing it (i.e. from royalties, since writers depend almost exclusively on a market of readers) and are thus obliged to live materially from activities other than the one by which they like to define themselves. They may be teachers, journalists, doctors, editorial advisers, engineers, they may have several, often precarious, 'bread and butter' jobs, but writers are rarely 'full-time' writers; the Flaubertian model of the writer of independent means who concentrates on his literary work and nothing else is not a generally applicable model for understanding the literary game as a whole. Flaubert, unmarried and childless, a man of independent means, with a 'second job', the 'man-pen' whose daily existence tends to amount to his writing (whether literary or epistolary) and the strength of whose literary dispositions makes him live in literature as his natural element, is the exception that confirms the rule of parallel activities:

> My life is a wound-up machine, which turns regularly. What I do today, I shall do tomorrow, I did it yesterday. I have been the same man for ten years. It has turned out that my organisation is a system, the whole without any deliberately adopted purpose, by the tendency of things in general, which makes the polar bear inhabit the ice and the camel walk on the sand. I am a man-pen. I feel by it, by reason of it, in relation to it, and much more with it.
>
> (G. Flaubert, Letter to Louise Colet, 31 January 1852)

The model of those who, like Flaubert, can give themselves 'body and soul' to their craft, who invest in it a time and energy sometimes judged 'unreasonable' by all those whose investments are less intense, is therefore also the model for actors who withdraw or disinvest the most from all other domains of existence (family, politics, sport, culture, etc.). High degrees of investment therefore presuppose the management (and acceptance) of this relation to other social universes. In taking as the model only those actors who have restricted extra-literary relations of sociability, limited their familial sociability, delegated everyday domestic tasks to others, found an 'understanding' (and sometimes even financially and/or psychologically 'supportive') partner or opted for a single life to devote all their time to literature, one would be looking at the literary game from the wrong end of the telescope and would fail to see that the great majority of the actors do not play the game in such 'ideal' conditions or at least in conditions 'favourable' to quasi-total investment in the game.

As Freidson puts it, literary writing is 'an activity that people engage in as a vocation and identification, without it constituting the main source of income' (Freidson 1986: 432). It presupposes an interest and a personal investment (temporal and affective) disproportionate to the irregular, unpredictable economic profits it can generate, which bear no relation to the hours of work and the intensity of the effort.

To appreciate the specificity of cultural producers in general, and writers in particular, in relation to the market, one has to imagine what would be the situation of lawyers or doctors who could only defend clients or treat patients capable of appropriating their own knowledge and know-how. If such were the case, one would no doubt see lawyers and doctors divided between those who, wanting to make a living from their occupation, strove to practise a simple and accessible form of legal defence or medical practice and others, chiefly concerned to practise their art in all its refinement, using another activity to provide their main means of subsistence. Although the writer, the painter, the lawyer or the doctor may all be considered 'experts' in their own areas, the great difference between cultural producers and the 'liberal professions' lies in the fact that the former sell the products of their knowledge and know-how to audiences who have more or less desire to appropriate them (and the competences to do so), whereas the latter sell their services to 'clienteles' who can derive benefit from them without needing to appropriate the knowledge that is put to work, i.e. without having to possess the cultural competences needed to understand them.

Turning to other cases, it can be seen that scientists are a parent case, situated between the cultural producers and the professionals mentioned. They are either employed by the State (as teacher-researchers or full-time researchers in public research organizations), or employees of large companies or private research laboratories. They are close to the cultural producers when their task is to create complex bodies of knowledge and pass it on to students, but clearly different in so far as they are (quasi-)civil servants whose income does not depend on the number of students trained. They may write and publish works for more or less extensive readerships (manuals, popular science, etc.), but their fees and royalties from publication are only a supplement relative to a main income guaranteed by the State. On the other hand, they are closer to lawyers or doctors in as much as their knowledge, while unintelligible to most people, can nonetheless lead more or less long term to technological, medical (etc.) innovations readily usable by consumers or from which the public can benefit with the aid of expert users (for example, the sophisticated equipment used in hospitals). Quite apart from the pedagogic mission training citizens in and through science, which justifies the strong state support for scientists, the State and private companies are also willing to employ scientists and invest in scientific research because the products of scientific knowledge can find their place on a market.

If field theory needs to be specified, this is because the situations of those who participate in the different social universes (medical, legal, political, journalistic, scientific, artistic, literary, etc.) varies greatly depending on the nature of the economic relationship between the potential audience and the members of these universes (purchase of a service and competences or purchase of symbolic goods), and the nature of the relationships between the State, the market and the universes in question. Thus, even with no audience or very restricted audiences, the full-time agents of the state-financed academic and scientific fields may continue to produce the most esoteric knowledge. The same is not true of the intermittent participants in a social game such as the literary game, subject to the market and enjoying much more limited State support. The hermetic poet may be a cousin of the esoteric scientist (there are in reality even mathematicians who write poetry), but s/he does not share the same conditions.

The writer's double life and literary interludes

Bourdieu clearly envisaged the cultural universes that he studied (artistic and literary ones) in terms of the model of the scientific field or the academic field, on the basis of the example of institutionalized social universes, codified and professionalized (in the economic sense of the term), that have largely settled the question of the economic conditions of the lives of their members. Whether in the regulation of the right of entry, based on examinations, competitions, certificates and elections, or the regulation of the different stages of the 'career', these institutionalized universes offer genuine professions to the main actors in their fields (researchers or teacher-researchers, philosophers, physicists, mathematicians, sociologists, etc.), who can and, by professional obligation in a sense, must devote themselves fully to the activity. These fields, which offer 'full-time' commitments to their members and thereby become the main social universes to which they belong, are rather different from those universes, such as the literary universe, to which individuals objectively attach themselves most often only secondarily, even if a proportion of those who join them consider this membership as their main identity. What relationship is there, in fact, between a writer who lives in parallel as a teacher, librarian, lawyer, journalist, doctor, psychologist, company director or farmer, and who exists in literature only part time or intermittently, and a doctor, a philosopher, a businessman or farmer who do their jobs full time in their respective social universes?

As a point of (structural, even structuralist) method, one might choose to consider only the works, independently of what their producers are and do (both 'in the field' and 'outside the field'), and also without regard for the concrete social conditions of their production. Structuralism applied to literary works thus effaces the writers in favour of the works. While notion of the 'field' may make it possible to break with a textualist structuralism exclusively concerned with works as signifying structures, it is very possible it is ultimately more suited to the differentiated positions and values of works and the publishing houses that support them than to study of the producers of works and their conditions of production.

However, in bracketing out the writing individuals, one would miss many central facts concerning the functioning of the literary universe. For example, it seems important to ask to what extent a cultural producer in general (and a writer in particular) situate themselves in the game or outside the game at particular moments in their trajectories. They are clearly in the game when they publish, but may withdraw from it more or less long term to devote themselves to other activities, only to reappear in the event of a new publication. These exits and re-entries to the literary game, with more or less long breaks, are not uncommon.

A sociologist interested in the intra-individual variations of behaviours and individual stocks (*patrimoines*) of dispositions cannot fail to wonder what 'type of person' (in Weber's sense) the social world shapes when it makes a more or less schizophrenic double life a social regularity, when it banalizes the permanent sense of frustration that arises from not being able to devote oneself to one's art, when it makes 'normal' the suffering linked to the gap between a subjective self-definition (as a writer) and a major part of one's objective conditions of existence. In contrast to all those who can experience their occupation as a central, permanent dimension of their personality, writers who have to pursue 'bread and butter' occupations for economic reasons have one (personal, 'cultural') foot in literature and another (material, sometimes also 'personal') foot outside it (the latter freeing the former from dependence on the constraints of the market).

Other 'mobilities' beyond entries and exits from the literary game can also be observed within the literary universe. It may also be wondered whether the same individuals can produce works occupying different positions within the literary game, whether they can come from the sector of restricted production and move to the sector of large-scale production, and conversely, or whether they can combine the production of works belonging to different sectors of the universe in question. One would then discover all the practices of literary double life (often with the use of pseudonyms) through which writers sometimes combine the production of personal literary works and the remunerative production of works belonging to 'industrial literature' or even practical literature.

The project of accounting for the specificity of the functioning of the literary universe requires the researcher, in any case, to expand the framework and ask what the actors identifiable in the literary universe are or do outside literature. Even from the standpoint of the questions that field theory poses (with its notions of *illusio*, habitus and investment), the double life that writers frequently lead is not an anodyne or insignificant fact but an absolutely central feature of literary life. How do writers manage their social investments when their literary activity exists only intermittently and depends on the 'gaps' that their other obligations – especially the familial and occupational ones – leave them? Can one 'invest' as intensely in different social universes whether or not they organize themselves in the form of fields of struggles? When they take part in different 'fields' (the literary field and the medical, journalistic, academic, diplomatic fields, etc.),[19] can they combine the different investments and types of *illusio* (in the sense of belief)? Can one belong to two different fields and have incorporated the *illusio* specific to each? The case of writers and the literary universe is just one case, more flagrant and acute than others, of synchronic and diachronic participation in heterogeneous social contexts characteristic of individual lives in differentiated societies (with a strong social division of labour, strong differentiation of functions, practices, stakes and types of *illusio*). Participation in differentiated social universes may range from the most durable presence to the most occasional and temporary investment in varied social contexts (family, groups or institutions). Torn between literature and the 'day job', not to mention other social frameworks such as family, writers constitute a somewhat particular but non-marginal case of social pluri-membership.

In the game and outside the game

If the overall global functioning of the social world is not indifferent to the fact that it is the same individuals who act, think and feel in very different

contexts of social life, and that these individuals experience tensions or contradictions linked to the permanent to-and-fro between one universe or sub-
universe and another, then it is crucial that sociologists take account of it as
systematically as possible in their field work and their analyses, which presupposes that the conditions of possibility and the tools of a sociology of
intra-individual variations in behaviours be made explicit (Lahire 2002b,
2004: 695–742). In this regard, field theory might be an unwitting contribution to the premature hyper-specialization of sociology[20] (with different
researchers becoming specialists of different fields) and induce blindness to
the phenomena of multiple social memberships or affiliations that are crucial
in highly differentiated societies.

However, it is clear that the reduction of individuals to their being-as-
member-of-a-field is even more problematic, and should be even more
apparent to the researcher, when those who participate in a field rarely have
both feet in the field but keep one outside it – the breadwinning foot that pays
for the other to 'dance'.

As I have already emphasized, it is as if the model of the 'literary field' had
been conceived on the basis of the very atypical figure of the *rentier* (Flaubert) who has the economic means to maintain a perfectly disinterested relation to his art, to devote himself entirely to it, to refuse all mercantile
literature, to delay publication until he judged his work worthy of it, to reject
literary fashions and despise unworthy and useless journalists and critics. It is
clearly not a matter of asserting that those who have worked on the 'literary
field' have systematically ignored the fact that writers are the most often to
pursue a 'second job',[21] but of seeing to what extent this basic *donnée* of the
functioning of the literary universe, like other artistic universes, has failed to
modify their way of talking about this 'field' and its principal actors (the
writers).

Another user of the concept of the field, Anna Boschetti, also underlines
the fact that 'to manage to live from one's royalties remains an entirely
improbable feat' (Boschetti 1991: 512–13) and that the great majority of the
writers of the period that she studies (1900–50) were obliged to practise a
second occupation, without the concepts of field and habitus being questioned
on the basis of this massive and major fact:

> Living from one's pen alone, i.e. exclusively from one's books, remained
> throughout this period the feat of a small minority. And it was not the
> case of the avant-gardes, except for some rare successes where scandal
> always played a determinant role. Without even mentioning the collec-
> tions of Éluard, whose print runs, in the 'age of the hundred thousand'
> were often below a hundred copies, even the sales figures of better known
> authors remained modest – 17,500 for Malraux's *Les Conquérants* in its
> first two years (1928–29), 5,000 for *Le Feu follet*, 8,843 for *Rêveuse
> Bourgeoisie* in the lifetime of Drieu la Rochelle. Sartre himself, who
> achieved the rare feat of living largely on his royalties, was able to give up

teaching mainly thanks to his plays and film scripts. It should be added that one success was not enough. Public favour is always conditional, always to be re-won, and writers' income also depended on the abundance and regularity of their production ... Being rich by birth, or kept, or a civil servant (increasingly, a teacher), having a second, or most often, several other paid activities – such was the writer's lot.

(Boschetti 1991: 512–13)

When Bourdieu acknowledges that 'the "profession" of writer or artist ... is one of the least capable, too, of completely defining (and nourishing) those who claim it, and who, quite often, cannot assume the function they take as their principal one unless they have a secondary profession to provide them with their main income', he only notes in this situation 'the subjective profits offered by this double status, with the proclaimed identity allowing one, for example, to be satisfied with all the small jobs described as being just to pay the bills, which are offered by the profession itself (such as that of reader or proofreader in publishing houses) or by related institutions (such as journalism, television, radio and so forth)' (Bourdieu 1996c: 227). Quite apart from the fact that writers do not derive all their economic resources from jobs in publishing or the media, the question of the economic precarity that can be generated by such a situation, the question of the time stolen by the 'second job' from the time for creation, the question of the effects of this double life on individual stocks of dispositions (which would inevitably challenge the notion of the habitus in as much as it is difficult to speak of a 'literary habitus' for actors who – as writer-doctors, writer-teachers, writer-journalists, writer-engineers, writer-manual workers, etc. – would then combine 'habitus' as theoretically non-cumulable), all this is more or less completely ignored by the author. One may even have the impression that, for Bourdieu, those who do not possess the economic resources that would enable them to invest totally in the literary universe belong only to 'literary bohemia'. This is in any case what is implied in his definition of literary bohemia in mid-nineteenth-century France, since it corresponds perfectly to the general situation of writers today: 'the bohemia of Murger, Champfleury or Duranty constitutes a veritable intellectual reserve army, directly subject to the laws of the market and often obliged to live off a second skill (sometimes with no direct relation to literature) in order to live an art that cannot make a living' (Bourdieu 1996c: 57).

One might even see a fairly clearly sign of theoretical forgetting of the question of the 'second skill' in Bourdieu's remarks on 'how interesting it is from this perspective to have studies of figures who have participated in a more or less "creative" manner in several fields ... and have produced, according to the typically Leibnizian method of possible worlds, several realizations of the same habitus (just as, in the order of consumption, the different arts give rise to objectively systematic expressions, as "counterparts" in Lewis's sense, of the same taste)' (Bourdieu 1996c: 379). The way in which

Bourdieu poses the problem presupposes that the habitus is unitary (systematic and homogenous) and that the objective of research is to see the effects of translation of the 'same habitus' into different properties and structurations of the possible. He appears not to see that the somewhat atypical situation that he thinks he is describing – the participation of the same individuals in several universes – is precisely the case of a very large proportion of the writers who combine literary activity with extra-literary activity, not necessarily in other universes of cultural production, or even in other non-cultural universes. The researcher is not therefore obliged to proceed in the manner of logicians and imagine realities that are in fact before his very eyes.[22]

A fleshless field

In its concern to analyse the struggles played out among agents belonging to the same universe, or those among agents from different fields, field theory has ended up neglecting the study of the nature and specificity of the activities that take place in the different universes in question. The research conducted on the literary, legal, scientific, educational (etc.) 'fields' never makes it possible to answer questions of the type: What is literature? What is law? What is science? What is education (or pedagogy)? Are these questions too 'anthropological' (in the philosophical sense of the term)? Are they typically essentialist or substantialist questions and therefore illegitimate for sociology? Certainly not. Similarly, field theory does not really make it possible to understand the specificity of a given literary work, a form of law, a particular scientific practice or a variant of schooling.

Yet the progressive autonomization of social functions (the 'literary', the 'legal', the 'educational', the 'religious', the 'political', the 'medical', the 'mathematical', etc.) is indissolubly linked to the process of constitution of specific traditions that are endlessly taken up, transformed, reworked from one generation to another, and which form a basis for the development of ever more specific modes of reasoning, objects and styles of expression. As Jack Goody explains, 'Throughout history, the specialization of scribes combines with the relative autonomy of the written tradition to promote the structural autonomy of the "great organizations" which tend to develop their own literary corpus, their own bodies of specialist knowledge' (Goody 1986: 172).[23]

The field therefore appears relatively skeletal and only shows us clearly – admittedly a significant gain from the analysis – spaces of positions, the strategies of agents engaged in struggles, relations of force and domination, unequal structures of distribution of kinds of specific capital.[24] How can we avoid the split between a formal approach to cultural products and a fleshless sociology of the producers, their power relations and their strategies? Should one conclude that Bourdieu can accurately study only the polemological dimension of the universes in question, while imagining that he is able to advance knowledge (of practices, activities, types of knowledge, their nature and their specific forms, at the same time as that of the struggles, strategies and relations of domination) at all levels? Or that the scientific programme is, in the present state of affairs, partially realized, but only requires filling out? Depending on the position one adopts in relation to field theory, the gaps will be seen either as the proof of a fundamental inadequacy or as a call to the enrichment of the research programme. In any case, scientific lucidity requires one not to proceed as if field theory, in the present state of the research work to which it has given rise, had managed to establish itself as a general and complete theory.

A literary field without literature

A sociology of literature that neglects literary texts in favour of the symbolic production of the value of works, the social construction of writers' trajectories, literary strategies, the structuring of the space of literary positions or the history of literary institutions is not without interest but clearly omits a central dimension of its object. Even if Bourdieu declared that he had superseded the 'lethal' dichotomy of external reading versus internal reading,[25] no empirical research exists to confirm this supersession in practice, and one can observe that, like many sociologists of literature, he remains outside the specific territory of the text, leaving to others the study of themes or style, having tacitly abandoned the ground to literary, aesthetic or formal analyses. How does one articulate determinations external to the works (and which ones – the writer's social class of origin, generation, gender, geographical origin, religion, literary training, position in the literary field ... ?) with the literary characteristics of the texts? It is on this kind of question that sociologists of literature very generally falter, and Bourdieu is no exception to the rule.

Bourdieu's sociology of the literary field is essentially a sociology of producers (rather than productions), and no existing analysis has really succeeded in showing that this sociology of producers makes it possible to grasp the order of productions in its specificity. This is partly explained by the fact that the specificity of the field (the specifically literary character of the 'products' that circulate) concerns all the agents of the field and partly transcends the differences (and struggles) internal to the field. Focused essentially on grasping the differences of position of the producers, their struggles and strategies to increase their literary capital or change the legitimate definition of literature, etc., the sociologist is not in a position to answer the question ritually posed by writers, critics, literary theorists or philosophers: 'What is literature?'

Presupposing this shared or common interest, which is rarely questioned as such (given, as Bourdieu puts it, the 'objective complicity' that exists among the various adversaries within the same field), the way of framing the phenomena specific to field theory explains why it is ill-placed to consider the nature ('literarity', the literary construction of the real) of the 'common'. A comparative historical sociology of the different social universes that sought to discover how the literary vision of the world (as a set of literary forms of construction of the world) distinguishes itself from the scientific, legal, philosophical, etc. visions of the world, and which therefore broadened the focus of its lens, would make it possible to answer the question 'what is literature?' Such an approach would reconnect with the Weberian and Durkheimian conceptions of religion or science and would avoid disincarnating the fields of force and struggle: in other words, it would not forget the specificity of the practices, behaviours and life orientations that unfold there. What is the specificity of aesthetic products? The answer that consists in saying that 'literature' is what literary institutions consider as such, that 'art' is whatever is put in an art gallery, that 'science' is whatever is published in a scientific journal, is clearly inadequate. While this tautology is useful in underlining the institutionalization by the social world of the meaning of acts or of the products of these acts, it does not answer the question of what characterizes these different symbolic constructions of the real. Nor can the question be answered by pointing to the social functions of art or science (e.g. the function of cultural distinction – the profit of distinction accruing from demarcating oneself from the 'vulgar').

Bearing in mind the problem of focal distance (and the priority given intra-field comparisons),[26] it is not surprising that such preoccupations are stronger among historians and anthropologists than sociologists. When the anthropologist or historian studies the encounter between mythical thought and religious thought, or between mythical thought and rational, philosophical or scientific thought, when they study the invention of rational thought, experimental science, philosophy or literature,[27] they are in a position to respond – in a scientifically quite serious way – to questions that some sociologists may judge too 'philosophical' or even 'metaphysical'.

It is indeed when they have to engage in epistemological reflections, when they have to situate themselves in relation to other forms of knowledge and intellectual know-how, that sociologists (like historians) consider the specificity of their construction of the world, the specificity of their (sociological or historical) gaze on the real.[28] What makes an historical narrative irreducible to a narrative, and thereby distinguishes it from a literary narrative? What makes the social sciences not comparable to (even the most realist) literature, or to (even investigative) journalism, or (even the most social or political) philosophy, or to the physical and chemical sciences, the life sciences or the logical-formal sciences? How does the sociological vision of the world differ from other scientific visions of the world?

It might be thought that in his work on Flaubert Bourdieu responds effectively to the objection that the sociology of the literary field is more interested in the producers than the works. However, what Bourdieu does in showing that *L'Éducation sentimentale* contains an implicit sociology of the social world in which Flaubert is himself immersed (as can also be shown for authors such as Proust (Belloï 1993; Bidou-Zachariasen 1997; Dubois 1997; Lahire 2011: 32–35), Stendhal (Dubois 2007), Pirandello, Simenon or Memmi (Lahire 2005a)) and in comparing 'sociology' (in fact *his* sociology) with literature (à la Flaubert)[29] in no way accounts for the social creation of a literary work (genre, style, registers, themes …). To detect what implicit sociological theory or 'sense of the social' there is in literary works is a good way of expanding one's sociological imagination, but does not fulfil the programme of a sociology of literary creation.[30]

Discourse producers without discourse

Each field is characterized by both the structure of positions and the structure of position-takings that corresponds to it. Depending on the case, the second term covers works (literary, pictorial, musical, scientific, etc.), practices or discourses (political, legal, religious, etc.), but in no case does field theory offer any tool for entering into the works, practices or discourses, prioritizing instead the establishment of correspondences (most often statistically based) between indicators of objective positions in the field and indicators of position-takings (types of production, types of discourse, religious and political affiliations, tastes, opinions or practices of all kinds).

Even before the systematic use of analysis in terms of fields, the tendency to prioritize the study of inegalitarian structures, relations of domination, gaps between social groups, etc., was strong in the works of sociology of education and culture. To take just the case of schooling, the absence of an analysis of the specificity of knowledges and practices is just as clear (Lahire 1999a, 2008). Thus the British educational sociologist Basil Bernstein was able to write in the 1980s that:

> [g]eneral theories of cultural reproduction … appear to be more concerned with an analysis of what is reproduced in, and by, education than with analysis of the medium of reproduction, the nature of the specialized discourse. It is as if pedagogic discourse is itself no more than a relay for power relations external to itself; a relay whose form has no consequence for what is relayed … Bourdieu and Passeron are more concerned with the *relation* to pedagogic communication, that is, with differences between acquirers with respect to how they have been positioned in their relations to legitimate pedagogic communication, than with the analysis of the relations *within* pedagogic communication.
>
> (Bernstein 1990: 166–67)

Relating the phenomenon of educational inequality to the unequal structure of the distribution of cultural capital and the phenomenon of cultural inheritance, Bourdieu and Jean-Claude Passeron ended up with an ahistorical (Passeron 1991: 89–109) and somewhat formal sociological vision of the social world, capturing only inegalitarian structures, gaps, differential proximities, etc., and leaving us no better informed as regards what makes the specificity of the school, namely the (historically variable) contents of the activities that go on there, the knowledges that circulate, the modes of study that are transmitted, the dispositions that are endlessly constituted, the forms of pedagogic relations (which are power relations) engaged there, etc. The more general focus of sociologists of education on the certification effect of the school (partly linked to the idea of 'diploma inflation') likewise led them to neglect what would belong to a 'sociology of pedagogic practices that takes as its object the content and organization of teaching, the criteria or mechanisms of selection' (Passeron 1982: 553). Equally, the notion of 'cultural capital', qui might have functioned both as a tool for understanding phenomena of social reproduction and cultural domination (this capital being unequally distributed) and as a means of designating cultural contents, practices, knowledges, skills, relations to knowledge, language, etc., was ultimately used more for the benefit of the former perspective (sociology of domination and power) than the latter (sociology of knowledge).

More generally, when the agents of a field produce (oral or written) discourses, everything takes place as if these were transparent and without form, and as if they could be summed up in a few properties readily expressible by the analyst. This neglect of discourses is explained in part that the sociologist aims to twist the stick in the opposite direction from those who believe that power lies in words. Around this classic question of 'how to do things with words', Bourdieu insisted on the social legitimacy of the spokesperson, on the authority conferred on him/her not by discourse but by what is regarded as external to it (State, government, administration, Church, party, union, the medical establishment, science, academia, etc.). He therefore declares that one can easily drop 'the naive question of the power of words' and the idea of 'looking within words for the power of words, that is, looking for it where it is not to be found' (Bourdieu 1991c: 107): 'authority comes to language from outside', and one cannot therefore 'find in discourse itself ... the key to the efficacy of speech' (Bourdieu 1991c: 109). The case seems closed and discourse is indeed a very minor aspect of things compared to the authority of the spokesperson: 'Language at most *represents* this authority, manifests and symbolizes it' (Bourdieu 1991c: 109).

The very researchers who would be outraged by the reduction of the destiny of scientific statements to the social force and position of the scientists do not hesitate to quarantine social discourses for fear of being caught out in a 'linguistic turn' or 'rhetorical turn' (Lahire 2011: 163–74). While they avoid entering discourses, they nonetheless read them (and how could they not, in order to characterize the 'points of view' of the social agents they seek to objectivate by relating them to the positions they occupy?), without any particular method but with a conviction of the self-evidence of their understanding of these texts. Paradoxically, those who insist on the need to arm oneself with conceptual and methodological toolboxes when it comes to objectivating positions, social structures or institutions often embark on the reading of discourses with nothing more than the common sense of a professional reader. When each 'position-taking' or 'point of view' has been reduced to what appears to the analyst an adequate abstract, summary or generative formula of an author's thought or a broader current of thinking, it only remains to slip these shorthand notes into the argument in order to concentrate on what makes such points of view possible (e.g. 'social Catholicism', 'elitism of competence', 'pastoral populism', 'economic humanism', etc.; Bourdieu and Boltanski 1976).[31] Having laboured to situate the field in question within the field of power and analyse its internal structure, the social trajectories and positions occupied by the agents, the researcher is indeed bound to arrive exhausted at the discursive gates, unable to do more than sketch the architectural style in broad terms.

This significant lacuna in field theory can be a starting point for understanding the recurrent critiques that Bourdieu made of Michel Foucault on account of his closeness 'to the semiologists such as Trier and the uses they have made of the idea of "semantic field"', because he 'explicitly refuses to search outside the "field of discourse" for the principle which would elucidate each of the discourses within it' (Bourdieu 1996c: 197). The critique is all the sharper because it makes it possible to avoid posing the question of the 'frontal' analysis of discourses (their invariants and their variations, their themes, their styles, the practices and institutions with which they are articulated and which they allow to be articulated). Rather than survey the discursive order from a distance, it would be useful, as Michel Foucault puts it, to study it 'in the exact specificity of its occurrence' (Foucault 2002: 30), and not as a reflection of a reality, the effect of a cause or the product of an underlying order – in short, to enter into the flesh of the discourse.

A problematic homology

Bourdieu's sociology of the fields of cultural production is thus fundamentally a sociology of the producers engaged in struggles to appropriate the capital specific to the field, applying strategies of conservation or subversion, and works are thus seen as marked by the positions and strategies of their producers. However, if the 'consumers' or 'receivers' of works are manifestly not the centre of interest of this sociology, what place *are* they given? The individuals of our social formations, belonging to the fields of power or not, dominant or dominated, who attend performances more or less frequently, 'consume' the products of the agents of the different fields with more or less regularity; they read novels, philosophical essays, works of social science, strip cartoons, newspapers and magazines; they go to the cinema, theatre, museum or gallery; they watch and listen to politicians on television, etc. What of the experiences of these multiple 'receivers' of shows, performances, texts, images, sounds?

The first way in which field sociology integrates the 'consumer' is by asking whether s/he possesses the cultural code assumed to be inscribed in the work: 'The work of art takes on meaning and interest only for someone who is provided with culture, or cultural competence, i.e. the code in which it is encoded' (Bourdieu 1996b: 2). For such a sociology of cultural consumption, the work of art possesses, locked within it as it were, the code that the 'consumer' needs in order to 'decipher' it. The modalities of reception remain very simple. The reasoning is sometimes binary ('possessing the code' or 'not possessing the code'; Bourdieu *et al.* 1991), sometimes ternary, so as to be able to integrate the relation to culture of the three major social classes (the cultural bourgeoisie as characterized by its 'mastery of the code', working classes by their 'non-mastery of the code' and the cultural petite-bourgeoisie by its 'pretension to mastery of the code' or 'partial mastery of the code'; Bourdieu 1984).

Proceeding in this way, Bourdieu ignores all the works on the sociology, and especially the history, of cultural reception (or appropriation) (Passeron 1991: 257–88; Chartier 1985, 1987; Ang 1985). In these approaches, the meaning of the work is not inscribed in the work, waiting to be unveiled or decoded, but is produced in the encounter between the work and its 'receivers' (who are therefore active producers of its meaning). There is therefore not 'a' meaning, but meanings produced in each encounter between audiences and works.

The interest taken in multiple modes of appropriation has the effect of avoiding the traps of cultural legitimism. Instead of proceeding as if the ideological, symbolic, cultural, religious or political effects aimed at by the various institutions of power were equivalent to the effects actually produced, instead of overestimating the capacities of the 'dominant' to acculturate the most 'dominated' populations, this conception is sensitive to the noisy or silent resistances at work in the ordinary acts of appropriation. Aesthetic, expert or erudite commentaries on the work are not the only possible ones, even if they claim to deliver 'the code', the 'true meaning' of the work, and one becomes aware of the legitimism that haunts the sociology of cultural consumption, which cannot describe and analyse experiences with works that are outside the norms and outside the codes. Those who do not possess the 'codes' are defined by (and reduced to) their 'cultural poverty' by analysts, unable to describe and analyse their practices, tastes and experiences (Grignon and Passeron 1989; Lahire 1993). The sociology (and history) of the reception of works is interested in all forms of experience or appropriation, from the most legitimate to the most bizarre, incongruous and unorthodox. It is concerned with real receptions, as they happen. However, the sociology of cultural consumption is also too legitimist in that it often credits the most cultivated 'receivers' with mastery of the 'code', when they are clearly not always potential art historians or literary critics.

It is clear what benefit the analysts of the present day would derive from adopting such interpretative approaches. Nowadays, when, much more than even in *Ancien Régime* societies, a large proportion of cultural products are present in all social milieux, in the form, among others, of television or radio broadcasts, it is important – if one wants to resist pessimistic and scientifically weak discourses on the uniformization, standardization and 'dumbing down' of tastes – to study how the same products, the same works, are subject to differentiated appropriations.

Another way of understanding the relationship between the producers (or products) and the consumer-receivers of works in the framework of field theory lies in the idea of a 'homology between the space of producers and the space of consumers' (Bourdieu 1996c: 249), which posits a correspondence between types of audiences and types of works (and of producers). In opposition to those who think that cultural, aesthetic sensibility is innate, this sociology seeks to show that there is a strong statistical correspondence between, on one side, the hierarchy of the arts (from the most legitimate to the least legitimate) and (within each art) the hierarchy of genres, and on the other side, the social hierarchy of the consumers (audiences).

Such a homology seems clear to Bourdieu, when it concerns, for example, the literary field (producers) and the field of power (consumers):

> The homology between the space of producers and the space of consumers, i.e. between the literary (etc.) field and the field of power, grounds the unintentional adjustment between supply and demand: at the temporally dominated and symbolically dominant pole of the field, writers produce for their peers (meaning for the field itself or even for the most autonomous section of this field), and, at the other extreme, writers produce for the dominant regions of the field of power ...
>
> (Bourdieu 1996c: 249)

By contrast, the coupling appears to him much looser when one moves outside the dominants into the overall social space, which is not so easily structured: 'The homology between positions in the literary (etc.) field and positions in the overall global social field is never as perfect as the one established between the literary field and the field of power from which the bulk of its clientele is usually recruited' (Bourdieu 1996c: 251).

Not only might one wonder what heuristic power can be attributed to this model of the homological correspondence between the space of producers and the space of consumers, if its relevance is essentially limited to 'communication' between the different categories of the 'dominant' (the social world is singularly reduced to its most legitimate poles, its spaces of power), but, more generally, this way of conceiving the consumers prevents one from grasping the plural appropriations of the same works. By assuming the existence of a 'reading contract ... between the sender and the receiver' drawn up 'on [the] basis of common premises' (Bourdieu 1996c: 384 n.31), Bourdieu gives too simplified an image – which does not take account of the gains from historical and sociological work on reception or cultural appropriation – of what a reading experience may involve (Lahire 2011: 89ff).

Concluding remarks: normative viewpoints on autonomy

As a pure analyst, Bourdieu can be content to study the genesis and evolution of fields, and coldly the degree of autonomy attained by each of them, the

gains and losses of autonomy observable in different epochs, different economic and political environments, etc. However, Bourdieu the sociologist,
explicitly adopting a normative position ('Postscript: For a Corporatism of
the Universal', Bourdieu 1996c: 337–48), marks the autonomy of the fields of
cultural production with a positive sign. Speaking of a 'conquest' of autonomy and concerned at the 'threats'[32] that weigh on it, Pierre Bourdieu makes
clear the positive value he attributes to it.

However, in parallel, the autonomy of some other fields (and in particular
the political field) is severely criticized, and one may speculate as to the reasons
for these different judgements (very positive or very negative) on autonomy,
depending on whether one is dealing with culture (in the broad sense) or
politics.[33] The political field is roundly criticized for its closure, which leads
politicians to be interested only in narrowly political stakes (*'la politique politi-
cienne'*) over the heads of the ordinary citizens whom they are supposed to
represent: 'The political world has gradually turned inward, absorbed in its
internal rivalries, its own problems, its own interests. Like the great tribunes,
politicians capable of understanding their constituents' expectations and
demands are becoming increasingly rare, and they are far from being in the
front rank of their organizations' (Bourdieu 2000b: 627).

This autonomy of the political microcosm is alleged to account for the
disaffection of the French with public affairs, and its similarity to the artistic
field is then noted, without any reflection on the variation in the judgement
being formulated:

> Primary apoliticism, which is now increasingly strong in the French
> political consciousness because the political field increasingly tends to
> close in on itself and function as an autonomous field, independent of it
> (in other words, ultimately like an artistic field), rests on a sort of confused
> awareness of the profound complicity between adversaries in the same field:
> they disagree with one another but they at least agree about the object of
> disagreement. It is a kind of complicity seen in particular in moments of
> crisis, i.e. when the very existence of the field is called into question.
>
> (Bourdieu 1989)[34]

One only has to apply the reasoning developed with regard to the political
world to the case of the literary game to arrive at an attitude critical of the
literary avant-garde and any formal refinement pursuing 'art for art's sake'.
This would lead to the following formulation: 'The literary world has gradually turned inward, absorbed in its internal rivalries, its own problems, its own
interests. Like the great artists, writers capable of understanding their readers'
expectations and demands are becoming increasingly rare.' It is clear that this
would amount to a critique of art for art's sake, a negative vision of the
'purest' literature, the literary avant-garde which, exclusively preoccupied with
its own interests (stylistic, formal, etc.),[35] supposedly cuts it off from the
literary tastes of the great majority of the population.

The passages in Flaubert's correspondence where he describes his endless battles with sentences, commas and semi-colons, where he writes that what seems to him 'beautiful' and what he most aspires to write is 'a book about nothing, a book without external attachments, that stands up by the internal strength of its style', since, from the standpoint of 'pure Art', there are 'neither beautiful nor ugly subjects' (Flaubert 1980, letter to Louise Colet, 16 January 1852), could be interpreted as marks of absolute disdain and indifference towards the real tastes of readers. Then it would be the authors of best-sellers or, at least, of novels reaching a wide readership, who would be praised for their openness and responsiveness to the expectations of the public.

Other intellectual traditions, in particular the pragmatist current,[36] develop in this regard a critical discourse, very different from that of Bourdieu, on the autonomization of art and on an aesthetics cut off from ordinary practices. The pragmatic philosophy expresses a profound disagreement with theories and practices (supported by institutions) that isolate art and its appreciation, cutting them off from other modes of experience. John Dewey deplored what he saw as an elitist tradition relegating art to the museum and making it a refuge to be enjoyed only in the pauses of real life, 'the beauty parlour of civilization'. A critique of Kant's aesthetic ideas, and then of the analytical philosophy of art, is therefore inseparable in pragmatic philosophy from a socio-political critique of the social tendencies to distinguish art from everyday life by putting it in museums, theatres or concert halls, i.e. confining it to specific places and times of social activity. Aesthetic theories that make art an autonomous object are historically linked to the economic and institutional conditions that set up a division between art and life (Shusterman 1992: 49). Advocates of 'art for art's sake' would no doubt denounce the 'populism' in the attitudes of these pragmatist philosophers, but it has to be recognized that even within philosophical culture there are ways of contesting the process of autonomization of the field of art on anti-elitist grounds.

Conversely, what would a positive vision of the self-enclosure of the political universe, the economic world or war making have to say? 'Art for art's sake', the emphasis on form rather than function, on the mode of representation rather than on the object represented, etc., would have its equivalent in a kind of 'art of politics for the sake of politics' (in which politics would become an end in itself rather than a means), an 'art of making economic profit for the sake of profit' (the amoral pursuit of economic interest for the sake of economic interest), an 'art of war for the sake of war', etc. However, politics for its own sake, economic cynicism, war raised to the status of an art – all of them judged perverse distortions (and not only by the sociologist) – like the 'art for art's sake' of science, letters or the arts – defended and valued by the author, as by a host of agents in the fields of cultural production – are only different expressions and manifestations of one and the same overall social logic, namely the progressive differentiation-autonomization of spheres of activity that increasingly function in closed circuits, make themselves opaque and cut themselves off from outsiders, through the invention and the development of a logic internal to each of these spheres, i.e. rules of the game, specific stakes, etc.

We are clearly faced with a practical and normative contradiction, but this is the kind of tough questioning that researchers have to confront if they want to make progress, and it should logically lead them to distinguish different types of social universes – and even different types of fields – according to their size, the nature of their activities, their social functions, their degree of competitiveness, their relations with their 'audiences', with the market, with the State, and more generally with all the other microcosms that make up the social formation.

Notes

1 This reflection, which has given rise to a first publication (Lahire 1999c), has led to the book *Monde pluriel. Penser l'unité des sciences sociales* (Paris: Seuil, Couleur des idées, 2012).

2 For reasons of space I shall not discuss here the ways in which Karl Marx (1974) or Georg Simmel (2009) addressed the question of the social differentiation of activities.

3 It will be seen, for example, that the family is not a field in the precise sense of the term.

4 Here one has to think in particular of all the informal everyday interactions between strangers or acquaintances, which are not always assignable to specific fields of activity and are the objects of interactionist or ethnomethodological analyses.

5 This does not mean that no competition is found within dominated groups or categories, but the existence of competitions or struggles is not sufficient to justify speaking of a 'field'.

6 On this conception of scientific debate, see 'Scene II: Pertinent Fields' in Lahire 2011: 211–22.

7 Notably in 'Some Properties of Fields' (in Bourdieu 1993: 8; Bourdieu 1980) and 'Le champ littéraire' (Bourdieu 1991a).

8 This is what a critical study would have to aim to do: to examine the real or fictitious, decisive or rhetorical, significant or weak contributions of the various case studies that have helped to install the notion of the 'field' durably in the vocabulary of contemporary sociology.

9 Bourdieu invites this kind of extension when he says, for example, that 'under certain historical conditions, which must be examined empirically, a field may start to function as an apparatus. When the dominant manage to crush and annul the resistance and the reactions of the dominated, when all movements go exclusively from the top down ... the struggle and the dialectic that are constitutive of the field cease ... Thus apparatuses represent a limiting case, what we may consider to be a pathological state of fields' (Bourdieu and Wacquant 1992: 102).

10 In universes of power where struggles of all against all are observed, the gap between the rarity of the distinctive places to be won and the number of competitors means that the level of frustration is particularly high. The philosopher Vincent Descombes shows on this subject how a poet like Baudelaire develops a fairly gloomy quasi-sociological analysis of the 'individualistic regime in the arts' (Descombes 1992: 127–28), in which everyone strives to be recognized for his originality. What Baudelaire calls the 'glorification of the individual' does not lead, in his view, to emancipation, autonomy and self-realization. 'It will mean the opposite: "doubt", "poverty of invention", the "chaos of an exhausting and sterile

freedom"'. Ultimately, it is harder for the great majority of artists to be happy in such an 'individualistic' regime. In the past, 'individual artists of lesser originality found their rightful place in a secondary function: "obedient to the rule of a powerful leader, and helping him in all his undertakings". No one in fact was required to demonstrate originality' (Descombes 1992: 127). Now, however, everyone is expected to offer a new solution to the artistic problems that present themselves, and since the great majority do not have the means to produce really original works, this leads to general malaise and doubt.

11 For example, linguistic practices in no way constitute a separate domain of practice, still less a 'field to be studied like any other field (political, economic, religious, legal, philosophical, etc.)'. Bourdieu nonetheless wrote – very problematically if one bears in mind the definition of the field as a relatively autonomous sub-space separated from other sub-spaces through an historical process of differentiation of functions: 'Fully to construct the space of life-styles within which cultural practices are defined, one would first have to establish, for each class and class fraction, that is, for each of the configurations of capital, the generative formula of the habitus that translates the necessities and facilities characteristic of that class of (relatively) homogeneous conditions of existence into a particular life-style. One would then have to determine how the dispositions of the habitus are specified for each of the major areas of practice, by implementing one of the stylistic possibilities offered by each field (the field of sport, or music, or food, decoration, politics, language, etc.)' (Bourdieu 1984: 208).

12 Affinities can be seen between the theory of fields (and of the *illusio* specific to each field) and Pascal's notion of 'diversion', although the latter does not necessarily lead to a field theory. The need for a certain investment in social activities and a certain belief in the importance of such activities may indeed be derived from some of his reflections, such as: 'Nothing is so insufferable to man as to be completely at rest, without passions, without business, without diversion, without study. He then feels his nothingness, his forlornness, his insufficiency, his dependence, his weakness, his emptiness'. Man needs to be 'caught up in the game', Pascal also writes: 'He must get excited over it, and deceive himself by the fancy that he will be happy to win what he would not have as a gift if he were not to play ... ' But these investments, which distract him from thinking about his miserable condition, are not necessarily investments in fields: 'the least thing, such as playing billiards or hitting a ball, is sufficient to amuse him' (Pascal 1965 [1670]).

13 The same presupposition reappears in Bourdieu's question: 'Why is it important to understand the field as a place which one has not produced and into which one is born, and not an arbitrarily instituted game?' (Bourdieu 1998: 86).

14 Leslie McCall (1992: 841) notes that for Bourdieu 'the social structure ... is defined by occupations and the capitals associated with them', and that the habitus has a 'largely public' dimension. As a consequence, the social practices of women, who are more present in the private spheres, contribute little to the – occupational and public definition – of the social space.

15 Within the abundant literature on this subject, see in particular Kohli *et al.* 1991.

16 I refer the reader here to the concept of 'individual heritage of dispositions', which leads one to present the habitus as one case of the possible – a particular one and not very frequent in differentiated societies (Lahire 2002a, 2004).

17 Men's propensity to abandon the domestic universe in order to invest in extrafamilial universes says much about the degree of recognition and prestige of domestic activities.

18 Moreover, on the fact that the influence of the 'professional spirit' is very relative, since it is not the only universe in which its members move and, in a differentiated society, each individual is aware of the non-universality of the rules specific to his professional activity, see Durkheim 1997: 243.

19 This is not the case for the less common but nonetheless real writer-manual workers, writer-clerks, writer-farmers, etc.

20 Which Bourdieu did not want to see (cf. Lahire 2005b).

21 Bourdieu speaks of 'this profession which is not really one (since it is almost always associated with a private income or activity "to pay the bills")' (Bourdieu 1991a: 15).

22 'To grasp the effect of the space of possibles, which acts as a discloser of dispositions, it suffices – proceeding in the fashion of logicians who admit that each individual has "counterparts" in other possible worlds in the form of the ensemble of people each could have been if the world had been different – to imagine what people such as Barcos, Flaubert or Zola might have been if they had found in another state of the field a different opportunity to deploy their dispositions' (Bourdieu 1996c: 235).

23 As a classic example of the reworking of a corpus, a pre-existing tradition, one could mention the case of myths. Once written down, they become the basis of a theological knowledge of the different gods and the relations among them.

24 It can also be observed that, focused on the question of power and the strategies for acquiring, reproducing or converting capital, Bourdieu often reduces sociability, inter-personal relations (including friendship) to a 'social capital' that can be mobilized for profit. In this case it is the nature of the social ties that is ignored. The reduction effected by the notion of 'social capital' can be seen *a contrario* from a reading of the work of Claire Bidart (1997).

25 'The notion of the field enables us to move beyond the opposition between internal reading and external analysis without losing any of the benefits and exigencies of these two approaches, traditionally perceived as irreconcilable' (Bourdieu 1996c: 205).

26 When inter-field comparisons are mentioned, it is essentially to stress the power relations between different fields or the competitive struggles among agents belonging to different fields.

27 See, among many others: Dupont 1999; Vernant 1982, 1983; Détienne 1986; Détienne and Camassa 1988; Gruzinski 1993; Havelock 1963; Goody 1977; Yates 1966; Lévi-Strauss 1966.

28 Borrowing the phrase from Everett Hughes, Bourdieu nonetheless invoked the 'sociological eye' – 'the gaze that could be called Spinozist, [that] takes things and people as they are, because it always strives to relate them to the causes and reasons they have for being what they are' (Bourdieu 1991b: 5).

29 However, psychoanalysts could no doubt show equally well that there is an implicit psychoanalysis in Flaubert or Proust.

30 It was to respond to this scientific challenge that I recently devoted a study to the work of Franz Kafka (Lahire 2010). In it I offer a sociological way of studying precisely the work of literary creation that brings out, by contrast, a whole series of other limits to the concept of the 'field'.

31 Bourdieu proceeds in the same way when he strives 'to bring out what seems to me to be the *generative formula* of Habermas's thought as regards politics' (Bourdieu 2000a: 66).

32 '*The threats to autonomy* result from the increasingly greater interpenetration between the world of art and the world of money' (Bourdieu 1996c: 344, emphasis added).

33 I make it clear here that I share Bourdieu's positive judgement on the autonomy of the fields of cultural production, and more especially of the scientific field.

34 Found also in shortened form in Bourdieu 1998: 78 (trans.).

35 'In so far as it manifests a rupture with external demands and a desire to exclude artists suspected of obeying them, the affirmation of the primacy of form over function, of mode of representation over the object of representation, is the most

specific expression of the claim to the autonomy of the field and of its pretension to produce and to impose the principles of a specific legitimacy as much in the order of production and in the order of reception of the work of art' (Bourdieu 1996c: 299–300).

36 The key work in this current, John Dewey's *Art as Experience* (Dewey 1980), first published in 1934, has still not been translated into French.

References

Ang, I. 1985. *Watching Dallas: Soap Opera and the Melodramatic Imagination.* London and New York: Methuen.

Bachelard, G. 1999. *La Formation de l'esprit scientifique. Contribution à une psychanalyse de la connaissance.* Paris: Vrin.

Belloï, L. 1993. *La Scène proustienne: Proust, Goffman et le théâtre du monde.* Paris: Nathan.

Bernstein, B. 1990. 'The Social Construction of Pedagogic Discourse'. In *The Structuring of Pedagogic Discourse* (*Class, Codes and Control*, vol. IV). London: Routledge.

Bidart, C. 1997. *L'Amitié un lien social.* Paris: La Découverte.

Bidou-Zachariasen, C. 1997. *Proust sociologue.* Paris: Descartes & Cie.

Boschetti, A. 1991. 'Légitimité littéraire et stratégies éditoriales'. In R. Chartier and H.-J. Martin (eds) *Histoire de l'édition française. Le livre concurrencé 1900–1950.* Paris: Fayard/Cercle de la Librairie, 511–51.

Bourdieu, P. 1971. 'Une interprétation de la théorie de la religion selon Max Weber'. *Archives européennes de sociologie*, XII-1, 3–21.

——1980. *Questions de sociologie.* Paris: Minuit.

——1982a. *Leçon sur la leçon.* Paris: Minuit.

——1982b. *Ce que parler veut dire. L'économie des échanges linguistiques.* Paris: Fayard.

——1984. *Distinction: A Social Critique of the Judgement of Taste.* Harvard University Press; London: Routledge

——1989. *Intérêt et désintéressement.* Cours du Collège de France, Cahiers de recherche du GRS, no. 7, Lyon.

——1990. *In Other Words: Essays Towards a Reflexive Sociology.* Stanford, CA· University Press; Cambridge: Polity Press.

——1991a. 'Le champ littéraire'. *Actes de la recherche en sciences sociales*, 89, 3–46.

——1991b. 'Introduction à la socioanalyse'. *Actes de la recherche en sciences sociales*, 90, 3–5.

——1991c. *Language and Symbolic Power.* Cambridge: Polity.

——1993. *Sociology in Question.* London: Sage Publications.

——1994. *Raisons pratiques. Sur la théorie de l'action.* Paris: Seuil.

——1996a. *The State Nobility: Elite Schools in the Field of Power.* Cambridge: Polity; Stanford, CA: Stanford University Press.

——1996b. 'Consommation culturelle'. *CD Encyclopædia Universalis*, Paris, 1–8.

——1996c. *The Rules of Art: Genesis and Structure of the Literary Field.* Cambridge: Polity; Stanford, CA: Stanford University Press.

——1996d. 'On the Family as a Realized Category'. *Theory, Culture & Society*, 13(3), 19–26.

——1998. *Practical Reason: On the Theory of Action.* Stanford: Stanford University Press.

——2000a. *Pascalian Meditations*. Stanford: Stanford University Press; Cambridge: Polity Press.

——2000b. *The Weight of the World*. Stanford: Stanford University Press.

Bourdieu, P. and Boltanski, L. 1976. 'La production de l'idéologie dominante'. *Actes de la recherche en sciences sociales*, 2–3, 3–73.

Bourdieu, P., Darbel, A. and Schnapper, D. 1991. *The Love of Art. European Art Museums and their Public*. Cambridge: Polity Press; Stanford, CA: Stanford University Press.

Bourdieu, P. and Grenfell, M. 1995. *Entretiens, Centre for Language in Education*. Occasional Papers, 37, May, University of Southampton.

Bourdieu, P. and Wacquant, L.J.D. 1992. *An Invitation to Reflexive Sociology*. Chicago, IL: University of Chicago Press; Cambridge: Polity Press.

Chartier, R. 1985. 'Du livre au lire'. In R. Chartier, *Pratiques de la lecture*. Marseille: Éditions Rivages, 62–88.

——1987. *Lectures et lecteurs dans la France d'Ancien Régime*. Paris: Seuil.

Descombes, V. 1992. *Proust: Philosophy of the Novel*. Stanford: Stanford University Press.

Détienne, M. 1986. *The Creation of Mythology*. Chicago: University of Chicago Press.

Détienne, M. and Camassa, G. (eds) 1988. *Les Savoirs de l'écriture en Grèce ancienne*. Lille: PUL.

Dewey, J. 1980 [1934]. *Art as Experience*. New York: Perigee Books.

Dubois, J. 1997. *Pour Albertine: Proust et le sens du social*. Paris: Seuil.

——2007. *Stendhal: une sociologie Romanesque*. Paris: Éditions la Découverte.

Dupont, F. 1999. *The Invention of Literature: From Greek Intoxication to the Latin Book*. Baltimore and London: Johns Hopkins University Press.

Durkheim, E. 1983. *Pragmatism and Sociology*. Cambridge: Cambridge University Press.

——1997 [1893]. *The Division of Labor in Society*. New York: Free Press.

Elias, N. 1991. *The Society of Individuals*. Oxford and Cambridge, MA: Blackwell.

Flaubert, G. 1980. *Correspondances*. Vol. 2. Paris: Gallimard.

Foucault, M. 2002. *The Archaeology of Knowledge*. London: Routledge.

Freidson, E. 1986. 'Les professions artistiques comme défi à l'analyse sociologique'. *Revue française de sociologie*, 27(3), 431–43.

Goffman, E. 1981. *Forms of Talk*. Philadelphia: University of Pennsylvania Press.

Goody, J. 1977. *The Domestication of the Savage Mind*. Cambridge: Cambridge University Press.

——1986. *The Logic of Writing and the Organisation of Society*. Cambridge: Cambridge University Press.

Grignon, C. and Passeron, J.-C. 1989. *Le Savant et le Populaire. Misérabilisme et populisme en sociologie et en literature*. Paris: Gallimard/Le Seuil.

Gruzinski, S. 1993. *The Conquest of Mexico: The Incorporation of Indian Societies into the Western World, 16th–18th Centuries*. Cambridge: Polity Press

Havelock, E. 1963. *Preface to Plato*. Harvard: Harvard University Press.

Kohli, M., Rein, M., Guillemard, A.-M. and van Gunsteren, H. 1991. *Time for Retirement: Comparative Studies of Early Exit from the Labor Force*. Cambridge: Cambridge University Press.

Lahire, B. 1993. *La Raison des plus faibles. Rapport au travail, écritures domestiques et lectures en milieux populaires*. Lille: Presses Universitaires de Lille.

——1995. *Tableaux de familles. Heurs et malheurs scolaires en milieux populaires*. Paris: Gallimard/Le Seuil

——1999a. 'La sociologie de l'éducation et l'opacité des savoirs'. *Éducation et sociétés. Revue internationale de sociologie de l'éducation*, 4.

——1999b. 'Pour une sociologie psychologique de la famille'. In H. Desmet and J.-P. Pourtois (ed.) *Réalités familiales aujourd'hui*. Paris: PUF.

——1999c. 'Champ, hors-champ, contrechamp'. In B. Lahire (ed.) *Le Travail sociologique de Pierre Bourdieu. Dettes et critiques*. Paris: Éditions la Découverte, 23–57.

——2002a. *Portraits sociologiques. Dispositions et variations individuelles*. Paris: Nathan, Collection Essais et Recherches, Série 'Sciences sociales'.

——2002b. 'Les variations pertinentes en sociologie'. In J. Lautrey, B. Mazoyer and P. van Geert (eds) *Invariants et variabilité dans les sciences cognitives*. Paris: Éditions de la MSH, 243–55.

——2004. *La Culture des individus. Dissonances culturelles et distinction de soi*. Paris: la Découverte, Laboratoire des sciences sociales.

——2005a. *L'Esprit sociologique*. Paris: Éditions la Découverte.

——2005b. 'Misère de la division du travail sociologique: le cas des pratiques culturelles adolescentes'. *Éducation et sociétés. Revue internationale de sociologie de l'éducation*, 16, 129–36.

——2006. *La Condition littéraire. La double vie des écrivains*. Paris: Éditions la Découverte.

——2008. *La Raison scolaire. École et pratiques d'écriture, entre savoir et pouvoir*. Rennes: Presses Universitaires de Rennes.

——2010. *Franz Kafka. Éléments pour une théorie de la création littéraire*. Paris: La Découverte.

——2011. *The Plural Actor*. Cambridge: Polity Press.

Lévi-Strauss, C. 1966. *The Savage Mind*. London: Weidenfeld and Nicolson.

Marx, K. 1974. *Capital*. Vol. 1. London: Lawrence & Wishart.

McCall, L. 1992. 'Does Gender Fit? Bourdieu, Feminism, and Conception of Social Order'. *Theory and Society*, 21(6), 837–67.

Pascal, B. 1965 [1670]. *Pensées*. Paris: Nouveaux Classiques Larousse.

Passeron, J.-C. 1982. 'L'inflation des diplômes. Remarques sur l'usage de quelques concepts analogiques en sociologie'. *Revue française de sociologie*, 4, 551–83.

——1991. *Le Raisonnement sociologique. L'espace non-poppérien du raisonnement naturel*. Paris: Nathan.

Shusterman, R. 1992. *Pragmatist Aesthetics: Living Beauty, Rethinking Art*. Oxford: Blackwell.

Simmel, G. 2009. *Sociology: Inquiries into the Construction of Social Forms*. Leiden: Brill.

Strauss, A.L. 1993. *Continual Permutations of Action*. New York: Aldine de Gruyter.

Vernant, J.-P. 1982. *The Origins of Greek Thought*. New York: Cornell University Press.

——1983. *Myth and Thought among the Greeks*. London: Routledge and Kegan Paul.

Weber, M. 1946. 'Religious Rejections of the World and their Directions'. In H. Gerth and C. Wright Mills (ed.) *From Max Weber: Essays in Sociology*. New York: Oxford University Press.

——1993. *The Sociology of Religion*. Cambridge, MA: Beacon Press.

——1996. *Sociologie des religions*. Paris: Gallimard.

Yates, F.A. 1966. *The Art of Memory*. London: Routledge and Kegan Paul.

3 The field

A Leibnizian perspective in sociology

Louis Pinto

Introduction

When reading one of Pierre Bourdieu's texts on the question of what it means to read an author – to read him or her non-scholastically (Bourdieu 1996a: 302ff) – one thinks first of all of Bourdieu himself. One has to imagine the kind of amused scepticism he must have felt when he described the fate inflicted by scholars on authors who were not automata generating texts destined to be treated as objects of commentary but historical individuals caught up in one of the games that the social world offers, games in which they involved themselves armed with knowledge, but also with passions that excited or blinded them, and 'know-how' that inclined them to do one thing or another. The scientific posture often tends to reduce the thinker to 'theses', exegetes study the different versions, researchers establish comparisons and filiations, and critics seek 'contradictions' either to highlight the author's lacunae or to offer themselves as ultimate recourses for surmounting them (Skinner 2002: 67ff). These temptations are inherent in such a posture, which is shared to some extent by all 'scholars', all scholastic individuals. However, there is another way of reading, one that adopts 'the point of view of the author' and which presupposes that one both contextualizes his action and makes explicit its principles which exist in the practical state. 'Homo academicus relishes the finished. Like the *pompier* (academic) painters, he likes to make the strokes of the brush, the touching and retouching disappear from his works' (Bourdieu and Wacquant 1992: 219). It is no accident that the aim that Bourdieu set himself in his lectures on Manet at the Collège de France was to recreate the painter's brushstrokes, his practice as such, in the context of the history of art but also beyond it. I can say from experience that, regarding his own concepts, such as habitus and field, in his teaching he was less concerned to theorize and 'situate' himself in relation to others than to show, like a 'sports coach',[1] in specific cases, how and for what purpose ideas could be used. One could also say that his texts on Weber's sociology of religions follow the same principle: with a peer on a series of problems far outweighs learned commentary and the aim of reconstructing the 'real' Weber – although it can at the same time be argued that the use one makes of an author, even when diverted from the letter of the texts, is a way of taking him seriously and asking him questions on which he had things to say but which he was not in a position to formulate explicitly, things that one can grasp precisely thanks to other authors: 'In postulating that magical or religious actions are worldly (*diesseitig*) in principle and must be done "in order to live a long life", Max Weber prevents himself from grasping the religious message as Lévi-Strauss does (that is, as the product of "intellectual operations" as opposed to "affective" or practical operations) and from raising the question of the strictly logical and noseological functions of what he considers a quasi-systematic set of responses to existential questions' (Bourdieu 1991: 4).[2]

The sensible and the intelligible

Have there ever been monolithic individuals and authors? It would be naïve to surrender to a conclusion of irreducible plurality, as many commentators do when they renounce the search for a unitary, unified work. Bourdieu was a bearer of the 'rationalist empiricism' which, according to Durkheim, is characteristic of sociology. This dual scientific attitude, which 'satisfies the two contradictory feelings that can be regarded as the motors *par excellence* of intellectual development: the sense of the obscure and faith in the efficacy of the human mind' (Durkheim 1897: 174). Whereas the first of these feelings induces the anxiety that precedes the will to know, the second sustains confidence in the possibilities of the mind. This is not simply an invitation to fight on two fronts, against pure rationalists and pure empiricists, but an encouragement to engage on a narrow path that finally leads to the privileged viewpoint where the opposing forces, 'rationalist' and 'empiricist', do not cancel each other out but escape from the partial view to which they seem condemned by their spontaneous inclination and combine to make previously inconceivable visions and programmes of work possible.

To illustrate this tension, one might be tempted to set on one side the concept of the habitus as an effort to account for practice in its singularity and on the other side the theory of fields as an effort to totalize and systematize. The insistence on confronting the obscurity of things is, of course, never more clearly expressed than in the warnings against intellectualism and the invocation of the practical sense, a reminder of the limits of a scientific viewpoint that is inclined, as in an expression of Marx often quoted by Bourdieu, to 'take the things of logic for the logic of things'. Agents do not confront the world as perceived and understood by a detached observer but, as Alfred Schütz showed, a world structured according to their practical interests, by different degrees of familiarity, relevance and urgency. This is what is contained in the idea of the habitus. The idea of the field, an essential component of the theoretical construction, attests, by contrast, to a strongly rationalist inclination.

Presented in this way, things would seem to be ultimately very simple, making it possible to point to the two sides of Bourdieu. However, that would be to forget that, as Rogers Brubaker puts it, his theory itself must be 'treated as a habitus' (Brubaker 1993). Far from being a set of theses belonging to the 'theory of the social', it is first of all, as a theory of knowledge of the social, or rather, as a theory of the practice of the sociologist, a way of working, a set of precepts valid in the working situation, more akin to an *ars inveniendi* than a formalized hypothetico-deductive apparatus.[3] The same is true of the concept of the field, which Bourdieu, who was very economical in 'theoretical' matters (Pinto 1999: 120, 142), warns us should first be regarded less as ontological thesis than as a work tool, a 'conceptual shorthand', or as 'a *pense-bête*, a memory jogger' as he put it (Bourdieu and Wacquant 1992: 228).

In contrast to ordinary empiricism, this concept raises to a high degree the ambition of maximum intelligibility that is characteristic of 'rationalist empiricism': it is the means of describing and explaining a set of phenomena with a small number of principles sufficiently fertile to account for the greatest diversity. This ambition is of a kind that could be called 'Leibnizian', bearing in mind that in his student years Bourdieu was an attentive reader of Leibniz (Bourdieu 1987: 13), and noting that – without seeking to unearth an author's hidden 'influences' – what the author has read may have supplied instruments, schemes of analysis for problems and solutions that could be invested in a quite different context and for quite different purposes. Indeed, Leibniz, one of the thinkers who might be encountered by a sociologist concerned to escape from the forced choice between theoreticism and empiricism, provided the incentive to bridge gaps and see continuity, in particular as regards the relationship between the intelligible and the sensible, unity and multiplicity, the finite and the infinite. So, where the empiricist sociologist, faced with a complex case, is tempted to abjure the prerogatives of theory and denounce the simplifications of all construction and the limitations of a thinking imprisoned in generality and powerless in the face of the profusion of individuals, one may wonder if it would not be better to take another route, admittedly more complicated and exposed to the most facile of criticisms, but making it possible to regard the deviations, the differences between theory and experience, as being as small as possible.

From this flows a typically Leibnizian ethic of the treatment of opposing paths (objectivism and subjectivism, structure and history, interest and disinterestedness, generality and singularity, etc.) which belongs to the style of Bourdieu. It is as if a forced choice required to be suspended so long as one was not convinced that it was something other than the imposition of a problematic, demanding that everyone take sides without having to examine its premises, and something other than a means of repressing a viewpoint from which the opposing terms cease to contradict one another. A choice of alternatives is never strictly speaking invalidated but is, in a sense, unlocked by a new gaze that makes it possible to grasp the immanent necessity of the partial viewpoints. Rather as Leibniz sought both to reconcile the physicist's view on the 'phenomenon' of matter and the metaphysician's view on spiritual 'substances' and to justify each of them in its order, Bourdieu, using Marx, Durkheim and Weber as emblems of scientific postures for the sociology of

religions, endeavoured to show the interest of 'situating oneself at the geometric vantage point in the various perspectives from which one can see, at
the same time, both what can and what cannot be perceived from each of
these separate points of view' (Bourdieu 1991: 2).[4]

The social force of a forced choice can often be regarded as a concession to
the immanent laws of the intellectual field which require everyone to limit
him- or herself to the most probable choices and to accept one view rather
than another on the basis of his or her position in the field. Invention in
sociology is rather the expression of a refusal to surrender to these laws, a
wager on unprecedented combinations, and therefore a total 'way of being', a
line of conduct. One has to strive to be at once 'ambitious and modest'
(Bourdieu 2004a: 103): such an blend of indissolubly moral and intellectual
qualities, generally regarded as opposed and even incompatible, is ultimately
the essence of the definition of the scientist that Bourdieu wanted to convey.
This is simply the aspiration of the sociological gaze to recognize problems
and issues wherever it is deployed, in order to make real use of them in
research and not, of course, to make them separate objects of dissertation
(like the 'theoretical' preliminaries commonly invoked in the introduction to
an article even when they have no cognitive consequences). 'Small' objects
worked on seriously and meticulously can – contrary to the dominant representations of the hierarchy of objects – give rise to innovations, and 'big'
objects, if not brought down to a manageable scale, can result in mere
academic exercises.

The 'greatest order' and the 'greatest variety'

The primary function of the concept of the field, used in physics and psychology to account for the fact that elements belong to an encompassing
configuration that has effects on their meaning and functioning, is to deal
with the question of the analytical unity of a plurality of elements while
sacrificing neither unity nor plurality. Striving to reconcile the specificity of
the parts of the social whole with their dependence on a totality, it aims to
explain a differentiated social world in which determinate regions cannot be
reduced to the overall structures of the society to which they belong. Just as
the concept of the habitus has to be understood as the relatively unified generative principle of appropriate practices that are at once spontaneous and
regulated, in Leibnizian terms one can say that the concept of the field has a
'monadological' status, inasmuch as it makes it possible to delimit a relatively
unitary and self-sufficient object according to immanent criteria of coherence
and not on the basis of external principles of vision and division provided by
common sense or by more or less scholarly traditions (legal, administrative,
political, literary, etc., or even frankly journalistic ones): the field is the
monad endowed with an individuality and an immanent force that make it
capable of acting by itself and therefore of not being determined from outside.[5] The concept applies a mode of thought that is 'relational' (Cassirer,

Bachelard) or structural (Lévi-Strauss); this consists in regarding the relative 'positional' properties (as opposed to 'conditional' or 'substantial' properties) of the elements as having, if not an exclusive value, at least a decisive role in the analysis.[6]

The object of analysis is not the interactions among empirical individuals who consciously oppose one another, as Bourdieu may have thought in an early stage (Bourdieu 1968); rather, it is the system of intelligible relations among relationally defined distinctive positions (priest/prophet, etc.) occupied by determinate agents: 'I must ... make sure that the object that I have given myself is not enmeshed in a network of relations that assigns its most distinctive properties' (Bourdieu and Wacquant 1992: 228). The Bachelardian language of 'object construction' was first intended in a general way as a negative recommendation to break with 'prenotions', but it was also, this time with a positive intention, an encouragement to construct the unit of analysis for which the field was a serious if not privileged candidate. The frontier of the field is what delimits the interior, characterized as the system of positions and/or relations and their game, and the exterior, where this system ceases to have effect.

The concept of the field is Leibnizian in another respect: it is the illustration *par excellence* of the principle of economy, since it satisfies the demand to obtain the greatest number of 'effects' with the smallest number of 'means', the 'greatest possible variety' being compatible with the 'greatest possible order' (quoted by Mahnke 1993: 163). One and the same opposition is often repeated in other forms either by transposition into another field, or by arborescence in the same field, as in the case of the production of symbolic goods:

> the principal opposition, between pure production, destined for a market restricted to producers, and large-scale production, oriented towards the satisfaction of the demands of a wide audience, reproduces the founding rupture with the economic order, which is at the root of the field of restricted production. This principle of differentiation is intersected by a secondary opposition that is established, within the sub-field of pure production, between the avant-garde and the consecrated.
>
> (Bourdieu 1996a: 121)

The concept of the field makes it impossible to surrender to the laziness of substantialist realism by suggesting a heuristics of comparison and perspectivization.

Analysis of the social space offers, *par excellence*, an illustration of what a structural analysis of the social classes can look like.[7] Once it is accepted that positions can be specified *ad infinitum*, it can be seen that one can try to give an account of it from a finite number of relations to the social space that reflect, among other things, the relation to culture, the educational system and the future of the group. In a hierarchized society, the gaps between classes demand to be considered in an ordinal mode that requires each position to

define itself by its position from the highest positions, the holders of excellence.[8] Far from being a contingent property, associated with a determinate
historical framework, such positions contain 'taste' as the sense of distinction
or distinction as a way of being distinct, distinctive, distinguished, in conformity
with an ideal of human accomplishment: it manifests itself in a *feeling* that leads
its possessors to privilege style, form, the indefinite play on nuance, but also
highly calculated ruptures (Proust's Madame Verdurin imposes an audacious,
unknown artist or the 'herb garden' fashion, while others cling to established
values ...); and if it is accompanied by self-assurance, this is precisely because
the mastery of legitimate manners acquired through a slow, invisible familiarization has nothing of conquest about it but seems to be the result of a inborn,
natural refinement. The intermediate position of the middle classes generates
the tension inherent in positions for which access to the legitimate practices is
not self-evident, if only because it takes place under the gaze of those for whom
'be' and 'ought to be' coincide, and who are led to perceive and disqualify
errors, clumsiness and, even more, 'pretension'. Expressing a mismatch between
the disposition to recognize the law of culture (which Bourdieu calls 'cultural
goodwill') and the limits of the means possessed, pretension is betrayed by traits
such as hypercorrection and falling for 'imitations'. These hierarchized positions are distinguished by more than cultural competence; or rather, in the
definition of this competence one has to include the relation to culture, which is
not reducible to the formal order of knowledge. The lower positions, for their
part, are structurally characterized by their not being in the game, because they
are deprived of the minimal conditions (in particular the economic conditions)
for entering it. In their case, a paradox emerges: the objective necessity that
imposes itself on them, through material conditions of existence and the at least
vague perception of a probable future, does not act directly, as one might think
(income dictating practices), but is mediated by a taste based on the propensity
to love that for which one is made in any case ('for the likes of us') and therefore
to exclude that from which one is excluded ('not for us'). This 'taste of necessity', the active and 'proud' assertion of what one is, as one is, at least has the
virtue of preserving one from ridicule, and also, more profoundly, of making it
possible to accept oneself as the author of one's acts, willing what must come;
confessing abstention from a hopeless commitment to a game from which one
would be disqualified, it contains no alternative assertion of legitimacy but
rather something like a demand to be recognized as being what one is.[9]

   To each position in this space there corresponds a point of view on the
other positions and on the other 'points of view', and it can be said that, as
the differences between points of view express the differences between positions, the points of view are linked among themselves by what Leibniz called
a relation of inter-expression The same social space is seen from different
positions 'as the same town, looked at from various sides, appears quite different and becomes as it were numerous in aspects [*perspectivement*]' (Leibniz
1966: 248); the move from one position to another takes place according to
one or more principles of variation which make it possible to conceive them

otherwise than, in empiricist fashion, as a simple juxtaposition of groups. A space such as the social space is not the simple product of the aggregation of a multitude of variables but reflects the historically conditioned unitary law of differences, which in a given society tends to make one factor or another pertinent, discriminant, i.e. socially efficient. This is the case, in societies such as ours, based on statistical reproduction predominantly through education, of the factors that Bourdieu calls economic capital and cultural capital: it is from their modes of combination that the different positions in the social space can be derived. One of the least well understood aspects of this type of analysis is the status given to socio-occupational category, which is supposedly privileged at the expense of other variables (which some critics are eager to champion, whether it be gender, ethnicity or religion, etc.). However, such critiques forget several things. The first is that the variables form a system: unskilled construction workers tend to be male immigrants, hired on short contracts, with few or no qualifications. Next, it is forgotten that occupation owes its analytical interest to its informative content: it is a variable that concentrates or associates the greatest number of variables (income, inheritance, etc.), which does not mean that it has the power to act by itself. So it is futile to seek to isolate in occupations such as nurse or secretary that which derives from this or that particular variable, since 'femininity' is an unofficial condition of access and determines a way of performing occupational tasks. In other words, a variable such as occupation envelops not only formal attributes (content of the tasks, status, etc.) but also a space of possibles that exist in the tacit mode of self-evidence (types of schooling, structure and limits of the matrimonial market, forms of inheritance of the different kinds of capital). Finally, this analytical value does not need to be raised to the rank of an ontological dignity. What interests the sociologist, beyond the content of the activities concerned, is the position occupied in a social space insofar as it procures or excludes profits and powers, and, through them, the instruments of social reproduction in the struggle among groups to appropriate different kinds of value. The volume and composition of the capital specific to a position are, therefore, as principles of variation (one vertical and the other horizontal in the diagram of the classes in *Distinction*), the privileged means for discerning the intelligibility of the representations and practices associated with the different positions in the social space, beyond the diversity of 'empirical individuals'. This privilege stems from the fact that if there is one aspect in which, in advanced capitalist societies, all positions can be (objectively) measured and, in some sense, measure each other (subjectively and in the political sense), it is indeed the one that concerns the distribution of the kinds of capital.[10] Only a misunderstanding of the intention and methods of this structural vision of the social space can lead one to counterpose, to the variables that are highly charged with information on the volume and composition of capital, other variables which, like gender, religion or ethnicity, are supposedly endowed with an autonomous force and an independent explanatory power.[11] For these variables, always linked to a system of variables, act in a space in which the appropriation of the types of value that are engaged in it constitutes the principle and the stake of the actions, or strategies, of the agents. It hardly needs to be said that a female academic is not split between two variables each acting in its own way, but that she is situated in a specific space with its own logic, the university field, in which the different variables possessed may, depending on the case, be suffered, valorized, neutralized, etc. Far from neglecting this or that variable, analysis in terms of the field aims to integrate them all by determining the relative place of each of them.

Thus the sociologist does not have to define objective classifications of agents, as most theorists of social class aim to do on the basis of apparently 'scientific' criteria (such as the relations of production, technology or status). Against the taxonomic ideal, a statistical version of the scholastic illusion that treats groups as objects of pure knowledge, one has to assert that the social space, understood as the site of distribution of the various properties, is the product of a set of struggles taking the form, among others, of a struggle over classifications and/or a struggle for the determination of the relative weight of a 'factor'. This is the case, for example, with the definition of the civil service (as opposed to the private sector) or relative value given either to certain qualifications or to 'experience'. Factors, says Bourdieu, are powers.

It is an effort of abstraction that dissociates variables that closely overlap in reality: to speak of a supermarket cashier is to speak as much of an occupational activity endowed with technical and economic attributes as of a female population subjected to part-time work and condemned to docility. One way of obtaining a simultaneous knowledge of the superimposition of the greatest possible number of methodically constructed variables is a technique of geometric analysis of data such as multiple correspondence analysis, much used by Bourdieu, which makes it possible to provide a spatial representation of three aspects: as an instrument appropriate to analysis in terms of field, it makes it possible both to show the relations between positions, the links between variables, and to provide an image of the unit of analysis as a real space of coexistence and conflict between positions. The principal axes, which rarely coincide with variables considered separately, reflect rather the specific principles of structuration and opposition of the space in question, generated by a specific history.

Action in relation to the field

The subject of action is the field, says Bourdieu. Such a formulation was bound to confirm the image of structuralist or anti-humanist 'holism' which, in the writings of his adversaries, often stands as a summary of his thinking. Such a proposition, however, does not aim to deny the spontaneity or freedom of the agents but to show that one cannot be content with a scholastic duality of the type structure/agency, filled out, in some cases, with attempts at reconciliation. Rather, it is an invitation to break with the philosophy of consciousness in which the subject is the ultimate principle of representations and practices, and to replace it with a theory of action capable of integrating the two monadological dimensions, that of the habitus and that of the field. Far from striving to paste structure and agent together, the sociologist is concerned to describe one and the same social reality, which are apprehended through two different aspects: as an order of succession, he deals with an individual (or collective) trajectory which relates a habitus to a series of states of the world (as a series of states of a series of fields), and, as an order of coexistence, he deals with this same trajectory, but envisaged in the space of the relations among simultaneous positions.[12] In both respects, the subject of idealist philosophies proves inadequate. The habitus has the virtue of showing that for the sociologist (if not for the philosopher),[13] the principle of representation and action of an individual is not a pure consciousness but a set of dispositions, schemes of perception, evaluation and action. The field has the virtue of showing a singular habitus in the space of possible habitus linked by the relation of coexistence: or, to put it another way – since the distinction must be made between a singular agent and the objective position in the field occupied by that agent – of making it possible to conceive a singular habitus-position couple in the space of habitus-position couples. The habitus is a capacity to act which includes the capacity to orient oneself in the field, in other words to take a position there, to take the position most appropriate to what one is, and to take the positions compatible with that position; conversely, the field is a machine for selecting and ordering the habitus that conform to it.

The most ambitious and most consistent expression of this conception was the postulate, suggested by Bourdieu, of a principle of systematic correspondence between three spaces, that of positions, that of dispositions and that of position-takings: to each point A in one of the spaces a point A′ and A″ in the other two tends more or less to correspond, which means that each of these spaces reflects the system of differences of the other two (A, A′, A″/B, B′, B″ ...). The order in one series corresponds to the order in another (*datis ordinatis etiam quaesita sunt ordinata*)[14]: A is to B as A′ is to B′, etc. Thus, the object of the sociological analysis of certain practices such as cultural practices is not, as some critics think, a term-to-term relationship between a socially defined agent and a socially defined product, but the system of relations between systems – classes of agents, classes of practices (and in particular practices of classification), classes of domains (classical music, jazz, rock, etc.) and the classes of objects in these domains. Within these different systems, the correspondences are made with a certain leeway. This is, first, because 'choices' of objects are always mediated and not immediate; second, because they are mediated by the habitus as the social principle of classification and orientation which makes it possible to discern what is and is not 'for me' ('it looks intellectual', 'it hurts', 'bling-bling'); and finally because, like any rule-governed practice, they contain an element of fuzziness, of error and correction ('after all, it's not that bad', 'no, I've decided I don't like it'), and varying degrees of commitment to and distance from a practice. It also needs to be remembered that the classifications specific to the different spaces considered are not immutable and that it would be absurd to postulate a universal competence regarding the state of the classifications, a competence that does not exist either in the set of agents or even in any one of them.

The articulation of the two concepts of field and habitus makes it possible to take a quite different view of the choice between objectivism and subjectivism, the terms of which, in a very Leibnizian way, demand not to be invalidated but rather considered as partial perspectives. The sociologist needs both the physicalist perspective which treats the social world as a set of forces and factors acting according to laws, 'as things', as Durkheim put it, and the phenomenological perspective which takes seriously the view that a subject, as a principle of action on the world, takes on the world. For a philosopher, this very ancient problem raises the question of the relationship between two distinct and legitimate logics, which are those, depending on the terminology one adopts, of mechanism and finality, causes and reasons; one has to try to explain the harmonization of the logics without forgetting what is heterogeneous in them. However, to escape from the paradoxical (Cartesian) solution of a causality between substances (thinking and extended) or the (Leibnizian) solution of a pre-established harmony, one can embark on a path that consists in doing justice to each of these logics by showing that they are in fact reconciled in the practical state in the work of research. 'It is the primary function of the concept of habitus to break with the Cartesian philosophy of consciousness and thereby overcome the disastrous mechanism/finalism alternative or, in other words, the alternative of determination by causes and determination by reasons' (Bourdieu 2003: 210–11). The sociologist deals neither with pure objective causes nor with pure subjects: as has been seen apropos of the different kinds of capital, causes are effective only in so far as they function as powers that agents can – or cannot – mobilize, and in so far as they tend to determine the order of possibles as it exists for an agent; and the agent is not reducible to an undefined consciousness, since, through his/her dispositions, he/she is marked by objective structures. So, if it can be said that visiting museums and galleries increases as a function of the factor *cultural capital*, this does not mean that this capital acts according to the mechanical model of billiard balls endowed with a mass and a velocity, but that such a cultural practice has very unequal chances of being judged desirable by agents, depending on their socially constituted capacities and tastes. Conversely, if it can be said that agents entertain certain cultural aspirations, these tend, whatever their spontaneity, to reproduce an objective order of conditional probabilities. There are no grounds for privileging either the causes or the reasons, but rather for seeing the reasons anew and more clearly, in the light of consideration of causes, and therefore seeing in a different way the sense of practice of an agent who, if he does what he likes or what he says he likes, at the same time does what he has been inclined to do by his position in a particular space. There is a 'causality of the probable' (Bourdieu 1974), which is not the direct action of a structure on an agent but the effect of an adjustment to social reality through an evaluation-anticipation that takes the pre-reflexive form of tastes, wishes and even indifferences towards possibles that are only vaguely posited. The belief in the value of the stakes in question (which Bourdieu calls the *illusio*) is not an accessory, 'subjective' property of the agents, but an essential condition of possibility of the functioning of the field. With a very 'Pascalian' twist, it is at the very moment when he refuses all philosophy of the subject that Bourdieu shows everything that, in the subject, comes into play without his being aware of it – habits, inclinations, expectations, all of them personal and inward things that are nonetheless adjusted to the order of the world.[15]

Fields in perspective

Bourdieu had the project of a general theory of fields which would have made it possible both to define the essential properties of a field and to account for the diversity of the degrees and forms of existence of fields. Let us start with the second point, since it concerns the very coherence of the project. The uses of the term range from weak versions, in which the field tends to be seen essentially as a space of positions, to strong versions (the scientific field), via intermediate versions (the field of fashion design). In the strong versions, the field is not simply a set of positions defined by their relations, but a region of the social world which has the property of being distinct, separate, limited in relation to the other regions: it possesses what Bourdieu called 'relative autonomy', a term that designates the power to exist per se, at least in part. 'Increasingly I see the social world as being like a Calder mobile, where there are little universes moving around in relation to one another in a multi-dimensional space' (Bourdieu 2000: 323). The autonomy of these 'little universes' is, for a sociologist, not the reflection of Platonic essences, but the result of the action of a set of agents who, beyond their differences, have in common that they are situated in relation to one another and therefore recognize what unites them: a game and certain stakes. The field is the product of a history and an effort of collective construction which are part of its definition and its mode of functioning. Its degree of autonomy is measured by the conditions of entry, which, manifesting the specificity of the game and its stakes, establish a frontier between qualified and non-qualified agents, between specialists and outsiders. That is why there is a continuum running from the most autonomous fields (Bourdieu 1976), to fields that tend to function as simple spaces of positions: the difference between these extreme configurations derives from the immanent duration that they have, i.e. the way in which, in order to exist and function, they conserve the collective memory of the states of the field and its struggles, in the objectified form of a specific capital and agencies of evaluation.[16] Some fields exist as a spatial coexistence of positions, a *mens momentanea* in which knowledge of the previous states, not being a prerequisite for membership, is as small as possible. In other fields, by contrast, the logic of monopolization of the specific goods tends to favour legitimate agencies, the holders of accumulated knowledge that is conserved through a particular history. Between them, one could distinguish cases in which reference to the past, without ever being detached from present interests, is made into an end in itself (erudition), those where it essentially serves a pool from which agents can draw tools or models for their current action (the history of political ideas), and those where it fulfils the two functions simultaneously (the history of the sciences by and for scientists). Finally, there is a field that has a quite particular status, primarily because here the question of autonomy (or non-autonomy) does not arise as it does in the others: this is the field of the social classes or the social space, a space in which every agent is situated, from which no one is excluded or disqualified (even if stigmatized). All the other fields relate to it more or less directly, many because they depend on it (the economic field), and others because they play a part in defining it, the social space being an essential stake in the social struggles that go on over classifications, representations and rights.

A general theory of fields has the task, among other things, of envisaging the different fields as so many elements in the same group of transformations. The relational mode of thought makes it possible on the one hand to analyse the relations between different fields,[17] and on the other hand through comparative analysis, to situate a given case in a space of possibles, strip away the 'local' particularities, extend the description so as to bring to light regularities and explanatory factors, and so to satisfy the demands of generalization.

An essential point, as has been seen, is the difference between fields in terms of autonomy, one indicator of which is the place given to the outside audience: whereas invocation of the public is not possible in mathematics or biology, the professionals in the political field – however self-enclosed it may be – cannot fail to appeal to the ordinary citizens whose spokespersons they aim to be, if only to secure their votes periodically. Another indicator is the degree of independence of the internal stakes relative to external determinations: in the most autonomous fields, the specific position-takings are governed by the logic of the field and cannot be deduced in a simple and direct way from properties of the agents, such as their social origin. To each field there corresponds a specific value that is current within it and is irreducible to external values. The mode of autonomy specific to each field governs how this value is accumulated, appropriated and distributed within it and how the agents are admitted, recognized and classified. Inevitably, between positions a set of oppositions is constituted: between holders of temporal power and holders of spiritual power; between the most autonomous and the least autonomous positions; between those of the dominant and those of the dominated; between those of the guardians of order and those of the agents of subversion (in accordance with the priest/prophet model); between those of the established and those of the challengers. This set of differential positions is, by its very logic, always prone to a certain instability, since the positions exist through struggles aimed at conserving or subverting the state of the power relations. Between fields, one finds fairly similar resources, taken up by some agents and rejected by others: recourse to the lay public, importation of goods or values from another field, codification of legitimate practices, imposition of an orthodoxy, especially through a corpus of texts of reference or canonical authors, etc.

Contrary to a received idea, the social world described by Bourdieu is not fixed, any more than that envisaged by Durkheim.[18] The field makes it possible to envisage the problem of change in a precise way: nothing obliges one to postulate immobility, but novelty cannot be treated, as it is by the sociologists of 'mutations', in the magical mode, as an upsurge *ex nihilo*.[19] The structural conception of change is opposed to a naïve binary conception in which, as in Aristotelian physics, there is either movement or rest: everything changes, or nothing. Change can be analysed rationally (and relationally) as a rule-governed transformation, and it is important always to take into consideration the conditions, the limits and, behind what varies, the invariants.

To his credit, the economist Robert Boyer (2004: 121) not only contests a certain fixist imagery, but also puts forward an outline of the factors and forms of change according to Bourdieu. Without entering into detailed descriptions, it can be said that, depending on the case, change flows from the struggles internal within a field, from conflicts and modifications of the frontiers between fields (Bourdieu 2004b), from discrepancies between the space of positions and the corresponding space of dispositions, for example through morphological upheavals, or again from modification by the State of the norms of selection and evaluation. For example, in the section of *Distinction* on the transformations resulting from the growing weight of the educational system, it is not a question of describing a 'mutation' ('mass schooling') but of bringing to light a complex process in which conservation of differences combines with a multitude of effects produced by the encounter between the immanent logic of the educational system and the systems of dispositions specific to groups previously remote from the system (the working and peasant classes, the self-employed fractions of the middle classes and even of the upper classes). These transformations concern several aspects at the same time: the educational strategies of the social groups, the restructuring and formation of new groups (new petite bourgeoisie, the salaried bourgeoisie of qualified executives), a new mode of domination, based on the 'velvet glove' (rather than the iron fist of overt authority), sometimes assimilated by semi-scientific sociology to an 'individualistic break-up' of society.

Conclusion

For all the reasons that I have tried to develop here, one can only be perplexed by what might be called eclectic uses of Bourdieu's concepts. Of course, everyone is entitled to propose corrections and amendments, but not if this entails evacuating the meaning of what constitutes the most precious gain from these concepts. Thus 'distinction', a form taken by the social sense of orientation, deserves more than to be reduced to the idea of snobbery, itself associated with a national French aberration, or to be hastily discarded with the argument of a growth in apparently atypical ('omnivorous') practices.[20] Properly understood and undiluted, the concept of distinction is inseparable from the functioning of a field in which positions inevitably 'differ' in many different modalities: it presupposes that the social properties of the agents, their volumes and types of 'capital', govern determinate practices, and that these practices, whether it be choices of objects or classifying operations, derive, along with a certain 'game', from a principle of homology between a space of positions and a space of position-takings. If one does not accept principles of this kind, one is free to adopt others, but not without making explicit the presuppositions of those that one prefers and testing them by comparing them with those that are rejected.

The 'ambition' of the sociologist as Bourdieu conceives it is what incites one to engage, if only provisionally, a vision of the 'monadological' totality capable of embracing both a determinate space of positions and the group of transformations to which it belongs, with which one can situate it, i.e. understand its specificity. If it is true that, as Leibniz said, a drop of water seen through a microscope appears as a differentiated lake, then relational thinking will never cease to identify structural oppositions, study the transpositions and regulated variations, apply the hypothesis of a continuity between extreme cases (symbolic goods/goods material[21]), and seek the highest generality, which implies increasingly powerful instruments capable of accounting for the details, in their tangible, specific singularity. In devising a law of variation, the sociological method avoids sacrificing diversity to unity, or the reverse. This might be seen merely as a heritage of structuralist intellectualism, but relational thinking in actuality, far from assigning a mysterious power to structures, helps to free us from the temptations of substantialism: even the variables, routinely treated as 'factors', demand to be conceived as active powers constructed by social practices and combined in a fundamentally historical constellation. The field, one should never forget, is all at once a support, a horizon and a product of practices.

Notes

1 'The sociologist who seeks to transmit a scientific habitus has more in common with a high-level sports coach than with a Professor at the Sorbonne' (Bourdieu and Wacquant 1992: 224).
2 For an empirical analysis of a state of the religious field, see Bourdieu and de Saint-Martin 1982.
3 Even if this temptation may at one time have been present, as evidenced by the 'formalized' first part of *Reproduction in Education, Society and Culture*, by Bourdieu and Passeron.
4 This Leibnizian style can be contrasted with the Kantian mode of resolution of 'antinomies' (on the self, on the world), which consists in attributing a common presupposition – which is judged to be 'illusory' because it is 'dogmatic' – to each of the competing positions.
5 'Each monad is harmonized with all others, which remain foreign to it, although it obeys its own force and the laws of its nature' Leibniz (1969: 102) declares.

6 On the opposition between these two types of properties, see Bourdieu 1966.
7 Critiques of Bourdieu on this point are often based on the inclination to envisage only substantialist propositions that are readily falsifiable: 'the lower-middle class like (or reject) this or that type of consumption', at the expense of relational, historically conditioned propositions.
8 Seeking to dispense with questions of legitimacy and recognition, one risks being locked in a binary vision (the dominated are either submissive or dissident) such as that of James C. Scott, whose critique of Bourdieu (Scott 1990) is eloquent. The whole question is whether thumbing noses at the dominant in private is an act of 'resistance'. The inventory of this type of practice, which is in fact well known, feeds the methodological populism of sociologists delighted to be shrewder than colleagues taken in by 'official' appearances. Domination, for Weber as for Bourdieu, goes far beyond explicit discourses, 'scripts', or public imagery. Rather, it designates a closure of the possibles, a precondition for the perpetuation of the political order of things.
9 This has nothing to do with the dominated being obsessed with the dominant, as those who denounce Bourdieu's 'legitimism' think. If there is 'obsession', it rather characterizes the groups who embody social pretension, or hopes of cultural salvation. In a certain sense, the dispossessed have the advantage of being freed from a game that excludes them, but having, despite everything, a representation of the social space, at least through their unhappy (and/or foreshortened) experience of the educational system, they have an awareness of the existence of a distant game that is played out above their heads. However, in a differentiated society, who can claim not to be dispossessed of any game?
10 The declarations of those who – having paid homage to Bourdieu – announce, for example, in a perfect illustration of the empiricism he combated, that 'now, in Britain', quite other variables are more important, can be seen as derisory.
11 The division of sociological labour has the effect of favouring the emergence of advocates for a variable, who constitute themselves as unofficial spokespersons for an unfairly treated group (women, homosexuals, immigrants, etc.) while appearing to conform to the demands of scientific rigour, and who strive to protest against the repression of 'their' variable by most of their colleagues. Sociological analysis must of course be ready to take into account every kind of variable, but not to grant them exceptional status. The initially unfavourable conjunction of the variables 'female' and 'immigrant origin' could, in a particular conjuncture, be reversed in an autonomous space such as the political field, where the logic of competition made it envisageable to take the 'risk' of appointing a person with such attributes as a minister. Such a reversal, which remains very marginal, in no way modifies the distribution of the different forms of capital among social groups, or the dependence of the different variables with respect to this distribution. A particular variable can also be a weapon of universalization to modify the state of the distribution of capital in favour of a group or class fraction.
12 Of course, while the concept of the field is first defined by coexistence, it can perfectly well receive a temporal dimension in the second stage.
13 Jacques Bouveresse has expressed some reservations regarding Bourdieu's dispositional conception in a text, 'Règles, dispositions et habitus,' reproduced in Bouveresse 2004.
14 'As the data are ordered, so the unknowns are also ordered' (Leibniz 1966: 351). This adage is generally taken as the classic formulation of Leibniz's principle of continuity.
15 The idea of a correspondence between the order of dispositions and the order of positions does not imply the idea of a functional relationship. Everything takes place as if, in the ordinary course of events, there were a harmony between the two orders, but there can also be critical situations in which habitus are not fully

adjusted to the state of a field, and such situations, too, are of course perfectly amenable to analysis.

16 This memory must be distinguished from the notion of 'reflexivity' in its common current uses, which tend to emphasize a capacity for self-monitoring either on the part of the agents (strategic anticipation of the images that agents have of one another) or even of the 'systems'.

17 On the relationship between the 'field of power' and field of institutions of higher education, see Bourdieu 1996b.

18 This is still the case. Bourdieu could have made his own the remarks of Durkheim, who on his supposed aversion to the 'dynamic' aspect, replied to a Bergsonian philosopher: 'I was greatly surprised to hear Mr. Wilbois make the more or less preponderance of the static viewpoint the essential characteristic of my sociological ideas ... He presents it as self-evident, as does the school to which he belongs, that change [*le devenir*] lies outside the scope of scientific thought, that is to say, distinct thought' (Durkheim 1914: 66–67).

19 A sociology of knowledge that takes as its object both the social sciences and the intellectual doxa would make it possible to analyse the differential profits of the emphasis placed, according to the discipline, either on creation, innovation (as opposed to routine, reproduction) or, in the manner of some historians, on the *longue durée*.

20 For some American authors, such as Richard Peterson, an 'omnivore' is an individual who mingles all cultural genres regardless of hierarchies: this would be a relatively new figure, manifesting a relaxed, independent relation to culture. It may be wondered whether the statistical plausibility associated with this metaphorical term is not based first on the technique of the questionnaire, which, through the formulation of the questions, the division of the categories and the coding operation, makes it possible to generate anomalies which are then simply recorded in an apparently neutral way. In any case, an analytical framework cannot be invalidated simply by 'facts' whose principle of construction first needs to be analysed; nor can it be tested by propositions separated from experience. Once it is observed that 'omnivores' are predominantly found in the middle and upper strata, one is entitled to wonder whether, assuming that it corresponds to something, the expansion of this sub-population is not more simply the expression of the transformations of the relation to culture of dominant groups who are assured of holding it at both ends (legitimacy *and* frivolity, at least – in the case of the youngest – until they reach the age of maturity). While the supply may have diversified, this does not mean that the hierarchy of cultural domains has been dismantled or attenuated. On questions of this type, the interview procedure, far from being supplementary, makes it possible to relate the coherence and dispersion of choices to determinate trajectories and to evaluate the relative importance of the different cultural registers in the tastes of the same agent. The statistical approach should be introduced only when informed by concrete cases that raise real sociological questions.

21 On this point one could point to Bourdieu's work on the field of publishing and also on the housing market.

References

Bourdieu, P. 1966. 'Condition de classe et position de classe'. *Archives européennes de sociologie*, 7, 2, 201–23.
——1968. 'Intellectual Field and Creative Project'. *Social Science Information*, 8, 2, 89–119.
——1974. 'Avenir de classe et causalité du probable'. *Revue française de sociologie*, XV, 1, 3–42.

118   *Louis Pinto*

——1976. 'Le champ scientifique'. *Actes de la recherche en sciences sociales*, 2–3, 88–104.

——1984. *Distinction: A Social Critique of the Judgement of Taste*, trans. Richard Nice. Cambridge, MA: Harvard University Press.

——1987. *Choses dites*. Paris: Minuit.

——1991. 'Genesis and Structure of the Religious Field'. *Comparative Social Research*, 13, 1–44.

——1996a. *The Rules of Art: Genesis and Structure of the Literary Field*. Cambridge: Polity; Stanford, CA: Stanford University Press.

——1996b. *The State Nobility: Elite Schools in the Field of Power*. Cambridge: Polity and Stanford: Stanford University Press.

——2000. 'Questions à Pierre Bourdieu'. In G. Mauger and L. Pinto (ed.) *Lire les sciences sociales, 1994–1996*, vol. 3. Paris: Hermès Science, 197–223.

——2003. *The Social Structures of the Economy*. Cambridge: Polity Press.

——2004a. *Sketch for a Self-Analysis*. Cambridge: Polity Press.

——2004b. 'From the King's House to the Reason of State: A Model of the Genesis of the Bureaucratic Field'. *Constellations*, 11(1), 16–36.

Bourdieu, P. and de Saint-Martin, M. 1982. 'La Sainte famille. L'épiscopat français dans le champ du pouvoir'. *Actes de la recherche en sciences sociales*, 44–45, 2–53.

Bourdieu, P. and Wacquant, L.J.D. 1992. *An Invitation to Reflexive Sociology*. Chicago, IL: University of Chicago Press; Cambridge: Polity Press.

Bouveresse, J. 2004. *Bourdieu, savant et politique*. Marseille: Agone.

Boyer, R. 2004. *Une théorie du capitalisme est-elle possible?* Paris: Odile Jacob.

Brubaker, R. 1993. 'Social Theory as Habitus'. In C. Calhoun, E. LiPuma and M. Postone (ed.) *Bourdieu: Critical Perspectives*. Cambridge: Polity Press; Chicago: University of Chicago Press, 212–34.

Durkheim, E. 1897. 'L'empirisme rationaliste de Taine et les sciences morales'. In *La Revue blanche* (repr. in E. Durkheim, *Textes*, vol. 1. Paris: Minuit, 1975).

——1914. 'Bulletin de la Société française de philosophie' (repr. in *Textes*, vol. 1. Paris: Minuit, 1975).

Leibniz, G. 1966. *The Monadology and Other Philosophical Writings*. Oxford: Clarendon Press.

——1969. 'De la nature en elle-même, ou de la force inhérent aux choses créées and de leurs actions'. In *Opuscules philosophiques choisis*. Paris: Vrin.

Mahnke, D. 1993. 'Le concept scientifique de l'individualité universelle selon Leibniz'. *Philosophie*, 39.

Pinto, L. 1999. *Pierre Bourdieu et la théorie du monde social*. Paris: Points-Seuil.

Scott, J. 1990. *Domination and the Arts of Resistance: Hidden Transcripts*. New Haven and London: Yale University Press.

Skinner, Q. 2002. 'Meaning and Understanding in the History of Ideas'. In Q. Skinner (ed.) *Visions of Politics*, 3 vols, vol. 1, *Regarding Method*. Cambridge: Cambridge University Press, 57–89.

Part II

Education, culture and organization

4 Collective agents in the school field

Positions, dispositions and position taking in educational and vocational guidance

Géraldine André and Mathieu Hilgers

Introduction

For more than three decades, the sociology of education in the French-speaking world was profoundly influenced by the work of Bourdieu. Analyses concerned with teachers' judgement of their pupils, for example, were particularly marked by his approach.[1] Numerous studies analysed teachers' judgement as a mechanism of social reproduction and emphasized the stability and consistency of the practices of the educational agents, which were then supported by structural dimensions.

In the early 1990s, new research highlighted the growing instability and many uncertainties of teachers' judgement, now characterized by the pluralization of its systems of reference (Derouet 1988, 1992; Baluteau 1993; Calicchio and Mabilon-Bonfils 2004). In this context, this judgement no longer appeared as decided in advance because framed by structural determinations (Derouet 1992). It became necessary to devise new theoretical and methodological tools to grasp the uncertain character of the decision making of the institutional actors (Derouet 1992, 2000). Researchers turned away from Bourdieu in their search for a better understanding of the new logics and interplay of actors (Rochex 1994; van Haecht 2006). In the view of sociologists of education, the 'massification' of schooling, the arrival of pupils with diverse social origins, the raising of the school leaving age, the appearance of new pedagogical references, new models of socialization and new forms of school governance, have profoundly reduced the autonomy of the educational institution and undermined the legitimacy of its agents (Derouet 1992; Dubet 2002).

We argue here that in this context of uncertainties, field theory remains extremely useful in shedding light on the sociological foundations of teachers' judgement. Our research shows that, in spite of these changes, teachers' judgement remains profoundly linked to certain structural influences, one of which is the position of their school in the school field. In order clearly to identify different schools' positions in a local field, one must first establish their economic capital and their cultural capital. This presupposes that certain concepts generally used to describe the positions of individual agents in an autonomized domain of activity be transposed to collective agents. By constructing the positions of three schools in a local field, we seek to establish the impact of position in the field on teachers' judgement and on the positions they take in the educational and vocational orientation of their pupils.

From the *grandes écoles* to secondary education

Teachers' judgement has a profoundly social function. Within the educational institution, it provides the relay for a classification that becomes effective in the field of power. To understand the role teachers play in this transmission, Bourdieu examined the 'genesis and functioning of the categories' through which the professors of the French *grandes écoles* perceive and evaluate their students and their performances and results (Bourdieu 1996: 166–67).[2] Bourdieu found a relative stability in professorial decision making, arising from a twofold constraint. First, the competence of the professors is structurally constrained by the habitus of their social group, which is strongly linked to an academic institution that has classified them favourably and which they serve in their turn. Structured by a practical sense of class affinities and distinctions, professors' evaluations bear mainly on the *hexis* of their students. Paradoxically, teachers' judgement makes relatively little reference to the performance officially required by the institution. They form their judgement on the basis of the bodily signs and attitudes of their students, their relation to language, their ease with culture rather than their actual knowledge. Finally, they pronounce their judgement and verdict in their capacity as representatives of the state, enjoying a status recognized by all (Bourdieu 1990).

Through the case of the field of higher education, Bourdieu shows that the autonomy of the academic field is relative. The *grandes écoles* are opposed, classified and distinguished depending on the access they give to more or less high and prestigious social positions in the field of power. There is: 1 a homology between, a) the opposition between the major *grandes écoles* and the less prestigious '*petites écoles*', and b) the opposition between the *grande bourgeoisie* and the *petite bourgeoisie*; and 2 a homology between the opposition between, a) the 'intellectual' *grandes écoles*, academically dominant but socially and economically dominated, and the schools of economic and political power, academically dominated but socially and economically dominant, and b) the opposition between the two poles that structure the field of power, the intellectual or artistic pole and the economic or political pole. This double homology constitutes, for Bourdieu, the principle of 'the specifically social effect' of the *grandes écoles*, i.e. the principle that structures them in relation to one another (Bourdieu 1996: 136). The logics of individual schools and their symbolic references are thus built up within a system of relations that exist among them based on their distinctive positions in the field of power. In addition, transformations in the field of power affect the reproduction strategies of the dominant and modify the positions of the schools. The rise of financial capital at the expense of industrial capital, for example, propels to the summit of the school hierarchy those schools teaching managerial skills rather than schools that teach technical competence (Bourdieu 1996). In other words, the structuring of the cultures of institutions follows the dynamics of the field of power and the symbolic struggles that run through it and which 'have as one of their stakes the hierarchy of the principles of ethical evaluation', the maintenance of this hierarchy, its modification or reversal (Bourdieu 1996: 44).

The dynamics of transformation that affect the field of power thus have repercussions on the frames of reference and pedagogical styles and, correlatively, on the positions of the different schools (Mangez 2008).[3] It can be hypothesized, following Mangez (2008), that the development of symbolic references associated with the private sector (New Public Management), the accompanying diffusion of an 'invisible' pedagogy (Bernstein 1977) and the refocusing of secondary education on skills have affected the flows of populations towards different schools and their positions in their local school fields. The demographic changes (numbers and social origins of pupils) reflect changes in the relative positions of schools correlated with the changes implied in the variation of the hierarchy of legitimate values in the field of power. This dynamics of relations among schools constitutes a decisive variable in the production of the categories of teachers' judgement. Bringing to light its effects helps to explain the certainties and uncertainties of the actors invested with the power of 'guidance' (*orientation*).

To analyse the effects of position on the production of teachers' judgement, a field study was carried out in three secondary schools in French-speaking Belgium.[4] The aim was to describe the judgement of teachers (and other actors) and its implications in terms of orientation and reorientation towards vocational schooling.[5] Three schools were at the centre of our investigations: *Saint-John Perse*, *Jacques Prévert* and *Maurice Carême*.[6] They were chosen because their offer is mainly centred on the 'general' curriculum, which places them relatively high in the local school hierarchy (Delvaux and Joseph 2003),[7] but also in a situation of relative competition. In terms of their average socio-academic and socio-economic levels, the three schools occupy relatively similar positions in the national school hierarchy; however, our survey brought to light significant differences in their respective histories, trajectories and cultures which lead them to occupy distinct places in the local school field. To grasp the cultures of the schools in which the teachers' judgement is deployed, participant observation was carried out in each of the schools (André 2012). Reconstructing the functioning of the local field and establishing the importance of the positions of these schools for the positions they take as regards 'orientation' requires one to define the volume and kinds of capital they possess and to identify the trajectory of each of them in the local school field.

Defining the capital and trajectories of collective agents

To differentiate the schools in the space of relations constituted by the local field, one has to identify their positions. In a field, this position is determined by the volume and structure of their different kinds of capital. The analyses that follow aim to specify the heuristic capacity of these concepts (economic capital and cultural capital) when applied to collective agents, in this case schools.[8]

The *economic capital* of schools depends on the different types of material resources at their disposal. In the French Community of Belgium, the public funding of secondary schools is proportional to the number of pupils enrolled. Compared to the other two schools analysed, *Saint-John Perse* has a large enrolment (1,300). The correspondingly large budget gives its agents a scope for action that enables them to convert economic capital into cultural capital, through material investments: modern buildings, an annexe with a multimedia centre for computing and language learning, sports facilities, etc. This conversion enables the agents of *Saint-John Perse* to present their school strongly in the local field and reinforces their tendency to maintain or improve their position in the school hierarchy. The material assets of schools accrue over time and help to structure the relative positions of the schools, their relationships and their practices. Economic capital is also defined by the sociological profile of the pupils and their capacity to participate, or not, in the activities of the school. In this form, it constitutes a condition of access to the school even if schooling is officially free to all.

The *cultural capital* of schools is strongly dependent on the aggregation of the social and academic properties of their enrolment. We here adapt the structure of this capital as defined by Bourdieu (1986) for use with reference to collective actors. The 'objectified state' of the cultural capital of a school refers to the cultural goods it possesses. Some schools have modern infrastructures, multimedia centres, theatres, cinemas, libraries, sports facilities, study rooms, works of art, gardens, etc. In the French Community of Belgium, secondary school cultural capital does not exist in the 'institutionalized state'. In contrast to other countries or other levels of education, there are no official 'league tables' by which secondary schools can be compared. However, such rankings exist implicitly. Finally, by the 'incorporated state' of cultural capital we mean the aggregate of the cultural references, axiological orientations and pedagogical properties effective in the institution and internalized by the agents who compose it. To refer to the incorporated state of cultural capital, we shall use here the notion of 'institutional culture' (*culture d'établissement*) (André 2012).[9] Institutional cultures derive from the histories of schools. Our observations indicate that in their constitution the dispositions of the pupils, their socialization within their families, their social origin and previous schooling, are more important than those of the teachers. However, it is true, as shown by the case of *Saint-John Perse*, set out in Box 4.1, that the institutional culture, the incorporated state of cultural capital, also depends on the dispositions of the teaching body (which has sometimes been carefully selected on this criterion). These dispositions have been acquired through the teachers' experience, their exposure to the values of the school and its pupils, or through a deliberate effort of inculcation by the school management.

Box 4.1 A dominant position

Saint-John Perse is a school located in the heart of a large urban centre. A modern eight-storey building is surrounded by extensive recreation areas. The school initially taught children from modest backgrounds in the tradition of the Brothers of the Christian Schools. It increasingly found itself in competition with the neighbouring Jesuit school, which attracted a more privileged population. In the 1950s, this rivalry was resolved by a division between the classical humanities (ancient Greek and Latin) for the Jesuits and the 'modern humanities' (mathematics and science) for *Saint-John Perse*.

Since the 1980s, the school has seen significant growth in its enrolment, which now amounts to 1,300 pupils. The 'general education' track has steadily expanded. The buildings are being modernized and extended. In its new development, the school pursues the objective of building up a community spirit – by constructing an environment sufficiently agreeable for the pupils to want to spend time there – and protecting the community from external intrusions – the new entrance no longer opens onto the playground, but leads directly into the buildings. The enclosure of a space of their own is one of the most typical acts of schools at the top of their hierarchy (Wagner 1998; Pinçon and Pinçon-Charlot 1989); it is much appreciated by the rising middle and/or upper classes (Bourdieu 1996) and facilitates the development of a common culture. This 'cloistering' is part of the work of constituting not only an 'educational community' in which the pupil benefits from a 'total education', but also an *esprit de corps* (Wagner 1998) among both pupils and teachers.

According to the head of the school, in the 1990s the declining intake of a well-regarded neighbouring school benefited his own institution which, with its scientific and mathematical orientation, attracted the children of the managerial classes. In addition to the assets acquired by *Saint-John Perse* thanks to its economic capital, the school has developed on the one hand cultural references linked to New Public Management, in which the head was trained, and on the other a commitment to the 'invisible' pedagogies that prioritize the person of the pupil. The 'learning contexts' are structured so that the pupils can 'explore', 'organize' and 'select'; the 'control procedures' are 'implicit' – the learner is more subject to peer regulation than to a hierarchical discipline (Bernstein 1977). The culture of the school is apparent in its spatiotemporal organization, in the discourse of the institutional agents, and in the body language and working attitudes of the teachers, who, for example, work together 'spontaneously' in teams. However, it is also expressed in the mission statement of the school (*projet d'établisse-ment*): socialization into the new technologies, languages, adaptability, sensitization to the economy through the importance of mathematics, valorization of the individual, individual's adaptation to a constantly changing world, ability to enter into the dynamics of collective work, responsibility for becoming the actor of one's own education. This school now occupies a dominant position in the local school hierarchy.

Like those of individual agents, the trajectories of collective agents are variable. Having described a school with a rising trajectory, in Box 4.2 we describe a school that has similar average socio-academic and socio-economic levels but which is undergoing a slow process of devaluation. This can be understood in terms of the dynamics of change in the field of power, which impacts on the frames of reference and the pedagogical styles valorized in the school field and therefore on the positions of the schools. The first school presented has placed its emphasis on an 'invisible' pedagogy and references linked to New Public Management. The school described has been unable to adapt to the new categories of the dominant evaluation and is suffering a decline in the average socio-economic level of its intake.

Box 4.2 A declining trajectory

The *Maurice Carême* school is more than 150 years old. Like *Saint-John Perse*, it was founded by the Brothers of the Christian Schools to educate the children of the labouring class. In the course of time, like *Saint-John Perse*, it specialized in the 'modern humanities' (mathematics and sciences) and increasingly attracted a population drawn from middle-class families of commercial proprietors. In the 1970s, it had 800 pupils. Teachers who have been at the school a long time like to recall that era, rich in options, with pupils from 'good families', when the curricula recommended 'visible' pedagogies, learning was structured by benchmarks and explicit forms of hierarchical control (Bernstein 1977) and discipline went without saying. Since the mid-1990s, the enrolment has declined, a fact the head teacher attributes to the geographical location. The average socio-economic profile of the pupils has changed. Having failed to attract the children of managers, in order to keep up its enrolment the school has again opened up to working-class children. Whereas over the same period the previous school was moving towards invisible pedagogy and a managerial ideology, the maintenance of a 'visible' pedagogic approach and the emphasis on the literary options[1] reflects the changing intake of *Maurice Carême*. In contrast to middle- and upper-class families who prefer invisible to visible pedagogies, working-class families favour more explicit pedagogical styles.

This difference can be detected in the different atmosphere. At the entrance to the courtyard of *Maurice Carême*, the teachers oversee the comings and goings in a quasi-parental and authoritarian manner. During the breaks, the head teacher backs up the supervising teachers. He stands at the top of a stone staircase and casts a severe gaze over the activities. At the end of the break the pupils line up and wait for their teachers. The values linked to the history of the school and its enrolment made up of the children of shopkeepers and independent professionals appear in the organization of the institution, in the discourses and dispositions of the teachers, who, in contrast to *Saint-John Perse*, do little teamwork – except in a hierarchical relation of initiation of younger teachers by more senior colleagues – in the hierarchization of disciplines, in the mission statement, and in the explicitly hierarchical forms of control and evaluation, which contrast with the emphasis placed on the personal involvement of the pupil at the top of the hierarchy. There is little place for use of and familiarization with new technologies, and language learning is not valorized. The school and its values increasingly attract working-class families. However, in contrast to the school described earlier, with an enrolment of now only some 600 pupils, the volume of economic capital available to *Maurice Carême* remains limited. This weakness restricts its material investments and impacts on the processes of 'orientation'.

Note

[1] In 'general' education in the French Community of Belgium, the literary options are less prestigious and less valorized then those centred on mathematics (Friant and Demeuse 2011).

The description in Box 4.2 indicates that the appearance of new values directly linked to the field of power has valorized certain pedagogical references (invisible pedagogy, managerial values, emphasis on skills) and affects the strategies, ethos and aspirations of schools. The third school in our sample (Box 4.3) shows that mere aspiration to the dominant values does not suffice to position a school in the higher segment of the local school field. Despite its wish to remain in the higher range of the school hierarchy, for example by extending the use of an invisible pedagogy, the *Jacques Prévert* school is on a downward trajectory owing to the change in its enrolment . The cultural values and invisible pedagogic style are close to those valorized at *Saint-John Perse*, but, with its technical and vocational streams, the school now recruits an increasingly large part of its intake from the working classes. In contrast to the other two schools, *Jacques Prévert* is located close to two well-to-do provinces. In former times its location was an advantage and, in the late 1950s, when the general track was opened, the school attracted young people from 'good families'. Nowadays, the combination of different tracks on the same site has become a negative factor since this population can easily find schools in the region that offer exclusively the 'general' track. The middle classes generally aim to keep their children as long as possible in this type of curriculum (van Zanten 2009). To limit defections, the teachers and their head maintain the historical demands of the school and assert values linked to the dominant rhetoric but their aspirations are less and less in accord with the values of their pupils and they have to adapt their practices. Academic heterogeneity engenders a social heterogeneity which does not enable the school to remain at the top of the hierarchy.

Box 4.3 *Jacques Prévert*

The *Jacques Prévert* school was initially a vocational establishment for girls from the working classes. In the late 1950s, a 'general track' centred on mathematics and science was created and developed, thus opening the school to higher social categories. In contrast to the two other schools, *Jacques Prévert* now has three tracks of secondary education (general, technical, vocational) on one site. With the reform known as *l'enseignement rénové* and the creation of options in the general track (the sciences and Latin were added to mathematics) and in the technical and vocational tracks (sales and hospitality), there was a strong surge in recruitment, and enrolment eventually rose to almost 1,300, mainly from middle- and working-class backgrounds. *Jacques Prévert* consequently has relatively high economic capital, visible in its modern infrastructure and recent investments. To the right of the main building, a large porch opens onto the annexes and also to a large well-maintained lawn. In the centre of the cluster of old grey stone buildings is a pleasant courtyard in which a recently built veranda houses the well-appointed Hospitality and Catering section.

The change in the school population has directly affected its cultural capital. The potential profitability of objective cultural capital always needs to be valorized by 'incorporated capital' (Bourdieu 1986). To realize their value, cultural goods (a silent study room, for example) require the individuals who make up the school collective to possess the dispositions needed to activate their cultural value. Here, the social origin of the pupils, misaligned with the dominant values, affects the institutional culture and limits the profitability of its objectified cultural capital. This explains why, in the constitution of the institutional culture, the dispositions of the pupils are more important than those of the teachers. An institution with high cultural capital can see it depreciate following a change in the composition of its enrolment. It may accumulate economic capital if it has a large number of pupils, without being able to convert it into effective cultural capital if the pupils are drawn from the lower fractions of the social hierarchy. This conversion, which is essential in order to attract pupils from more advantaged backgrounds, presupposes that the intake is relatively homogeneous and drawn from the higher levels of the social hierarchy, or else requires the implementation of a selection which paradoxically has to operate without reducing the numbers.

We now aim to establish how the positions of the schools affect the positions taken by the schools' agents as regards 'orientation'.

Positions and position-takings

As regards academic and vocational orientation, there are significant differences, which can be understood by analysing the positions, and changes in the positions, of the schools within the school field. As has been shown, their positions are defined by the volume and structure of their capital, i.e. the proportions of economic and cultural capital, but also the objectified, institutionalized and incorporated components of the latter.

The *volume of economic capital* held by each school affects the decision making of the teachers in the class conferences. At the top of the hierarchy, at

Saint-John Perse, the large number of pupils enables the institutional agents to engage fully in an act of orientation understood above all as a strategy for maintaining and reproducing the values of the institution. Academic orientation, and more especially the move from the first to the second cycle of secondary education, is an important process, as evidenced by the number of institutional agents mobilized and the plethora of activities related to it. 'Orientation project sessions' are provided for pupils 'in academic difficulty'. A major orientation project entitled '*Once upon a time there was a choice*', for pupils in their second year of secondary school, takes place all year long in several stages: career discussions, information on the structure of secondary education, collective sessions in which the different routes and options are presented, questionnaires on interests, all followed by individual, personalized meetings with an agent of the Psychological, Medical and Social Centre (CPMS) attached to the school. The rigour with which the various activities are carried out shows how seriously the matter is taken. While they consider that many parents have an influence on the life of the school, the teachers approach their role in orientation as autonomous experts and consider themselves all the more legitimate in their decision making in that the many actors and procedures converge.[10] In this school, orientation proceeds as a strategy for reproduction of the position of the institution within the field. It makes it possible to establish a clear frontier between the 'normal' and the 'abnormal', to put it in terms of emic categories, or between pupils considered 'virtuous' or 'non-virtuous' (Bourdieu 1996), according to the logic of the institution. This distinction appears from the earliest orientation conferences (see Box 4.4).

Box 4.4 Orientation conference, *Saint-John Perse*

Formal objective: to monitor the pupils' progress.

The class teacher comments on the situation of a pupil from a working-class background: 'M. has an average of 63% with a fail in maths, 9/50!'

The teacher of French: 'That girl really has very little ability.'

Maths teacher: 'The problem is, she understands nothing!'

Class teacher: 'Well, 63% is not yet totally decisive [*orientatif*]. We must wait until January, when it will be clearer.'

Another pupil has a similar average. The French teacher stresses the boy's earlier results and the family background, which is high in the school and social hierarchy: 'He comes from a good family and he had very good primary results with the Brothers.[1] I'm both pleased and a bit disappointed by his marks.'

The economics teacher provides excuses for the pupil and stresses his qualities for the institution: 'He's cultured and interested; he just doesn't do any work!'

The reference to 'laziness' has a twofold significance, since the negative judgement, a lack of commitment to school work, subtly underlines the pupil's presumed intelligence and his ability to succeed.

> The maths teacher goes further: 'Yes, and he's not in the same situation as M., who understands nothing. He's intelligent and he's backed by his parents. We can give him a hand. It won't be wasted.'
> The teachers decide to assign remedial hours.
> (Second year class conference, *Saint-John Perse*, November 2007)
>
> **Note**
>
> [1]   The other very well-regarded school in the town centre, of which this school sees itself as a rival.

While their official purpose is to evaluate the pupils' difficulties, provide necessary support and guide them in their choice of track, the orientation conferences seem to be structured around a different aim. They distinguish, separate, discriminate and co-opt groups of pupils according to their proximity to the culture of the institution. From the start of the year, it is a question of orienting the pupils least embodying the values of the school towards vocational education and retaining those whose values, representations and practices are closest to those favoured by the teachers. In the example in Box 4.4, pupils with similar results but different social profiles are treated differently.

In the schools with a lower volume of economic capital, and especially *Maurice Carême*, situated at the bottom of this fraction of the field, and with a smaller number of pupils, the orientation process is different. First, it is not an important issue: there are no modules, no 'mission', no special curricula, no specific activities. The decisions taken in terms of orientation are less precise and less numerous at the beginning of the school year. Second, the teachers distance themselves from their role. They call into question an orientation process entirely guided by the agents of the school. They consult the pupils and parents more often to establish choices of orientation. Finally, in the first secondary cycle at *Maurice Carême*, because of the low number of pupils, the *logic of the market* is important in the construction of the judgement. It aims consciously and deliberately to maintain or expand the economic capital of the institution by increasing the number of pupils. In this way the school can preserve in the short term a position threatened by devaluation, but at the cost of a deterioration of the social quality of its intake, which, in the long term, leads systematically to a worsening of its position in the school field. Hence many decisions aim to keep pupils in the school and avoid awarding certificates of orientation that would channel pupils towards courses not offered by the school. It is important to note that this is not the *only* logic that operates in the class conferences. It can conflict with other decisional logics, which explains the instability of the teachers' judgement noted by some authors. For teachers, orienting pupils in the name of an explicitly formulated market logic is hard to accept.

If the number of pupils enrolled in each school shapes teachers' judgement in terms of academic orientation, *the structure of the schools' cultural capital* also exerts a considerable influence on the outcome of decision making. To understand this, one has to grasp the dynamics at the heart of orientation judgement that are present in the class conferences of the three schools. The social affinities between the pupils and the teaching body, family cultures and attitudes towards the school, underlie the decisions as much as 'purely' scholastic competences and results. The perception of the pupils' scholastic performance is constructed on the basis of a gaze that establishes the proximity of the pupil to the values of the school. It constitutes a decisive element because it is possible to present results so as to favour pupils capable of integrating themselves into the school (or already integrated) and to exclude pupils who are out of line with the values promoted by the institutional actors. This phenomenon, highlighted by Bourdieu in his work on education (Bourdieu and Passeron 1979) and on the field of the *grandes écoles* (Bourdieu 1996) retains all its efficacy today. As the next description indicates, the repeated year that enables pupils to remain in the school is granted to those regarded as most deserving, i.e. those who recognize and share the values of the teachers. Re-orientation to other schools is generally recommended for the pupils least open to the values of the institution, in other words those who do not possess the incorporated cultural capital needed to valorize the objectified cultural capital of the institution and who therefore, by their mere presence, tend to diminish the overall cultural capital of the school, but also limit its capacity to convert economic capital, partly linked to their enrolment in the school, into cultural capital.[11]

Box 4.5 Orientation conference, *Jacques Prévert*

In the orientation conferences at *Jacques Prévert*, all the pupils are reviewed by the teachers who meet in a separate session for each class. Two pupils have failed in all areas but are not treated in the same way. The class teacher exclaims with reference to a girl of working-class background, who is described as talkative and liking to move around the classroom, and whose parents chose the school because it was close to home: 'A. has failed in everything!'

The deputy head reminds the meeting of the recommendation recently made to the family: 'We advise vocational year 3, sales.'

The gym teacher opposes this recommendation since it implies that the girl remain in the school, whereas the teacher considers she has the profile for a purely vocational school. She exclaims: 'But she's more like year 3 hairdressing at *Emile Zola*![1] Every day she sits there with her little mirror. But we aren't at *Emile Zola* here, and that is something she has never understood.'

So the teachers arrive at a recommendation for an option that the school does not offer. A little later, the class teacher comments on the results of a pupil whose parents are pharmacists and are strongly involved in their son's schooling: 'J. has failed everywhere and I don't understand why; his general culture is extraordinary!'

The teacher of French underlines the pupil's relation to the school and his conduct in class as especially positive.

'The problem is, he's in his third year in the first cycle, and he can't stay here if we don't let him through', the first cycle coordinator explains.
The maths teacher proposes special treatment: 'He has to be saved!'
To the relief of all, the CPMS representative provides a psychological argument for special treatment, which she had not done in the previous case: 'He's emotionally deprived relative to his sister, there's a lack of affection and recognition from his parents'.
The teacher of French makes his contribution to justify a verdict more favourable to the pupil. After some ingenious calculation, he points to a difference between the results of the two pupils by processing them differently from the method announced at the start. The legitimacy of this special treatment is grounded on 'the objectivity of the results' and ratified by all the teachers.
The class teacher even suggests a type of examination designed to help this pupil: 'We could raise his confidence with an oral exam?'
These suggestions are unanimously approved.
                              (Orientation conference, *Jacques Prévert*, April 2007)

Note

1 A vocational school situated at the bottom of the local school hierarchy.

The teacher's judgement in Box 4.5 appears as a central element in a strategy aimed at maintaining or increasing the cultural capital of the institution, and the social perception of the pupils by the teachers and the institutional culture constitute essential supports in decision making. Analysis in terms of position brings to light another important phenomenon. With the exception of the head teachers, who are led and forced by their function in the school to objectivate and develop reproduction strategies for the maintenance or improvement of the position of their school in the local hierarchy, the degree of objectivation of these strategies by the teaching body varies directly according to the position of the school. From a dominant position, at *Saint-John Perse*, the use of academic orientation as a tool of reproduction dominates the class conferences. However, for the institutional agents of the school, this orientation for and by reproduction takes place in a 'non-objectivated' way, i.e. by spontaneously and quasi-non-reflexively mobilizing the values of the school: academic excellence, active participation in group work, time management, speed, efficiency, striving for improvement. In our observation of a class conference to award letters of congratulation, these three sets of virtues (excellence, commitment, efficiency) are clear to see (Box 4.6).

Box 4.6 Orientation conference, *Saint-John Perse*

The class teacher (also teacher of Dutch): 'She has 94%. She's quick, effective and conscientious.'
Geography teacher: 'She's always ready to do more! That girl will go far! She doesn't rest on her laurels!'

Teacher of French: 'She automatically gets a letter of congratulation. She has all the qualities one could wish for! Some pupils boast of their successes, but she helps the others, and she's really well integrated. She's brings the whole class along with her.'
Class teacher: 'M. pays attention and works quickly.'
Maths: 'Too quickly, in my view. His work is often good, but a bit slapdash.'
Class teacher: 'True, he sometimes lacks rigour. But he's a good pupil. He knows what he is capable of. Shall we give him a letter?'
(Orientation conference, *Saint-John Perse*, 2006)

For the teachers and other educational agents of *Saint-John Perse*, the quantity and social quality of their enrolment confirms the pertinence of the values and references that structure the school; they are the benchmarks for the practices of orientation. In this case, the values of the school, its culture and their own legitimacy in the field enable the teachers to concern themselves relatively little with the implications and consequences of their academic orientation practices. Here, without uncertainty or self-doubt, the teachers and other institutional agents make decisions sending some of their pupils into forms of education that they consider devalued and devaluing, such as vocational training. From their dominant position the agents have little need to objectivate a selection strategy, since the *practical mode of decision* operates and spontaneously legitimates the selection mechanism.

In the two other schools, the uncertainties of the teachers' judgement are greater. At *Maurice Carême* the symbolic references and pedagogic style linked to the cultural past of the school structure the decisions made in the class conferences, but a twofold discrepancy – between these references and the dominant values and between these references and the new social quality of their intake – causes the decisions and judgement made in class conferences to be uncertain. Numerous tensions emerge between different sets of criteria governing decision making. No final decisions regarding orientation are taken until the end of the school year. As seen in the interview extract below, there are tensions between the logic of reputation, the logic of the market, a democratic logic favouring access to education, and the logic of excellence valorizing support for pupils who are struggling but have strong potential.

Like other teachers, I think, I'm always concerned to help someone who's struggling. But the school culture is to help the best, they have to be pushed because afterwards comes university, higher education, and we want results and so on at that level … And at the same time, I say to myself, I'm disappointed with orienting. I really think you have to be wary of orienting a pupil towards 'electricity' at the age of 14 when he's just an idler going through a crisis that will be over in a year or two … Pupils and parents choose their schools on the basis of reputation, that's how a school becomes elitist. It's true this is a high-level school. I try to help the weakest, but it isn't easy! I remember how, when I arrived here, the head said 'You have to put pressure on them, that's the way it is here!' I started off in top gear, worked like crazy, setting the level of my classes very high. I said to myself: 'I am going to push them hard, try to get the results.' But the problem is, it's contradictory! You push the pupils to the limit, but they mustn't fail, because then the head comes down on you, and the pupils change school and our numbers drop. And the same goes for orientation. I've been through all that. It's not easy!

(Geography teacher, *Maurice Carême*, June 2007)

When they appear to the teachers as the only guide for a choice that seems to be made at the expense of the pupil, strategies *explicitly* aimed at improving the school's position in the local field induce moral questioning in the minds of the institutional actors. The mismatch between the declared pretensions and the real cultural capital that the teachers perceive in their everyday work raises doubts in the class conferences. In the absence of a higher moral reason embodied in the culture of the school, the act of orientation is fraught with various logics which may contradict one another. This is why the institutional actors of schools where heterogeneous logics prevail ask themselves more questions about the future of a young person oriented towards the bottom of the school hierarchy.

G.A.:   And is it difficult to 'orientate'?

TEACHER: Yes and no. Making decisions for a young person isn't easy, these are responsibilities, decisions that he or she isn't in a position to take. Sometimes the parents aren't either. So it's a heavy responsibility! You start off wondering if you are making the right decision for the young person's future. Sometimes she can't decide for herself and you have to decide for her. It's true that we are professionals, but that doesn't mean it is necessarily the right decision. We often get it wrong … It has to be said, it's not just a question of orientation, you know, when we decide, the reputation of the school is also at stake.

(Maths teacher, *Jacques Prévert*, June 2007)

The schools that possess the highest incorporated cultural capital, i.e. a strong, coherent, legitimate institutional culture shared by the pupils and teachers, mobilizes the most implicit reproduction strategy, i.e. the one least subject to debate and therefore least contested. In the class conferences, symbolic affinities, the relations and modalities of distinction maintained on the basis of the social origin of the pupils and the image the teachers have of their school and the other schools in the school field combine in the teachers' judgement to constitute an 'incorporated' reproduction strategy (Bourdieu 1986). When they exist in 'incorporated' form, reproduction strategies operate spontaneously and largely unconsciously and are in any case barely objectivated. The reputation of the school goes without saying and is defined instinctively. When the incorporated part of cultural capital declines, the agents are led to objectivate orientation as a reproduction strategy. Objectivated reproduction strategies then appear as explicitly aiming to maintain or improve the position of the school in the local hierarchy – and sometimes at the expense of the pupil. Because they are in contradiction with a democratic moral order, because they do not enjoy the legitimacy of a strong, coherent school culture, because they are not backed by a position at the top of the hierarchy, these strategies give rise to moral doubts in the minds of teachers who experience their subjective power as objectively threatened by logics capable of harming the pupils.

Conclusion

In French-speaking sociology of education, under the impact of the social changes that have marked the educational system (massification, the influx of pupils with social origins different from those of the past), many authors have emphasized the uncertainties, the instability and the dynamics of co-construction that now affect teachers' judgement. They have moved away from Bourdieu's perspective. This text has aimed to show how useful it can be to pursue the analysis of the positional relations among institutions situated in the school field in order to understand the construction of teachers' judgement.

The school field is linked to the overall social space and to the field of power. It is not static. The dynamics of transformation in the field of power have repercussions on the frames of reference and preferred pedagogical styles and therefore on the positions of the different schools. The system of virtues and the principles of hierarchization that structure a culture specific to each institution in accordance with its position in the field are manifested in its activities and in the categories of teachers' understanding, their appreciation and perception of pupils. In the field of secondary education, the development of new values and pedagogical references (invisible pedagogy, managerial values, emphasis on skills) has an impact on the flows of populations towards schools and on their positions. When the positions change, the agents experience a mismatch between practices linked to the history of the school and those demanded by the new position occupied in the field. They objectivate more the logical orders that shape their practices. The contradictions, uncertainties and moral malaise affect their relation to their role, their convictions and their practices. These contexts are more marked by a moral plurality and generate uncertainties and ethical questioning in the teachers' minds. The approach through field theory thus not only enables one to interpret the continuities and stability of the judgement of school agents but also to bring to light the principle of the uncertainty and self-questioning of the agents about their practices, and the work of adjustment that they undertake.

Symbolic affinities, power relations and symbolic relations with pupils, and the image of the institution linked to its position in the field, shape the strategies of reproduction in class conferences. Field theory enables us to identify clearly the positions whose legitimacy facilitates the stabilization of the judgement of the school agents. If the teachers and other educational agents at the top of the hierarchy engage in the practice of academic orientation as if it were a vocation, even when it channels some young people to forms of education of which they personally do not approve, this is because they do so in accordance with the ethic implied by the ethos of their institution. In order for agents to reproduce the structure of the school field through their practices of academic and vocational orientation, this structure has to be understood as significant at their level. It is easier to understand the difficulty teachers have in engaging in the practice of orientation when the logics constituted by reasons linked to the market or those linked to the reputation of the school are not incorporated but objectivated and perceived by the teachers as purely strategic and lacking in concern for the pupil. In this case, the teachers improvise their decisions on the basis of the culture of their school and multiple logics. In this way, field theory has the potential of shedding light on the sociological foundations of teachers' judgment that desends on the positions and capitals of collective agents within the choold field.

Notes

1 To cite just a few: Pourtois *et al.* 1978; Marchand 1979; Zirotti 1980; Legrand *et al.* 1983; Mathey-Pierre 1984; Balazs and Faguer 1986; Terrail 2002.
2 *Les catégories du jugement professoral* (1975, in *Homo Academicus* (1988: 194–226 – 'The Categories of Professorial Judgement') and *The State Nobility* (1996) are the two texts in which teachers' judgement is at the centre of Bourdieu's analysis. There are also passages discussing teachers' evaluations in *Reproduction in Education, Society and Culture* (Bourdieu and Passeron 1977) and *The Inheritors* (Bourdieu and Passeron 1979).
3 It should nonetheless be noted that in the case of secondary education, schools transmit competence less directly linked to the field of power, if only because the aim of the teaching is to lead the pupils to higher education. In France, schools distinguish themselves from one another by the 'mission statements' (*projets d'établissement*) through which they attract a socially differentiated population (Devineau 1998). In the French Community of Belgium, schools are required to draw up a 'project' through which they can be situated in relation to one another, but comparisons are mainly based on informal criteria.
4 Secondary education in the French Community of Belgium is composed of three levels of two years each. At the first level, there is theoretically one track (*filière*), the 'general track'. From the second level, there are three different tracks: 'general', 'technical' and 'vocational'. The 'general' – more academic – track mainly consists in theoretical courses and leads to higher education. The 'technical' and 'vocational' tracks, and especially the latter, do not lead to higher education, but teach a trade through practical courses. Schools may offer all three tracks, but in general they either offer a mainly or totally general curriculum or offer the technical and vocational courses.
5 In French-speaking Belgium, as in France, the 'class conference' (*conseil de classe*) is the key moment for the evaluation of pupils: there the teachers come to decisions relating to academic 'orientation' (advance to the next class or cycle, assignment to a track) and the award of diplomas, certificates of successful completion, and failure. While teachers' judgement was essentially studied in class conferences,

observation was expanded to other contexts, for example academic orientation meetings. Finally, in addition to the orientation courses arising from school-specific initiatives, everyday interactions between teachers and the pupils they 'orientate' were closely observed. For a presentation of the fieldwork methodology see the introduction to André 2012.

6 The names have been changed.

7 If one refers to Delvaux and Joseph (2003), who described the local school hierarchy in the school district of Charleroi in terms of the 'average socio-economic level' and the 'average academic level' of the pupils of each school, the schools in our study occupy relatively close objective positions.

8 At the individual level as at the collective level, *symbolic capital* constitutes the capital of recognition an agent enjoys in a domain of activity. It gives him his legitimacy and his weight in the field and is therefore specific to the field. It did not seem necessary to specify its usage for a collective agent.

9 In this sense, one could identify different 'habitus' of different schools, as do some authors who apply Bourdieu's concept to whole schools and identify 'organizational habitus' (McDonough 1997) or 'institutional habitus' (Reay 1998). However, the diversity of profiles raises problems and the use of this term is liable to make the school appear as a 'reality transcending its members' (Atkinson 2011).

10 For example, the results provided by the CPMS agents from their tests and questionnaires support the decisions made by the teachers in the class conferences.

11 Not to mention the fact that some of them have an individual economic capital that limits their participation in the activities of the school.

References

André, G. 2012. *L'orientation scolaire. Héritages sociaux et jugements professoraux.* Paris: PUF.

Atkinson, W. 2011. 'From Sociological Fictions to Social Fictions: Some Bourdieusian Reflections on the Concepts of "Institutional Habitus" and "Family Habitus"'. *British Journal of Sociology of Education*, 32, 331–47.

Balazs, G. and Faguer, J.-P. 1986. 'Un conseil de classe très particulier'. *Actes de la recherche en sciences sociales*, 62–63.

Baluteau, F. 1993. *Le Conseil de classe: peut mieux faire!* Paris: Hachette.

Bernstein, B. 1977. *Class, Codes and Control. 3. Towards a Theory of Educational Transmissions.* London: Routledge.

Billemont, H. 2006. *L'écologie politique: une idéologie des classes moyennes.* Université d'Evry Val d'Essone, doctoral thesis, tel.archives-ouvertes.fr/docs/00/12/24/90/PDF/These-sociologie_sur_Ecologie-Politique.pdf.

Boltanski, L. and Chiapello, E. 1999. *Le nouvel esprit du capitalisme.* Paris: Gallimard.

Boltanski, L. and Thevenot, L. 1991. *La justification. Les économies de la grandeur.* Paris: Gallimard.

Bourdieu, P. 1986. 'The Forms of Capital'. In J. Richardson (ed.) *Handbook of Theory and Research for the Sociology of Education.* New York: Greenwood Press, 241–58.

——1988. *Homo Academicus.* Cambridge: Polity Press; Stanford, CA: Stanford University Press.

——1990. *In Other Words: Essays Toward a Reflective Sociology.* Stanford, CA: Stanford University Press.

——1996. *The State Nobility: Elite Schools in the Field of Power.* Cambridge: Polity; Stanford, CA: Stanford University Press.

Bourdieu, P. and de Saint Martin, M. 1975. 'Les catégories de l'entendement professoral'. *Actes de la recherche en sciences sociales*, 3, 68–93.

Bourdieu, P. and Passeron, J.-C. 1977. *Reproduction in Education, Society and Culture*. London: Sage Publications.

——1979. *The Inheritors: French Students and their Relation to Culture*. Chicago: University of Chicago Press.

Buisson-Fenet, H. 2005. 'Des professions et leurs doutes: procédures d'orientation et décisions de réorientation scolaire en fin de seconde'. *Sociétés contemporaines*, 59–60, 121–38.

Calicchio, V. and Mabilon-Bonfils, B. 2004. *Le conseil de classe est-il un lieu politique? Pour une analyse des rapports de pouvoirs dans l'institution scolaire*. Paris: L'Harmattan.

Delvaux, B. and Joseph, M. 2003. *Les Espaces d'interdépendance entre écoles: étude de cas en Belgique francophone* (research report). Cerisis-UCL.

Derouet, J.-L. 1987. 'Une sociologie des établissements scolaires: les difficultés de construction d'un nouvel objet scientifique'. *Revue française de pédagogie*, 78, 86–108.

——1988. 'Désaccords et arrangements dans les collèges (1981–86). Éléments pour une sociologie des établissements scolaires'. *Revue française de pédagogie*, 83, 5–22.

——1992. *École et justice. De l'égalité des chances aux compromis locaux?* Paris: Métailié.

——(ed.) 2000. *L'École dans plusieurs mondes*. Bruxelles: De Boeck.

Devineau, S. 1998. *Les projets d'établissement*. Paris: PUF.

Dubet, F. 2002. *Le déclin de l'institution*. Paris: Seuil.

Dutercq, Y. 1998. 'La résistible ascension de la cause des parents d'élèves en France'. In M. Hardy *et al.* (eds) *L'École et les changements sociaux*. Montréal: Logiques, 181–200.

——2000. 'Le sens de l'orientation. Les problèmes d'interprétation de nouvelles procédures d'orientation des élèves'. In J.-L. Derouet (ed.) *L'École dans plusieurs mondes*. Bruxelles: De Boeck, 56–76.

Friant, N. and Demeuse, M. 2011. 'Un modèle du prestige des options dans l'enseignement secondaire de transition en Communauté française de Belgique. *L'orientation scolaire et professionnelle*, 40/2, 183–200.

Legrand, M., Nizet, J. and van Haecht, A. 1983. *La psychologie dans l'école: éléments pour une analyse sociale des centres psycho-médico-sociaux en Belgique francophone*. Namur: Presses Universitaires de Namur.

Mangez, É. 2008. *Réformer les contenus d'enseignement: Une sociologie du curriculum*. Paris: PUF.

Marchand, F. 1979. *Evaluation des élèves et conseil de classe*. Paris: Epi.

Mathey-Pierre, C. 1984. 'La différence institutionnalisée, Pratique d'orientation d'établissement et origines sociales des élèves'. *Cahiers du Centre d'étude de l'emploi*, 26, 141–90.

McDonough, P. 1997. *Choosing Colleges: How Social Class and Schools Structure Opportunity*. Albany: State University of New York Press.

Pinçon, M. and Pinçon-Charlot, M. 1989. *Dans les beaux quartiers*. Paris: Seuil.

Pourtois, J.-P. *et al.* 1978. 'Le niveau d'expectation de l'examinateur est-il influencé par l'appartenance sociale de l'enfant?' *Revue française de pédagogie*, 44, 34–37.

Reay, D. 1998. '"Always Knowing" and "Never Being Sure": Familial and Institutional Habituses and Higher Education Choice'. *Journal of Education Policy*, 13, 519–29.

Rochex, J.-Y. 1994. *Normes et normativité en sociologie de l'éducation*. escol.univ-paris8.fr/IMG/pdf/rochexnorme.pdf.

Terrail, J.-P. 2002. *De l'inégalité scolaire.* Paris: La Dispute.

van Haecht, A. 2006. *L'École à l'épreuve de la sociologie. Questions à la sociologie de l'éducation.* Bruxelles: De Boeck.

van Zanten, A. 2009. *Choisir son école. Stratégies familiales et mediations locales.* Paris: Presses Universitaires de France.

Wagner, A.-C. 1998. *Les nouvelles élites de la mondialisation: une immigration dorée en France.* Paris: PUF.

Zirotti, J.-P. 1980. 'Le jugement professoral: un système de classement qui ne fait pas de difference'. *Langage et Société*, 14, 3–42.

5 The literary field between the State and the market[1]

Gisele Sapiro

Introduction

Contrary to the ideology of the uncreated creator, the concept of the 'literary field' forged by Pierre Bourdieu implies that literary activity does not escape the constraints governing the social world. However, unlike the Marxist theory of art as pure reflection of reality, the concept of field suggests that cultural universes have a specific logic of functioning and their own rules, which means that they enjoy a certain degree of autonomy (Bourdieu 1966, 1971, 1991, 1992). This autonomy has not existed in all times and places. It results from a double historical process: that by which literary activities freed themselves from different types of external constraints, related to its conditions of production, and that whereby, starting in the nineteenth century, intellectual activities were progressively differentiated. The historical and sociological studies that have been realized in line with Bourdieu's theoretical approach, as well as the development of the history of publishing, make it possible to attempt a provisional account of the types of constraints that literary activity has to face regarding its conditions of production.[2]

The situation of national literary fields depends on two main factors: the degree of economic liberalism and the degree of political liberalism. Historically, these two factors have been associated. On the one hand, ideological control during the *Ancien Régime* in France or in authoritarian regimes required strict market regulation and control of professional organization. On the other hand, claims to political liberalism (freedom of speech, freedom of association) have often accompanied or concealed the liberalization of economic exchange, from the French Revolution to the neoliberal policy in the second half of the twentieth century. It is thus possible to class national literary fields according to their relative degree of dependence upon the State or upon the market, while keeping in mind the distinction between these two factors. Furthermore, as we shall see, mainly with the French case, whereas the market has favoured the literary field's relative liberation from State control, the State can help it, nowadays, to preserve a certain degree of autonomy from the market. Although the most typical expression of this process of

'autonomization' is the emergence of a worldly literary field relatively autonomous from external constraints (Casanova 1999), the effects of different
political and economic configurations on literary activity should be taken into
account at both the national and international levels (Heilbron and Sapiro
2007; Sapiro 2010).

Ideological control and economic regulation

On the side of State control, we can place all authoritarian regimes in which
economic exchanges are strictly regulated and cultural products entirely controlled by an apparatus created for this purpose and/or by the institutional
centralization of the means of production and consecration of cultural productions. In these regimes, the State is an instrument of control put at the
service of an ideological system – e.g. religious, fascist, communist – with a
totalitarian ambition. Ideological demand determines the supply of cultural
goods. The more these systems succeed in monopolizing legitimate violence,
both physical (army and police forces, administrative power) and symbolic
(justice, education, media, and other means of propaganda and morals), the
more severe the control exerted on cultural production. I shall leave aside the
forms of physical violence and repression inflicted on intellectuals suspected of
dissidence, since they are not specific to this population.

Censorship and repression

The instruments of ideological control are well known. The degree of control
can be ranked on a scale, but it also depends on the extent to which these
instruments are employed in practice, and on the ways in which they are used.

Authorization to print is the most selective instrument of control, but also
the most costly. The system of control promulgated by the Catholic Church in
1564 required a double authorization, from the bishop and the inquisitor of
the diocese. As Claude Savart (1985: 298) puts it, 'even if we suppose that
such severe specifications could readily have been entirely applied without
difficulty, they were bound to become largely inoperative where they lacked
the support of the "secular arm"'. The absolute monarchy developed its own
system of control: authorization to print was delivered in the name of the
king. During the eighteenth century (see Chartier 2000; van Rees and Dorleijn 2001), the growth of the book market favoured the liberalization of
printed matter. This was due to the fact that, while the publishing regime had
not changed, the strict control of writing became more and more difficult to
assure. Conversely, in some cases, preliminary authorization could be reques-
ted by the publisher, for whom it would have been more costly to have a book
banned after publication. For example, in Italy, during the fascist regime,
although preliminary authorization was not compulsory in theory, publishers
preferred to ask for it (Milza and Berstein 1980).

Preliminary control before printing through censorship is based on the opposite principle – only litigious writings must be forbidden – but it requires an organization similar to that employed in the preliminary authorization model (a group of specialized and faithful agents in charge of this job) and its cost is high. Systems of authorization and censorship are often compounded with a third instrument: lists of banned books, modelled on the *Index* catalogue, the catalogue of prohibited books which the Catholic Church began to publish in 1564. Lists of banned books are established when a strict ideological system coexists with or succeeds a more liberal regime. This is the case when a change of regime occurs or in a situation of military occupation (as in France during the Second World War). It is also the case when the ideological system does not succeed in monopolizing the State apparatus.

As a consequence of the liberalization of the book market and the modernization process, and more specifically the secularization movement, which began with the French Revolution and led to the separation of Church and State in France in 1904, the Catholic Church lost control of book production during the nineteenth century and had to redefine its strategy. With the consolidation of the Roman pontifical power, the application of the *Index* became much more severe from 1850 on, provoking in France an acute debate between Gallicans and Ultramontanists (Savart 1985: 252–313). The following step was the promulgation in 1864 of the *Syllabus*, which mentioned in its list of the 80 modern errors the idea that every truth is good to say and the principle of freedom of expression. From the 1880s onward, as the republican regime developed a laicized patriotic moral code opposed to religious morals, the religious stance ceased to be supported by the State and protected by the law. The Catholic Church lost its power of excommunication after its separation from the State in 1904, although from time to time it condemned authors such as André Gide. It thereafter developed a new system of control of cultural production, which combined lists of banned books with the *imprimatur*, a mark appended to authorized books at the author's request (the *imprimatur* was compulsory for all books published by clergymen). Specific committees called 'vigilance councils' were entitled to authorize or proscribe books for the clergymen and Catholic laymen lectorate (Serry 2004).

By laying down the principle of freedom of publishing, the liberal regimes radically differentiated themselves from the previous ones. This freedom was promulgated in laws that simultaneously imposed restrictions on this freedom in certain cases. On the basis of these restrictions – which are either political (offence to State security, incitement to crime), or moral (offence to high morals and religion) – books could be banned after publication. We thus moved from a preventive to a repressive system of publishing (Dury 1997), although, as we have seen, both are usually combined in the first case. This repressive liberal system has prevailed in France since 1819 for the book market and since 1830 for the press (nevertheless, preliminary authorization was imposed upon political periodicals during the Second Empire), while censorship was maintained for the theatre until 1905. Yet, the degree of liberalism varied with the political regimes and the laws were more or less strictly applied at different historical stages. Despite the liberalization introduced by the Third Republic, namely the 1881 law abolishing censorship, 14 writers were tried between 1880 and 1910, and 174 trials for 'pornography' took place between 1910 and 1914, in application of the law against offence to morality, which was maintained by the liberal law of 1881 (Leclerc 1991; Mollier 1997: 78; Sapiro 2011). In wartime (1914–18, 1939–40), the democratic regime imposed a system of preliminary censorship. However, this type of military censorship in a situation of national crisis should be distinguished from the previous one because of its exceptional character. The four years of the Vichy Regime must be considered separately, because of this regime's proximity to the authoritarian category with regards to the control of printed matter and of cultural production in general (see Fouché 1987; Thalmann 1991; Loiseaux 1995).

The professional organization as an instrument of ideological control

Prevention, repression and economic measures (such as value-added tax),[3] are not the only means by which authoritarian regimes exert control on cultural production. Apart from the system of direct gratification (temporal and symbolic) which sought to reward the intellectuals most devoted to the regime (see Karabel 1996), the major instruments of control are centralization of the means of production, unification of the profession, surveillance of professional institutions, and ideological supervision. As they ensure a certain homogeneity of professional recruitment, these means help to limit heretical behaviours or to track them down more easily. This is especially true of literary activity, access to which is not regulated by organized training or a formal title (such as a diploma), as opposed to the 'professions' (*professions libérales* in French). Illiberal regimes have all imposed a kind of professionalization and bureaucratization on the activity of the writer, which have systematically helped to improve the ideological control of intellectual production. This observation contradicts the association that is usually made in the sociology of professions between professionalization and autonomization.

In Italy, a Fascist National Institute of Culture was founded in 1925, which edited four series of books and a magazine, and opened centres in more than 150 provincial towns. Yet this apparatus was not able to replace the old academic system, which was too prestigious to be abolished. This is why in 1926, Mussolini created the Academy of Italy, which was inaugurated in 1929. The Academy was divided into four classes of academicians: physical sciences, moral sciences, letters, and arts (Milza and Berstein 1980: 205–20). In a similar way, the Third Reich created a *Reichschriftumskammer* (Literature Chamber of the Reich), which delivered a card allowing members to publish in the authorized magazines. The Vichy Regime imposed a system of censorship for the press, theatre and book publishing. A commission for the distribution of paper, created in 1942, was in charge of the censorship of books (see Fouché 1987, vol. 2: 13–18). The Vichy Regime also developed a corporatist project partly imitating the fascist regimes or Salazar's Catholic authoritarian regime, which was defined in the *Charte du travail*. In this perspective, every intellectual or liberal profession had to found its own *ordre*. For example, an *ordre des médecins* was created in 1940, but it was reorganized in 1942 under a more liberal form (Muel-Dreyfus 1996: 301–11). However, the programmes of this corporatist project failed in the case of journalists (Delporte 1998: chap. 10), artists (Bertrand-Dorléac 1990, 1993: 155–68), and writers (Sapiro 2004).

It was probably the communist regimes that deployed the greatest efforts in order to organize the intellectual professions and to exert an ideological control on literary production. The unions of writers, professional associations modelled on trade unions, were in fact centralized agencies controlling the means of publishing and the instruments of consecration (specialized journals, prizes, etc.). Formally, they were not affiliated with the communist party, but the communists, who represented the most important group among their members, exerted a close ideological control, and their formal independence was highly illusory (on the Soviet Writers' Union, see Garrard and Garrard 1990; on the Romanian one, Dragomir 2008).

The regime wanted not only to control but also to orientate more directly cultural production. 'Socialist realism', defined in 1934 by Andrei Zhdanov as a 'method of creation', was imposed as a critical category as well as an exclusively authorized method in the USSR (Robin 1986; Aucouturier 1998). At the end of the 1930s, several waves of repression 'purged' the intelligentsia. After the war, in what has been called the Zhdanov period, beginning in 1946, the control became more severe and 'socialist realism' was imposed on all the arts (literature, art and music) in a move against Western influences and 'bourgeois' literature. Condemning individualism, pessimism, subjectivism, decadence and eroticism in the name of the education of youth, Zhdanov opposed 'socialist realism' both to formalism and to naturalism. While the former was an expression of art for art's sake and of modernism, naturalism reduced realism to the simple photography of reality. On the contrary, 'socialist realism' had to take a moral stance in the realistic description of reality. A work of art had to be classical and realistic in its form, whereas its content should embody 'revolutionary romanticism'. Literature had to perform a didactic task: it had to promote 'good feelings' and 'the Soviet man's virtues', while showing people 'what they must not be' (Zhdanov 1950).

The Soviet Union imposed this model of organization and of orientation of cultural production on all Eastern European countries. The creation of a school of writers in Romania in the beginning of the 1950s (Dragomir 2003) illustrates both the will to develop a corporative organization of the profession and the policy of ideological control and training.

Thwarting strategies and 'field effects'

In all authoritarian regimes, cultural producers develop strategies in order to escape the political constraints. These strategies of resistance, which prevent the unification of the professional group (*corps professionnel*), can be described in Pierre Bourdieu's (1985) terms as 'field effects'. Contrary to the attempts to unify the 'corporation' (*corps*) and to increase professional homogeneity, the logic of the field opposes the dominant agents, who hold the monopoly of the means of formal consecration, and the dominated, who resist this system. However, the autonomy of this field remains relatively weak, since the political struggle determines the antagonism between the 'heretical' dissidents and the 'orthodox' dominant agents (i.e. those who submit to the dominant ideology).

Three main strategies of thwarting can be identified: thwarting censorship in legal publications or in places like theatres by using a metaphorical code, allegory, or allusion; publishing abroad; and illegal or clandestine publishing.

Inspired by an idea borrowed from Bertolt Brecht, who theorized the use of ruse as a means of revealing truth in the midst of the Nazi regime's generalized lie, the use of coded language, a technique called 'literary contraband', was developed by the communist writer Aragon during the 1939 war, when the Communist Party was outlawed in France, and during the Vichy Regime, as a mode of resistance to the German occupation and to the new regime. Poetry was the privileged genre of this 'literary contraband'. The code was provided by a metaphorical use of French history in order to speak about the present, allegories of the situation, and allusions to it. Thanks to the complicity of some censors, 'literary contraband' spread through small literary magazines, until it became too dangerous and was abandoned in favour of underground activity (Sapiro 1999: 423–66). This technique was widespread in theatres during the communist regime. Actors used intonation to draw the attention of the public to the political message that the text conveyed. 'Literary contraband' has also been used, in reference to Brecht and Aragon, by communist authors in France, like Pierre Courtade or the playwright Antoine Vitez, in order to thwart the constraints the Communist Party imposed on them (Lambert and Matonti 2001; Matonti 2003).

Some intellectuals in authoritarian regimes chose or were obliged to emigrate and have continued their activities abroad. However, cultural products can also be 'exiled'. During the German Occupation in France, books and literary reviews by writers who were at odds with the Vichy Regime were published in Algeria and Switzerland. The review *Fontaine* and the publisher Edmond Charlot (Albert Camus's first publisher) were based in Algeria. In Switzerland, several reviews like Albert Béguin's *Cahiers du Rhône*, and publishing houses like Éditions de La Baconnière and Éditions des Trois Collines, edited dissident poets like Aragon or Paul Éluard. Manuscripts circulated clandestinely from France to these places, as did books or journals, once they were published. Similar channels have been identified for Eastern European authors during the communist regime: writers who had emigrated founded publishing houses in countries like Germany or France and published original works by dissident authors (see Popa 2002, 2010).

The final strategy of resistance is illegal publishing. In France, during the Occupation, a real underground literary field was organized. A publishing house was created by two authors, Pierre de Lescure and Vercors, which published 24 booklets from 1942 to 1944, printing between 500 and 1,500 copies of each (see Simonin 1994). The manuscripts were provided by an illegal organization, the National Committee of Writers (Comité national des écrivains), which assembled around 50 writers at the end of the Occupation period (see Sapiro 1999: chap. 7). The National Committee of Writers also published a clandestine literary journal, *Les Lettres françaises*, which printed around 3,000–4,000 copies in 1943 and 12,000 in 1944. In this journal, anonymous articles denounced the structures of intellectual collaboration with the Nazis and the cultural conditions of production, while reviews were devoted to the clandestine books published by the Éditions de Minuit. A similar organization existed in the communist countries of Eastern Europe, which produced underground publications entitled *samizdat*. First created in the USSR, they developed in the 1970s, most notably in Czechoslovakia, where three banned authors, Ludvik Vaculik, Vaclav Havel and Jan Vladislav, founded the three main *samizdat* publishing houses: Edice Petlice, Edice Expedice and Edice Kvart (Popa 2002: 61).

Writing practices and professional deontology

The systematized control of printed texts conditions writing practices. Without pretending to give an exhaustive account, I will suggest some hypotheses for further research. Writers who submit to the dominant ideology tend to adopt classical forms in poetry and in prose: realistic novels, 'revolutionary romanticism', regionalism (in Vichy France), etc. Their products are likely to bear features of the 'ideological novel', such as a clear message, typical characters, clear-cut oppositions and monologism (see Suleiman 1983; Robin 1986). Literary criticism and essays with a didactic orientation are the dominant agents' preferred non-fiction genres.

This does not result, of course, from the intrinsic properties of genres, but from their historical evolution and their position in the genre hierarchy relative to the changes in both the external constraints on literature and the inner struggles in the literary field. For example, the novel was a despised genre till the middle of the nineteenth century and became dominant with the development of the book market, whereas poetry, which had, along with theatre, been the most praised genre by the upper social classes, was marginalized and became a hermetic genre practised in the most autonomous and closed segment of the literary field, which set itself against the values of the market. It was the genre most used for experimenting with new artistic trends and modernity.

Poetry and theatre, which were at that time more hermetic and codified genres than the novel, in which metaphor and allegory are commonplace, are an excellent means of conveying 'literary contraband', as already seen. Thus the privileged genres of clandestine writings during the twentieth century were poetry, allegory, the realistic novel, meditation, the lampoon and testimony. Apart from the fact that its short form is more suited to the conditions of underground circulation, poetry is a genre in which emotion and indignation in the face of horror and injustice can be expressed indirectly. It can also convey a subversive message. As Paul Éluard puts it in his anonymous preface to the clandestine poetry volume *L'Honneur des poètes*: 'Une fois de plus, la poésie mise au défi se regroupe, retrouve un sens précis à sa violence latente, crie, accuse, espère.'[4] Allegory – namely in the form of the novella – is an indirect but less expressive genre, which symbolically represents the situation in a fictional plot. A famous example is Vercors's *Le Silence de la mer* (*The Silence of the Sea*), the first novel published by the underground Éditions de Minuit in 1942, which symbolizes the Occupation through the refusal of a young woman to speak with the German soldier who settles in the house where she lives with her uncle, although she becomes more and more susceptible to his charms (he represents the 'good' German, in love with French culture). Allegory was also chosen by Camus in order to represent the period of the Occupation in *La Peste* (although it was published in 1947, after the liberation, he began to write it during this period). The realistic novel seems to have been less used in clandestine publications. This is probably for different reasons, namely its length (Minuit published only parts of André Chamson's *Le Puits des miracles* for this reason) and the features of the genre, such as individualism, the complexity of the characters, and ambiguity. The political representation of the situation in order to convey a political message requires, indeed, a certain degree of generalization (for example, Chamson's characters are archetypes) and clear-cut oppositions. Yet, these requirements threaten to routinize its effect and to reduce it to propaganda, with stereotyped characters and unambiguous oppositions ('monologism'). This kind of political use of literature was precisely what dissidents in all authoritarian countries denounced in the name of the field's autonomy. Meditation is a genre allowing self-examination in a situation of loss of references; it can retrace the path from doubt and despair to hope, as in Francois Mauriac's *Cahier noir* (1944), where self-examination combines with indignation and denunciation, as we see in the lampoon as well (Angenot 1982). Finally, although it is not a specific literary genre, testimony about the legally inexpressible socio-political reality has proven the best means of telling the truth when information is entirely controlled by propaganda. This purpose also justifies the risks implied by illegal publishing activities. Aragon, for instance, gave form to the testimonies about the Chateaubriant hostages who were executed in 1941 in a piece called 'Le témoin des Martyrs', which was copied and passed on from one person to another. During the Algerian war of independence, Minuit published direct testimonies about torture in a series called 'Documents', which were banned and seized (see Simonin 1996). A proscribed author like the Romanian Paul Goma built his entire *oeuvre* on the testimonies he collected about the communist regime's prisons.

The system of control exerted on literary production also partly determines the deontology of the profession of writer. For instance, in face of different forms of censorship or repression, telling the truth has become a literary value as important as the defence of beauty, disinterestedness and sincerity. The principle of art for art's sake was partially devised in defence of the writers charged with offence to morality. Against the conception of public morality as defined by the public prosecutor during the trials, the theory of art for art's sake (Cassagne 1997) developed a professional deontology, based on the writer's probity, his sincerity, and his concern with 'truth' when he paints or describes reality (Sapiro 2011).

In return, this deontology formed the basis of the political commitment of writers willing to defend literary autonomy, from Victor Hugo to Émile Zola, and to the writers of the Resistance, including Sartre: the values they championed in their political mobilization were those professional values, freedom of speech and truth, which they universalized. For instance, the 'intellectuals' headed by Émile Zola who campaigned for the revision of Captain Dreyfus's trial advocated the establishment of truth in the judicial investigation, whereas their opponents of the conservative camp sought to restrict the quest for truth on behalf of '*Raison d'État*', that is, in order to safeguard social order and the army's prestige, which are extra-intellectual values (see Charle 1990).

In this sense, the struggle against the political control of cultural production has contributed to the foundation of the principle on which the relative autonomy of the literary field rests, even though, as we have seen, in authoritarian regimes the defence of autonomy is associated with a political struggle to which it is subordinated.

The law of the market

In contrast with a market determined by a strict ideological control of supply, economic liberalism has imposed the idea of a market governed by its own rules, those of free competition arbitrated by consumers. Production has to adjust to the demand that it has, in fact, helped to create, since it is even less the case for the market of symbolic goods than elsewhere that demand pre-exists supply. However, the demand, or the presumed expectations of the public, can be estimated only on the basis of the sales of previous products. Therefore, the risk of standardization is inherent in the logic of the market, and in conflict with the expectation of innovation, which stems from the unique and inimitable character of the product.

Although there is no example corresponding to the idealized view of the liberal market, the book market in the United States and in the United Kingdom today is probably the closest to the model, with the intervention of the State being minimal, and the expensive production of worldwide best-sellers in standardized genres like thrillers. This market, which is more and more concentrated around big conglomerates, is ruled by literary agents who are mainly interested in economic profit (Thompson 2010). It is also expressed in the legislation on copyright, which is based on a conception of the work of art ('*oeuvre*') as a good produced by both its author and its publisher, and as beholden to economic law: the author can transfer his right to the publisher, unlike in the French legislation on the *droit d'auteur*, in which the moral right (the right to divulge, the right to respect, the right to repent) is inalienable.

Short-term profit vs. long-term investment

Historically, the development of the book market helped literary activity to free itself from the supervision of the State. During the *Ancien Régime* in France, to earn a living by producing literature was considered indecent. However, the unprecedented expansion of the book market during the eighteenth century opened up new possibilities. Suddenly, the population of writers making a living from their writing, whom the writers bribed by the State and holding official functions as well as seats at the prestigious Académie française stigmatized as 'the riff-raff of literature' ('*canaille écrivante*'; Darnton 1971: 95; Darnton 1983), increased. In the nineteenth century, thanks to the economic and political liberalization of the press, the book market developed quickly, as the mode of production became industrial. This configuration gave birth to the view of the writer as an 'entrepreneur', best represented by Balzac. He was one of the founders, in 1838, of the Société des gens de lettres, the first professional society of writers,[5] which was to be a model for men of letters in other countries. Facing the enlightened amateurism of the elite, the writers became more professional. This professionalization process can be described as market-driven, in contradistinction to the State-controlled professionalization described above. However, the development of what Sainte-Beuve called '*littérature industrielle*' ('industrial literature') and the figure of the 'mercenary writer', ready to sell his pen for any price, provoked a reaction on the part of the men of letters concerned with professional deontology. Contrary to the law of the market and to the sanction of the large public (measured according to sales) that prevailed at the pole of large-scale production, a pole of small-scale production emerged, promoting the judgement of peers as opposed to the taste of the profane public (Bourdieu 1971, 1983, 1992). Thus, in the second half of the nineteenth century, the French literary field achieved the principal phase of its autonomization. Heavily favoured by the liberalization of the press under the Third Republic, the autonomization process was exemplarily manifested in the growth in the number of literary magazines and reviews, which constituted privileged spaces for dialogue between peers, secure from economic and political constraints. It was not long before the judgement of peers and of literary experts (critics) was recognized by both of the authorities that determine literary activity: the market and the State.

The industrialization of the book market, the liberalization of printed matter and the growth in the number of readers as a result of the generalization of school attendance increased the need for intermediaries between the supply and the public. This need was first defined by the Catholic Church and Catholic and conservative writers who worried about the alleged harmful effects of 'bad books' – namely, on the youth, on women and on the 'people' (Chartier and Hébrard 2000; Sapiro 2011). This anxiety also existed in left-wing movements, both socialist and communist, according to which literature had to contribute to the education of the masses. Lacking the monopoly of the means of production, both these trends developed instruments such as specialized publishing houses, series and networks of distribution in order to select praiseworthy books and guide the public's choices.

However, the need for intermediaries soon appeared as a necessity inherent in the logic of a market in a perpetual state of overproduction. For economists of culture (Cave 2000) as for Bourdieu (1977), the market of symbolic goods is characterized by a high degree of economic uncertainty, which induces permanent risk for agents operating in its sphere. Publishers manage this risk by overproduction and by attempts to control the distribution. As the economist Françoise Benhamou explains, 'the consumer is all the more dependent on the judgement of the critics and on the impact of book launches on the media that his means of acquiring information are limited, that the number of products is high, and that the goods are singular, a fact that increases the cost of information' (Benhamou 2002: 67, my translation).

The success of literary prizes and the way in which this success has been exploited by the publishers is a good example of this need for intermediaries (for an economic approach, see English 2008). Beginning in the 1920s, the winner of the Goncourt Prize (founded in 1903) could have close to 100,000 copies of his book printed. This anticipated success has consequences for the choices of the jury, which adjusts more or less to what it perceives as the demand of the general public as reflected by the press (Sapiro 1999: chap. 5). The publishers, on their part, have developed more and more sophisticated and costly strategies of launching books (with costs as high as the expected return on investment), along with means of controlling the intermediaries: publicity in the media,[6] close relations with the critics and the members of literary juries, representation of their houses in the juries, etc. (see Lane 1998). The role of professional literary critics has also increased over time, although it does not suffice to determine the success of a book.

Publishers tend indeed to dissociate what they call the success of esteem from a public success. This division corresponds to what Pierre Bourdieu (1977, 1999) has identified as two distinct kinds of strategies in the publishing world: the logic of short-term profit, staked on quick sales and ephemeral success, and the logic of long-term investment, for the constitution of a stock of books likely to become 'classics'. In continuity with the sociologist's distinction, economists distinguish the segments of the market characterized by a high degree of innovation and those that are standardized. It is possible, as suggested by Bourdieu (1977, 1999), to class publishers between these two poles: Robert Laffont, who organized publicity campaigns unprecedented in France for his series of 'best-sellers' (which number about 200 titles, most of them translated from the US market), is typical of the commercial pole, while Minuit, the publisher of Beckett and of the authors of the *Nouveau Roman*, represents the innovative pole of restricted production (see also Simonin 1998). Apart from small publishers like Minuit, this duality exists in most cases within the publishing houses, whether independent or affiliated with a group, which can be classed according to the proportional weight of innovation as compared to standard production or reproduction (exploiting the backlist). This is notably the case for the major literary houses, Gallimard and Le Seuil, which share the literary prizes at the end of the year while keeping a place in certain series for more difficult works destined for a restricted public. In that respect, some independent houses like Flammarion or Albin Michel are much closer to Laffont.

In fact, the profits from ephemeral successful products often finance more risky enterprises – that is, they redeem the manufacturing expenses of the product. Most publishers and editors, including those working in houses that are affiliated with large conglomerates, express the need to balance quick sales and long-term investment for the development of the stock. This is all the more important considering that the exploitation of the backlist can in return help in managing situations of tight financial flows, as the vice-president of an old French publishing house now affiliated with a group explains:

> You see, the more intense the financial flows, the economic pressure, the more, to refer to what I called tradition before, the beautiful tradition of the profession, you have to impose the long term, that is to impose distance, to see far ahead. That is, to try and see far away. Because you will resist the assaults of the financial flows if you are able to impose a real long-term, that is a living list, not a fictive list, not an illusory list, but a backlist, that is, a book which will last after its first exploitation to sell over 100 copies a year. This is the backlist, it is not the beautiful book, or the good book, unfortunately. But often, the good book or the beautiful book is a book which, indeed, after the first year of exploitation, will sell 100 copies a year. The book of the backlist happens to be a reference book. But it is not because it is a reference book in your mind that it will be sold like a reference book. And if you have lots of reference books that don't score as 'novelties' or 'summer books' on the market, so that they generate losses, and that in addition are not sold in the long term, then you have lost on all sides. And these are the books that must be hunted.

In other words, the good backlist books are those that really generate funds. And this is not easy to foresee. This is the literary editor's work, and it is ours in our favourite domain [non-fiction].

(Interview, 7 June 2002, my translation)

This logic can be observed in the policy of literary translation (Sapiro 2008, 2010). The risk of publishing a new author in translation is lower than in the original language, owing to the fact that in general, the titles proposed for translation have already passed the gate of publication and had a certain success, be it in critical esteem or in sales, in the authors' own countries and, sometimes, elsewhere. However, the cost of the translation increases this risk considerably. Most series of foreign literature of quality generate losses – apart from American and British authors, whom only large publishers can afford to publish. The investments are seldom recovered in the first exploitation: sales stagnate around 1,500–2,000 copies, whereas 3,000 are needed to redeem the translation and manufacturing expenses. This is why publishers strictly limit the number of translations in a year and often ask for institutional or State support (see below). These publications at loss are compensated for by more commercial translations or by the exploitation of the backlist. The groups have accelerated the chase after great best-sellers which require expensive advances on fees (Thompson 2010). On the other hand, publishers affiliated to a group 'have at their disposal a financial groundwork which allows them to bear some failures or losses over several years, and hence to pursue long-term strategies', as Claudie Schalke and Markus Gerlach (1999) explain in relation to the German case, though these strategies are confronted with the logic of rationalization and profit which prevail in these groups.

The value of the proper name

Conversely, in this dual economy, the balance between the short-term cycle and the long-term cycle is a result of the long-term process of constituting a backlist, which is necessary to the durability of the company, both at the economic level – in order to manage tense financial flows (see the quotation of the interview above) – and at the symbolic level, that is, to ensure the prestige associated with the name of the firm. The fact that the symbolic capital accumulated becomes, in the long term, a source of economic profit is evidence of the social recognition that the principle of aesthetic quality claimed by the pole of small-scale production has acquired.

Given the degree of uncertainty that governs the innovative pole of publishing and the singularity of the goods supplied, the condition of survival for an author is to 'achieve a name'. Like the label in haute couture, the proper name is the sign of the symbolic capital accumulated (Bourdieu 1984). This principle is also operative in editors' strategies: they want to establish authors rather than isolated titles.[7] A writer's *oeuvre* is built along with the author's reputation, as explained by the editor of foreign literature at Gallimard, the most prestigious big literary publisher in France:

> In a general way, I say to myself that, in my profession as an editor, I shouldn't work in an ivory tower, I do want to reach readers. That is one point. But the other point is as important, and a balance has to be found between these two, it is our exactingness for quality. We want texts which harbor a real literary expression, coherent, autonomous, original, strong, a real literary quality. And then we can say two things. We stop when there is no more quality. And we continue when quality is present but not the sales. This is really the policy that my publishing house observes in all domains, and I think that there are still publishers in France that function like that, even within the big groups.[8] Maybe they have more difficulties than we do sometimes, but there are some who still do it very well. But at Gallimard, this is really the prevailing rule. We want to take the time to build an *oeuvre* and, slowly, to find the public for this *oeuvre* in France. And, for the authors that don't sell very well, I have time ahead. I can persuade Antoine Gallimard, saying: I really believe in it, maybe we'll never have a very large public but we will have a public, and book after book, we have to build his [or her] reputation, his [or her] renown in France.
>
> (Interview with Jean Mattern, 14 May 2002; quoted in Sapiro 2002, my translation)

The proper name is also the name of the publishing house, which, in many cases, is the family name of its founders and owners, like Gallimard or Flammarion. The name of 'Gallimard' as well as that of 'Minuit' function as a label of quality. It is a mark that orientates the reader's choice, the value of which is, therefore, inestimable. Some studies have been concerned with the publishers strategies of accumulation of symbolic capital. Founded in 1909, Gallimard has benefited from a transfer of the symbolic capital accumulated by André Gide and Jean Schlumberger's prestigious *La Nouvelle Revue française*, after which the publishing house was first named (Éditions de la Nouvelle Revue française), before taking the name of its manager and owner (Assouline 1984; for the deployment of this strategy in the interwar period, see also Boschetti 1990). On the contrary, when the founders of the firm are endowed with a slight cultural and social capital, translation can be a strategy of accumulation of literary capital (Serry 2002). Les Éditions de Minuit, the publishing house born in the Resistance during the German occupation, earned its position as an innovative literary house in the 1950s by reconverting the subversive legacy of the underground period to a double literary and political avant-garde strategy during the Algerian war (Simonin 1994, 1996).

In the 1980s, the value of Gallimard's business was estimated 2 billion francs, which was 90 times its turnover. However, according to Bernard

Guillou and Laurent Maruani (1989: 222), if Gallimard were to be launched today, it would cost much more than this. From an economic standpoint, the name is considered a rare resource. This explains the strategy of acquisition that the big groups deploy in the domain of publishing: external growth, buying existing houses, is much less costly and risky than internal growth, that is, creating new publishing imprints (see Guillou and Maruani 1989; Reynaud 1999; Schalke and Gerlach 1999). However, as Benedicte Reynaud (1999) explains, only the physical capital can be surrendered to an outsider, since the social capital and the symbolic capital are linked to those who possess the proper name, and can be transmitted only within the family. In a similar way, in order to ensure good management of the symbolic capital, it is, in general, necessary to keep the editors and the exterior signs such as the cover, the dummy, etc.

Observers generally agree on the fact that small literary publishing houses are more qualified to play the role of 'discoverer', which is necessary in order to innovate in the domain of books of quality – all the more since the large and medium-sized publishers, confronted with the competition of the conglomerates, tend to abandon this function, preferring to confine themselves to reliable values and to 'asset management at the expense of innovation' (Bourdieu 1999: 4; English transl. 2008: 124). Although their number has grown as a result of both the merging process in the book industry, which has made space for market 'niches', and new technologies, which facilitate access to publishing, these small publishers have to face material difficulties multiplied by the concentration occurring in the book production and distribution sectors (Schiffrin 1999). In the case of large and medium-sized publishing houses, the tendency to delegate the selection and the representation of authors to specialized agents – scouts attached to the house or independent literary agents – results from this double requirement to limit the risks and to build the name as a label of quality.

Criticism and cultural journalism as intermediaries

In the process of constructing the name as a label of quality, the critics and press editors play a major role: 'For decades, the fiction editor of *The New Yorker* has controlled the velvet rope at the gateway to literary stardom, welcoming a fortunate few into the prestigious inner circle of short story writers and a career of lucrative book contracts.'[9]

Criticism must be divided between a pole of large-scale circulation, which ratifies the success of a book in the media and in sales (journals with a large circulation, popular weeklies, women's magazines, etc.), and a pole of small-scale circulation, where the aesthetical judgement and a certain exactingness prevail (intellectual daily journals, cultural weeklies, literary magazines, literary broadcasts on public radio stations like France-Culture, etc.). However, the margin of autonomy at the pole of small-scale circulation tends to diminish because of harsh competition with the commercial pole, the relations of dependency that result from the publicity publishers pay for in the written press, and the integration of media and publishers into large conglomerates (the radio station Europe 1 belongs to the Lagardère group, for instance). In the last two cases, it is the magical effect of consecration itself that is being threatened: the charismatic effect of consecration is, indeed, attributable to the fact that the consecrator's selection as well as his judgement are 'disinterested' (Bourdieu 1977). The channel of recognition is more likely to produce its full effect if the person consecrated cannot be suspected of any connivance with the consecrator (kinship, hierarchical dependency, financial dependency, etc.), both at the stage of publication as well as at that of critical judgement.

More than traditional criticism (though the borders tend to disappear), it is cultural journalism, namely on television, that has become a major inter-mediary between the public and the market. In this respect, the literary pro-gramme *Apostrophes* with Bernard Pivot played an unequalled role from 1975 to 1990. An invitation to Pivot's programme represented consecration with effects comparable or even superior to those of winning one of the literary prizes. For example, when Pivot invited Marguerite Duras in 1984 to talk about her novel *L'Amant* (The Lover), almost 100,000 copies of the book had already been sold. After the broadcast, which was entirely devoted to her, sales jumped to 300,000 copies even before she won the Goncourt Prize. It was the first time an author of the *Nouveau Roman*, published by Minuit, had received the award. The prize amplified the enormous success of the book: with more than 700,000 copies sold in a few months, the novel was translated into 26 languages and became a worldwide best-seller.

Gathering between 2 and 5 million viewers every Friday night on the public channel Antenne 2, *Apostrophes* became an 'institution'. Born at a time when criticism was increasingly dominated by academics, Pivot's broadcast legiti-mated 'a non-academic ... non-pedagogical, more convivial, spontaneous and popular way of talking with writers and intellectuals and of speaking about books' (Pivot 2001: 31, my translation). Its presenter, who describes himself as a cultural journalist (a 'columnist') rather than a critic, praises the merits and the charm of an eclecticism that allows him to reach the most diversified public. In a subtle mixture that seldom infringed upon the limits of good taste, he mingled legitimate culture and popular culture, stars and debut authors, breaking the routine with a controversial debate between politically or intellectually opposite trends or between people who would have no chance to speak with each other elsewhere (like the academic linguist Claude Hagège and the comic Raymond Devos). This eclectic formula, which must be con-sidered in light of the State policy of democratization of culture underway at the same time (see below), met with great success among the newly cultivated public born of the sudden expansion of secondary and higher education in the 1960s and the growth of the intellectual and semi-intellectual professions during this period (primary and secondary school teachers, assistants and '*maîtres assis-tants*' at the universities, librarians, etc.).[10] The competition of private chan-nels, which reduced the broadcast's audience, eventually overcame the 'institution', a feat Pivot's rival, Patrick Poivre d'Arvor, did not succeed in achieving via his own programme, *Ex-libris* on France's first private channel (TF1), despite his best efforts.

It is significant that when the first channel was privatized, Gallimard and Le Seuil took a share in the capital, hoping to have influence over the programming devoted to books on the new channel, but as they probably understood how slight their proportional weight was, they retracted soon thereafter. This episode is a sign of the increased dependence of the modes of consecration on the media. It is this dependence that leads publishers to borrow more and more techniques of promotion from the star system (Benhamou 2002), where the focus is on the person rather than on his or her *oeuvre* – a focus well adapted to the small amount of space and time devoted to culture in the written or audiovisual media.

The constraints imposed by the economic laws of the market have contributed to modify the literary landscape. While standardized literary genres like mysteries, thrillers and romance flourish, poetry and theatre, which have been threatened by the domination of the novel since the end of the nineteenth century, have almost disappeared. They exist only in the margin of the market, thanks to subventions allocated by the State.

Cultural policy

The policies of control and repression against which the fields of cultural production affirmed their autonomy contributed to forge the representation of antagonism between the arts and the State (Dubois 1999: 24–38). Yet, while the market helped literary activity to free itself from the supervision of the State, the State can also become an instrument for saving the rights and freedom of creation from the merciless sanction of the market and the risks of being exploited that cultural producers endure. Copyright law (*droit d'auteur*) and policies aimed at helping artistic creation, illustrate this principle. They both mark a step in the process of the writer's recognition by the State, which has been a condition for the literary field's autonomization since the French Academy acquired official status in the seventeenth century (Viala 1985).

Copyright law: the author's right

As described by Foucault (1969), while the State first imposed the 'author function' in order to control the circulation of discourse, writers deployed it against the State in their struggle for the recognition of their moral right and of literary property as an individual's property, a struggle which culminated in 1777 with the recognition in France, by a royal decree, of literary works as the fruit of the author's own labour and the author's right to gain an income from them. The principle of intellectual property was born of the claims of the powerful community of booksellers and printers to have their privilege to print, which the king had granted them as a grace, recognized as a right.

Although they sought to reinforce their monopoly, the decree, which aimed at protecting the kingdom's market from foreign counterfeiting, contested this monopoly in recognizing the author's right to print and sell his books. Though it recognized the grace as founded in justice, the decree refused to transform it into a right: whereas the author, who was at last recognized, and his heirs, could enjoy the privilege forever (except if it was sold to a third party), the booksellers benefited from the grace only during the author's lifetime.

The French Revolution confirmed the principle of literary property but limited it to ten years after the author's death (the 1793 Lakanal law). It was a compromise between the conception of property as a natural right and the notion of 'public domain', to which all ideas belong. The notion of literary property was freed from its ties to private interests and privileges, and transformed into a reward for the author's good services to the nation (Hesse 1990: 109–37; Chartier 1992: chap. 2).

The struggle for the prolongation of the author's right was led by the epoch's literary societies which developed, as we have seen, in the context of political liberalization (Société des gens de lettres, Association littéraire et artistique internationale, etc.). The Société des gens de lettres undertook a project in order to extend this right to 50 years. In 1841, the project was presented to the Chamber of Deputies by the poet and deputy Lamartine, but it was rejected (Mollier 1992). It was only in 1866 that the extension was approved. Meanwhile, the International Literary Congress, at its 1858 meeting in Brussels, called for the international recognition of literary and artistic property. The first international convention of literary property was signed in 1886 in Berne. Established on the model of the convention for industrial property, signed in Paris three years earlier, the Convention of Berne was revised several times before the Universal Convention of the author's right was signed in Geneva in 1952. In 1957, a law for literary and artistic property was promulgated in France. Revised in 1985, it was included in the Code of intellectual property in 1992.

Support of creation

In parallel, the development of a State policy of aiding literary creation is a way to compensate for the sanctions the market exerts by supporting the producers or the products situated at the pole of small-scale circulation.

The system of privileges and permissions of the *Ancien Régime* ensured, if not a legal statute, at least a social status and material resources to an elite group of writers. After this system was abolished, the State did not cease to help men of letters in difficult situations, with life annuities or conditional allowances. Yet, the funds allocated to this policy had become grossly insufficient in face of the growth, during the nineteenth century, of the body of writers. It was during the interwar period that the first attempts to develop a real policy in favour of the intellectual milieu were made. In 1924, the minister of public instruction and of the beaux-arts, Léon Bérard, suggested creating in his ministry a literary department in charge of writers' interests. In 1927, Édouard Herriot, the leader of the Radical Party, who had been at the head of the government of the 'Cartel des gauches' in 1924, filed a project of law for the creation of a National Fund for the letters, arts and sciences, which would be funded by fees charged on works of art in the public domain. The project did not succeed, but the idea of a Fund for the letters was to be achieved in 1930. The finance law of 16 April 1930 set up a Caisse nationale des lettres (National Fund of Letters) which was aimed at encouraging literary production, awarding prizes or scholarships, and helping impecunious authors as well as their families (Sapiro 2004). Suppressed in 1935 because of financial restrictions, the National Fund for the Letters reappeared in 1946, and became active ten years later (Surel 1997). Its main task was to redefine the social and material conditions of professional writers, and to elaborate a system of social protection, which was adopted in 1975 (Sapiro and Gobille 2006). In 1973, the Caisse nationale des lettres was replaced by the Centre national des Lettres (CNL), which, besides the State's allowance, draws an income from taxes charged on big publishing houses and on photocopies (this second tax is the CNL's main resource today). The CNL was renamed Centre national du Livre in 1992.

Both the development of the CNL and the legislation on authors' rights occurred in the same period as the establishment, in 1958, of the Ministry of Culture. Headed by the prestigious figure of the writer André Malraux, it has favoured the development and the rationalization of a cultural policy aiming at the safeguarding of the national cultural patrimony, the democratization of access to legitimate culture, and the encouragement of cultural creation. The cultural policy has, from the beginning, privileged professional artists and their works rather than the cultural activities of local amateurs (see Urfalino 1996; Dubois 1999; Lebovics 1999).

From the 1970s onwards, the cultural policy in the literary domain changed its orientation from creation to production and consumption. As a result of the claims of publishers facing the merging of publishing houses into big groups, which tend to overshadow books with restrained readerships, as well as a crisis that appeared to be both conjunctural and structural, a book policy was developed, hailing from 1948 with the export of the French book abroad (Surel 1998). A 'Direction du livre et de la lecture' was created in 1975. The aid to literary creation through scholarships, a direct form of State mecenat, was maintained, but represented less than 10% of the budget of the CNL between 1989 and 1993 – that is, around one third of the sum allocated to the publication of books or periodicals implying an economic risk. The demands would be submitted to commissions of experts designated to this end, who would judge the aesthetical or intellectual quality of the project of publication or translation (into French or from French into another language). The CNL would grant either a loan without interest that the publisher would have to repay over five or ten years, or a subvention for unprofitable products like poetry, theatre, or magazines. Between 1981 and 1993, the amount of loans that the CNL allowed grew threefold (from 7 to 21.9 million francs) and the number of subventions grew sixfold (from 2.2 to 16.9 million francs). The latter indicates that the CNL was transformed into a real 'mecene' of low-profit literary publishing (Surel 1998: 531).

This policy was partially the result of the autonomy achieved by the literary field and of the State's recognition of aesthetical values, as well as of the development of a certain professional expertise, promoted by creators and critics. Aimed at regulating the market by reducing the uncertainty and the risks that derive from it for the publishers, such a policy, although often criticized, assures the preservation of a certain degree of autonomy for the pole of small-scale production in the face of the market's sanctions and especially in the face of the barrier that the logic of profit imposes on products reputed to be difficult regarding their chances of being published.

The establishment of a single price for a book, in application of a decision made by the socialist government in 1981, responded to literary publishers' claims. Headed by Jérôme Lindon, the PDG (CEO) of Minuit, in 1977, they founded an association in order to protect traditional bookstores against the development of large chains such as the FNAC, and against the liberal policy of the right under Valéry Giscard d'Estaing. The adoption of a single price for a book is the best illustration of this market regulation policy, developed in response to the demand by agents of the pole of small-scale production. It was extended with the development, in the globalization era, of the State policy in support of the export of French culture abroad.

Conclusion

Literary activity has evolved from ideological constraints to mercantile constraints. In authoritarian socio-political configurations, where the economic field depends upon the political field, the ideological demand of the ruling class (or of an institution like the Church) determines the supply of literary goods. Along with the control of publishing through preliminary examination (authorization or censorship) and lists of banned books, the professional organization and centralization of writers have been important means of guaranteeing their submission. Thus, a form of State-controlled professionalization and bureaucratization of culture have reinforced the heteronomy of the production of symbolic goods. The strategies of resistance developed by dissident writers have prevented the unification of the corporation and generated field effects, although the ideological issues at stake still determine the opposition between dominant and dominated, or orthodox and heretic.

In ultra-liberal configurations, it is the competition between publishers for the largest public that conditions the supply. This configuration threatens the autonomy of the literary field by encouraging the production of standardized best-sellers and by limiting the chances of more innovative and difficult works being published (when it does not almost suppress this chance, as in the case of poetry and theatre), while creating the space for 'niches'. The gap has widened between, on the one hand, the professionalized authors of best-sellers who are paid high advances on fees, sell hundreds of thousands of copies of their books, and have made their fortunes with literature,[11] and on the other hand, innovative writers who sell between 1,000 and 5,000 copies per publication, who are often exploited by their publishers (who do not pay any advance), and who have to bear the financial costs and risks of pursuing creative work alone.

Whereas the market has helped the literary field to free itself from State control, in the liberal-democratic regime the State has developed a cultural policy in order to support the pole of small-scale production. This is, however, the result of the process by which the literary field gained autonomy. Professional expertise in literature has been recognized both in the market, where the symbolic capital accumulated in a literary list has an inestimable value, and by the State, which has recognized the author's right and has become the principal 'mecene' of art and literature, although literary publishers today benefit from this support more than the creators themselves. The consequences of these different socio-economic and political configurations for writing practices, only suggested here, deserve to be investigated thoroughly.

Another conclusion of this overview is that, contrary to the assumption, contended by the sociology of professions, that professionalization necessarily implies autonomy, a thorough analysis of systems of constraints bearing upon the literary field clearly reveals three different paths of professionalization: a State-controlled path aiming at the control of cultural producers; a market-driven one, which can be measured through sales and by the rhythm of production; and a ficld-orientated mode of professionalization, based on the accumulation of symbolic capital with the field.

Notes

1 This paper is a revised and updated version of the article published under this title in the journal *Poetics* in 2003 (vol. 31, 441–64). I would like to thank Jasmine van Deventer for helping me revise it on a linguistic level.
2 I shall leave aside, here, the process of differentiation of intellectual activities, as well as constraints owing to the social origins of writers and their trajectories. For a comparative approach to intellectuals in Europe, see Charle 1996. For a study of the division of expert labour (which does not include cultural producers), see Abbott 1988. I have provided an analysis of the effects of the division of intellectual labour on the literary field in Sapiro 2003.
3 For example, in 1850, a supertax was imposed on the serial novel in France.
4 *L'Honneur des poètes*, Éditions de Minuit, 14 July 1943, republished in 1945, p. 10. Free translation: 'Once more, challenged, poetry regroups, rediscovers a precise meaning in its latent violence, cries, accuses, hopes.'
5 The Société des auteurs dramatiques already existed (it was founded by Beaumarchais in 1777), but it was only for playwrights.
6 Apart from on TV, where publicity for books is forbidden in France.
7 This tendency, which characterizes traditional literary publishing, is no longer true in the Anglo-American market of 'big books' (Thompson 2010).

8 The interview was conducted before Vivendi Universal sold its publishing group, so there were at that time two groups in France, the other one being Lagardère, which owns Matra-Hachette, which finally bought VU publishing.
9 David Carr and David D. Kirkpatrick, 'The Gatekeeper for Literature is Changing at *New Yorker*', *The New York Times*, 21 October 2002, C1.
10 Between 1960 and 1981, the teaching staff of the universities in France grew four-fold, from 10,015 to 41,311; the number of full professors rose from 1,969 to 12,123 (Passeron 1986; Kauppi 1990: 86).
11 For example, John Grisham's foreign annual earnings are said to exceed US$10 million (Cave 2000: 284). He is one of the authors translated in the above-mentioned 'best-seller' series of Robert Laffont.

References

Abbott, A. 1988. *The System of Professions. An Essay on the Division of Expert Labor.* Chicago and London: The University of Chicago Press.

Angenot, M. 1982. *La Parole pamphlétaire. Typologie des discours modernes.* Paris: Payot.

Assouline, P. 1984. *Gaston Gallimard. Un demi-siècle d'édition française.* Paris: Balland.

Aucouturier, M. 1998. *Le Réalisme socialiste.* Paris: PUF.

Benhamou, F. 2002. *L'Économie du star-system.* Paris: Odile Jacob.

Bertrand-Dorléac, L. 1990. 'L'Ordre des artistes et l'utopie corporatiste: les tentatives de régir la scène artistique française, juin 1940–août 1944'. *Revue d'Histoire moderne et contemporaine*, 64–88.

——1993. *L'Art de la défaite 1940–44.* Paris: Seuil.

Boschetti, A. 1990 [1985]. 'Légitimité littéraire et stratégies éditoriales'. In R. Chartier and H.-J. Martin (ed.) *Histoire de l'édition française, t. 4: Le livre concurrencé.* Paris: Fayard, 511–50.

Bourdieu, P. 1966. 'Champ intellectuel et projet créateur'. *Les Temps modernes*, 246, 865–906.

——1971. 'Le marché des biens symboliques'. *L'Année sociologique*, 22, 49–126.

——1977. 'La production de la croyance'. *Actes de la recherche en sciences sociales*, 13, 3–43.

——1983. 'The Field of Cultural Production, or: The Economic World Reversed'. *Poetics*, 12(4–5), 311–56.

——1984. Haute couture et haute culture. *Questions de sociologie.* Paris: Minuit, 196–206.

——1985. 'Effet de champ et effet de corps'. *Actes de la recherche en sciences sociales*, 59, 73.

——1991. 'Le champ littéraire'. *Actes de la recherche en sciences sociales*, 89, 4–46.

——1992. *Les Règles de l'art. Genèse et structure du champ littéraire.* Paris: Seuil (English trans.: *The Rules of Art*. Cambridge: Polity Press, 1996).

——1993. *The Field of Cultural Production. Essays on Art and Literature.* Intro. and ed. R. Johnson. Cambridge: Polity Press.

——1999. 'Une révolution conservatrice dans l'édition'. *Actes de la recherche en sciences sociales* 126–27, 3–28 (English trans. 'A Conservative Revolution in Publishing'. *Translation Studies* 1(2), 2008, 123–53).

Casanova, P. 1999. *La République mondiale des lettres.* Paris: Seuil (English trans. *The World Republic of Letters*. Cambridge, MA: Harvard University Press, 2005).

Cassagne, A. 1997 [1906]. *La Théorie de l'art pour l'art en France chez les derniers romantiques et les premiers réalistes.* Paris: Champ Vallon.

Cave, R.E. 2000. *Creative Industries. Contracts between Art and Commerce.* Cambridge and London: Harvard University Press.

Charle, C. 1990. *Naissance des 'intellectuels' 1880–1900.* Paris: Minuit.

——1996. *Les Intellectuels en Europe au XIXe siècle. Essai d'histoire comparée.* Paris: Seuil.

Chartier, R. 1992. *L'Ordre des livres. Lecteurs, auteurs, bibliothèques en Europe entre le XIVe et XVIIIe siècle. Aix-en-Provence: Alinéa.*

——2000 [1990]. *Les Origines culturelles de la Révolution française.* Paris: Seuil.

Chartier, A.-M. and Hébrard, J. 2000 [1989]. *Discours sur la lecture (1880–2000).* Paris: BPI-Centre Pompidou/Fayard.

Darnton, R. 1971. 'The High Enlightenment and the Low-life of Literature in Pre-revolutionary France'. *Past & Present. A Journal of Historical Studies,* 51, 81–115.

——1983. *Bohème littéraire et révolution. Le monde des livres au XVIIIe siècle.* Paris: Gallimard/Seuil.

Delporte, C. 1998. *Les Journalistes en France (1880–1950). Naissance et construction d'une profession.* Paris: Seuil.

Dragomir, L. 2003. 'L'implantation du réalisme socialiste en Roumanie'. *Sociétés et représentations,* 15, 309–24.

——2008. *L'Union des écrivains, une institution littéraire transnationale à l'est: l'union des écrivains.* Paris: Belin.

Dubois, V. 1999. *La Politique culturelle. Genèse d'une catégorie d'intervention publique.* Paris: Belin.

Dury, M. 1997. 'Du droit à la métaphore: sur l'intérêt de la définition juridique de la censure'. In Pascal Ory (ed.) *La Censure en France a l'ère démocratique (1848– ...).* Bruxelles: Complexe, 13–24.

English, I.F. 2008. *The Economy of Prestige. Prizes, Awards, and the Circulation of Cultural Value.* Cambridge, MA: Harvard University Press.

Foucault, M. 1969. 'Qu'est-ce qu'un auteur?' *Bulletin de la Société française de Philosophie,* LXIV (reprinted in *Dits et écrits, t. I, 1954–1988.* Paris: Gallimard, 1994, 789–821).

Fouché, P. 1987. *L'Édition française sous l'Occupation 1940–1944.* Paris: Bibliothèque de littérature française contemporaine de l'Université Paris VII, 2.

Garrard, J. and Garrard, C. 1990. *Inside the Soviet Writers' Union.* New York and London: The Free Press/Macmillan.

Guillou, B. and Maruani, L. 1989. *Les Stratégies des grands groupes d'édition. Analyses et perspectives.* Paris: Ed. du Cercle de la librairie/Observatoire de l'économie du livre.

Heilbron, J. and Sapiro, G. 2007. 'Outlines for a Sociology of Translation: Current Issues and Future Prospects'. In M. Wolf (ed.) *Constructing a Sociology of Translation.* Amsterdam and Philadelphia: John Benjamins Press, 93–107.

Hesse, C. 1990. 'Enlightenment Epistemology and the Laws of Authorship in Revolutionary France, 1777–93'. *Representations,* 30, Spring, 109–37.

Karabel, J. 1996. 'Towards a Theory of Intellectuals and Politics'. *Theory and Society,* 25, 205–23.

Kauppi, N. 1990. *Tel Quel: la constitution sociale d'une avant-garde.* Helsinki: The Finnish Society of Sciences and Letters.

Lambert, N. and Matonti, F. 2001. 'Un théâtre de contrebande. Quelques hypothèses sur Vitez et le communisme'. *Sociétés et représentations,* 11, 379–406.

Lane, Ph. 1998. 'La promotion du livre'. In P. Fouche (ed.) *L'Édition française depuis 1945*. Paris: Éditions du Cercle de librairie, 594–627.

Lebovics, H. 1999. *Mona Lisa's Escort. Andre Malraux and the Reinvention of French Culture*. Ithaca and London: Cornell University Press.

Leclerc, Y. 1991. *Crimes écrits. La littérature en procès au XIXe siècle*. Paris: Plon.

Loiseaux, G. 1995 [1984]. *La Littérature de la défaite et de la collaboration, d'après 'Phonix oder Asche?' de Bernhard Payr*. Paris: Fayard.

Matonti, F. 2003. '"Il faut observer la regle du jeu". Réalisme socialiste et contrebande littéraire: La Place rouge de Pierre Courtade'. *Sociétés & Représentations*, 15, 293–308.

Milza, P. and Berstein, S. 1980. *Le Fascisme italien 1919–1945*. Paris: Seuil.

Mollier, J.-Y. 1992. 'L'édition en Europe avant 1850: Balzac et la propriété littéraire internationale'. *L'Année balzacienne*, 13, 157–73.

——(ed.) 1997. 'La survie de la censure d'État (1881–1949)'. In P. Ory (ed.) *La Censure en France a l'ère démocratique (1848– …)*. Bruxelles: Complexe, 77–87.

——2000. *Où va le livre?* Paris: La Dispute.

Muel-Dreyfus, F. 1996. *Vichy et l'éternel féminin. Contribution à une sociologie politique de l'ordre des corps*. Paris: Seuil (English trans. *Vichy and the Eternal Feminine. A Contribution to a Political Sociology of Gender*. Durham: Duke University Press, 2002).

Ory, P. 1991. 'Le rôle de l'État: les politiques du livre'. In R. Chartier and H.-J. Martin, *Histoire de l'édition, t. 4, Le livre concurrencé 1900–1950*. Paris: Fayard/ Promodis.

——(ed.) 1997. *La Censure en France à l'ère démocratique (1848– …)*. Bruxelles: Complexe.

Passeron, J.-C. 1986. *1950–80. L'Université mise en question: changement de décor ou changement de cap? Histoire des universités en France*. Ed. Jacques Verger. Toulouse: Bibliothèque Historique Privat, 367–420.

Pivot, B. 2001 [1990]. *Réponses à Pierre Nora. D'Apostrophes à Bouillon de culture*. Paris: Gallimard.

Popa, I. 2002. 'Un transfert littéraire politisé. Circuits de traduction des littératures d'Europe de l'Est en France, 1947–89'. *Actes de la recherche en sciences sociales*, 144, 55–69.

——2010. *Traduire sous contraintes. Littérature et communisme (1947–1989)*. Paris: CNRS Éditions.

Renard, H. and Rouet, F. 1998. 'L'économie du livre: de la croissance a la crise'. In P. Fouché (ed.) *L'Édition française depuis 1945*. Paris: Editions du Cercle de librairie, 640–738.

Reynaud, B. 1999. 'L'emprise de groupes sur l'édition française au début des années 1980'. *Actes de la recherche en sciences sociales*, 130, 3–11.

Robin, R. 1986. *Le Réalisme socialiste. Une esthétique impossible*. Paris: Payot.

Sapiro, G. 1999. *La Guerre des écrivains (1940–53)*. Paris: Fayard (English trans. *French Writers' War (1940–1953)*. Durham: Duke University Press, 2014).

——2002. 'L'importation de la littérature hébraïque en France. Entre communautarisme et universalisme'. *Actes de la recherche en sciences sociales*, 144, 70–79.

——2003. 'Forms of Politicization in the French Literary Field'. *Theory and Society*, 32, 633–52.

——2004. 'Entre individualisme et corporatisme: les écrivains dans la première moitié du XXe siècle'. In S. Kaplan and Ph. Minard (eds) *La France malade du corporatisme*. Paris: Belin, 279–314.

——(ed.) 2008. *Translatio. Le marché de la traduction en France à l'heure de la mondialisation*. Paris: CNRS Éditions.

——2010. 'Globalization and Cultural Diversity in the Book Market: The Case of Translations in the US and in France'. *Poetics*, 38(4), 419–39.

——2011. *La Responsabilité de l'écrivain. Littérature, droit et morale en France (XIXe–XXIe siècles)*. Paris: Seuil.

Sapiro, G. and Gobille, B. 2006. 'Propriétaires ou travailleurs intellectuels? Les écrivains français en quête de statut'. *Le Mouvement social*, 214, 119–45.

Savart, C. 1985. *Les Catholiques en France au XIXe siècle. Le témoignage du livre religieux*. Paris: Beauchesne.

Schalke, C. and Gerlach, M. 1999. 'Le paysage éditorial allemand'. *Actes de la recherche en sciences sociales*, 130, 29–47.

Schiffrin, A. 1999. *L'Édition sans éditeurs*. Paris: La Fabrique.

Serry, H. 2002. 'Constituer un catalogue littéraire. La place des traductions dans l'histoire des Éditions du Seuil'. *Actes de la recherche en sciences sociales*, 144, 70–79.

——2004. *Naissance de l'intellectuel catholique*. Paris: La Découverte.

Simonin, A. 1994. *Les Éditions de Minuit 1942–1955. Le devoir d'insoumission*. Paris: IMEC.

——1996. 'La littérature saisie par l'Histoire. Nouveau Roman et guerre d'Algérie aux Éditions de Minuit'. *Actes de la recherche en sciences sociales*, 111–12, 69–71.

——1998. 'L'édition littéraire'. In Pascal Fouché (ed.) *L'Édition française depuis 1945*. Paris: Éditions du Cercle de la librairie, 30–87.

Suleiman, S. 1983. *Authoritarian Fictions. The Ideological Novel as a Literary Genre*. New York: Columbia University Press.

Surel, Y. 1997. *L'État et le livre. Les politiques publiques du livre en France (1957–1993)*. Paris: L'Harmattan.

——1998. 'L'État et l'édition'. In P. Fouché (ed.) *L'Édition française depuis 1945*. Paris: Éditions du Cercle de la librairie, 517–39.

Thalmann, R. 1991. *La Mise au pas. Idéologie et stratégie sécuritaire dans la France occupée*. Paris: Fayard.

Thompson, J.B. 2010. *Merchants of Culture. The Publishing Business in the Twenty-First Century*. Cambridge: Polity Press.

Urfalino, Ph. 1996. *L'Invention de la politique culturelle*. Paris: La Documentation française.

van Rees, K. and Dorleijn, G.J. 2001. 'The Eighteen-century Literary Field in Western Europe: The Interdependence of Material and Symbolic Production and Consumption'. *Poetics*, 28, 331–48.

Viala, A. 1985. *Naissance de l'écrivain. Sociologie de la littérature à l'âge classique*. Paris: Minuit.

Zhdanov, A.A. 1950. *On Literature, Music and Philosophy*. London: Lawrence & Wishart Ltd.

6 A heuristic tool

On the use of the concept of the field in two studies in the sociology of culture

Julien Duval

Pierre Bourdieu, who always argued that the social sciences should be at once theoretical and empirical, would sometimes point out that the word 'theory' comes from a Greek verb meaning 'to see', 'to contemplate'. In making that point, he wanted to challenge the relationship that sociologists generally have with theory. He set little store by over-theoretical approaches that turn into somewhat gratuitous contemplation and end up saying little about the social world itself. However, he set himself no less apart from purely empirical sociologies and considered that the positivist ideal of a science without theory was a myth. Returning to the etymology of the word 'theory', he explained, against such postures, that theory is comparable to an instrument of vision, that it is essential in the 'conversion of the gaze' that accompanies the progress of knowledge. It is one of the instruments that are interposed between the researcher and his objects and which, like a pair of spectacles – alluding to a quotation from Heidegger that Bourdieu invoked several times with reference to statistical sociology (see, for example, Bourdieu *et al.* 1991: 108) – may either help one to see or prevent one from seeing.

So as not to disconnect theoretical questions from empirical research, this text is based on two works in which the concept of the field is implemented. The concept is considered an instrument of research and the aim is to identify some of its contributions. This intention should not, however, be taken too literally, first, because the concept, and therefore its specific contribution, cannot be entirely isolated. The concept of the field belongs to a system of concepts (Bourdieu and Wacquant 1992: 96), so that it would be artificial to try to isolate its specific contribution from the gains secured more generally by the set of notions to which it is linked, such as the concept of capital. Next, being a concept devised by and for research, the field is not separable from the empirical operations implied by its implementation. Reasoning in terms of the field, for example, when it leads a researcher to construct a 'square-table of pertinent properties' (Bourdieu and Wacquant 1992: 230) or make use of correspondence analysis (Le Roux and Rouanet 2010), leads him to address in systematic fashion a set of questions on the limits of the universe being studied or on the properties and groups of agents that are 'efficient' there: these questions are productive in themselves and the concept should be credited with the contribution from the operations linked to its empirical implementation. Finally, one has to stress the risks of an approach that consists in describing works from a standpoint other than that from which they were undertaken. The notion of the field was implemented in a deliberate fashion in the two works discussed here, but its use was not the only objective aimed at; moreover, these works are not totally separable from other research carried out at much the same time with common theoretical instruments and on closely related empirical objects.[1]

These two works were thus not undertaken with the intention of 'testing' the concept of the field; nor were they conceived as exemplary implementations of the concept with a view to mobilizing the totality of its potentialities. Likewise, while they bear in one case on economic journalism and in the other on the cinema, they provide only some elements of responses to the question of the pertinence of the notions of the 'journalistic field' or the 'cinematographic field'.[2] What they do show is the interest that the concept presents for raising research questions, producing original findings or bringing out the specificities of the universes studied. Three points stand out in particular. First, the concept proved useful, especially in the work on economic journalism, in breaking with common representations and problematics and seeking to renew them. Second, as the work on cinema more clearly shows, it constitutes a kind of question generator and makes it possible to construct a fairly ambitious model, which is important at a time when sociology is confronted with the rise of economic models that it is difficult for sociology not to see as 'reductive'. Finally, comparison with the literary field, which seems to have played a privileged role in the formation of the concept, proves a productive approach, in particular in bringing to light some specificities of the universes studied.[3]

What the field reveals

Although, at the time when *Le Métier de sociologue* (Bourdieu *et al.* 1968) was being written, some concepts (notably that of the field) were not yet fully formed, the set of notions that Bourdieu progressively developed and refined can be seen as an array of tools enabling the social sciences to achieve the objectives set out in that book. When undertaking to identify the contribution made by the concept of the field, one is therefore often brought back to principles set out in *Le Métier de sociologue*, for example the break with common sense or the principle of 'non-consciousness'. In particular, the concept helps one to move beyond realism and the artificial debates of 'common sense'. Thus, to speak of the 'journalistic field', rather than 'the press', underlines that the latter is characterized by internal differentiation, and at the same time, it guards against unwarranted generalizations.

The study of economic journalism was made at a time when the question of the ideological uniformity of 'the press' was much debated in France. Those who complained, especially after the strikes and protests of 1995, that 'the press' had very largely adopted a monolithic *pensée unique*,[4] were answered that 'the press' was still 'pluralist' and that critiques of neoliberalism occupied an important place in some publications, such as *Le Monde diplomatique*, the satirical magazine *Charlie Hebdo*, or *L'Humanité* (until 1994 the 'central organ of the French Communist Party'). This discussion was something of a 'false debate': two theses face to face, mutually exclusive but each based on objective arguments. The notion of the field helps one to move beyond this forced choice and to integrate the two apparently contrary points of view. Depending on their position in the field, media outlets are unequally led to visions of the world marked by economic liberalism, but they differ, just as much, in their functional weight. Constructing the space leads one to reject the hypothesis of a uniform adherence to '*la pensée unique*', without accepting the illusion of pluralism fostered by radio round-ups of the press which juxtapose the editorials of *Le Figaro* and *L'Humanité*. There is no symmetry between *Le Figaro* and *L'Humanité*. The former, in stark contrast to the latter, is published by a large group; it has many more journalists (who collectively can be much more competitive as suppliers of information), a greater proportion of whom have received the most prestigious professional training. Its reader-ship is more numerous and socially higher placed, and in the 'newspaper business' it carries an authority that used to make it obligatory reading in the editorial committees of other publications. In short, the notion of the field prevents one from treating 'journalism' as a uniform entity, but also from accepting the false symmetries of spontaneous sociology. It reintroduces power relations, the relations of domination internal to the journalistic universe, which the enchanted vision of 'pluralism' masks.

More generally, it invites one to consider that the social world is more complex than is generally supposed. In media analysis, there is an equivalent of 'reflection theories', with which the model of the literary field breaks by considering that works should not simply be related to the generic properties of their authors (in particular, class membership), but that account must also be taken of the specific mediation of a field possessing a power of 'refraction' (Bourdieu 1996: 220). Changes in editorial policy, seen for example in 'new formats', are often ascribed to general transformations, changes in the 'mood of the time'. Thus the development of economic sections and supplements in the 1980s and 1990s is frequently explained by 'mutations' such as 'the redis-covery of enterprise', the 'public enthusiasm' for the stock exchange and the growth of share holding. When they create sections devoted to 'stocks and shares', 'the market' or 'company news', newspaper editors often invoke factors of this kind, their concern to keep up with the 'mood of the times' or the chan-ging interests of their readers. Some observers of the media, even in the aca-demic world, produce similar explanations. These may, however, be more akin to justificatory rhetorics.

They are not adequate. First, they are tautological: what is called 'the mood of the time' (*l'air du temps*), which press editors and managers supposedly follow, quite often corresponds to themes recurrent in the media discourses of the moment. They also lack rigour: the 'readership', too, is not a uniform entity, constant over time; and what is presented as change in its interests may be no more than an effect of its ageing or a transformation of its structure, sometimes linked to a commercial strategy of 'repositioning'. The struggles of the daily newspapers and weekly news magazines to 'capture' readers attractive to advertisers on account of their strong purchasing power, for example, exerts an influence on editorial policy. Finally, analyses in terms of 'reflection' amount to ad hoc explanations. To consider that in expanding and reorienting their coverage of the economy the French media have 'mirrored' their times, one has to see no more than 'the rediscovery of enterprise' in a period that has equally been marked by the institutionalization of mass unemployment and more precarious working conditions, two developments that go against analysis in terms of 'reflection'. The concept of the field, by contrast, leads one (also) to seek the origins of editorial changes in factors specific to the space being studied. It raises the question of why the space has 'reflected' certain social and political changes rather than others. It orients the inquiry towards aspects specific to the journalistic universe – to certain internal developments that are generally repressed: the changes in the corporate and capital structure of the press in the 1980s and 1990s, the changes in the recruitment of journalists, the competitive relations among press undertakings, etc.

Analysis in terms of field also made it possible to put forward a structural view of the relations between journalism and the economy, and renew the approach taken to a question that is almost always reduced to spectacular intentional 'pressures' and 'manipulations' to be denounced and deplored, being seen as comparable to the practices described by Zola in his novel *L'Argent*. Even if many people believed that in the 1990s such practices had become rare, the way the problem was addressed had not fundamentally changed: attention was mainly focused on the biases that in media owned by big industrial or financial groups, could affect the treatment of information about the activities of those groups. 'Scandals' regularly emerged concerning business leaders who had 'censored', in their own papers, information that could damage them. Since the nineteenth century, debate on 'the press and money' has tended to be reduced to a normative problematic with a strong moral dimension. It is based on the opposition between the model of an 'independent' journalism and a journalism subject to influence, either weak or 'corrupt', that allows itself to be 'bought' rather than serving its 'readers' and the values of 'truth' and 'objectivity' that should govern the profession. In this logic, there is nothing more to be said about the relations between journalism and the economy as soon as no 'pressure' is observed and no economic power is seeking to 'buy' editors or journalists.

In an analysis in terms of field, no journalist can be credited with absolute independence. They are all, to a varying extent, structurally dependent on the economic world, for several reasons. Their activity requires considerable economic investments. It is often financed by advertising revenues coming pre-dominantly from private companies operating for profit, and by readers who, especially as regards economic information, are strongly integrated into the 'economic cosmos'. One has to abandon the hypothesis, implicit in ordinary discussions, that there is a 'free and independent' journalism separated by a difference in nature from 'venal' journalism. These conceptions never appear in a pure form in reality and are, at best, the two ends of a continuum. Similarly, sociological analysis leads one to see censorship, direct pressure and blackmail as just the extreme forms of practices that, in reality, almost always take a gentler, less perceptible form.

Companies do not need to own media or crudely display their power in order to influence information. Those with big advertising budgets, for example, have a powerful weapon at their disposal. Big corporations also invest in communication strategies through which they can 'manipulate' all the more efficiently because this instrument largely escapes collective repro-bation and tends to set up long-term exchanges between journalists and the economic powers, which differ from specific censorship or localized pressure as the logic of the deferred gift differs from commercial exchange. Journalism can thus serve economic interests (which are never reducible to the interests of a particular company but also cover the interests specific to the whole eco-nomic field) by serving the interests of readers who are strongly integrated into the economic order. It does so, moreover, through a spontaneous adjustment between the journalists and the economic agents. Examination of the social and educational properties of economic journalists shows that many of them are very close in their origins and trajectories to managers and even directors in the private sector. In these conditions, they do not need to be called to order to serve the interests of the economic world and put forward a coverage of 'economic affairs' that is truncated in the sense that it is marked by the preoccupations, the blind spots and the interests shared by the social categories most integrated into the economic world as it is.

They tend to espouse a vision of the world that reduces it solely to the issues pertinent in the economic world (at the expense of social, ecological or cultural issues), not so as to respond to express demands made of them, or through conscious ideological choices, but as an effect of a structural depen-dence which they rarely experience as such. They can then feel free (and be perceived as such), but simply because they are only weakly aware of the dependences to which they are subject. There is in this sense a 'twofold truth' of economic journalism, as Bourdieu put it in relation to work (Bourdieu 2000: 202–5). In short, analysis in terms of fields substitutes a structural vision for a moral problematic and in place of the traditional question of 'independence' it poses the problem of the relative (and historically variable) autonomy that the journalistic universe enjoys with regard to the economic world. Attention is then focused on the powerful relationships that are only rarely materialized in dramatic interactions or visible material exchanges and are most often established through spontaneous adjustments.

A model against economism

Like journalism, the cinema is a very reflexive universe. 'Cinema people', or some of them at least, have the resources and dispositions necessary to reflect deeply on the functioning of the world in which they are involved. Moreover, the sector has its 'observers' – critics and specialist journalists, experts involved in cultural policy, etc. These agents contribute to a kind of collective reflexivity and help to produce or maintain certain representations of the cinema, for example the division into two sectors. The universe is thus often described in terms of the coexistence of two sectors, one 'commercial', the other 'independent'. The classifications are somewhat fuzzy and fluid, which suggests that they are not (solely) the product of rigorous analysis: the expressions 'popular cinema' and '*cinéma d'auteur*', for example, are not unrelated to the first two, but cannot be directly substituted for them. Faced with these classificatory categories, the sociology of the cinema oscillates between two postures. Sometimes it adopts them, no doubt because it recognizes in them the echo of the opposition between the expanded market and the restricted market that organizes fields of cultural production. Sometimes it rejects them, considering that they constitute a 'binary Manichean division' or 'common-sense oppositions stemming from arbitrary preconceptions' (Laroche and Bohas 2005: 61, 75). One may in fact think that 'native' reflections and knowledge, while limited by the practical objectives for which they are formed, are never without some measure of sociological truth. In any case, neither of these two positions appears to be adequate. It is preferable to construct empirically the cinematographic field, so as to determine to what extent a sociological analysis is able to endorse the commonly accepted bipartition.

Empirical construction of the space shows that the categories 'commercial cinema' and 'independent cinema' are pertinent if they are understood as polarities between which the different film-making entities tend to distribute themselves, forming a continuum of positions whose extremities are, in a sense, never reached. However, the operations through which the field can be constructed, in this case multiple correspondence analysis, are as instructive as the findings that emerge. They oblige one, in particular, to address the question of the limits of the field and of national frontiers. The need to construct a statistical population requires one to consider whether it is pertinent to construct a national population. There are arguments to be made on both sides. It may be considered that French cinema, like all European cinemas, has to reckon with the commercial hegemony of the American industry and therefore cannot be analysed as a field. A field tends to constitute a system of self-sufficient relations and therefore a unit that it is pertinent to isolate; it does not derive the essential part of its properties from its insertion in a larger whole (Bourdieu and Wacquant 1992: 228). However, taking into account the linguistic and cultural barriers or the still largely national character of film financing, at least in France, one is inclined to conclude that it is appropriate to construct a French field.

In other words, statistical analysis requires one to provide a clear-cut answer to a question to which there is, in reality, no simple response. The difficulty of establishing a set of pertinent variables for an international population weighed in the final decision, but the argument is not purely technical since it arises from the arbitrary character that such a population has, at least at the present time. It was therefore decided to limit the inquiry to the national statistical population but to take care, at the moment of sociological interpretation of the statistical analysis, to allow for the international context of 'French cinema'. In practice, this question of international insertion resurfaces at every stage of the work. The decision to define a national statistical population raises difficulties, for example, because co-productions are not uncommon. Nor are professional migrations (which are no doubt particularly important in the case of France, where *auteurs* who cannot finance their projects in their country of origin often work). Likewise, among the criteria that generate distinctions within a national population in the sector, some have a strong international dimension – the selections and prizes of the major international festivals such as Venice, Cannes or Berlin, for example.

Once the space is constructed, it can be seen that the major opposition based on volume of capital relates in part to the degree of internationalization: the undertakings that occupy the highest positions in the national space have, in a certain number of cases, the specificity of having a market and a reputation abroad. The second factor in terms of structure of capital sets undertakings mainly characterized by their commercial successes (whose protagonists are able to work, intermittently, in Hollywood) and undertakings that primarily enjoy a strong symbolic recognition, won or confirmed at the major European international festivals. This opposition seems to be the form taken, at national level, by the international opposition between a more 'commercial' definition of cinema dominated by the 'Hollywood industry' and a more 'artistic' conception historically dominated by Europe.

The concept of the field, and its empirical implementation, also lead one to give particular attention to the symbolic stakes that structure the space. Economic studies of the sector (surveys made by the Centre national de la cinematographie, private bodies and companies, etc.) often use box office receipts or data on the profitability and export sales of French films. Analysis in terms of field also takes account of factors that are much less often objectivated: presence at festivals, critical acclaim, etc. Because the sociological work has to populate indicators that do not pre-exist it, new tools have to be devised (the same is true moreover for work on the media).

Through the questions that it brings up, the reading in terms of field develops by stages a rich model. As an example one can mention the analysis it enables one to outline of the 'New Hollywood'. The social sciences, often inspired on this point by economic science, have sometimes dealt with it. One overview restates arguments that have often been put forward: the development of television in the United States (and in Europe) in the late 1950s and early 1960s marked a turning point in the history of the 'Hollywood industry' because it threatened one of its foundations. Confronted with competition that led to lower cinema attendance, the producers responded with the big-budget 'blockbusters' (*Doctor Zhivago*, made in 1965, is the classic example), then tried the model of the '*film d'auteur*', before returning to the former, more profitable genre (Greffe 2002: 76–77). With the aid of the information in a well-documented journalistic work on the 'New Hollywood' (Biskind 1998), and, on the other hand, of what has been said above regarding the cinematographic field, a fuller analysis is possible.

First, while the development of television did indeed have an impact on the cinema (and it is in any case certain that it seemed at the time to 'compete' with it), the consequence was not only a fall in cinema going but also a change in the structure of cinema audiences in favour of younger and better-educated categories. It should also be noted that the late 1950s and early 1960s also correspond to the rise of an '*auteur* cinema' in Europe, with in particular the so-called 'modern' cinema, and in France the '*Nouvelle Vague*' (Mary 2006b). This phenomenon, which with a few exceptions was economically very marginal, was very important in the world of festivals and criticism (Baumann 2007). It was not unconnected with the rise of television since it concerned essentially an educated public whose relative weight was increasing (Darré 2000). Finally, in the history of the Hollywood studios, the period was marked by a generational renewal: the managers, who in some cases had been in place since their creation, were disappearing through death or retirement.

These factors must be borne in mind in order to understand the emergence of a *cinéma d'auteur* in a 'Hollywood industry', which was then organized in accordance with a bipolar structure of the type brought to light in the case of French cinema. A young generation of directors – and also screenwriters, actors and producers – often influenced by Europe, made films in Hollywood manifesting more pronounced artistic ambitions than their predecessors and sometimes inclinations towards political and social subversion (sharpened by the post-1968 context). They aspired to symbolic recognition, especially in Europe, and in the studios enjoyed the support of young producers who were sometimes close to them in their properties and who were, in any case, always very different from the generation of the studio founders. The trajectories of this group were affected in the 1970s by the fact that several large companies came under the control of consortia that were essentially interested in short-term profitability and which generalized the making of blockbusters, big-budget productions carefully marketed to bring in massive profits very quickly. The most art-oriented positions that some directors had managed to create could not withstand this change, but some of them stayed, cutting back their experimental leanings (Spielberg and, even more, Lucas) or seeking to strike a balance by occupying, simultaneously or successively, different positions in a bipolarized field.

Whereas the economic approach tends to make Hollywood a quasi-autarkic universe, systematically governed by 'commercial' objectives and ultimately reducible to the trying out of competing economic models (with the most profitable prevailing), a reading in terms of field sees it as a space marked by the struggles characterizing the international field in which it is set. The economic approach adopts a point of view that is only concerned with the pursuit of profitability. It is no doubt close to the view that characterizes the studio managers, who have always been answerable to their shareholders – even if it is not certain that it truly 'represents' their view, since the demands of immediate profit are not exerted at all times with the same strength on the various managers. Sociological analysis enables one to gain a fuller perspective that can encompass other points of view, more attentive, for example, to what are called 'artistic' questions. In particular, it can account for the 'twofold truth' of some Hollywood films (lucrative products from some points of view, especially in the eyes of those who finance them; goods with artistic ambitions for other points of view, such as European critics, but also for those who conceive them), a duality that explains the multiple receptions to which they can give rise. In a general way, the field seems to favour the construction of more complete models than the economic approach. In this respect the concept allows one to implement an ambitious modelling, the principles of which had already been set out in *Le Métier de sociologue* (in passages where the critique of the simplified models of economic science was already put forward). It is an important contribution in a context marked, in the study of domains of culture as in other specialisms where the sociological approach had previously tended to be dominant, by the growing influence of analyses inspired by economic science.

The model of the literary field

Given the role it played in the maturation of the concept of the field (Bourdieu 1996), the case of the literary field no doubt has an exemplary value for all analyses in terms of fields. However, this is even more true when one turns to domains such as journalism and the cinema, since the comparison with literature is, in a sense, then already present in the object. Groups of individuals who have played an important role in the genesis of these worlds cited the example of writers. On this point journalism and the cinema remind one of painting: pictorial art achieved its autonomy somewhat later than literature in France, and on that account, in his analysis of the impressionist revolution, Bourdieu put forward a study of the support that writers like Zola or Mallarmé had given it.

The close relations between journalism and literature in France go back to the *Ancien Régime*, when the treatment of artistic and scientific questions in the gazettes was less subject to censorship than political subjects (Ferenczi 1993). This close relationship continued in the nineteenth century. 'Literary Bohemians' who lacked private incomes found in journalism a distinctly more lucrative means of survival (Bourdieu 1996; Charle 1996). When, at the end of the century, France began to adopt American methods of reporting, it brought into them literary ambitions that were absent from the genre on the other side of the Atlantic, as the examples of Gaston Leroux or Albert Londres attest (Ferenczi 1993). It is not surprising, then, that the journalistic field shares some features with the literary field. There is, for example, a clear kinship between the values that a paper like *Le Monde* proclaimed (the refusal of 'commercial' concessions and 'compromises' with the temporal powers) and the values that founded the autonomy of the literary field. More generally, one should perhaps see a borrowing from the fields of intellectual production in the French journalistic traditions that have most valorized investigation and/or independence from power. The figure of the 'intellectual' is moreover closely bound up with the press and it is no accident that Zola, who made a decisive contribution to its invention, played an important symbolic role in the early days of the professional organization of the journalist's craft.

The closeness between literature and cinema in France is even more manifest. The very particular literary capital concentrated in France played a major role in the emergence of Paris as 'the capital of film culture' (Casanova 1999). Moreover, in Europe, most of the figures who have most powerfully contributed to endowing the cinema with the dualist structure of the literary field have been linked, if not directly to that field, then to other already strongly autonomized artistic universes. This is true of the major representatives of the interwar 'art cinema', and also several *Nouvelle Vague* directors who, like Éric Rohmer or Jean-Luc Godard, had envisaged a literary career before coming into cinema (via criticism) (Mary 2006b). In the 1920s, writers, and not only surrealists, brought their symbolic capital into cinema (and moreover took the risk of losing it by investing in a domain whose artistic and cultural legitimacy was still very low; Andreazza 2006). The same was seen during the Second World War and into the early 1960s, as seen for example when one studies the composition of the juries at the Cannes Festival (del Toso 2008).

The case of the film director Robert Bresson[5] combines many aspects of the relationship between the literary and cinematographic fields. With a radicalism and success almost without parallel, he developed a conception of pure art in the cinema. He did so, moreover, in an unpromising context: the cinema had learned to 'talk' (and had therefore become more expensive and less open to avant-garde work), but the portable equipment that made the *Nouvelle Vague* possible did not yet exist and the 'French cinema world' in which he moved was, at the time, subject to very strict professional organization (Darré 2000). Throughout his career Bresson remained closely connected with more legitimate artistic universes. Throughout his life he painted, he was a professional photographer, in his early years he was fairly close to the surrealists, he filmed with actresses from the *Comédie française* and collaborated with recognized writers (Giraudoux or Cocteau). Several of his films were inspired by consecrated works (Diderot, Dostoyevsky, Bernanos, Tolstoy). He claimed the status of an artist and rejected the craftsman status that others assigned to themselves; in interviews he compared himself to a writer or painter. He declared himself to be concerned only with form and the 'truth of art', irreducible to naturalism. He defended the 'cinematographer', an artist whose vocation was not to adapt or serve other more legitimate arts, but to borrow from them a disposition: the 'act of creation' must lie in the cinema itself, which had its own language and its own means. The radicalness of his position was seen in his rejection of many of the cinematic conventions of the time (refusal to use professional actors in favour of 'models', to use background music, to have happy endings, etc.). In using the term *cinématographe* (which had already dropped out of use at the time), he asserted his aspiration to purity ('original purity') while distancing himself from all those who just made 'films'. In 1955, he confessed that he '[went] very little to the cinema', declared he had never seen a film by Hitchcock and would not even acknowledge Charlie Chaplin ('It's brilliant, but it's music-hall, it's not cinema').

Such an enterprise, in the cinema world even more than in literature, could only develop in a microcosm isolated from economic reality. Bresson's first film was financed by a painter and art critic and his later films by atypical producers who, as in publishing, covered their losses with the profits from their successes, or thanks to the personal intervention of a minister. One of his producers spoke of his 'remoteness from realities', his inability to 'sell his film to a producer' ('all his energy is concentrated on his art'). He only rarely achieved public success, to which, according to a critic, he was nonetheless 'sensitive'. He is exemplary of directors whose importance is almost entirely linked to the success achieved among their peers. A critic lists the film makers of different generations and different countries who have, or say they have, been influenced by him (Frodon 2008: 87).

However, when comparing the field of literature with the fields of journalism and film making, one has to bear in mind that the former enjoys a 'seniority' (which places it, in the exchanges that have been discussed, in the position of 'creditor'), which implies greater legitimacy. There are not only common points but also differences between these universes. Economic journalism, for example, does not have exactly the structure of the most autonomous fields of cultural production (Bourdieu 1996). It is indeed organized around a main opposition in terms of 'volume of capital' (between newspapers owned by big groups, with highly professionalized editorial teams, and publications not supported by big groups, whose readerships are smaller and whose editorial teams are always at risk of being seen as more 'politically motivated' than 'professional'). A second opposition is apparently very similar to that seen between the expanded market and the restricted market of the fields of cultural production (here it is the cleavage between mass-audience audiovisual media and printed press outlets, which are often professionally more legitimate, tend to produce more information – at least at the time of the study – and have a smaller but more selective and socially more homogeneous audience). However, the professionally most legitimate pole as regards economic journalism is not the pole most independent of temporal powers and, importantly, the opposition, at the summit of the space, between different degrees of internal legitimacy, corresponds, in terms of audience, to an opposition between the 'general public' and a restricted public made up of categories highly integrated into the economic order, and not, as tends to be the case in the literary field (or cinema), to an opposition between economically and culturally rich fractions of the dominant class.

It is true that economics is not the area of journalism that has the closest relations with the literary field or more generally with the fields of cultural production, even if (in *Le Monde*, for example) there is a long tradition of economic journalism close to the university world. In fact, this specificity in structure also seems to be found among other producers (or distributors) of economic discourses: among economists, professional legitimacy does not seem necessarily to imply much more than among journalists an independence with regard to the temporal powers. Their microcosm seems to be characterized by the same 'power denial' (Lebaron 1997). This does not mean, however, that the difference in structure observed can be reduced to the specificity of economic publications and sections.

Although the phenomenon may be more accentuated in this area of the press, it seems to express ambiguities and characteristics common to the whole of the journalistic field. While internal recognition is no doubt always difficult to objectivate, as shown by the case of scientific prestige in the academic world (Bourdieu 1988), it is especially so in the journalistic profession. It is not that the notion has no meaning there, but its forms are particularly non-institutionalized. The value 'independence' seems particularly ambivalent: as has been seen, the claim to be 'independent' of the economic or political powers may denote a will to 'serve the reader' which, in other universes, would immediately appear as highly mercantile. One might also ponder the issue of the relation to posterity, which is problematic in a universe that by definition produces supremely perishable goods soon to be superseded. The prophets, the agents 'ahead of their time', play an important role in autonomous universes which, perpetuating pre-capitalist logics, require renunciation of short-term, worldly profits (Bourdieu 1996) in favour of beliefs in 'the judgement of posterity' that make it possible to see failure and incomprehension ('flops') as the signs of possible subsequent election. It is not quite the same in journalism. Hubert Beuve-Méry, the founder of *Le Monde*, while renowned for his asceticism, also owes his place in the professional mythologies to the temporal success of his project, measured by the growth in the paper's readership under his editorship or the influence it won in government circles. Being 'of one's time', being simply a 'witness' to the *Zeitgeist*, is perceived positively, and the apparent exceptions are entirely relative (e.g. the homage to Pierre Viansson-Ponté for publishing his article 'France is Bored' two months before May 1968).

While the cinema has a structure comparable to that of the most autonomous fields of cultural production, it also has some important differences from the literary field. In particular, the fact that the production costs of its 'works' are much greater has consequences. The pursuit of 'pure art', intended for a very restricted audience (in the limiting case, no more than the peers) seems to be much more difficult, especially in any sustained way. The tensions between 'art' and 'commerce' are manifest even at the heart of the most autonomous institutions, such as the international festivals (del Toso 2008) or the journals. In France, 'uncompromising' directors such as Jean-Marie Straub and Danièle Huillet are an interesting example in this regard. They enjoyed significant recognition from autonomous institutions, but this was always limited, as if it had reached a plateau. Their films were regularly presented at the international festivals, but in parallel sections rather than the official competition; critics rejected them in particular on the grounds of their lack of public success, and journals that supported them would not take the commercial risk of displaying them on their covers. In a general way, the implementation of autonomous projects no doubt presupposes more elaborate strategies than in other spaces. A study would be required to verify this, but it is possible that those who occupy very autonomous positions, without being marginal, have often previously achieved recognition in the sector of wider distribution. Robert Bresson, for example, started by acquiring a form of academic legitimacy in other artistic sectors and, among the Hollywood directors most acclaimed by the critics, a number have been actors who first gained recognition through their performances in highly successful productions (Charles Laughton, even Orson Welles, or, more recently, John Cassavetes or Clint Eastwood).

Comparison of journalism and the cinema with the literary field at least gives rise to two hypotheses. First, it could be that the history of a field that is increasing its degree of autonomy necessarily moves through a phase of primitive accumulation implying relations with fields of more longstanding autonomy. Second, the journalistic field and the cinematographic field are perhaps strongly condemned to a lower degree of autonomy than the spaces on which they have modelled themselves. While, for example, a specific capital has been formed in the cinematographic field (as shown by the fact that the proportion of writers and, more generally, of artists external to the world of cinema has sharply declined), it is not certain that this capital has become totally independent of all literary, theatrical or painterly capital, relative to which it no doubt remains dominated. Patrick Champagne's remarks on the journalistic field point, in some respects, in the same direction: journalism oscillates between universes more powerful and often more autonomous than itself (the economic, political and intellectual fields) and the autonomy that it may win at a given moment with respect to one of them always seems to be offset by increased dependence on one of the other two (Champagne 2007).

Conclusion

This text has aimed to illustrate the usefulness of the notion of the field in work on areas such as journalism and cinema. As a concluding question: could studies devoted to areas often classified among the 'cultural industries' – because they demand greater economic investment than literature, for example, and have a larger audience – contribute in their turn to the analysis of older spaces that have been an important reference in the constitution of field theory? Is some respects one might think so. The most autonomous fields are currently changing. With, in particular, processes that have been called 'commoditization' or 'the [growing] grip of journalism' (Bourdieu 1998), they seem to be acquiring some of the properties previously reserved for the 'cultural industries'.

Notes

1 The study of economic journalism is linked to a set of works on the journalistic field. Pierre Bourdieu himself was taking not a new but an increased interest in this universe, of which *On Television and Journalism* (Bourdieu 1998) bears the mark. Incidentally, it should be pointed out that Bourdieu's 'intervention', often reduced in France to its most polemical passages, also aimed to make the notion of the field known to a non-academic readership and to apply it to journalism. The other study described here, on the cinema, is partly linked to a set of works which, continuing the path marked out by the work of Yann Darré, but making significantly more use of the field, have implemented sociological tools in their approach to the cinema (Andreazza 2006; Mary 2006a, 2006b).
2 As regards journalism, these questions are dealt with more fully elsewhere. See in particular the remarks by Patrick Champagne (2004, 2007) on the notion of the journalistic field, and Dominique Marchetti (2004) on the notion of a specialized sub-space.
3 For fuller discussion on the points relating to economic journalism and the cinema sketched in this text, see Duval 2004, 2006.
4 This expression, current in left-wing movements in France from 1995, refers to the dominant adherence to the 'liberal model' in political and media circles. It could be seen as a French equivalent of the British Thatcher government's 'There is no alternative'.
5 The information concerning Robert Bresson, and the quotations, are taken from 'Une mise en scène n'est pas un art' (lecture at the Institut des hautes études cinématographiques, IDHEC, in December 1955), *Cahiers du cinéma* 543b, and Frodon 2008.

References

Andreazza, F. 2006. 'La conversion de Pirandello au cinéma'. *Actes de la recherche en sciences sociales*, 161–62, 32–41.
Baumann, S. 2007. *Hollywood Highbrow: From Entertainment to Art*. Princeton, NJ: Princeton University Press.
Biskind, P. 1998. *Easy Riders, Raging Bulls: How the Sex-Drugs-and-Rock 'n' Roll Generation Saved Hollywood*. London: Bloomsbury.
Bourdieu, P. 1988. *Homo Academicus*. Cambridge: Polity Press; Stanford, CA: Stanford University Press.
——1996. *The Rules of Art: Genesis and Structure of the Literary Field*. Cambridge: Polity; Stanford, CA: Stanford University Press.
——1998. *On Television and Journalism*. London: Pluto.
——2000. *Pascalian Meditations*. Cambridge: Polity; Stanford, CA: Stanford University Press.

Bourdieu, P., Chamboredon, J.-C. and Passeron, J.-C. 1968. *Le Métier de sociologue*. The Hague: Mouton (trans. *The Craft of Sociology*. New York and Berlin: De Gruyter, 1991).

Bourdieu, P., Darbel, A. and Schnapper, D. 1991. *The Love of Art. European Art Museums and their Public*. Cambridge: Polity Press; Stanford, CA: Stanford University Press.

Bourdieu, P. and Wacquant, L.J.D. 1992. *An Invitation to Reflexive Sociology*. Chicago, IL: University of Chicago Press; Cambridge: Polity Press.

Casanova, P. 1999. *La République mondiale des lettres*. Paris: Le Seuil.

Champagne, P. 2004. 'The "Double Dependency": The Journalistic Field Between Politics and Markets'. In R. Benson and E. Neveu, *Bourdieu and the Journalistic Field*. Cambridge and Malden, MA: Polity Press, 48–63.

——2007. 'L'étude des médias et l'apport de la notion de "champ"'. In E. Pinto (ed.) *Pour une analyse critique des médias*. Broissieux: Éditions du Croquant, 39–53.

Charle, C. 1996. *Les Intellectuels en Europe au XIXe siècle: Essai d'histoire comparée*. Paris: Le Seuil.

Darré, Y. 2000. *Histoire sociale du cinéma français*. Paris: La Découverte.

del Toso, J. 2008. *Le festival de Cannes, un certain regard sur le cinéma. Naissance et transformations d'une institution cinématographique*. Master's dissertation in social sciences, École des hautes études en sciences sociales.

Duval, J. 2004. *Critique de la raison journalistique. Les transformations de la presse économique en France*. Paris: Le Seuil.

——2006. 'L'art du réalisme. Le champ du cinéma français au début des années 2000'. *Actes de la recherche en sciences sociales*, 161–62, 96–115.

Ferenczi, T. 1993. *L'invention du journalisme en France: Naissance de la presse moderne à la fin du XIXe siècle*. Paris: Plon.

Frodon, J.-M. 2008. *Robert Bresson*. Paris: Cahiers du cinéma/Le Monde.

Greffe, X. 2002. *Arts et artistes au miroir de l'économie*. Paris: Économica.

Laroche, J. and Bohas, A. 2005. *Canal + et les majors américaines*. Paris: Pepper.

Lebaron, F. 1997. 'La dénégation du pouvoir. Le champ des économistes français au milieu des années 1990'. *Actes de la recherche en sciences sociales*, 119, 3–26.

Le Roux, B. and Rouanet, H. 2010. *Multiple Correspondence Analysis*. Thousand Oaks, CA: Sage.

Marchetti, D. 2004. 'Subfields of Specialized Journalism'. In R. Benson and E. Neveu, *Bourdieu and the Journalistic Field*. Cambridge and Malden, MA: Polity Press, 64–82.

Mary, P. 2006a. 'Le cinéma de Jacques Tati et la "politique des auteurs"'. *Actes de la recherche en sciences sociales*, 161–62, 42–65.

——2006b. *La Nouvelle Vague et le cinéma d'auteur*. Paris: Le Seuil.

Part III
The State and public policy

7 The field of power and the relative autonomy of social fields

The case of Belgium

Eric Mangez and Georges Liénard

Introduction[1]

Pierre Bourdieu's sociology invites us to aim to understand everything in relation to its social conditions of production, circulation and use – in short, to understand everything in relation to its social conditions of possibility. Can the same principle be applied to the concept of the field itself? Does the concept of the field still function in the same way (and as effectively) when translated into a context other than that of French society? Is it equally pertinent in all contexts marked by a form of differentiation of spheres of activity? To answer these questions, we examine the problematic of the relative autonomy of fields in the Belgian context, focusing on the relationship between the field of power and different specific fields. Studying this context requires us to consider not only the process of functional differentiation that gives rise to fields but also a process of cultural fragmentation from which emerge what Belgian and Dutch intellectuals habitually call the 'pillars' (Dobbelaere and Voyé 1990; Seiler 1997; de Munck 2002, 2009; Vanderstraeten 2002) or 'segments' of society (Lijphart 1979, 1985).

The autonomy of the field as a central theoretical issue

The concept of the field arises from the need to understand the historical origin, the progressive construction and the functioning of differentiated social 'universes', 'worlds' or 'microcosms' (Bourdieu and Wacquant 1992: 97). It thus serves to designate the social and symbolic spaces that are constituted around a specific activity and a specific stake (art, education, health, science, etc.), by considering them as structured spaces of relations among positions. This societal differentiation is linked to the general process of rationalization and differentiation of activities in modern social formations. The concrete process of the formation of any given field must not, however, be understood as the response to some historical necessity but rather as a process of power: for example, the formation of the field of literature and the very definition of what it means to be a writer 'is the product of a long series of exclusions and excommunications trying to deny existence as writers worthy of the name to all sorts of producers who could live as writers in the name of a larger and looser definition of the profession' (Bourdieu 1996b: 224).

In his various studies of different fields, Bourdieu often presented the field as a theoretical means of escaping from two extreme postures: a naïve posture and a posture that he sometimes described as the 'Marxist short-circuit' (Bourdieu 1977b: 116; Bourdieu 1991: 169). The naïve posture presupposes a 'bracketing out of the social' (Bourdieu 1991: 55) and consists in not sociologizing social activities, in other words considering, for example, that there can be such a thing as 'pure' art, independent of all forms of social condition of possibility. It is the non-sociological, naïve posture, of the purity of the law, or even the purity of science. At the other extreme, the 'Marxist shortcut' consists in seeing all social activities as the direct expression of social relations, played out at the level of relations between classes and class fractions, with no particular mediation, i.e. without taking account of the social logic linked to the specific stakes of the different fields.

The concept of the field aims to escape from these two postures by identifying *relatively* autonomous social spaces constituted around a particular activity, which have been constructed historically through struggles and power relations and have succeeded in generating their own rules of functioning, their own principles of evaluation, their own institutions, their own mechanisms of legitimation and recognition, their own systems of classification and, thereby, their own structures of relative positions.

The importance and centrality of the question of the relative autonomy of fields immediately becomes apparent. It is this dual logic (both *autonomy* and its *relative* character) that enables one to escape both the naivety of the pre-sociological position and the oversimplifying radicalness of the Marxist shortcut.

In theoretical terms, the relative autonomy of a field can be understood as the resultant of the relationship between two kinds of forces that can be effective within a given field: on the one hand, the forces linked to the exercise of power within the field itself; on the other, the forces linked to the exercise of power in other fields and especially within the field of power. As Hilgers and Mangez point out in the Introduction to this volume, according to Bourdieu, each field is in reality structured by two opposing principles of hierarchization: 'an external or heteronomous principle of hierarchization that applies to the field the hierarchy prevailing in the field of power, and an internal or autonomous principle that hierarchizes in accordance with the values specific to the field' (Mounier 2001: 71). Each field of cultural production is subject to these two principles of hierarchization and its degree of relative autonomy 'is revealed by the extent to which the external principle of hierarchization is subordinated to the internal principle of hierarchization' (Bourdieu 1996b: 217). To grasp the relationship between these two kinds of forces at work in the specific fields, it is necessary to understand what the field of power is and how it exerts effects on the specific fields.

The field of power and its effects on the specific fields

Bourdieu introduces the concept of the field of power in the text 'Champ du pouvoir, champ intellectuel and habitus de classe' (1971); he returned to it and developed it, mainly in *La Noblesse d'État* (1989) and *Les Règles de l'art* (1992). But what precisely is it? The concept is often misunderstood. First, it should not be confused with the political field (or field of political power), which is a specific field like others (Vandenberghe 1999: 53). In contrast to the other fields, whose content can in a sense be grasped intuitively, the field of power has a more abstract character: 'The field of power is a sort of "metafield" that regulates the struggles for power throughout all fields' (Vandenberghe 1999: 53). It is not linked to a specific activity. Rather, it is bound up with the social structure and more especially with the social and symbolic relations among the social fractions dominant within the social structure. As Bourdieu (1983: 319) indicates and Vandenberghe (1999: 53) underlines, 'the field of power … is … situated at the dominant pole of the field of class relations'.

The field of power is thus 'the site of struggles between holders of different powers (or kinds of capital)'. More precisely, it is 'the space of relations of force between agents or between institutions having in common the possession of the capital necessary to occupy dominant positions in the different fields' (Bourdieu 1992: 300; Bourdieu 1996b: 215). The field of power is fundamentally structured by the opposition between the dominated fractions, and the dominant fractions of the dominant classes, which consists in reality, for Bourdieu, in an opposition between cultural capital (dominated) and economic capital (dominant). This structuring of the field of power by a relation between cultural capital and economic capital produces effects on the structure of the specific fields.

Each field of production may be more or less autonomous with respect to the field of power. The weaker its relative autonomy, the more permeable the field is to the forces exerted from the field of power. According to Bourdieu, these forces are then capable of shaping the structure of the specific fields by generating within them two opposing poles: a pole corresponding structurally to the positions of dominated fractions in the field of power and another corresponding to the dominant fractions in the field of power (Bourdieu 1996b: 217–18).

So it can be seen that part of the structure and the dynamics of the specific fields derives from the structure of the field of power and, more precisely, of the relation of domination that hierarchizes cultural (dominated) capital and economic (dominant) capital. Indeed, as Vandenberghe emphasizes, 'the state of the structure of the field of power determines the structure of oppositions of the subfield and thus also the possible alliances that can be formed in the subfield, and also between the members of the subfield and those of their environment' (Vandenberghe 1999: 53).

It is in the light of the theoretical propositions set out above that we propose to examine a specific historical situation that questions field theory.

Functional differentiation and cultural fragmentation in Belgium

The process that gives rise to the emergence and development of fields is a process of functional differentiation which progressively distinguishes different spheres of activity. By functional differentiation, we do not mean to suggest that this process corresponds to a functionalist dynamic or some 'natural' evolution of societies, but simply to indicate that this process differentiates and constructs distinct functions (health, art, education, etc.). As has been indicated, the specific fields arise from struggles for the recognition of new forms of specific cultural capital: they do not respond to an historical necessity but are constituted through power relations.

If such a process of functional differentiation is at work in modern societies, it needs to be stressed that certain social formations are also marked by a process of cultural differentiation/fragmentation. This process distinguishes different sociological communities within a social formation, generally on the basis of philosophical orientation (Bader 2003), language or ethnic origin. This process of cultural fragmentation is itself dependent on power relations and becomes fully realized only when the sociological communities concerned manage to organize themselves through pressure groups, associations and political movements.

Some European countries have been particularly marked by this process of cultural fragmentation (Papadopoulos 2003; Lorwin 1971). For example, the political and social history of the Netherlands is characterized by the presence and action of liberal, Catholic and Protestant cultural communities (Kickert 2003); Austria is also marked by a high degree of cultural fragmentation. The case that will concern us specifically is that of Belgium. We will start from this case in order to study the relation of relative autonomy between the specific fields and the field of power. In Belgium, several processes of cultural differentiation are at work and have given rise to two main divisions: a linguistic-cultural divide which distinguishes and opposes French speakers and Dutch speakers; and a philosophical-cultural divide which distinguishes the Christian world from the secularist world. These cleavages divide the elites and structure the space of their relative positions. They constitute inescapable dimensions of the field of power.

The field of power

While the opposition between cultural capital and economic capital is clearly present in the field of power in Belgium, this field is also strongly structured by two other kinds of capital: linguistic-cultural capital (French-speaking/Dutch-speaking); philosophical-cultural capital (Catholic/secularist). So the space of power has to be understood in its multipolarity. It is not simply a bipolar space in which the possessors of cultural capital are opposed to the possessors of economic capital. In Belgium, the field of power is structured by three oppositions which intertwine to form six poles: cultural capital/

economic capital; French-speaking/Dutch-speaking; Catholic/secularist. How do the dynamics of the specific fields unfold in the context of a multipolar field of power? We shall first examine the effects of the linguistic-cultural divide on the functioning of the specific fields.

The linguistic-cultural divide

The linguistic-cultural divide, which has significantly marked the social and political history of the country, opposes French speakers to Dutch speakers. In recent decades, this divide within the field of power has given rise to the pure and simple splitting of most of the specific cultural fields. Many organizations (associations, youth movements, political parties, universities, ministries, administrations, etc.) have been split in two. It would be a mistake to suppose that these divisions have led to a simple polarization of the specific fields around two poles, French-speaking and Dutch-speaking. In reality, in many cases, the break has been such that it has given rise to a doubling of the fields. If one takes the case of the educational sector, one has to consider that actors in French-speaking education and actors in Dutch-speaking education no longer belong to the same field, but to two distinct fields. They are no longer either linked or divided by anything[2] – neither the services and products they generate,[3] nor the users of the services in question, nor the definition of the conditions of access to education and the educational professions, nor the definition of the conditions of exercise, nor even the struggle for the legitimate definition of education and its stakes. They no longer belong to the same space of relative positions.[4]

Many fields have thus split and become doubled as a result of this linguistic-cultural division of power. Only the areas of activity that are most autonomous with respect to this component of the field of power have been able to maintain the existence of unitary fields in which both French-speaking and Dutch-speaking actors act. This is true to some extent of the fields of sport and the economy. We shall return to the specific case of the field of political power.

The philosophical-cultural divide

Let us now examine how the philosophical-cultural divide produces effects on the functioning of specific fields. This case is more complex and requires a longer analysis. To grasp the scale of this division, one has to go back to the origins of the country: the Belgium of 1830 was characterized by a major demarcation line within the elites and the population. It opposed the Catholics to anti-clericals. One of the main conditions of possibility of Belgium as a nation-state was the construction, in 1830–31, of a fundamental compromise between these two communities, which agreed to live together only on condition that they were granted a certain number of freedoms, in particular to organize their collective lives (Mabille 2000). In a range of sectors (fields), each of these communities then set up a number of organizations which together constitute what Belgian and Dutch intellectuals have come to call a pillar[5] (Dobbelaere and Voyé 1990; Seiler 1997; de Munck 2002, 2009; Vanderstraeten 2002) or a segment (Lijphart 1979, 1985). The concept of the pillar – and 'pillarization' – designates this process through which a cultural community organizes its collective life by setting up a number of organizations active in different fields. Thus, within the secularist world (in its socialist branch more than its liberal branch), one finds a number of organizations[6] (hospitals, youth movements, trade unions, universities, health insurance and cooperative bodies in the field of insurance and banking, etc.). The Catholic side likewise has a wide range of organizations active in various fields (health, schooling, culture, higher education and research, leisure, youth movements, banking, insurance, etc.), constituting the Christian pillar (Jelen and Wilcox 1998). This pillarization has developed more strongly in the service sectors (education, health, leisure, trade unions ...) than in the less personalized sectors (finance, industry, etc.) (Vanderstraeten 2002).

Based on these elements, a simple empirical fact observed in the Belgian context can be understood: many fields are divided and structured along similar lines of demarcation. Thus, in the field of health there are institutions, actors, organizations, associations and insurance schemes specific to the Catholic world and others associated with the secularist world or the State. Schooling is mainly divided between denominational (mostly Catholic) schools and the so-called 'official' schools run by the public authorities (communes, provinces, federated entities). The field of higher education and research has its Catholic universities and universities of free-thinking tradition or attached to the State. In the world of labour, the trade union organizations are also divided between Catholic unions on one side and secular (mainly socialist but also liberal) ones on the other. These different fields thus exhibit a 'family resemblance' (Quaghebeur and Rebérioux 1997). They are all divided by the same line of demarcation.

The philosophical-cultural divide, thus rooted in organizations in various fields, has also established itself historically in the field of political power through political parties. Both on the Catholic side and on the socialist side, and to some extent also among the liberals, a logic of reciprocal support has been set up between the different fields and the field of political power. Thus the Catholic (or socialist) organizations in the different fields have nurtured and consolidated the Catholic (or socialist) presence in the field of political power, which has, in turn, contributed to the strengthening of those organizations. In this sense the political segment of the pillars is crucial on account of its pivotal role.[7]

It can be seen that the concepts of the field and the pillar designate different realities, which are articulated with one another. While the 'field' groups a number of actors around a specific stake which creates the *illusio* of the field, the 'pillar' tends to group, around a certain cultural identity, actors who are active in different fields and mobilized by different stakes specific to each of their respective fields. The pillar thus runs through various fields; it is transversal to them.

While these different fields also produce lines and norms that are specific to them in accordance with an internal principle of hierarchization (which is the sign of their relative autonomy), it seems clear that this demarcating line which runs through them and structures them is, in a sense, 'external' to them.[8] It does not result from a symbolic labour specific to each of them. None of the field of schooling, field of health or field of research produces, through its own social and symbolic dynamic, the Catholic/anti-clerical divide on which the pillars are based. The divide originates from the field of power (in particular, the way the Church/State relationship is organized in Belgium) and from the sociological characteristics of the Belgian social formation.

According to Bourdieu's field theory, the fact that a field is structured by lines of division and classification that do not result from the debates, struggles and power relations strictly internal to that field is the indicator of a deficit of relative autonomy of the field in question with respect to the field or fields that have produced those lines of division. We know that an autonomous field normally furnishes itself with reference values, rules of functioning, legitimate means of action, principles of recognition of self and others, lines of division, etc., that are specific to it. We are thus led to interpret the existence of pillars within a social formation as the sign of an autonomy deficit of the specific fields concerned by pillarization, vis-à-vis the field of power, but is such a diagnosis satisfactory?

Pillars versus fields?

It seems at first sight that the two types of differentiation/fragmentation stem from forces working in opposite directions. The birth of a field (functional fragmentation) arises from the social and symbolic labour of agents who progressively manage, through power relations, to secure the recognition of a specific domain of activity and to gain internal control of the conditions of entry and the rules of the game, etc. The construction of a pillar (cultural fragmentation) is a process that runs partly counter to autonomization of fields, since it creates links and draws lines that are transversal to them. Two dynamics seem to be in tension: one is conducive to the autonomy of the field; the other structures social and symbolic links between actors from different fields. Following Bourdieu, one would be led to consider the resultant of this dual dynamic purely in terms of the relative autonomy of the field. Thus the presence of pillars in a social formation would be synonymous with a deficit in the autonomy of its fields and, conversely, the weakening of cultural fragmentation would contribute to the autonomy of the fields. The current situation in Belgium, characterized by a relative weakening of the pillars, should then be understood as favourable to the autonomy of the fields affected by (de-)pillarization.

Such a diagnosis, which sees pillarization only as an autonomy deficit of the specific fields, is unsatisfactory, or more precisely, incomplete, since it fails to account for the specific effects of pillarization. These include the consolidation of the resources and positions of the actors most strongly integrated into the pillars. The interaction of cultural fragmentation (the pillars) with functional fragmentation (the fields) produces specific effects that cannot be reduced to forms of 'deficit'. In the remainder of this text, two particular effects are distinguished: an effect of solidarity, which arises within each pillar between different fields; and an effect of inter-segment (inter-pillar) discretion that operates within different fields.

Solidarity within the pillar

It is not sufficient to conclude that fields have an autonomy deficit. The pillar also and mainly has the effect of holding together fractions of different fields, who recognize one another, beyond the limits of their respective fields, by their membership of the same cultural community and a shared philosophical-cultural orientation. This mutual recognition, resulting from a common membership, produces effects of reciprocal support (solidarity) that enhance the means of action of the central actors in the fields in which they act (in particular the volume of information at their disposal, but also, to some extent, their symbolic, social and sometimes economic resources). Thus there is a form of solidarity among the Catholic actors in the different fields, and likewise among the actors of the secularist (socialist or liberal) organizations in different fields. This solidarity, which gives the actors enveloped in it additional means of symbolic and social action, has often enabled them to act more pertinently and with more means of action in one field or another. The bonds existing within a pillar between its different constituent associations and political segment are of particular importance. The dynamics of mutual support in which the functional 'segments' of the fields support and are supported by their political segment in the field of power have strongly marked the Belgian system (to the point of producing effects regarded by some (van Brabant 1998) as 'perverse', such as the politicization of the civil service or various functions in different fields).

These 'transversal' bonds among the actors in different fields help to explain a certain number of phenomena, particularly as regards the Belgian model for the management of potential social conflict. This complex arrangement produces effects on the (political) dispositions of the actors, who are thus linked to one another beyond the stakes specific to their field: the disposition towards compromise, in particular, flows from pillarization (van de Craen 2002). If one takes the case of the Catholic world, which has constructed a quasi-ideal-typical form of the pillar, it can be noted for example that this pillar links (Catholic) trade union leaders and (Catholic) employers' representatives, beyond the opposition of interests that structure their relationship in the field of labour relations. In other words, this specific (pillar) arrangement in some way smoothes and moderates the power relations that may exist between actors in potentially conflictual positions in a given field, because they are united by their shared membership of the same world. Observers of Belgian social and political life are well aware that Catholic union actors often opt for positions more open to compromise with power than their socialist equivalents. This probably helps to explain why the Catholic world in particular produces elites well versed in the art of compromise and disinclined to engage in direct conflict (a power relation through domination).

So it can be understood why, in the social sciences, Belgian intellectuals (Quaghebeur and Rebérioux 1997) tend to produce works that envisage power relations in theoretical forms other than that of the habitual relation of domination, with, for example, Jean Rémy's concept of transaction (Rémy *et al.* 1978, 1980) or Georges Liénard's theory of power (Liénard 2010). In terms of the sociology of knowledge, it is clear that the analytical tools forged in a given context owe some of their specific characteristics to the specificities of the context in question, into which they were created and developed, which they were designed to explain.

Between the pillars, a certain discretion

While the pillar holds together actors in different fields, it also has the effect of separating different worlds. The political history of the country (Mabille 2000) is indeed fundamentally marked by the need to enable distinct worlds to live together while allowing them a certain autonomy, even a degree of discretionary power. This history makes sense once one has grasped its central problem, which has been to find ways of behaving that enable different groups to live together while preserving, at least in part, their autonomy in collective existence. These ways of behaving that allow for coexistence in a segmented society are, for example, proportional voting, the granting and maintenance of a certain autonomy for organized collective actors (especially through constitutional liberties), public funding of activities organized by these collectives when considered to be in the public interest (following the principle of 'subsidized liberty', for example), and the negotiation of various forms of 'pacts' (for schooling, culture, associations) thought to guarantee a sharing of social and symbolic power (Mangez 2009). It is clear, for example, why the Belgian authorities now define their relationship with the world of associations (especially non-profit bodies) as a 'complementarity'.

Within various fields, these practices maintain and update a sharing of social and symbolic power. Belgium's way of organizing a form of peaceful cohabitation among its constituent segments has thus long been accompanied by a principle of discretion (van Brabant 1998). This need for discretion should not be taken for a form of reluctance to 'divulge' information that, as such, could endanger anyone. Rather, it is a habit of prudence or diplomacy which, in the consociational context (Lijphart 1979), is the bearer of a

fundamental political utility (Byrne 2001; Gabel 1998): it concretizes seg-
mental autonomy and at the same time creates the possibility of inter-segmental
compromise. The notion of 'discretion' is then to be understood in both
senses: it means leaving a certain number of choices to the discretion of the
organized actors (guaranteeing their autonomy in practice), but also maintaining a certain discretion in the sense of not meddling in one's neighbours'
affairs (which creates the potential for compromise).

Let us take as examples the field of schooling and that of educational
research. The field of schooling, like many others, is marked by the process of
cultural fragmentation peculiar to Belgium, being mainly segmented between
a network of 'free' Catholic schools and the 'official' network, historically
invested by the anti-clerical sociological fractions of the population.

When studying the educational sector, one cannot fail to be struck by certain particularities that are interesting in terms of the functioning of the field.
For example, for the greater part of its history, the field of schooling has not
really been equipped with instruments for the evaluation of pupils that were
common to all schools and all pupils. Nor was there a common syllabus: the
curricula of the Catholic network differed significantly from those of 'official'
schooling (Mangez 2004, 2010). Until recently (September 2008), the field
also lacked a corps of inspectors with the same prerogatives in all networks.

It constitutes a field which, in its functioning and its history, has not generated these various devices, which are in reality instruments of measurement
and evaluation, systems of classification, but also programmatic instruments
that define what schooling is and what its stakes are. This observation, which
derives from the history of the field, well illustrates the principle of discretion:
the symbolic and social labour that, in other contexts, gives rise to such
devices common to the whole field, is here left to the discretion of the main
'segments' resulting from the phenomenon of cultural fragmentation.

In theory, within a field, the actors and groups are indeed engaged in social
and symbolic relations that bear precisely on the principles of functioning of
the field, on the very legitimacy of the criteria of classification, etc. However,
when one observes the relationship between the Catholic segment and the
'official' segment, one has to conclude that there has been a form of
arrangement that does not result from social and symbolic struggle, but is
rather based on a lasting, if not permanent, suspension of struggle over a
certain number of stakes. It can be hypothesized that this suspension stems
from a relative equilibrium among the various participants in the political
field and among the various segments of the rival camps that were forced into
compromise after a period of crisis (cf. the 'schools war' that peaked in 1954–
58 and led in 1959, after a change of government and political majority, to
the signing of the School Pact).

Outside these periods of 'open warfare' over schooling, a kind of implicit
pact reigns over the field: don't meddle in your neighbours' affairs, don't try
to evaluate them, above all don't make comparisons. In other words, if the
field of schooling has not generated the devices in question, it is not because

the symbolic relations were too tense, but rather because it was decided that some questions should not be handled at the level of the field as a whole. It is a kind of peaceful cohabitation, made possible by the (social, political and also legal) recognition of an equivalence between the opposing camps. The School Pact of 1959 durably established the recognition and autonomy of the parties, and this equilibrium was consecrated even more clearly when, in 2001, the Constitutional Court of Belgium recognized the 'free' education network (very largely Catholic) as a 'functional public service', thus establishing a quasi-total equivalence of treatment between State education and recognized 'free' education.

The field of research is equally marked by this need for discretion (Mangez and Mangez 2011). The following can be observed: first, the same demarcation lines are found there as in the field of schooling – just as there are Catholic schools and 'official' schools, so there are Catholic universities, publishing their own journals and pursuing their own research programmes, and 'free-thinking' or State-run universities. In the field of research, most research in education is mono- and intra-segmental. It is mono-segmental in the sense that the scope of its enquiry is often limited to a single network (Catholic or official), and intra-segmental in the sense that the research team often belongs to the same segment as its object. Researchers in education know from experience that, socio-politically, it is extremely problematic to try to set up a research framework whose scope includes both the Catholic and the 'official' school systems. Certain conditions have to be fulfilled, in particular the creation of a consortium of universities belonging to different segments and/or a supervisory committee comprising representatives of the various stakeholders. Such a committee may then impose a certain number of constraints on the type of data that can be gathered and made public. This does indeed mean that the autonomy of the field of educational research remains limited. It also means that there are research questions that cannot be addressed and research programmes that cannot be conducted.

The multipolarity of the field of power produces effects on a variety of fields. Our analysis makes it possible to understand, for example, the recent troubles in the management of the DEXIA Bank. This Franco-Belgian undertaking was run by a Franco-Belgian Board of Directors whose functioning and some of its problems stem precisely from the clash of logics governing the organization of two national fields of power. On one side a Jacobin logic prevails in which binding instructions flow directly from the highest authority of the State (CEO Pierre Mariani is close to former President Nicolas Sarkozy), while on the other the Belgian representatives are appointed to meet complex considerations of balance (rather than for their competence) and headed by a person whose role is to reconcile divergent positions rather than lay down a strong line. On the French side, the technocratic vision of *énarques* who share a certain way of thinking; on the other, the obligation to respect an equilibrium that goes far beyond a single board, because in Belgium the balance of the pillars is a complex, national stake reflected in countless arrangements. To put it another way, every action in one of these structures has an impact on overall relationships and requires adjustments designed to maintain the balance of power rather than meet objectives of efficiency, competence, etc. Appointments to one board are often made so as to offset an imbalance resulting from appointments to other boards. This social and political dynamic can have varied effects. It can lead to situations in which individuals occupy positions for which they lack the specific competence (as seems to have happened at DEXIA), but it can also endow them with social, symbolic, economic, etc., resources useful to the exercise of their mandate.

Conclusion: multi-dimensionality of power and field theory

Field theory is particularly adequate for understanding functional differentiation (between spheres of activity) in a social formation that is relatively homogeneous in cultural terms (such as France). Our aim has been to show that for a society such as Belgium, marked simultaneously by a functional fragmentation (fields) and a twofold cultural fragmentation – both linguistic (communities) and philosophical (pillars) – one has to use more complex theoretical tools. More precisely, the theoretical objective of this article is to refine the problematic of the relations between the field of power and the specific fields.

It is the multi-dimensionality of the field of power in Belgium that requires one to adopt a more complex approach to the way in which different forces that stem from the field of power produce effects in the functioning and structure of the specific fields. The specificity of the field of power in Belgium lies in the fact that it is structured by more salient lines of division than simply the opposition between cultural capital and economic capital.

Just as Bourdieu observes that the specific fields (art, research, literature, etc.) translate the cultural capital/economic capital opposition characterizing the field of power, by generating within themselves an opposition between a sub-space devoted to the 'pure' activity (art for art's sake, fundamental research, etc.) and a sub-space responding to an external demand (commercial art, applied research, etc.), so it can be observed that the complexity of the field of power in Belgium (characterized not only by a cultural capital/ economic capital opposition but also a Catholic elites/secularist elites opposition and a French-speaking elites/Dutch-speaking elites opposition) produces multiple structuring effects on the specific fields, which are partly homologous with the field of power itself.

In addition, our analysis has shown that the field of power can produce other effects on the specific fields that the simple diagnosis of a deficit of relative autonomy cannot grasp. In certain cases, the effect of strong tensions within the field of power can lead to the actual splitting of fields. In other cases, the social management of power relations within the field of power through the pursuit of equilibrium may require the suspension of particular stakes in some fields. This is no doubt much more a Belgian than a French

phenomenon. In so far as symbolic relations over the principles of functioning of the field are determinant for the definition of positions and therefore
the distribution of power, it can be said that the sustained suspension of
symbolic relations also entails a power sharing and an agreement on its conditions. In Bourdieusian terms, this could be expressed as the establishment of
a fixed (and balanced) rate of exchange between different kinds of capital.
The specificity of fields in the Belgian context no doubt stems from this
capacity to divide power durably, to work out pacts in which each side concerns itself with its own affairs. This particular historical situation requires
one to refine the concept of the field in order to recognize fields with particular forms, nurtured and structured by power relations other than those
between holders of cultural capital and holders of economic capital.

The need to take account of the multidimensionality[9] of the field of power
requires and enables us to refine our grids of analysis of the relative autonomy
of specific fields. Three general theoretical propositions can thus be
formulated:

- *Different specific fields can be marked differently by a given line of division
within the field of power.* By recognizing a certain plurality of the lines of
division within the field of power, one is able to understand how different
specific fields can be marked differently by a given line of division within
the field of power. In other words, when the complexity of the field of
power is brought to light, one can formulate the hypothesis that the relative
autonomy of a given field may vary depending on whether one considers its
autonomy vis-à-vis one or another of the lines of division that structure the
field of power: a given field may have, for example, strong autonomy vis-à-vis
the power relation between Catholics and secularists, and at the same time
weak autonomy in relation to economic power.
- *A given field may see its relative autonomy increased with respect to one
dimension of the field of power and decreased with respect to other dimensions structuring the field of power.* For example, while it is clear that fields
such as health, education or research have traditionally been marked by
the philosophical-cultural power relation, these fields are now seeing a
relative gain in autonomy vis-à-vis this line of division, at the same time as
their relative autonomy with respect to economic power is being reduced.
This process is seen, in refracted form, in the increasingly clear hierarchization of two criteria of the recognition and valorization of knowledge – in both research and education, the evaluation of knowledge in
terms of its use value is gaining the upper hand over the valorization of
knowledge for its own sake (i.e. as a contribution to the accumulation of
knowledge) (Mangez 2008).
- *Actors who are opposed within a given field in a particular respect (for
example in their philosophical-cultural positions) may at the same time
form an alliance to try to consolidate the autonomy of the field with respect
to another component of the field of power.* Thus the socialist and Catholic

health insurance bodies, which are opposed in philosophical-cultural terms and compete with each other, may form alliances to resist the demands of the doctors' unions, for example. In the field of schooling, the intermediate educational specialists (pedagogic advisers, inspectors, etc.) in the Catholic and 'official' school networks may ally in some conditions to resist the demands that economic power applies to their field.

Notes

1 This chapter was conceived thanks to the support of the European Union's Sixth Framework Programme for Research – socio-economic sciences and humanities theme (contract no. 028848-2 – project KNOW and POL). The information and views set out in this article are those of the author(s) only and do not necessarily reflect the official opinion of the European Union.

2 The situation in Brussels, where French speakers and Dutch speakers coexist, requires some refinement of the analysis. Some forms of discussion have developed between French speakers and Dutch speakers, particularly concerning the educational infrastructures that will be required to cope with the demographic development of the city.

3 Their funding, however, still depends on political negotiations at federal level. It is the federal executive, made up of both French speakers and Dutch speakers that funds the specific governments (the Flemish government and the government of the French Community), which are in charge of organizing education for their respective communities.

4 For some authors (Lawn and Lingard 2002), an international educational field is now developing, particularly as a result of the instruments for international measurement and comparison. The French-speaking and Dutch-speaking actors in Belgian education can be regarded as acting in this field, each on a similar footing to other actors from other national spaces.

5 It is generally considered that there are two main pillars in Belgium (Seiler 1997): a Catholic pillar, and an anticlerical (or secularist) pillar with two branches – a socialist branch and a liberal branch. Each of these branches is in turn self-organized through various fields. In practice, the Christian pillar is indisputably the most structured: for a long time it has represented a quasi-ideal-typical form of the pillar. Then comes the socialist branch of the anticlerical world, which also contains a large number of organizations and forms a relatively well-integrated pillar. The liberal branch has fewer organizations and is less strongly integrated.

6 While both the secularist and the Christian world have each created a pillar of organizations and collective actors active in various fields, it has to be emphasized that the process of pillarization has been and remains more intense and more complete on the Christian side. In the secularist camp, the actors have articulated two dynamics, one of developing their own organizations and the other of investing in public services (in particular, the public authority schools) and, in some periods, of struggling against the Catholic grip on public services.

7 Current social and political history, however, is marked by the predominance of the linguistic-cultural divide over the philosophical-cultural divide and by a more instrumental (than philosophical) logic of affiliation of individuals to organizations linked to the pillars, which has weakened the structuring force of the pillars in the political field. Two developments ensue from this: 1 the political actors are no longer the champions of a single pillar; and 2 the members of the pillars in each field attach themselves pluralistically to several participants in the political field, who are no longer the spokespersons of a single pillar.

8 It should also be noted, however, that the fact that the Catholic/secularist dividing line is in a sense 'external' to the specific fields does not mean that it is not highly significant for the development of the specific activities within the fields.

9 In addition to the dimensions examined here, one should no doubt also take account of the extranational actors and international dimensions that also contribute to complexifying the field of power. It can be seen, for example, that international bodies (such as the Organisation for Economic Co-operation and Development, or OECD, the World Bank, etc.) produce or try to produce effects on specific fields.

References

Bader, V. 2003. 'Religions and States. A New Typology and a Plea for Non-Constitutional Pluralism'. *Ethical Theory and Moral Practice*, 6(1), 55–91.

Bourdieu, P. 1971. 'Champ du pouvoir, champ intellectuel et habitus de classe'. *Scolies*, 1, 7–26.

——1977a. 'Sur le pouvoir symbolique'. *Annales E.S.C.*, 32(3), 405–11 (translated as 1977b).

——1977b. 'Symbolic Power'. In D. Gleeson (ed.) *Identity and Structure: Issues in the Sociology of Education*. Driffield: Nafferton Books, 112–19.

——1983. 'The Field of Cultural Production, or: The Economic World Reversed'. *Poetics*, 12, 311–56.

——1989. *La Noblesse d'État. Grandes écoles et esprit de corps*. Paris: Éd. de Minuit (translated as 1996a).

——1991. *Language and Symbolic Power*. Cambridge: Polity.

——1992. *Les Règles de l'art. Genèse et structure du champ littéraire*. Paris: Seuil (translated as 1996b).

——1996a. *The State Nobility: Elite Schools in the Field of Power*. Cambridge: Polity; Stanford, CA: Stanford University Press.

——1996b. *The Rules of Art: Genesis and Structure of the Literary Field*. Cambridge: Polity; Stanford, CA: Stanford University Press.

Bourdieu, P. and Wacquant, L.J.D. 1992. *An Invitation to Reflexive Sociology*. Chicago, IL: University of Chicago Press; Cambridge: Polity Press.

Byrne, S. 2001. 'Consociational and Civic Society Approaches to Peacebuilding in Northern Ireland'. *Journal of Peace Research*, 38(3), 327–52.

de Munck, J. 2002. 'La Belgique sans ses piliers? Du conflit des modèles au choix d'une politique'. *Les semaines sociales du MOC*, 95–115.

——2009. 'Que reste-t-il des clivages en Belgique Replacement?' *La Revue Nouvelle*, 10, 45–57.

Dobbelaere, K. and Voyé, L. 1990. 'From Pillar to Postmodernity: The Changing Situation of Religion in Belgium'. *Sociological Analysis*, 51, Special Presidential Issue Sociology of Religion: International Perspectives, S1–S13.

Gabel, M.J. 1998. 'The Endurance of Supranational Governance: A Consociational Interpretation of the European Union'. *Comparative Politics*, 30(4), 463–75.

Jelen, T.G. and Wilcox, C. 1998. 'Context and Conscience: The Catholic Church as an Agent of Political Socialization in Western Europe'. *Journal for the Scientific Study of Religion*, 37(1), 28–40.

Kickert, W.J.M. 2003. 'Histoire de la gouvernance publique aux Pays-Bas'. *Revue française d'administration publique*, 105/106, 167–82.

Lawn, M. and Lingard, B. 2002. 'Constructing a European Policy Space in Educational Governance: The Role of Transnational Policy Actors'. *European Educational Research Journal*, 1(2), 290–307.

Liénard, G. 2010. 'Entre travail, responsabilité et action: quelles articulations'. Louvain-la-neuve, Charleroi, *Cahiers du CIRTES no.2*, Université Catholique de Louvain.

Lijphart, A. 1979. 'Consociation and Federation: Conceptual and Empirical Links'. *Canadian Journal of Political Science/Revue canadienne de science politique*, 12(3), 499–515.

——1985. 'Non-Majoritarian Democracy: A Comparison of Federal and Consociational Theories'. *Publius*, 15(2), 3–15.

Lorwin, V.R. 1971. 'Segmented Pluralism: Ideological Cleavages and Political Cohesion in the Smaller European Democracies'. *Comparative Politics*, 3(2), 141–75.

Mabille, X. 2000. *Histoire politique de la Belgique: facteurs et acteurs de changement*. Centre de recherche et d'information socio-politiques.

Mangez, E. 2004. 'La production des programmes de cours par les agents intermédiaires: transfert de savoirs et relations de pouvoir'. *Revue française de pédagogie*, 146, 65–77.

——2008. *Réformer les contenus d'enseignement. Une sociologie du curriculum*. Paris: PUF.

——2009. 'De la nécessité de discrétion à l'Etat évaluateur'. *La Revue Nouvelle*, juillet–août, 32–37.

——2010. 'Global Knowledge-based Policy in Fragmented Societies: The Case of Curriculum Reform in French-speaking Belgium'. *European Journal of Education*, 45(1), 60–73.

Mangez, C. and Mangez, E. 2011. 'Producing Dangerous Knowledge: Researching Knowledge Production in Belgium'. *European Educational Research Journal*, 10(2), 252–58.

Mounier, P. 2001. *Pierre Bourdieu, une introduction*. Paris: Agora.

Papadopoulos, Y. 2003. 'Gouvernance et transformation de l'action publique: quelques notes sur l'apport d'une perspective de sociologie historique'. In P. Laborier and D. Trom (eds) *Historicités de l'action publique*, Paris: PUF, 119–35.

Quaghebeur, M. and Rebérioux, M. (1997). 'Intellectuels en Belgique et en France: "piliers", citoyenneté, état'. *Le Mouvement social*, 178, 89–115.

Rémy, J., Voyé, L. and Servais, E. 1978. *Produire ou reproduire?* Vol. 1. Bruxelles: Vie Ouvrière.

——1980. *Produire ou reproduire?* Vol. 2. Bruxelles: Vie Ouvrière.

Seiler, D.-L. 1997. 'Un système consociatif exemplaire: la Belgique'. *Revue internationale de politique comparée*, 4, 3, 601–24.

van Brabant, K. 1998. 'Civil Society and Substantive Democracy: Governance and the State of Law in Belgium'. *Development in Practice*, 8(4), 407–18.

van de Craen, P. 2002. 'What, if Anything, is a Belgian?' *Yale French Studies*, 102, 24–33.

Vandenberghe, F. 1999. '"The Real is Relational": An Epistemological Analysis of Pierre Bourdieu's Generative Structuralism'. *Sociological Theory*, 17(1), 32–67.

Vanderstraeten, R. 2002. 'Cultural Values and Social Differentiation: The Catholic Pillar and its Education System in Belgium and the Netherlands'. *Compare*, 32(2), 133–48.

8 The fields of public policy[1]

Vincent Dubois

The notion of the field was conceived as a transposable tool capable of explaining the logics specific to each differentiated space of relationships and practices. As such, it is by definition applicable to all areas of sociological research, all the more so since the constitution of these areas very often replicates the differentiation of social spaces, as in the cases of sport, medicine, law, science, religion, politics, etc. It is, however, used to unequal degrees in the different cases. While it is central in sector sociologies, where it has given rise to many studies, such as the sociology of art or journalism, it is less present in transversal specialisms such as the sociology of work, occupations or deviance. My concern here is with what is commonly called public policy analysis. It is an area of social science research where the concept of the field is very little used.[2] My aim will therefore be not so much to draw up a critical assessment of its uses as to explore its potential contributions, from the more general standpoint of the sociologization of a research specialism whose dominant approaches are sometimes only distantly related to the conceptual and methodological tools forged by sociology. After a rapid presentation of the main competing concepts currently deployed in this area and their limits, I shall set out how the principles of field sociology can be applied to give an account of the space of production of public policies. Finally, on that basis I shall formulate propositions for a relational analysis that accounts for the modes of domination and legitimation at work in public policy.

Public policy without the field

Research in public policy analysis remains dominated by approaches that are remote from the concepts and methods of sociology (Dubois 2009). Inherited from the *policy science* developed in the United States in the 1950s, it first concentrated on analysing processes (most commonly agenda setting, decision making, development, implementation and evaluation), with the often pragmatic aim of improving governmental practices. It conceived policy as a chain of sequences rather than in terms of a sociological analysis of the groups involved in making it. Specifically sociological concerns mainly appeared in the analysis of the social construction of public problems, which represents a major contribution to the critical understanding of policies (Gusfield 1981). This latter trend, working from a symbolic interactionist perspective, is little concerned, however, with systematic objectivation of the systems of positions of the actors. Public policy analysis is nonetheless rich in concepts devised to account for the configurations, systems and social milieux in which policies are produced. For lack of space, I shall give here only the main examples (for a fuller discussion, see Hassenteufel 2008).

Public policy networks: empirical unfolding and normative assumptions

In the study of the production and implementation of public policies, analysis in terms of networks is no doubt the approach most frequently adopted. Developed in the 1970s in the United States and Great Britain, it has given rise to the concept of the *policy community,* which designates the set of actors, of varying status – politicians, civil servants, experts, representatives of interest groups, etc. – who interact in defining a policy. Subsequently, the concept of the *issue network* has come to designate more specifically the network formed around the resolution of a certain type of problem (Le Galès and Thatcher 1995). The initial intention is very simple. Essentially it is to underline that public actors are not the only actors who determine the orientations of policies, and to integrate into the analysis their relations with private actors, essentially the interest groups who, as is well known, are present in the American political system of *lobbying*. From this flows a whole series of notions. Members of the specialist Congressional committees, civil servants in the relevant federal agencies and the corresponding interest groups are linked in *iron triangles*. The actors in heterogeneous positions brought together by a problem on which they share a common vision form *advocacy coalitions* (Bergeron *et al.* 1998). The experts, civil servants, politicians and other promoters of public policies who have the same ways of thinking and analysing make up an *epistemic community* (Haas 1992), and so on.

The use of these concepts raises several problems. The variants that have been mentioned may serve as useful descriptive labels, but their analytical scope in the sense of the capacity to generate new hypotheses seems limited relative to the abundance of theoretical discussions to which they give rise. The heterogeneity of their intellectual and disciplinary origins is compounded by the diversity of sectoral and national terrains and the distinctive dynamics of a scientific sub-field whose development and autonomization have grown considerably since the early 1980s. The proliferation of new ad hoc concepts has prevailed over the effort to transpose generic concepts that have already proven their worth in the social sciences.

In these theories, the overarching concept of the network is itself used in heterogeneous senses. They are descriptive or metaphorical, making little use of the conceptual tools and techniques of the sociology of networks (Mercklé 2004). There is little recourse to quantification, which plays a decisive role both empirically and analytically in network sociology. Ultimately, these uses derive from a theoretical and political presupposition – that public policy stems from horizontal cooperation among weakly or non-hierarchized actors, whose hierarchization, so far as it exists, is in constant flux. Playing down the power relations and the phenomena of domination and concentration of power, this way of conceiving networks therefore has strong affinities with the thesis that a system of *multi-level governance* has replaced the State – or should do so. As such, the concept of the network may turn out to be more prescriptive than descriptive.

Analysis of public policies in France makes extensive use of these frameworks of analysis. It nonetheless has its particularities, notably the fact that it is strongly marked by two currents: Michel Crozier's strategic analysis and the cognitive approach stemming from the work of Bruno Jobert and Pierre Muller. Each has developed their own conceptualization of the systems of relationships that lie behind policies.

Concrete action systems in public policy making

The concept of *concrete action systems* occupies an essential place in the conceptual apparatus of the sociology of organizations as formalized by Crozier and Friedberg (1981). By drawing attention to the real relations between actors and so moving beyond the juridical analysis of formal organizations, it has shed light, in particular, on the modes of functioning of bureaucracies, the management of reforms and the power games behind local policies (Dupuy and Thœnig 1983; Grémion 1976).

However, beyond its general limitations (such as weak historicization or the failure to take account of the social characteristics of the actors), the action system concept raises a whole set of problems when applied to public policy. Some of these limits have long been made clear (Jobert and Leca 1980). Three will be mentioned briefly here.

First, while strategic analysis, through the concept of the concrete action system, has an undeniable critical strength in comparison with conventional decisionist models and the over-politicized vision generally associated with them, it has the vice of its virtues. Adopting the opposite perspective, it postulates that everything derives from a play of interactions and power within which the political is only one actor among others and where party affiliations, the specific constraints of the craft of politics and ideological orientations are not pertinent variables. It thus presents a depoliticized vision of public intervention, detached from the electoral game and more generally from relations of political exchange. This may in some cases result from empirical observation, but it is a debatable preconception if taken as an initial postulate.

Second, the conception of a power present at the level of each relationship among actors and the postulate of the non-hierarchization of action systems (it is posited *a priori* that no system can exert pressure on the others) make it impossible to account for the phenomenon of the concentration of powers. The notion that the State only exists in the diffraction of the games of concrete and localized powers constitutes an advance on demiurgic visions that make it an abstract, homogeneous entity (the vision of jurists and also of one strand of Marxism), but masks the general structuring of the relations of domination in and through the historical process of accumulation of the resources that constitute it.

A third limitation can be added: it lies in the fact that the strategic and interactionist vision prevalent in the concept of the action system leads to neglect of the symbolic dimension of the exercise of power and therefore of the conduct of policies. However, it is an essential dimension, both because public intervention also consists to some extent (which varies from case to case) in acting on social representations (accrediting the vision of a problem and thereby orienting behaviours) and because it is bound up with the symbolic exchanges in which the political process is played out par excellence: the legitimation of political power and of those who claim the right to exercise it (Lagroye 1985).

Sectors and frames of reference

The symbolic dimension (which in this case is termed 'cognitive') is, by contrast, central to the model of analysis formalized by Jobert and Muller (1987). Without entering into the detail of a system of interpretation that has given rise to many commentaries (see in particular Desage and Godard 2005), I shall focus here only on what is directly relevant to a possible comparison with field sociology. Jobert and Muller's analysis shares with field sociology – and indeed with many others – the initial hypothesis of a growing differentiation of spheres of social activity inspired (distantly, in this case) by Durkheim's thesis of the progress of the division of labour. Thus the authors consider that under the combined effect of the Industrial Revolution, the development of means of communication, the proliferation of specialist occupations and the growth of a State apparatus that is both centralized and internally specialized, territorialized societies (where social identity, the representation of interests and the regulation of conflicts had a local base) have been replaced by sector-divided societies (in which identities and interests are more occupationally defined and where social regulation is conducted more by sector of activity, at national level, or at least is no longer strictly attached to a place). One example would be the substitution of the farmer, a member of an occupation organized into unions and a specialized actor in an economic sector regulated as such, for the peasant, a polyvalent social figure defined by his attachment to a territory that constitutes his social and political horizon. Another would be the transformation of the systems of solidarity, with the creation of the welfare state substituting national redistribution based on social, generally occupational, status for public or private charity operating on a local basis – prolonging in this respect the church aid dispensed to the parish poor.

In a sector-divided society such as France, the political risk is no longer so much a break-up through the secession of territories, as disintegration, since each sector tends to function by imposing its own logic.[3] Beyond the handling of the problems specific to each sector, the function that defines public policies consists in 'managing the relationship between the sectors and the whole', i.e. regulating the relations among interdependent sectors (such as industry and transport), dealing with the effects of each sectoral policy (the modernization of agriculture in the 1950s accelerated the rural exodus, creating new housing needs in the cities, the fulfilment of which led to urban planning problems with their own social impact), and finally and most importantly, adjusting each sector to the dominant social and political model (winding down traditional agriculture when society required 'modernization', making the universities 'efficient' to fit the model of competition and the market).

This analysis, while in many respects compatible with the tools of field sociology, makes no reference to it. The authors use the term 'sectors' to designate broadly spheres of activity that could be analysed as fields. They define a sector as 'a vertical structuring of social roles (generally occupational) that defines the rules by which it functions, selects its elites, develops its specific norms and values, and draws its boundaries' (Jobert and Muller 1987: passim). While they note that a sector is riven with dissensions, they do not, as one would for a field, establish the polarities that structure it or explain the logics of its internal competitions. To designate the actors intermediate between a sector and the public authorities, who play a decisive role in the orientation of policies, they use the concept of the mediator, a kind of organic intellectual of sectoral policies who produces a system of representation (a 'sector frame of reference [*référentiel*]'; Jobert and Muller 1987: passim), linked to power relations and practices of intervention. However, by limiting themselves to identifying a few individual mediators, whose decisive role is deduced intuitively rather than systematically demonstrated, they avoid the need to reconstruct the system of positions specific to each sector, which is the only way to understand sociologically the structure of the kinds of capital and the relationships that underlie the positions of influence.

This approach is called 'cognitive', in that it puts social representations, regarded as the matrix of policies, at the centre of the demonstration. 'To devise a public policy amounts to constructing a representation, an image of the reality on which one wants to intervene. It is by reference to this cognitive image that the actors organize their perception of the system, compare their solutions and define their proposals for action' (Jobert and Muller 1987: passim). It is the frame of reference of policy, defined as 'the set of norms or images of reference by which the criteria of State intervention and the objectives of the public policy in question are defined' (Jobert and Muller 1987: passim). The 'sector frame of reference' is deduced empirically from the discourse of the mediators, which is then akin to the shorthand for a representation articulated with practices, which has primacy at a given moment over rival representations because of its compatibility with the 'overall frame of reference'; by contrast, field sociology would seek to reconstruct systematically the genesis of the norms and rules that specify it. The 'overall frame of reference' has a still more uncertain status and empirical foundation. It corresponds to very general principles (modernization in the period 1945–75, then the social market economy), for which a social history would have to reconstruct precisely that which is here only alluded to: the producers, the sites of production, the forms in which they are presented, through a methodical study of a clearly identified corpus – as Bourdieu and Boltanski did in their article on 'the production of the dominant ideology' (Bourdieu and Boltanski 1976).

In short, not only is field sociology almost totally ignored by Anglo-American work in this area, but it is also neglected by French research that claims to analyse public policies, even when, as has been seen, it could at least provide some useful complements and correctives.[4]

The space of production of a policy

The approach in terms of field can, more ambitiously, be mobilized to ground a truly sociological analysis of public policy. This will become apparent as I give a first glimpse of how it might be used to construct the space of policy production.

Propositions

One postulate and two initial hypotheses

The mobilization of the concept of the field in order to construct the space of production of a policy is based on a postulate that makes it possible to construct the policy as a sociological object. This postulate breaks as much with the classic conceptions of public policy as the product of a 'will', a decision, and/or of a rational progression of thought, as with contemporary analyses that see it as an unpredictable effect of interaction – the 'garbage can model' (Cohen *et al.* 1972) – or of ideas considered as matrices of action (*Revue française de science politique*, 2000). It consists in regarding public policy as the product of the practices and representations of the agents involved in it, these practices and representations being determined by the social characteristics, interests and objective positions of the agents, and therefore the structure of the relationships among them. By making it possible to objectivate the structure of the positions, of the corresponding position-takings and the relationships, analysis in terms of field enables one to bring to light the social foundations of a policy and so put forward a sociological analysis.

This postulate leads to the formulation of two main basic hypotheses. The first takes up one of the axioms of field sociology, positing a relation of homology between positions and position-takings, and consists in relating the options and orientations competing in the definition of a policy (reducing costs for employers or reducing working time to create jobs, preferring road or rail transport) to the positions and interests of those who advocate them (employers' representatives or senior civil servants and activist experts in the Ministry of Labour; auto industry lobbyists or ecologist politicians). A second hypothesis, more original and rarely tested empirically, consists in establishing a correspondence between the content of a policy (its orientation, its style), and the relational structure of the space of the agents involved in its production. It is this hypothesis that I propose to develop by considering a policy as the objectivation, in a politically legitimated mode of intervention, of a provisional state of the power relations within the field of struggles over the legitimate definition of this intervention.

Applications and scope of a concept

Pierre Bourdieu gave an example of this in his work on housing, analysing the space of positions and position-takings underlying the production of housing policies (Bourdieu 2003). He shows how change in the relative values of the kinds of capital within the bureaucratic field (cf. *infra*) in the latter half of the 1970s, during the presidency of Valéry Giscard d'Estaing, facilitated a conjunctural alliance between young technician graduates of the École Polytechnique and young financial administrators from the École Nationale d'Administration to gain the upper hand over the positions previously established in housing policy making – civil servants in the Ministère de l'Equipement, local politicians and representatives of joint public-private undertakings. The former were thus able to impose the 'modern' and 'liberal' vision attached to their own position and interests, relegating the ideas of the latter as 'archaic'. One then understands the social and also ideological foundations of the decline of building subsidies (*aide à la pierre*) in favour of personal subsidies (*aide à la personne*), the technical translation of an individualization of the housing question (financial support for households rather than building social housing), signalling the start of the move to neoliberalism.

The same framework of analysis can be applied to French language policies in France in the late 1980s (Dubois 2006a). Since their development in the mid-1960s, the making of these policies had been dominated by agents with traditional positions, in particular members of the Académie Française who found a way of reinvesting capital that was being devalued within the literary field. Their orientation was then purist or at least defensive, against the 'invasion' of English. The occupants of 'progressive' positions, more open-minded and hostile to purism, were found in particular among the linguists, who were more or less excluded from the space of production of language policies, just as they were kept out of the Académie Française. It was the valorization of the scientific capital of expertise within the bureaucratic field, in the reformist moment that corresponded to the appointment of Michel Rocard as prime minister in 1988, that for the first time allowed linguists to be brought into influential positions: adviser to the prime minister (Pierre Encrevé), vice-president of the Conseil supérieur de la langue française (Bernard Quémada), Délégué général à la langue française (Bernard Cerquiglini).

It was the incoming of new personnel that lay behind the (partially abortive) shift to a policy that sought to be more open to change (spelling reform, feminization of the names of occupations) and linguistic diversity (recognition of regional and minority languages).

Through these examples it can be seen that, considered in this light, the contribution of field sociology to the analysis of public policy goes far beyond the simple morphology of the governing groups, the elite 'decision makers' with social properties that can be established. It is much more a matter of showing what the properties of the agents and the logic of their relationships induce in terms of position-takings, i.e. symbolic production (expert opinions, ideological constructions, legitimate visions of the world) and, inseparably, practices of intervention (laws, regulations, budget decisions, reforms, institution building, resource allocation, etc.).[5]

It can also be seen that this application goes far beyond the slightly sophisticated version of Marxism to which the critics of field sociology often try to reduce it (see, for example, Alexander 1995). What the empirical mobilization of this sociology shows in this case is that the field of production of a policy is rarely reducible to the mechanical reflection of a class relation, and that the dominant groups in established positions have not always won the game in advance. One frequent characteristic of such a field is that it is composite: civil servants whose hierarchical positions, the generations, corps and institutions they belong to are different – experts, representatives of industries, trade unions and diverse interests, etc. Alliances are constantly made and unmade, and these fluctuations can explain the changes of orientation.

Finally it can be seen that objectivating the structure of such a field does not lead to a fixist vision of an immutable order whose reproduction consists in a replication of the *status quo ante*. Giving an account of its successive states makes it possible, on the contrary, by identifying the shifts in the power relations, better to understand political changes that can no more be ascribed to the individual 'wills' of the decision makers or their replacement than to a simple 'adaptation' of public choices to the objective development of the situations on which they bear.

Questions

The perspective of which the main foundations have just been outlined leads one to formulate a set of questions that make it possible both to test the rigour of the use of the concept of the field and make it function as a tool for the formulation of empirically oriented hypotheses. Starting out with five classic questions in field sociology (Bourdieu 1992, 1993), I shall reformulate them and apply them to the space of production of public policies.

A field constitutes itself by defining a stake that is specific to it, irreducible to those of other fields. A first question consists in establishing what stake specifies the space of production of a policy. One can answer this by positing that it is the power to regulate a particular sphere of practices (immigration, housing, education, health, etc.) by mobilizing resources (financial, legal, administrative, etc.) specific to a public institution (national government, local authority, European Union (EU), etc.), or one linked to the public authorities (a joint public-private agency, a para-public body, an association financed with public funds, a social security body, etc.).

Second, how does one define and delimit this space? As with any field, its periphery cannot be posited *a priori*, but results from the reconstruction performed in the course of the study. In his research on housing policy, Pierre Bourdieu starts by identifying those whom he calls the efficient agents, on the basis of institutional positions, reputation analysis and a survey of position-takings; this then serves as a basis for a systematic reconstruction of the whole through successive crosschecks and additions. In many cases, the ad hoc committees set up to address a particular problem or domain can be analysed as the objectivation of the 'hard core' of the field in question and as such can be the object of a specific study. This is, for example, what I set out to do in reconstructing the formation of a legitimate space for the working out of cultural policies in France in the 1960s starting from the cultural committees of the National Plan (Dubois 1999). Here as elsewhere, indeed more so, the definition of the limits of the field is a stake in the struggle, because being 'inside' or 'outside' here corresponds to obtaining, or not, official recognition of the right to intervene in the regulation of a sphere of activity and the potential to contribute effectively to it. In the case in question, it was thus possible to establish how and for what reasons artists were – counter-intuitively – initially excluded from the field of production of cultural policies.

The existence of a field presupposes a degree of autonomy, short of which a field ceases to function as such, because it is subject to external logics. Far removed from the theoretical debates of the Marxist tradition (see in particular Poulantzas 1973) on the autonomy of the State relative to the dominant classes, field sociology invites one to reconstruct empirically the historical configurations of the power relations internal to each field and the respective chances their different fractions have of bearing on the orientation of the policies. In complementary fashion it invites one to establish the state of the political and bureaucratic fields that determines the possibilities of alliances and the types of exchange with these different fractions, the regulation of their differentiated access to the sites of power and public resources, the capacity or propensity to gain the upper hand over them or to convert their demands into official policy. In other words, it is a matter of establishing the systems of relations among different systems of relations (or fields), following the logic of a conception of the State as a meta-field (cf. *infra*), which clearly opens more on to sociological research than to general, abstract discussion of its autonomy.

Fourth question: what are the principles of opposition that structure the field of production of a policy? The answer has to be established case by case, but some recurrent principles can nonetheless be identified. The pole of the agents who successfully claim to speak for the general interest (e.g. senior civil servants, 'qualified persons') is opposed to the pole gathering those who are thrown back on the defence of particular interests (e.g. trade union representatives, locally elected politicians); this opposition may overlap with that which separates generalist agents from sector specialists. The two competing principles of legitimacy – competence and political legitimacy – oppose the experts to elected representatives, in a game of mutual delegitimation between 'technocrats' who are seen as aspiring to take over power and 'politicians' chiefly concerned to be re-elected (Dubois and Dulong 1999). Within the bureaucratic field, one generally observes a combination of hierarchical, vertical oppositions (central State versus local authorities, senior versus junior civil servants), functional oppositions (e.g. financial departments versus spending departments) and institutional competitions between 'bureaucratic fiefdoms' (Allison 1969) defending divergent interests and orientations. At the level of the individual agents, this corresponds to competitions between different kinds of bureaucratic capital, also linked to generational oppositions: experience versus technical knowledge; internal competences and legal or practical mastery of the rules of the game versus sectoral competences, transposable outside of the bureaucracy.

These principles of opposition combine with principles of grouping and solidarity, such as the classic *esprit de corps* observed among senior members of the different branches of the French civil service. These often confer a strategic importance on the intermediate positions that emerge at the interface between these polarities, such as those of the 'mediators' mentioned above in Jobert and Muller's analysis – multipositioned experts, the professionalized trade unionists close to administrative circles, those who move from one branch to another, and the ex-civil servants who have been headhunted by the private sector (the *'pantoufleurs'*). No less strategic are the intermediate spaces – conferences, think tanks and 'neutral sites' (Bourdieu and Boltanski 1976) where employers and civil servants, experts and trade unionists, or elected officials from different camps meet and forge a common language.

Fifth and final question: what are the products of these competitions? They are politically legitimated ways of seeing a 'problem' or a sphere of activity (objectivated, for example, in speeches and official reports) and handling it (materialized in projects and reforms). These products are formally legitimated by their endorsement by an agent endowed with political authority (a mayor, a minister, etc.) or sanctioned by a vote. They are also legitimated by the very logic of the functioning of the field, by observance of the procedures, by the claim to technical or scientific competence, by the accumulation of symbolic capital, by recourse to public opinion, by more or less theatrical consultation or the regulated confrontation of rival points of view aimed at producing a more or less illusory consensus – similar to what happens in the committees discussed above, which are nothing less than 'power technologies', machines for generating legitimacy. For example, Pierre-Édouard Weill shows with reference to the expansion of home ownership and the '100,000 euro house' scheme that the creation of a space of deliberation mobilizing 'civil society' in the name of the 'mutualization of competences' was accompanied by a quasi-monopoly retained by the traditionally dominant agents (the minister and his *cabinet* of advisers) in the orientation of the scheme and by strongly personalized political profits (the dwellings were known as 'Borloo houses', named after the minister). The case reveals the more general invention of an apparently paradoxical mode of 'authoritarian consultation' that disguises a very conventional centralist State interventionism under the modernist trappings of neoliberal governance (Weill 2007).

Mobilizing field sociology in order to reconstruct the space of production and the modalities of production of public policy thus makes it possible to understand the product (public policy) and, most importantly, the conditions and modalities of legitimation.

Clarifications

At this point three clarifications regarding method are called for. First, the objectivation of the fields of policy production is not limited to an approach by sector (family, transport, tourism, etc.) but can be used to identify spaces that have a transversal role in as much as their products affect all fields of public intervention or at least several of them. Once again I am thinking of Bourdieu and Boltanski's (1976) seminal article on the dominant ideology, or studies that objectivate the spaces of production of the praxeologies of public policy, neoliberalism (Denord 2007) or thinking in terms of risks (Daccache 2008).

Second, while for the purposes of presentation the preceding pages set out a 'hard' or 'orthodox' version of analysis in terms of fields, it should be noted that mobilizing field sociology does not mean seeking at all costs to demonstrate the existence of a field, by subjecting each and every space to a multiple correspondence analysis (MCA) from which polarities and systems of opposition can always be derived. Likewise, it is not a matter of posing in this respect a quasi-theological question (is this or is it not a 'true' field?), but of formulating it in and for a sociological reasoning in practice (what can one see by analysing this space as a field that one would otherwise not see?). This implies that one should neither forget the demands imposed by the rigorous use of a concept that takes on its full meaning only when the whole set of concepts with which it is logically articulated (in particular, autonomy, habitus, capital, rules, stakes, specific principles) is mobilized, nor forego the contributions that field sociology can make (in particular, understanding positions relationally, establishing polarities, associating positions with position-takings so as to analyse spaces that strictly cannot usefully be designated as fields).

Finally, the foregoing presentation could give the impression that analysis of public policy in terms of fields is limited to the dominant positions and to the – admittedly essential – phase of the social genesis of public policies (called 'elaboration' in public policy analysis). On the contrary, this analysis also makes it possible to account for the concrete production of policies 'on the ground', involving agents at all levels (what is generally called 'imple-mentation'); Bourdieu's work on housing again gives a good example of this (Bourdieu 2003). One could go even further and imagine a sociology of public policy that would take the programme of field sociology to its logical con-clusion and articulate the reconstruction of the space of policy producers with that of the space of its 'recipients' – beneficiaries, target populations, groups indirectly affected, etc. In short, this sociology can be useful in the analysis of policies far beyond the analysis simply of dominant groups and the moments of genesis.

Public policy from the inter-field to the meta-field

It is clear, then, that while systematic reconstruction of the space of produc-tion of a policy is a first essential contribution from field sociology, it would be reductive to stop there. This sociology also invites one to account for the relations between social spaces that are constitutive of public policy and, in doing so, to grasp the complexity of the relations of domination and legitimation that characterize the intervention of the public authorities.

Public policy as a product of the relations among fields

Like every social object, public policy has to be analysed as the product of social relations. In this case, the multiplicity of these relations and the diver-sity of the positions of the agents engaged in them are such that they cannot easily be circumscribed to a single field. While, as has been seen, there is a gain from reconstructing the specific space of the making production of a policy with the aid of field sociology, this approach must therefore be com-bined, at a second level, with an analysis of the relations among the fields or fractions of fields mobilized in the pursuit of a policy. In other words, beyond a purely monographic use of the concept of the field, one has to establish (systems of) relations among (systems of) relations.

Bilateral relations

The simplest form that these relations among systems of relations can take concerns the exchanges, collaborations, confrontations, etc., that are estab-lished bilaterally between the fraction of the governmental space mobilized in the public handling of a particular domain (e.g. the civil servants and political agents at least temporarily in charge of a particular sector or dossier) and the corresponding field. What is called 'cultural policy' can be analysed from this standpoint as the product of the relations between the field of culture and the group of administrative and political agents who intervene on cultural ques-tions within the governmental space. The history of cultural policy is then defined as the history of these relations. Reconstructing them makes it possible, in particular, to understand the formation of inter-field alliances which could not have happened at other times, and in which one finds the principle of the major innovations or reorientations in this domain – even if credit for them may be claimed by or attributed to singular agents. The first political formalization in France of a 'republican policy for the arts', for example, sprang from the encounter, in the late nineteenth century, between reformist administrators, the composite milieu of the 'industrial arts' and the avantgarde of the artistic field; it was facilitated by political agents who were both novices and multipositioned, and made possible by a political conjuncture favourable to innovation (Dubois 2001). The institutionalization of policies for culture in the modern sense of the term corresponds to a moment when the field of culture was sufficiently established for the intervention of the State to be seen as a support rather than external interference, and when the central administration was strengthening itself in a modernizing direction that favoured the opening up of new areas of intervention. The collaborations that could then be established gave a social foundation to the principle of 'cultural democratization' as a rallying cry whose dual political and cultural connotation clearly indicated its origin: a technocratic humanism taking up and neutralizing the political velleities of the artists in a compromise between agents of the bureaucratic and cultural fields – much more than in the 'genius' attributed to the minister André Malraux, which is not to say that he played no part in the working out of these compromises, and then thanks to them (Dubois 1999). Such a perspective enables one to reformulate in sociological terms the question of the role of 'the State' in 'culture' as it is naïvely posed in public debates and philosophical or legal essays, by orienting research towards identifying the objective, historically situated positions and relations rather than speculating on the desirable relationship between two abstract entities.

Beyond this particular case, this approach can be applied to any policy that touches on the functioning of a field constituted as such – education, science or sport, for example – even when this field is itself constituted within public institutions, as in the case of the field of justice. It is especially fertile when it is seeking to account for the genesis of new categories. The notion of 'mental health', for example, is in part the product of the relations established between the agents of the administrative field of public health and the agents of a fraction of the field of psychiatry, who had integrated the critique of anti-psychiatry and were arguing for a more social definition and an extension of their speciality (Courtin 2006).

The concordance of fields

It would, however, be too simple to consider that a policy stems only from the binary confrontation between the political-bureaucratic space on one side and the field concerned on the other. That is a possible configuration, especially when the question is very specific and circumscribed and/or the field is strongly self-enclosed and its functioning has little effect on the functioning of other fields, as in the case of measures that are presented as 'technical' and receive little publicity. This kind of closure is also found when governmental control is such that it restricts the relationships to face-to-face dealings with select groups, a case exemplified by the corporatist system of authoritarian regimes. In most cases, the multiplicity of the spaces and sub-spaces involved in generating a policy in fact entails a much more complex set of interrelations.

To confirm this, one only has to observe the production of the 'reforms' that are now proliferating to the point of becoming almost synonymous with 'government policies'. At least as regards reforms on a certain scale, understanding their emergence and their conditions of realization implies not only reconstructing the field of the reformers or the 'reforming nebula' (Topalov 1999) but also establishing the state of the internal power relations in the various fields concerned and ways in which they became interrelated. Even a seemingly technical question, internal to the bureaucratic field, such as the reform of the State, originates and derives its logic from its handling in different spaces and through their interrelation: the airing of the administrative question in the press; its transformation into a stake in electoral competition; the intellectual and literary investments of senior civil servants in devising and diffusing reformist arguments (Baruch and Bezès 2006). The 'Juppé Plan' for reform of social security (Lebaron 2001) and the closer checks on the unemployed in the 'Social Cohesion Plan' in France (Dubois 2006b) have been analysed in this way.

These reforms give rise to intense mobilizations in the political and bureaucratic fields. Their economic and social stakes mobilize the field of the employers (through its representatives) and the field of the trade unions, which together constitute the institutionalized space of power relations (known as the 'social partners') in which the regulation of employment relations and the management of the 'social State' are in part debated and defined. In a social and political system where both the legitimation of governmental reforms and the success of the mobilizations that try to inflect them are partly played out in the media, one has to add the specific contribution of the journalistic field. In a complex domain, and in an age when 'competence' – especially in economics – is a major political resource, one finally has to add the composite space of the production of expertise, at the interface between the bureaucratic and scientific fields.

The dominant poles of these different fields are, for reasons that may differ, favourable to reform or have an interest in it. At the very least, as the case of the trade union field shows, the logic of relations with the governmental fields has the consequence that only the positions (opinions) that run in this direction can be heard, which in turn reinforces the positions (places) of those who express them in the power relations internal to this field. Reform projects that are attributed to the governmental 'will' are thus possible only in and through the convergence of logics and interests that are (partially) specific to distinct but interrelated spaces of interrelation. To some extent, they arise from this convergence, in so far as the governing politicians (who are not necessarily their only or main initiators) have integrated them into the space of the politically possible only because they knew they could count on a favourable convergence.

This convergence does not, however, spring from pure chance or from the quasi-spontaneous alignment described by analyses in terms of 'windows of opportunity' (Kingdon 1984). Linked to the power relations internal to the different fields, it stems from the collusions that may be established between one field and another and the power relations among the fields. Examples would be the relations between employers, the press and politicians, or the exchanges between trade unionists and experts. While it would once again be too simple to consider that these convergences are produced solely by a government capable of making and unmaking the positions within each field, this orchestration could indeed have a 'conductor' – to reverse Bourdieu's celebrated formula – in so far (and only in so far) as the distinctive feature of the field of political power is its capacity to act simultaneously in several fields, in particular by distributing positions of power to agents (appointing them to committees, entrusting them with missions, designating them as favoured interlocutors, etc.), thereby securing the means of exercising power over the internal equilibrium of the fields to which they belong.

The complexity of the relations of domination and legitimation

The structural and relational approach of field sociology makes it possible to account for the specification of spaces endowed with their own logics of functioning (the bureaucratic or scientific fields) and to reconstruct the relationships in which they engage in a realist manner, i.e. in terms of systems of objective positions, thus avoiding the reifying abstractions that interrelate pure concepts ('State' versus 'civil society'). Its use in analysing public policy makes it possible, in return, to shed light on the links between the socio-historical dynamics of the autonomization of social spaces and the transformations of the modes of exercise and legitimation of political power. Some partly counterintuitive hypotheses can be formulated about them: political power is not necessarily exercised at the expense of the autonomy of the social fields; this autonomy in turn is not necessarily an obstacle to the exercise of political power, but may on the contrary assist in its legitimation.

Paradoxes of the autonomization of fields and threats to autonomy

Public intervention in a field leads in the first analysis to action from outside on its functioning and therefore to a reduction of the autonomy that constitutes it as such, or even a threat to its existence. The limiting case arises in dictatorial regimes, where all spheres of activity are more or less subject to the rules of the political-bureaucratic apparatus – as in the Zhdanov model of scientific policy – to the point where the use of the concept of the field becomes problematic. Beyond this limiting case, public policy, like any external intervention (by the Church, or economic power) represents for the field in question the risk of having heteronomous logics imposed on it, unless this intervention can be seen as a neutral support merely recording the state of its internal power relations. This can sometimes be the case but the instances clearly cannot be generalized. The history of public policies is indeed strewn with examples where they play a decisive role in changing the internal power relations, such interventions being denounced as unacceptable political interference by those whose interests they compromise.

In contemporary liberal democracies, what more generally follows is the – at least partial – submission of public regulation of social relations to – at least formal – respect for the principle of self-organization of the differentiated social spaces. This is no doubt the central element in the sociological definition of such regimes. The – again partially realized and never definitively established – extension of the principle of the separation of powers to fields that have not managed to impose their autonomy as a social norm to be respected (the 'freedom' of the artist or entrepreneur, the 'independence' of the journalist or scientist, the irreducible specificity of the rules governing sporting or medical activity) marks the dual history of these political regimes and of the differentiation of the societies in which they have developed. This extension also marks the conditions and forms of intervention by the public authorities – if only because they must therefore, here in particular, 'observe the formalities', by following formal procedures and/or deploying all the technologies of power that distinguish their intervention from sovereign arbitrariness. This explains, for example, why, even if Western democracies have created ministries of sport and their leaders regularly attend sports events involving their national teams, it is unthinkable for them to intervene in the game (unlike the brother of the Emir of Kuwait, who came on to the pitch in the 1982 football World Cup to overrule the referee …).

Historical analysis of the genesis of fields enables one to see public intervention from another angle than that of the potential or actual reduction of their autonomy. Contrary to the spontaneous image of pre-existent fields in which the public authorities intervene in a second stage, this analysis, coupled with that of the historical formation of the State, reveals a process that is very often blended. Pierre Bourdieu, among others,[6] has shown the limits of the opposition between the State and the market, which underlies the political denunciation of public intervention as an illegitimate *dirigisme*, pointing out what the historical formation of the economic field owed to the State, notably through monetary unification, a *sine qua non* for the creation of a national market (Bourdieu 2003). The national academies, created under the aegis of the State and later denounced as the instrument of its interference in the artistic and literary fields, provided some of the earliest sites of debate, organization and consecration specific to literature and art, and were thus decisive steps in initiating their process of autonomization (Viala 1985). The development of sports policies in France in the 1960s, in a period of strong centralized public interventionism, greatly contributed to the autonomization of the sporting field in its contemporary forms (Defrance 1995).

Limiting ourselves to recent times, we can say that for half a century – broadly from the interwar period to the mid-1970s, and in ways that vary between countries and between fields – when the contemporary modes of public intervention were shaped, this intervention made a paradoxical contribution to constituting or preserving the autonomy of fields. It contributed to this autonomy, because political-bureaucratic structuring ratifies the differentiation of fields and strengthens it, reproducing the distinction of the different fields (sport, science, health, culture) in institutional structures (such as the sectoral ministries). It also contributed to autonomy because it is generally conducted at least in part in the name of the defence of the logics specific to these different fields, in particular against the risks of domination by the heteronomous logics of the economic field. The cultural policies of the 1960s were devised in the name of the principle of an artistic creation shielded from the laws of financial profitability, and a democratization of access to genuine art, which was thought to be unattainable purely through the free play of the market, and even blocked by the domination of the products of 'mass culture' imposed by the 'cultural industries'. The same observation could be transposed on a number of other sectoral policies.[7]

This contribution of public intervention to autonomization is at the same time paradoxical, inasmuch as the autonomy of fields is both won partly against the State and granted by the State. Moreover, at the same time as the State contributes to the autonomization of a field, its intervention is accompanied by the imposition of heteronomous principles (i.e. specific to the political and bureaucratic fields) or the formation of hybrid principles and beliefs, produced in the transactions between a specialist field and the political and bureaucratic fields. Belief in economic progress driven by science, social integration through sport, the democratization of culture, the principles of public health or equal opportunity in education, for example, are norms worked out in these relations between fields in the course of the development of public intervention and partly absorbed within each of the fields concerned.

In contrast to this paradoxical contribution to their autonomy, what is too hastily and in part wrongly called the withdrawal of the State – it is rather a neoliberal swing in public policies sometimes accompanied by a return to traditional forms and forces of the State, e.g. in security matters – has very largely consisted in imposing the logics of the economic field on the other fields. This can be seen in the areas of health, with the managerial reforms of the hospital system (Pierru 2007), higher education and research (Montlibert 2004; Bruno 2008), sport (Smith 2000) and culture, with the encouragement of corporate sponsorship and the growing submission of cultural activities to the needs of economic development at local level in EU cultural programmes – and the list is clearly not closed. The redeployment of public intervention is leading this time more to the heteronomization of the various social fields. The paradox previously identified may then be pushed to its extreme, since, contrary to common conceptions, it is 'interventionism' that, in certain conditions, favours the autonomy of fields and 'liberalism' that works in the other direction.

Longer legitimation circuits and more complex relations of domination

The question whether public policy is produced in bilateral relations between two spaces of positions (the governmental field and the specific field) or results from a much more complex system of interdependence involving several fields, sub-fields or fractions of fields is less theoretical than empirical. The situations vary from one case to another and according to the historical configurations. However, one can hypothesize a long-term trend towards the multiplication and diversification of interrelations in the conduct of public policy, corresponding to the lengthening of the circuits of legitimation, itself associated with a growing complexity of the relations of domination in contemporary societies (Bourdieu 1996: 382–89).

From this standpoint the intervention of multiple agents is a necessary condition for the legitimation of a public decision that could not easily be envisaged solely on the basis of the political legitimacy of the person who endorses it. This is seen in particular in the mechanisms for the delegation of judgement. When a government sets up a 'committee of wise persons' to clarify decisions with an ethical dimension, panels to choose an architect or artist from whom a work is to be commissioned, or a group of experts to settle an environmental controversy, it does so to avoid taking political responsibility for the choice, not so much because the questions are intrinsically complex but rather because they touch on fields of struggle over the definition and possession of the legitimate competence needed to handle them. The 'Borloo houses' mentioned earlier certainly sprang from the personal initiative and self-promotion of a minister, but their (relative) political success derived from the production of a consensus only made possible by the (relative) convergence of agents and groups in very different positions (local politicians of various hues, construction companies, financers of social housing, journalists, etc.) around home ownership as an ideal and as an answer to social and urban problems.

This intervention by agents in multiple positions, i.e. situated in different social spaces, does not so much lead to the dilution of the exercise of political power, as constitute a condition and modality of its legitimation. It is by demonstrating their capacity to gather 'competent persons' around themselves and 'organize the widest possible dialogue' that governments demonstrate their aptitude to govern and their legitimacy to do so. The agents appointed for their competence or intervening in various capacities in the making of a policy are all the more effective as auxiliaries of political power when they do not appear in that light but present themselves as independent of it, i.e. as the agents of a field whose rules and logics are irreducible to those of government. Just as the autonomy of the legal field permits the neutral translation of social power relations and so helps to perpetuate domination, and just as the autonomy of the cultural field permits the denial of the social that makes the strategies of distinction possible and effective (Bourdieu 1984), so the autonomy of fields is from this perspective not merely a constraint limiting interventionist velleities but also a resource for the exercise and legitimation of political power.

Conclusion

Public policy can thus be seen sociologically as a politically legitimated mode of regulation of the relations between fields, favouring their autonomy or not, correcting their relations of subordination or not – so long as this regulation is not seen as a form of centralized piloting but analysed as the product of power relations among these fields, and between each of them and the field of policy production. Here the sociology of public policy joins up with the sociology of the State as a 'meta-field' (Bourdieu 1994; Dubois 2007), whose power can be exerted by means of the accumulation of the resources available in the different fields, enabling it in return to intervene in them. Just as this analysis enables one, as has been seen, to avoid a simplifying vision of the relations between public intervention and the autonomy of social fields, so it allows the classic question of the autonomy of the State and its intervention to be examined in a less univocal and theoretical way than that of, for example, the 'armchair Marxists', one which brings to light the practices and objective relationships that underlie the system of generalized interdependence that characterizes contemporary Western societies.

Notes

1 This chapter was originally written in June 2009 for a francophone readership.
2 A few papers advocate the use of the notion of the field, mainly in education policy: Thomson 2005; Lingard *et al.* 2005; Lingard and Rawolle 2008; see also Duffy *et al.* 2010 on urban policy.
3 The fact that this contribution is part of a collective reflection conducted with Belgian colleagues immediately brings to light the nationally situated character of this type of analysis.
4 Beyond the concept of the field, Pierre Bourdieu's whole sociology is generally neglected by this work, almost the only exception being episodic references to *The State Nobility* for the sociology of the *grandes écoles* and the governing circles (Bourdieu 1996). It would take too long to examine here the reasons for this exclusion, which stem alternately (or simultaneously) from a demarcation from French political sociology (where reference to Bourdieu is very present), the potency of English-language references or competing sociologies such as Crozier's, and struggles between institutions (with, for example, the central role of the Paris *Institut d'Etudes Politiques*). Its consequence is that generations of researchers are trained without reference to and/or with an intellectual and/or political aversion to Bourdieu's sociology.
5 The currently fashionable theme of the instruments of public action, though aiming to bring together the symbolic or cognitive dimensions ('political theorization') and

the practical uses of the apparatus, ignores the social characteristics of the groups who produce and use these instruments (Lascoumes and Le Galès 2005).

6 See, for example, the work of economists on collective agreements.

7 One would need to be able to establish systematically the set of conditions required for public intervention to favour the autonomy of fields, which is beyond the scope of this chapter.

References

Alexander, J.C. 1995. *Fin de Siècle Social Theory: Relativism, Reduction and the Problem of Reason*. London: Verso.

Allison, G.T. 1969. 'Conceptual Models and the Cuban Missile Crisis'. *American Political Science Review*, 63(3), 689–718.

Baruch, M.-O. and Bezès, P. 2006. 'Généalogies de la réforme de l'Etat'. *Revue française d'administration publique*, 4(120), 625–33.

Bergeron, H., Surel, Y. and Valluy, J. 1998. 'L'advocacy coalition framework. Une contribution au renouvellement des études de politiques publiques'. *Politix*, 41, 195–223.

Bourdieu, P. 1984. *Distinction: A Social Critique of the Judgement of Taste*. London: Routledge; Cambridge, MA: Harvard University Press.

——1993. 'Some Properties of Fields'. In *Sociology in Question*. London: Sage Publications, 72–76.

——1992. 'The Logic of Fields'. In *An Invitation to Reflexive Sociology*. Chicago, IL: University of Chicago Press; Cambridge, MA: Polity Press, 94–115.

——1994. 'Rethinking the State: Genesis and Structure of the Bureaucratic Field'. *Sociological Theory*, 12(1), 1–18.

——1996. *The State Nobility: Elite Schools in the Field of Power*. Cambridge: Polity; Stanford, CA: Stanford University Press.

——2003. 'The State and the Construction of the Market and the Field of Local Powers'. In *The Social Structures of the Economy*. Cambridge: Polity Press, 89–147.

Bourdieu, P. and Boltanski, L. 1976. 'La production de l'idéologie dominante'. *Actes de la recherche en sciences sociales*, 2–3, juin, 4–73.

Bruno, I. 2008. *A vos marques, prêts … cherchez! La stratégie européenne de Lisbonne, vers un marché de la recherché*. Bellecombe-en-Bauges: Le Croquant.

Cohen, M.D., March, James G. and Olsen, J.P. 1972. 'A Garbage Can Model of Organizational Choice'. *Administrative Science Quarterly*, 17(1), 1–25.

Courtin, E. 2006. *Entre impératif gestionnaire et idéal militant. La politique publique de 'santé mentale' (1990–2005)*. Master's dissertation in social sciences of politics, IEP Strasbourg.

Crozier, M. and Friedberg, E. 1981. *Actors and Systems, the Politics of Collective Action*. Chicago: Chicago University Press.

Daccache, M. 2008. *La gestion des risques entre savoir et pouvoir. Genèse, structure et fonctionnement d'un champ de production des discours sur le risque*. Doctoral thesis in sociology. Paris: Ecole des Hautes Etudes en Sciences Sociales.

Defrance, J. 1995. 'L'autonomisation du champ sportif. 1890–1970'. *Sociologie et sociétés*, 27(1), 15–31.

de Montlibert, C. 2004. *Savoir à vendre. L'enseignement supérieur et la recherche en danger*. Paris: Raisons d'agir.

Denord, F. 2007. *Néo-libéralisme version française*. Paris: Demopolis.

Desage, F. and Godard, J. 2005. 'Désenchantement idéologique et réenchantement mythique des politiques locales'. *Revue française de science politique*, 55–4, 633–61.

Dubois, V. 1999. *La politique culturelle. Genèse d'une catégorie d'intervention publique.* Paris: Belin.

——2001. 'Le ministère des Arts ou l'institutionnalisation manquée d'une politique artistique républicaine (1881–82)'. *Sociétés et représentations*, 11, 229–61.

——2006a. 'La linguistique, science de gouvernement? Les linguistes et la politique de la langue française (1966–90)'. In O. Ihl (ed.) *Les sciences de l'action publique.* Presses Universitaires de Grenoble, 233–44.

——2006b. 'Le contrôle des chômeurs'. GSPE-DARES, ministère du Travail.

——2007. 'Etat'. In *Abécédaire de Pierre Bourdieu.* Éditions Sils Maria/Vrin, 63–67.

——2009. 'Action publique'. In A. Cohen, B. Lacroix and P. Riutort (eds) *Nouveau manuel de science politique.* Paris: La Découverte, 311–25.

Dubois, V. and Dulong, D. 1999. *La question technocratique. De l'invention d'une figure aux transformations de l'action publique.* Strasbourg: Presses universitaires de Strasbourg, coll. Sociologie politique européenne.

Duffy, M.M., Binder, A.J. and Skrentny, J.D. 2010. 'Elite Status and Social Change: Using Field Analysis to Explain Policy Formation and Implementation'. *Social Problems*, 57(1), 49–73.

Dupuy, F. and Thœnig, J.-C. 1983. *Sociologie de l'administration française.* Paris: A. Colin.

Grémion, P. 1976. *Le pouvoir périphérique. Bureaucrates et notables dans le système politique français.* Paris: Seuil.

Gusfield, J.R. 1981. *The Culture of Public Problems. Drinking-Driving and the Symbolic Order.* Chicago: University of Chicago Press.

Haas, P. 1992. 'Epistemic Communities and International Policy Co-ordination'. *International Organization*, 46(1), 1–35.

Hassenteufel, P. 2008. *Sociologie politique: l'action publique.* Paris: Armand Colin.

Jobert, B. and Leca, J. 1980. 'Le dépérissement de l'Etat. À propos de L'acteur et le système de Michel Crozier and Ehrard Friedberg'. *Revue française de science politique*, 30(6), 1125–71.

Jobert, B. and Muller, P. 1987. *L'Etat en action. Politiques publiques et corporatismes.* Paris: PUF.

Kingdon, J. 1984. *Agendas, Alternatives and Public Policies.* Boston: Little, Brown.

Lagroye, J. 1985. 'La legitimation'. In M. Grawitz and J. Leca (eds) *Traité de science politique*, vol. 1. Paris: PUF, 395–467.

Lascoumes, P. and Le Galès, P. (eds) 2005. *Gouverner par les instruments.* Paris: Presses de Sciences-Po.

Lebaron, F. 2001. 'Chômage, précarité, pauvreté. Quelques remarques sur la définition sociale des objectifs de politique économique'. *Regards sociologiques*, 21, 67–78.

Le Galès, P. and Thatcher, M. (eds) 1995. *Les réseaux de politiques publiques. Débat autour des policy networks.* Paris: L'Harmattan.

Lingard, B. and Rawolle, S. 2008. 'The Sociology of Pierre Bourdieu and Researching Education Policy'. *Journal of Education Policy*, 23(6), 729–41.

Lingard, B., Rawolle, S. and Taylor, S. 2005. 'Globalising Policy Sociology in Education: Working with Bourdieu'. *Journal of Education Policy*, 20(6), 759–77.

Mercklé, P. 2004. *Sociologie des réseaux.* Paris: La Découverte.

Pierru, F. 2007. *Hippocrate malade de ses réformes.* Bellecombe-en-Bauges: Le Croquant.

Poulantzas, N. 1973. *Political Power and Social Classes.* London: Secker and Warburg.
Sabatier, P.A. and Schlager, E. 2000. 'Les approches cognitives des politiques publiques'. *Revue française de science politique*, 50(2), 209–35.
Smith, A. 2000. 'Comment le néolibéralisme gagne sur le territoire. A propos de certaines transformations récentes du rugby'. *Politix*, 50, 73–92.
Thomson, P. 2005. 'Bringing Bourdieu to Policy Sociology: Codification, Misrecognition and Exchange Value in the UK Context'. *Journal of Education Policy*, 20(6), 741–58.
Topalov, C. (ed.) 1999. *Laboratoires du nouveau siècle. La nébuleuse réformatrice et ses réseaux en France 1880–1914*. Paris: Editions de l'Ecole des Hautes Etudes en Sciences Sociales.
Viala, A. 1985. *Naissance de l'écrivain: sociologie de la littérature à l'âge classique.* Paris: Minuit.
Weill, P.-E. 2007. *La maison à 100 000 euros: une 'affaire' d'Etat*. Master's dissertation in social sciences of politics, IEP Strasbourg.

9 Field theory and organizational power

Four modes of influence among public policy 'think tanks'

Thomas Medvetz

How do power and influence accrue within organizations? The prevailing social scientific answer to this question has been that an organization becomes powerful by specializing in a particular function and monopolizing the resource or resources associated with that function. This view is consistent with Marx's claim that the bourgeoisie exercised power over workers, intellectuals and the state by controlling the means of production. The later interventions of Marxists in organizational theory reflected a similar assumption. As Scott summarized, in the Marxist view, 'organizational structures are ... power systems designed to maximize control and profits', as opposed to 'rational systems for performing work in the most efficient manner' (Scott 1992: 115).

While Weber's theory departed from the materialism in Marx's approach, he nonetheless described the power of a bureaucratic organization in broadly similar terms by emphasizing functional specialization. For Weber, quite simply, 'bureaucracy has been and is a power instrument of the first order' that 'rests upon ... a functional specialization of work, and an attitude set for habitual and virtuoso-like mastery of single yet methodically integrated functions' (Weber 1946a [1915]: 228–29). More broadly, Weber argued that modernity itself was marked by a growing separation among 'life orders' or 'value spheres' – that is, increasingly distinct domains of action dedicated to particularized functions (Weber 1946b [1915]). Science, art, politics, law, religion and domestic life: each realm acquired its distinctiveness and irreducibility through the development of its own institutions, themselves administered by specialists with particular skills.

In contemporary theory, the idea that an organization's power is based on functional specialization has received its most extensive treatment in the work of Pierre Bourdieu, and more broadly in the family of approaches known as field theory.[1] In Bourdieu's rendering, for example, the power circulating in a field depends on its inhabitants' ability to monopolize and even define a given socially valued resource. As Wacquant explains, a field is a system of relations 'in which participants vie to establish monopoly over the species of capital effective in it – cultural authority in the artistic field, scientific authority in the scientific field, sacerdotal authority in the religious field, and so forth'

(Bourdieu and Wacquant 1992: 17). The most straightforward interpretation of the role of organizations in this theory is that they acquire power by coordinating social action in the competitive pursuit of some specialized form of value.

This chapter extends the scholarly discussion about the relationship between organizations, power and fields by identifying four ways of thinking about organizational power from a standpoint informed by field theory. To provide an empirical anchor for the discussion, I will focus on the growing but ambiguous breed of organizations known as public policy 'think tanks'.[2] Think tanks provide a useful case for thinking about power in organizations by virtue of their complex morphology and functioning. In the following section, I will consider four approaches to the question: What kind of power might a think tank hope to exercise? The first of these approaches grasps think tanks as *inhabitants of a larger field* populated by multiple kinds of organizations, all of them engaged in the competitive pursuit of a socially valued resource. The second approach, while similar to the first in certain respects, treats think tanks as making up a *field unto themselves*. To speak of think tanks in these terms is to emphasize their novelty as an organizational type and, more to the point, to suggest that they are carriers of a novel form of power.

While each of these approaches has certain benefits, neither is sufficient for capturing what is significant about think tanks. The third approach thus treats think tanks as drawing a certain kind of power from their ability to *span multiple fields*. While the idea of functional specialization remains vital to this approach, the kind of power it implies rests on a kind of 'second order' specialization. Boundary-spanning organizations claim for themselves a certain mediating role in the social structure, and thus a power that consists in regulating flows of resources, information and people among fields. The fourth approach I will discuss takes this idea a step further by grasping think tanks not as merely spanning boundaries, but in constituting them. Drawing on insights from Eyal's concept of the *spaces between fields*, I introduce the idea of *boundary organizations*, or organizations that become influential for their role in creating and maintaining institutional separations, including boundaries between fields. In this approach, the potential power of an organization is akin to *symbolic power* in Bourdieu's sense, or the power to impose meaning and legitimate distinctions, to designate and define, and to alter or reinforce systems of classification.

There is a general logic in my ordering of these approaches. Put simply, whereas the first and second fit comfortably within the logic of field theory as it is normally applied, the third and fourth approaches begin to draw out certain tensions within this framework. My purpose in this chapter, however, is not to undermine field theory per se, but to strengthen and extend it by highlighting the importance of analytic construction, even when one is working within a seemingly integrated framework such as field theory. My argument is that to remain coherent, a sociology based on field theory must be capable of moving flexibly among different modes of analysis. There is a related purpose behind my use of a single category of organizations as the empirical basis for this discussion. By looking only at think tanks, I wish to emphasize that the forms of power described here do not correspond to discrete organizational 'types'. Nor do they refer to distinct moments in the development of an organization (or set of organizations) over time. Instead, they refer to the relations of power within which organizations are embedded. In this way, the discussion has implications that extend well beyond the world of think tanks.

Four forms of organizational power

At the broadest level, this chapter is oriented to the question of how power and influence accrue within organizations. For the sake of clarity and concreteness, however, I will address this question by referring to a particular empirical case: namely, the organizations known as think tanks. Think tanks offer an ideal empirical device for thinking about organizational power precisely because of the uncertainty surrounding their most basic properties, aims and influences. To investigate their power, then, means remaining open minded with respect to a series of fundamental questions: What is a think tank? What does it mean for an organization to succeed or fail as one? What is at stake in the competition among think tanks?

In this section, I will outline four ways of thinking about the potential power of a think tank. Each approach sets out from an analytic stance informed by field theory. However, as we will see, the four approaches also bring out certain tensions in field theory itself. The view I will put forward is that none of the four approaches is sufficient on its own. Instead, the most compelling application of field theory is one that remains flexible and continuously attentive to the problem of analytic construction.

Approach #1: organizations as members of a larger field

How does a think tank become powerful? The first and most straightforward approach is to conceptualize the power of a think tank in terms of its capacity to produce effects within a larger or more established field. This is the approach most scholars have brought to the study of think tanks, if only implicitly, in their focus on *policy outcomes* as the relevant target of a think tank's actions. On this view, a think tank might be described as powerful to the degree that it exercises direct effects on the policy-making process.

Not all scholars focus narrowly on policy outcomes as the site of a think tank's effects. Some, especially those working in the institutionalist tradition, have broadened the analytic lens somewhat to capture a wider range of possible effects. For our purposes, what is significant about both approaches is that they implicitly treat think tanks as members of a particular field – typically the political field (that is, the system of struggles among parties, politicians and other political specialists over the powers of delegation and representation) or the bureaucratic field (Bourdieu 1991). In Bourdieu's taxonomy of fields, the *bureaucratic field* refers to the array of public institutions 'entrusted with the maintenance of the economic and legal order … [and] the sustenance of the dispossessed and the provision of public goods' (Wacquant 2004: 8).

Doubtless this approach has a certain commonsense appeal, in the term's best sense. In the first place, there is no question that think tanks try to influence the policy process – and a commonsense view would hold that their success or failure in doing so is the best measure of their power. Nevertheless, I would argue that even the most open-ended versions of this approach have important limitations. The first sign of a problem is that the theory does not align very well with the actual strategies and practices adopted by many think tanks. While all think tanks try to establish some form of access to the political and bureaucratic fields – for example, by cultivating network ties to politicians, bureaucrats and party officials – this fact alone does not begin to tell the whole story of their organizational strategies. Indeed, to anyone familiar with this sphere, it is clear that many think tanks also strategically *turn down* certain forms of political access. Consider the Heritage Foundation, a think tank with extensive ties to the Republican Party (Callahan (1999), for example, refers to the organization as 'the de facto research arm of the GOP [Grand Old Party]'). Heritage's Republican ties notwithstanding, it is worth noting that the organization has long been careful to maintain a certain distance from the party. The reason is simple: to remain a standard bearer of American conservatism, Heritage must reserve the right to critique Republicans who stray too far from conservative principles. Of course, one could argue that Heritage's adherence to conservative principles merely indicates another form of connection to the political field. Yet this would miss a larger and more significant point. Put simply, organizations like Heritage must take care to balance their ties to certain agents, organizations and groups within the political field as a way of managing their relations with other fields.

This idea – that think tanks are engaged in a kind of balancing act – brings to mind other relevant examples, some of them quite different from Heritage. Consider one of Heritage's chief opponents, the Economic Policy Institute (EPI), a think tank established in 1986 by a set of liberal economists, including soon-to-be Secretary of Labor Robert Reich. Over its 25-year history, EPI has established a clear reputation as an organization that speaks on behalf of workers and the labour movement. While EPI has often disputed the label 'labour-backed think tank', in years past it has accepted up to 40% of its funding from unions. However, it is clear that EPI has a complex relationship with the labour movement and the label 'labour-backed'. At one level, the association is an albatross around EPI's neck. Its conservative opponents in particular are often keen to point out that labour unions supply a significant share of EPI's funding, the implication being that EPI is simply a mouthpiece of the labour movement, not a bona fide supplier of expertise. (Thus, a 2009

Heritage Foundation *Backgrounder Report* titled 'Big Labor Admits Employer Violations Rare in Elections' peremptorily dismisses EPI as 'a union-funded think tank', while a 2011 article by the *Weekly Standard* is simply titled, 'Just a Reminder: The Economic Policy Institute is Dominated by Labor Interests'.[3]) Given the drawbacks of its association with organized labour, it should come as no surprise that EPI spends considerable time and energy fighting off the appellation 'labour-backed'. A section of its website, for instance, advises journalists on the organization's preferred description: 'Is it accurate or appropriate to call EPI labor-supported or labor-backed? No. Foundations provide about twice as much of EPI's funding as unions do, so "foundation-supported" would be accurate but "labor-backed" is not.'[4]

However, to stop the analysis there would be to miss the key fact that, in other contexts, EPI's ties to the labour movement serve a positive role for the organization. Many of EPI's practices, in fact, are manifestly designed to bolster its ties to organized labour. For example, EPI cofounded the Global Policy Network, a set of 'policy and research institutions connected to the world's trade union movements', which lists among its goals 'forging links between institutes connected to unions and labour movements in developed and developing countries' and 'furthering international solidarity and engaging the common challenges posed by globalization'.[5] EPI's Briefing Papers series suggests yet another facet of this complex relationship. In certain instances, EPI makes a direct claim to speak on behalf of labour unions to an audience of policy makers. (The list of EPI Briefing Papers includes such titles as, 'How Unions Help All Workers' and 'Still Open for Business: Unionization has No Causal Effect on Firm Closures' (Mishel and Walters 2003; DiNardo 2009).) From this vantage point, EPI's connection to organized labour is not an albatross around its neck at all, but the organization's calling card – i.e. a signal to journalists that EPI will always be ready with a quotable expression of the pro-labour side of a debate, a cue to labour unions that EPI is an ally and thus a worthy recipient of donations, and a pointer to pro-labour politicians that they can always count on EPI for a useful statistic, a private briefing, or an expert witness for a legislative hearing. In short, in a crowded 'marketplace of ideas', EPI has what every think tank needs: a recognizable identity and a corresponding audience or clientele.

The point of this discussion is that there is a certain danger for a think tank in achieving 'too much' political access, or in any case, access of the wrong form. Doubtless the greatest danger is that of becoming transparently tied to a single party, interest group, or political candidate (even if the strategy may have short-term advantages). Indeed, the history of think tanks is replete with cases of organizations that enjoyed a brief moment in the sun by virtue of some privileged form of access to a specific political network or agency, only to be pushed to the margins of the think tank world when that access either evaporated or lost its value. The Progressive Policy Institute (PPI), for example, a think tank once considered influential as the intellectual base of the New Democrat movement, offers a clear case in point. By the end of the

Clinton presidency, PPI's status among think tanks had fallen considerably along with that of the Democratic Leadership Council (DLC) that sustained it. (Not surprisingly, PPI recently disaffiliated itself from the DLC in an effort to refashion its public image.) The overarching point is that think tanks must generally carry out a dynamic balancing act that involves establishing various ties and relations of exchange with organizations in multiple fields.

The question one must ask when treating think tanks as members of a larger field is to which field they 'belong'. By this point, however, it should be clear that there is no final answer to this question. In order to move beyond this approach, let us entertain a second possible way of thinking about the relationships among organizations, power and fields. In fact, this approach has already been signalled in this discussion, particularly where I have referred to think tanks as embedded in a semi-distinct network of relations, as members of a distinct 'type' of organization, or to the 'world' of think tanks. Put simply, the possibility raised by these formulations is that we can treat think tanks as a kind of field unto themselves.

Approach #2: organizations as a field of their own

If it is not entirely satisfying to conceptualize think tanks as members of a single field or as organizations that span multiple fields, then perhaps it is better to apply the field concept in a different way – by considering think tanks as making up a field-like space of their own. To examine think tanks in this way is to foreground the *relations among them* and to take seriously the distinctive social forms they have developed, by which I mean their unique strategies, intellectual products and practices, their modes of judgement and their internal hierarchies. Central to this approach is a basic historical proposition: as the organizations known as think tanks increasingly came to orient their judgement and practices to one another, they gradually formed a network and thereby acquired a kind of weak autonomy. Like the other approaches discussed in this chapter, I believe this idea has something important to recommend it. Its main insight is that there is a dimension of a think tank's existence that cannot be reduced to its relationships to more established fields. To understand fully the products and practices of a Brookings Institution or a Heritage Foundation, for example, it is not enough merely to consider how each organization expresses the interests of its audience or its sponsors. Instead, part of what is created by Brookings and Heritage is determined by the relationship between Brookings and Heritage.[6]

The notion that one can treat think tanks as a field-like space, an approach I have developed elsewhere (Medvetz 2012), is thus driven by a relational impulse. Its basic premise is that a rigorous sociology of think tanks would need to shift its focus away from the organizations per se – understood as entities or 'things' – and focus instead on the social relations in which they are embedded. It is also a resolutely historicist approach in its focus on the formation of network ties that permitted certain organizations to differentiate themselves from more established institutions – especially those of the market, academia and politics – even if their ability to do so remains an ongoing and precarious achievement. On this view, it was not just the appearance of certain organizations that inaugurated the birth of think tanks, but also the process by which these organizations became oriented to one another in their judgements and practices.

However, once again, I believe this approach has some important limitations. Despite its propensity to take think tanks seriously as members of their own field, the first problem lies in the risk of trivializing their importance. In short, because think tanks are constitutively dependent on more established fields for their resources and credibility, the inevitable conclusion of such an approach, to quote Eyal, is that 'we would be guided toward conceiving of this field as a lesser one' (Eyal 2013: 164). Even more problematic, however, is the fact that this approach essentially brings us back to square one with respect to the initial question: What forms of power might think tanks exercise? In other words, it may well be that think tanks have acquired certain field-like properties of their own – in other words, that they have carved out their own jurisdiction and invented certain unique products and practices; that they have their own internal hierarchies; and even that their members have established a degree of control over entry into their ranks (such as through rudimentary forms of credentialing, especially in emergent disciplines such as 'public policy studies'). However, it is not at all obvious what *kind* of field this is. What, in other words, is at stake in the 'social game' played by think tanks? To invoke Bourdieu's language, what is the form of capital generated in this space? The approach is useful, then, for conveying a sense of the growing distinctiveness of think tanks – and thus for suggesting that they possess some sort of power – but it cannot tell us much about what kind of power it is.

Approach #3: organizations as boundary spanners

If there are important limits to thinking about a think tank's power either in terms of efficacy within a larger field or as a member of its own field, then what are the possible alternatives? A third possibility, already signalled in the discussion above, is that think tanks crosscut or overlap multiple fields at once. The main inspiration for this approach, which is drawn from organizational theory, is the concept *boundary spanner* – a term normally applied to actors who derive their power from their strategic locations within and among organizations. Applied to the present case, its starting point is to discard the assumption that think tanks are first and foremost 'political' or 'intellectual' organizations – or indeed organizations of any specific type. To do so would be to assign them a kind of intrinsic character, purpose or essence that they do not possess.

In its original applications, the term *boundary spanner* referred to individuals located at strategic points of juncture, either within an organization or at the meeting point between organizations. To adapt the concept for the present use would require extending it 'upwards' from the actor to the organization. Just as certain individuals, we could say, derive their power and influence from their opportune locations within or among organizations, so there are organizations that acquire influence from their locations within larger systems of organizations.[8] Before I turn to the second step, let me point out an immediate advantage of this approach. Put simply, it allows us to put aside what was once the most paralyzing theoretical split within the study of think tanks: namely, the opposition between elite and pluralist theories. By and large, the early academic studies of think tanks fell into one of two camps. On the one side were the studies carried out in the theoretical tradition inaugurated by C. Wright Mills, which depicted think tanks as the intellectual machinery of a closed network of corporate, financial and political elites.[9] On the other side were studies based on the pluralist model, which grasped public policy making as the result of a dynamic interplay among organized interest groups, each with their own resources, strategies and aims.[10] According to the latter view, think tanks should be analysed not as weapons of ruling-class power, but as one kind of organization among many in an array of societal groups competing to shape public policy. In light of the foregoing discussion, it is possible to reinterpret this debate as an argument about where think tanks 'truly' reside relative to the state, the market and civil society. Yet as the discussion also suggests, this is a futile question.

 Thus, the main point of conceptualizing think tanks as boundary spanners is to suggest that they are involved in the business of gathering and assembling resources generated in multiple fields and assembling these into novel packages. But which resources do they gather, and from which fields? Based on my investigation of the organizations most commonly labelled as think tanks, the answer is that they assemble heterogeneous samplings of academic, political, economic and media capital. By the term *academic capital,* I mean visible markers of scholarly proficiency, especially academic degrees and titles. By *political capital,* I refer to competence in specifically political forms of expression, including the ability to generate knowledge and make pronouncements effective in the competition for control over the state (e.g. polling data, demographic statistics, 'talking points' memoranda, speeches, slogans and strategic advice). By *economic capital,* I mean not just money (which think tanks typically receive in the form of donations), but also the means of acquiring it, including the skills needed to rise funding and to 'market' one's intellectual wares effectively. By *media capital,* I mean direct or indirect access to the means of publicity, including through the ability to assist journalists and media institutions in their work (Bourdieu 1986). Most think tanks gather all of these resources at once, albeit in different quantities, forms and ratios.

In the language of field theory, then, the point is that think tanks operate by constituting themselves as relevant, albeit marginal, players in each of four relatively institutionalized fields: namely, those of academics, politics, business

To clarify this point, consider the example of the RAND Corporation, which is by many accounts the largest think tank in the world. Where would we locate RAND with respect to the state, the market and civil society? Channelling the elite theorists, one could point out that RAND was founded as a joint project of the US Air Force and the Douglas Aircraft Company, and that, since its inception, it has conducted strategic defence analyses on behalf of the US Defense Department.[13] For these reasons, one could say, RAND looks very much like an arm of the state, its claims to 'independence' notwithstanding. On the other hand, channelling the pluralists, one could emphasize that RAND is not, after all, an official agency of the government, nor is it subject to direct governmental controls. Furthermore, one could cite the occasional cases of RAND's 'intellectual rebelliousness' – or those cases in which the organization asserted its autonomy by questioning the basic premises of its research assignments (for examples, see Dickson 1971). For these reasons, one could say, RAND should be located outside of the state and within civil society.

Without denying any of the empirical facts put forward by either side, I would argue that neither argument offers a very satisfying answer. On the one hand, the pluralist approach arbitrarily privileges the official jurisdictional categories of the state instead of using specifically analytic categories. From a social scientific standpoint, why should it matter whether or not RAND is officially inside or outside the government? On the other hand, by suggesting that RAND's formal separation from the state is somehow 'false', the elite theory approach tends to imply that its success in appearing independent is the product of a kind of Machiavellian strategy. What neither approach can see is that RAND's independence from the state is the result of a never-ending project of boundary work, in the sociological sense of the term. This boundary work is necessary because the effect of independence is an important aspect of RAND's influence. It is this independence, for example, that allows a Pentagon official intent on a particular course of military action to point to a RAND study as corroborating evidence for his position, even if the study itself was commissioned by the Pentagon with a particular conclusion in mind and produced by former Pentagon officials.

However, while it is possible to say that RAND spans the boundary and exists in various domains at once, even this formulation does not quite go far enough. To call RAND a 'boundary spanner' would be to imply that the boundaries were already there to be spanned. Broadening our lens beyond the United States, in fact, shows that the exact reach or jurisdiction of the state, the market and civil society is not always and everywhere the same. In many countries, for example, studies similar to those carried out by RAND would actually be produced inside the official boundary of the state. For example, the closest equivalents to the RAND Corporation in Canada (Defense Research and Development Canada) and France (Defence Procurement Agency) are both official government agencies. From this standpoint, the location of the boundary between the state and civil society in the United

States begins to appear less a straightforward fact than a partial effect of RAND's practices (along with those of other defence-oriented think tanks, such as the Hudson Institute, the Center for Naval Analyses, the Mitre Corporation).

It is possible to make a similar point with respect to the boundary of the market by citing the example of the Competitive Enterprise Institute (CEI), a free-market think tank founded in 1984. While CEI does not make a profit or sell things in any overt fashion, it nonetheless takes a significant portion of its funding from private corporations. ('I probably have as much business funding as any group out there', says Fred Smith, Jr, CEI's founder and president, in an interview.[14]) While CEI's directors would not likely embrace the label corporate think tank, neither do they make any secret of their ultimate purposes as advocates for corporate interests. Smith describes his organization's mission in these terms: 'We have to illustrate that business needs allies in the war for survival ... We're sort of a "battered business bureau". Businessmen who get in real trouble may well then decide they need allies, and they'll reach out and say, "Is there anyone out there we can help whose work parallels our interests?"'[15] Of course, CEI's officers would likely point out that if businessmen can look to their organization as an ally in the 'war for survival', then labour unions can also depend on certain think tanks (such as EPI) for intellectual support.

The overarching point of this discussion is that the boundary spanner concept tends to reify the boundaries that are being traversed by a think tank. In my view, it is better to say, as Eyal (2006) does in his analysis of expertise in Arab affairs, that the boundary is part of what is at stake inside the organization. Put differently, the organization is the boundary. The power of a boundary organization, then, lies precisely in its ability to determine where one activity 'officially' ends and another begins – in this case, where political, market and media production end and the production of 'expertise' begins. The point acquires added significance when we consider the question of the 'conversion rates' among different forms of capital. One reason Bourdieu referred to institutionalized resources using the metaphor of capitals was to raise the question of the conditions under which one form of power could be converted into another. By mobilizing and reinvesting his or her capital in a particular way, a savvy agent can convert one form into another. The general implication of my argument is that with respect to the relationship among academic, political, economic and media capitals, the conversion rates are worked out largely in the struggles among think tanks. If a relatively scholarly think tank such as the National Bureau of Economic Research does battle with a more activist-oriented think tank – say, the Cato Institute – then what is at stake in this competition is more than simply a specific policy outcome. The same struggle can also be read as part of a macro-structural competition among holders of scholarly credibility (especially as scholarliness is defined in the field of economics) and holders of ideological credibility.

Before concluding this section, let me consider one possible objection to this argument. Based on everything I have said, the reader might sensibly wonder what kind of organization is not in some way a boundary organization? After all, we would only have to look at a think tank's nearest neighbours in the social structure (e.g. universities, government agencies, activist networks, political parties, business corporations, etc.) to see that there is no such thing as a purely academic, political or economic organization.

There are two possible lines of defence against this objection. The first would be to agree in principle while pointing about that the objection simply underscores the main contribution of field theory itself: namely, the fact that it requires us to think about power in relational terms. There is always the temptation, in other words, to think of power as an entity, or something you can possess. One can possess money, for example, but we all know that money's power lies in the institutionalized social relations that ensure its ready exchangeability for goods or services. If these social relations break down, then the money loses its power. This is a familiar point, but one that deserves repeating, the more deeply institutionalized a particular bundle of power relations becomes.

The second, and more ambitious, line of defence would be to insist that there is actually something special about think tanks, which in turn belong to a broader, historically emergent category of organizations whose most salient feature is their capacity to mediate the relationships among fields. The existence of these organizations would depend in turn on the formation of 'interstitial fields', itself indicative of a kind of hyper-rationalization. On this view, such boundary organizations could be regarded as powerful to the degree that they succeeded in transcending the 'spaces between fields' and acquire field-like properties of their own.

Conclusion

By one leading count, the number of American think tanks has more than quadrupled since 1970 (Rich 2004).[16] Think tanks have also become highly visible players on the policy scene, issuing studies aimed at politicians and the wider public, hosting symposia, press conferences and political speeches, and offering a 'government in exile' for sidelined officials awaiting a return to public office. Their affiliated policy experts also commonly supply informal briefings for politicians, Congressional testimony and news media punditry. It is in this context that think tanks have influenced some of the major political issues of the day. An early blueprint for the Iraq War, for example, was sketched in the late 1990s by a group of neoconservative foreign policy specialists operating in a think tank called the Project for the New American Century. The zero-tolerance policing method known as the 'broken windows' approach originated in the Manhattan Institute in the early 1980s. The anti-evolution intelligent design movement was born in the Seattle-based Discovery Institute during the 1990s. Think tanks have also been visible players in debates surrounding environmental, tax and regulatory policies.[17]

However, what kinds of power do these organizations have? I have suggested four kinds, each one rooted in a particular analytic approach. In the first approach, the organization in question is understood as part of a field inhabited by other kinds of organizations, each competing to accumulate some species of capital. In the second, the organization is understood as a member of its own field. The main difference between the two approaches is that while both locate an organization's power in its ability to compete successfully for a specific institutionalized resource, the second approach places far greater emphasis on the novelty and distinctiveness of the organization – and thus of the species of capital over which it might be said to compete.

To address the limitations of these approaches, I have argued that it is also possible to consider think tanks as organizations that span multiple fields in the context of a strategy for mediating the relations among holders of different forms of power. In this case, their power rests on their ability to accumulate multiple forms of capital and thereby play a crucial mediating or brokering role in the social structure. On this view, is not so much in the volume of capital, but in its ability to regulate the passage of resources, information and people among fields that a think tank acquires its power. Extending this idea, I have also suggested that a think tank's structural positioning, reach and ability to span or overlap multiple fields can become a source of power in another respect. This is the capacity to partake in the drawing of institutional boundaries themselves – that to determine what *sort of* practice a particular social action comes to be known as (e.g. an 'intellectual', a 'political', an 'economic' act) and what sort of actor a person is.

I see no irreconcilable tensions among these four ways of thinking about organizational power. Instead, I believe they are analytic tools or modes of analysis that can be deployed as the occasion demands and according to the priorities of the analyst. What they share in common, above all, is the implication that organizational power must be grasped in relational and processional terms.

Notes

1 On the notion of the field, see for example, Bourdieu 1985, 1990, 1993, 1996 [1989]; and Bourdieu and Wacquant 1992.
2 For prominent studies of think tanks, see Dickson 1971; Smith 1991; Stone 1996; Abelson 2002; and Rich 2004.
3 Sherk 2009: the headline is from blog.heritage.org/2009/06/18/big-labor-admits-employer-violations-rare-in-elections/ (accessed 30 June 2011); Warren 2011: www.weeklystandard.com/blogs/economic-policy-institute-dominated-labor-interests_552391.html (accessed 30 June 2011).
4 See www.epi.org/content.cfm/newsroom_describing_epi (accessed 20 November 2008). EPI also points out that its main rivals – Heritage, Brookings, Cato and AEI – 'are generally not labeled according to their funding sources'.
5 See www.gpn.org/statement-purpose.html.
6 Here I am paraphrasing Bourdieu on the French journalistic field: 'To understand a product like *L'Express* or *Le Nouvel Observateur*, there is little point in studying

the target readership. The essential part of what is presented in *L'Express* and *Le Nouvel Observateur* is determined by the relationship between *L'Express* and *Le Nouvel Observateur*' (Bourdieu 2005: 45).

7 There is a large literature on this topic. Key early sources include Keller and Holland 1975; Aldrich and Herker 1977; Leifer and Huber 1977; Tushman 1977; Leifer and Delbecq 1978; and Tushman and Scanlan 1981.

8 A few other organization scholars have spoken about organizations as boundary spanners. See, for example, Fennell and Alexander 1987.

9 See, for example, Dye 1978; Peschek 1987; and Domhoff 1999.

10 For a brief but informative intellectual history of the concept *pluralism*, see Ellis 2001.

11 Author interview, Paul Weyrich, Free Congress Foundation, 29 June 2004.

12 See www.hoover.org/about (accessed 4 December 2008).

13 On the history of the RAND Corporation, see Kraft 1960; RAND Corporation 1963; Smith 1966; Digby 1967; Dickson 1971; and Amadae 2003.

14 Author interview, Fred Smith, Jr, Competitive Enterprise Institute, 16 December 2003.

15 Author interview, Fred Smith, Jr, Competitive Enterprise Institute, 16 December 2003.

16 For other attempts to codify the concept think tank or catalogue the category's members, see Hellebust 1996; Innis and Johnson 2002; and United Nations Development Programme 2003.

17 On the role of think tanks in the promotion of 'broken windows' and zero-tolerance policing, see Wacquant 2009. On the Iraq War, see Abelson 2006. On welfare reform, see Medvetz 2012.

References

Abelson, D. 2002. *Do Think Tanks Matter? Assessing the Impact of Public Policy Institutes*. Montreal, Canada: McGill-Queen's University.

——2006. *A Capitol Idea: Think Tanks & U.S. Foreign Policy*. Montreal: McGill-Queen's University.

Aldrich, H. and Herker, D. 1977. 'Boundary Spanning Roles and Organization Structure'. *Academy of Management Review*, 2(2), 217–30.

Amadae, S.M. 2003. *Rationalizing Capitalist Democracy: The Cold War Origins of Rational Choice Liberalism*. Chicago: University of Chicago Press.

Bourdieu, P. 1985. 'The Genesis of the Concepts of Habitus and Field'. *Sociocriticism*, 2(2), 11–24.

——1986. 'The Forms of Capital'. In J. Richardson (ed.) *Handbook of Theory and Research for the Sociology of Education*. New York: Greenwood, 241–58.

——1990 [1986]. 'The Intellectual Field: A World Apart'. In *In Other Words: Essays Toward a Reflexive Sociology*. Stanford, CA: Stanford University Press, 140–49.

——1991. 'Political Representation: Elements for a Theory of the Political Field'. In J. B. Thompson (ed. and introduction) *Language and Symbolic Power*. Cambridge, MA: Harvard University Press, 171–202.

——1993. *The Field of Cultural Production: Essays on Art and Literature*. Ed. R. Johnson. New York: Columbia University Press.

——1996 [1989]. *The State Nobility: Elite Schools in the Field of Power*. Stanford, CA: Stanford University Press.

——2005. 'The Political Field, the Social Science Field, and the Journalistic Field'. In R. Benson and E. Neveu (eds) *Bourdieu and the Journalistic Field*. Cambridge: Polity Press, 29–47.

Bourdieu, P. and Wacquant, L. 1992. *An Invitation to Reflexive Sociology*. Chicago: University of Chicago Press.

Callahan, D. 1999. *$1 Billion for Ideas: Conservative Think Tanks in the 1990s*. Washington, DC: National Committee for Responsive Philanthropy.

Dickson, P. 1971. *Think Tanks*. New York: Atheneum.

Digby, J. 1967. *Operations Research and Systems Analysis at RAND, 1948–1967*. Santa Monica: RAND Corporation.

DiNardo, J. 2009. 'Still Open for Business: Unionization has no Causal Effect on Firm Closures'. *EPI Briefing Paper #230*. www.epi.org/publications/entry/bp230/ (accessed 2 June 2011).

Domhoff, G. W. 1999. *Who Rules America 2000*. New York: Simon & Schuster.

Dye, T.R. 1978. 'Oligarchic Tendencies in National Policy-making: The Role of the Private Policy-planning Organizations'. *Journal of Politics*, 40(2), 309–31.

Ellis, R.J. 2001. 'Pluralism'. In N.J. Smelser and P.B. Baltes (eds) *International Encyclopedia of the Social & Behavioral Sciences*. Oxford: Pergamon, 11516–20.

Eyal, G. 2006. *The Disenchantment of the Orient: Expertise in Arab Affairs and the Israeli State*. Stanford, CA: Stanford University Press.

——2013. 'Spaces Between Fields'. In P. Gorski (ed.) *Bourdieu and Historical Analysis*. Durham, NC: Duke University Press, 158–82.

Fennell, M.L. and Alexander, J.A. 1987. 'Organizational Boundary Spanning in Institutionalized Environments'. *Academy of Management Journal*, 30(3), 456–76.

Hellebust, L. (ed.) 1996. *Think Tank Directory: A Guide to Nonprofit Public Policy Research Organizations*. Topeka, KS: Government Research Service.

Innis, M. and Johnson, J. 2002. *Directory of Think Tank Publications*. London: Methuen Publishing.

Keller, R.T. and Holland, W.E. 1975. 'Boundary-spanning Roles in a Research and Development Organization: An Empirical Investigation'. *Academy of Management Journal*, 18(2), 388–93.

Kraft, J. 1960. 'RAND: Arsenal for Ideas'. *Harper's*, July.

Leifer, R. and Delbecq, A. 1978. 'Organizational/Environmental Interchange: A Model of Boundary Spanning Activity'. *Academy of Management Review*, 3(1), 40–50.

Leifer, R. and Huber, G.P. 1977. 'Relations Among Perceived Environmental Uncertainty, Organization Structure, and Boundary-spanning Behavior'. *Administrative Science Quarterly*, 22(2), 235–47.

Marx, K. 1990 [1867]. *Capital*. Trans. B. Fowkes. London: Penguin Books.

McGann, J.G. 1992. 'Academics to Ideologues: A Brief History of the Public Policy Research Industry'. *PS: Political Science and Politics*, 25(4), 733–40.

Medvetz, T. 2012. *Think Tanks in America*. Chicago: University of Chicago Press.

Miller, Louis. 1989. *Operations Research and Policy Analysis at RAND, 1968–88*. Santa Monica: RAND Corporation.

Mishel, L. and Walters, M. 2003. 'How Unions Help All Workers'. EPI *Briefing Paper #143*. 26 August. www.epi.org/publications/entry/briefingpapers_bp143/ (accessed 2 June 2011).

Peschek, J. G. 1987. *Policy-planning Organizations: Elite Agendas and America's Rightward Turn*. Philadelphia: Temple University Press.

RAND Corporation. 1963. *The First Fifteen Years*. Santa Monica: RAND Corporation.

Rich, A. 2004. *Think Tanks, Public Policy, and the Politics of Expertise*. Cambridge: Cambridge University Press.

Scott, W. Richard. 1992. *Organizations: Rational, Natural, and Open Systems.* Third edn. Englewood Cliffs, NJ: Prentice Hall.

Sherk, J. 2009. 'Organized Labor Concedes: Employer Violations Rare in Secret Ballot Elections'. *Backgrounder #2287.* Washington, DC: Heritage Foundation.

Smith, B.L.R. 1966. *The RAND Corporation: Case Study of a Nonprofit Advisory Corporation.* Cambridge: Harvard University Press.

Smith, J. 1991. *The Idea Brokers: Think Tanks and the Rise of the New Policy Elite.* New York: Free Press.

Stone, D. 1996. *Capturing the Political Imagination: Think Tanks and the Policy Process.* London: Frank Cass.

Tushman, M.L. 1977. 'Special Boundary Roles in the Innovation Process'. *Administrative Science Quarterly*, 22(4), 587–605.

Tushman, M.L. and Scanlan, T.J. 1981. 'Boundary Spanning Individuals: Their Role in Information Transfer and their Antecedents'. *Academy of Management Journal*, 24(2), 289–305.

United Nations Development Programme. 2003. *Thinking the Unthinkable: From Thought to Policy.* Bratislava: UNDP Regional Bureau for Europe and the Commonwealth of Independent States.

Wacquant, L. 2004. 'Pointers on Pierre Bourdieu and Democratic Politics'. *Constellations*, 11(1), 1–15.

——2009. *Prisons of Poverty.* Minneapolis, MN: University of Minnesota Press.

Warren, M. 2011. 'Just a Reminder: The Economic Policy Institute is Dominated by Labor Interests'. *The Weekly Standard*, 23 February.

Weber, M. 1946a [1915]. 'Bureaucracy'. In H.H. Gerth and C. Wright Mills (eds/trans/intro.) *From Max Weber.* Oxford: Oxford University Press, 196–244.

——1946b [1915]. 'Religious Rejections of the World and their Directions'. In H.H. Gerth and C. Wright Mills (eds/trans/intro.) *From Max Weber.* Oxford: Oxford University Press, 323–59.

10 Crafting the neoliberal State

Workfare and prisonfare in the bureaucratic field

Loïc Wacquant

Three analytic breaks have proven necessary to elaborate the diagnosis of the invention of a new government of social insecurity wedding restrictive 'workfare' and expansive 'prisonfare' propounded in *Punishing the Poor*, and to account for the punitive policy turn taken by the United States and other advanced societies following its lead onto the path of economic deregulation and welfare retrenchment in the closing decades of the twentieth century.[1]

The first consists in breaking out of the crime-and-punishment poke, which continues to straightjacket scholarly and policy debates on incarceration, even as the divorce of this familiar couple grows ever more barefaced. The second break requires relinking social welfare and penal policies, since these two strands of government action toward the poor have come to be informed by the same behaviourist philosophy relying on deterrence, surveillance, stigma and graduated sanctions to modify conduct. Welfare revamped as workfare and prison stripped of its rehabilitative pretension now form a single organizational mesh flung at the same clientele mired in the fissures and ditches of the dualizing metropolis. They work jointly to invisibilize problem populations – by forcing them off the public aid rolls, on the one hand, and holding them under lock and key, on the other – and eventually push them into the peripheral sectors of the booming secondary labour market. The third rupture involves overcoming the customary opposition between materialist and symbolic approaches, descended from the emblematic figures of Karl Marx and Émile Durkheim, so as to heed and hold together the instrumental and the expressive functions of the penal apparatus. Weaving together concerns for control and communication, the management of dispossessed categories and the affirmation of salient social boundaries has enabled us to go beyond an analysis couched in the language of prohibition to trace how the expansion and redeployment of the prison and its institutional tentacles (probation, parole, criminal databases, swirling discourses about crime and a virulent culture of public denigration of offenders) has reshaped the socio-symbolic landscape and remade the State itself.

A single concept sufficed to effect those three breaks simultaneously: the notion of bureaucratic field developed by Pierre Bourdieu ([1993] 1994) in his lecture course at the Collège de France in the early 1990s to rethink the state as the agency that monopolizes the legitimate use, not only of material violence (as in Max Weber's well-known capsule), but also of symbolic violence, and shapes social space and strategies by setting the conversion rate between the various species of capital. In this article, I extend Bourdieu's formulation to draw out the theoretical underpinnings and implications of the model of the neoliberal government of social insecurity at century's dawn put forth in my book *Punishing the Poor*. In the first section, I revise Piven and Cloward's classic thesis on the regulation of poverty via public assistance and contrast penalization as a technique for the management of marginality in the dual metropolis with Michel Foucault's vision of the place of the prison in the 'disciplinary society,' David Garland's account of the crystallization of the 'culture of control' in late modernity, and David Harvey's characterization of neoliberal politics and its proliferation on the world stage. In the second section, I build on these contrasts to elaborate a thick sociological specification of neoliberalism that breaks with the thin economic conception of neoliberalism as market rule that effectively echoes its ideology. I argue that a proactive penal system is not a deviation from, but a constituent component of, the neoliberal Leviathan, along with variants of supervisory workfare and the cultural trope of 'individual responsibility.' This suggests that we need to theorize the prison, not as a technical implement for law enforcement, but as a core organ of the state whose selective and aggressive deployment in the lower regions of social space is constitutively injurious to the ideals of democratic citizenship.

When workfare joins prisonfare: theoretical (re)percussions

In *The Weight of the World* and related essays, Pierre Bourdieu has proposed that we construe the State not as a monolithic and coordinated ensemble, but as a splintered space of forces vying over the definition and distribution of public goods which he calls the 'bureaucratic field' (Bourdieu 1994, 1999). The concept is sketched analytically in Bourdieu ([1993] 1994), illustrated in Bourdieu ([1993] 1999), and deployed to probe the political production of the economy of single homes in France in Bourdieu ([2000] 2005). Several issues of the journal *Actes de la recherche en sciences sociales* offer further cross-national empirical illustrations, including those on 'The History of the State' (nos. 116–117, March 1997), 'The Genesis of the State' (no. 118, June 1997), the transition 'From Social State to Penal State' (no. 124, September 1998), and 'Pacify and Punish' (nos. 173 and 174, June and September 2008), 'Field Theory' (no. 200, December 2013). The constitution of this space is the end result of a long-term process of concentration of the various species of capital operative in a given social formation, and especially of 'juridical capital as the objectified and codified form of symbolic capital', which enables the State to monopolize the official definition of identities and the administration of justice (Bourdieu 1994: 2, 9). In the contemporary period, the bureaucratic field is traversed by two internecine struggles. The first pits the 'higher State nobility' of policy makers intent on promoting market-oriented reforms against the 'lower State nobility' of executants attached to the traditional missions of government. The second opposes what Bourdieu calls the 'left hand' and the 'right hand' of the State. The left hand, the feminine side of Leviathan, is materialized by the 'spendthrift' ministries in charge of 'social functions' – public education, health, housing, welfare and labour law – which offer protection and succour to the social categories shorn of economic and cultural capital. The right hand, the masculine side, is charged with enforcing the new economic discipline via budget cuts, fiscal incentives and economic deregulation.

By inviting us to grasp in a single conceptual framework the various sectors of the State that administer the life conditions and chances of the lower class, and to view these sectors as enmeshed in relations of antagonistic cooperation as they vie for pre-eminence inside the bureaucratic field, this conception has helped us map the ongoing shift from the social to the penal treatment of urban marginality. The present investigation fills in a gap in Bourdieu's model by inserting the police, the courts, and *the prison as core constituents of the 'right hand'* of the State, alongside the ministries of the economy and the budget. It suggests that we need to bring penal policies from the periphery to the centre of our analysis of the redesign and deployment of government programmes aimed at coping with the entrenched poverty and deepening disparities spawned in the polarizing city by the discarding of the Fordist-Keynesian social compact. The new government of social insecurity put in place in the United States and offered as model to other advanced countries entails both a shift from the social to the penal wing of the State (detectable in the reallocation of public budgets, personnel and discursive precedence) and the colonization of the welfare sector by the panoptic and punitive logic characteristic of the post-rehabilitation penal bureaucracy. The slanting of State activity from the social to the penal arm and the incipient penalization of welfare, in turn, partake of the *remasculinization of the State*, in reaction to the wide-ranging changes provoked in the political field by the women's movement and by the institutionalization of social rights antinomic to commodification. The new priority given to duties over rights, sanction over support, the stern rhetoric of the 'obligations of citizenship', and the martial reaffirmation of the capacity of the State to lock the troublemaking poor (welfare recipients and criminals) 'in a subordinate relation of dependence and obedience' towards State managers portrayed as virile protectors of the society against its wayward members (Young 2005: 16): all these policy planks pronounce and promote the transition from the kindly 'nanny state' of the Fordist-Keynesian era to the strict 'daddy state' of neoliberalism.

In their classic study *Regulating the Poor*, Frances Fox Piven and Richard Cloward forged a germinal model of the management of poverty in industrial capitalism. According to this model, the State expands or contracts its relief programmes cyclically to respond to the ups and downs of the economy, the corresponding slackening and tightening of the labour market, and the bouts of social disruption that increased unemployment and destitution trigger periodically among the lower class. Phases of welfare expansion serve to 'mute civil disorders' that threaten established hierarchies, while phases of restriction aim to 'enforce works norms' by pushing recipients back onto the labour market (Piven and Cloward 1993: xvi and passim). *Punishing the Poor* contends that while this model worked well for the Fordist-Keynesian age and accounts for the two major welfare explosions witnessed in the United States during the Great Depression and the affluent but turbulent 1960s, it has been rendered obsolete by the neoliberal remaking of the State over the past quarter-century. In the era of fragmented labour, hypermobile capital, and sharpening social inequalities and anxieties, the 'central role of relief in the regulation of marginal labour and in the maintenance of social order' (Piven and Cloward 1993: xviii) is displaced and duly supplemented by the vigorous deployment of the police, the courts and the prison in the nether regions of social space. To the single oversight of the poor by the left hand of the State succeeds the *double regulation of poverty by the joint action of punitive welfare-turned-workfare and a diligent and belligerent penal bureaucracy.* The cyclical alternation of contraction and expansion of public aid is replaced by the continual contraction of welfare and the runaway expansion of prisonfare.

This organizational coupling of the left hand and right hand of the State under the aegis of the same disciplinary philosophy of behaviourism and moralism can be understood, first, by recalling the shared historical origins of poor relief and penal confinement in the chaotic passage from feudalism to capitalism. Both policies were devised in the sixteenth century to 'absorb and regulate the masses of discontented people uprooted' by this epochal transition (Piven and Cloward 1993: 21).[2] Similarly, both policies were overhauled in the last two decades of the twentieth century in response to the socio-economic dislocations provoked by neoliberalism: in the 1980s alone, in addition to reducing public assistance, California voted for nearly 1,000 laws expanding the use of prison sentences; at the federal level, the 1996 reform that 'ended welfare as we know it' was complemented by the sweeping Crime Omnibus Act of 1993 and bolstered by the No Frills Prison Act of 1995.

The institutional pairing of public aid and incarceration as tools for managing the unruly poor can also be understood by paying attention to the structural, functional and cultural similarities between workfare and prisonfare as 'people processing institutions' targeted on kindred problem populations (Hasenfeld 1972: 256–63). It has been facilitated by the transformation of welfare in a punitive direction and the activation of the penal system to handle more of the traditional clientele of assistance to the destitute – the incipient 'penalization' of welfare matching the degraded 'welfarization' of the prison. Their concurrent reform over the past 30 years has helped cement their organizational convergence, even as they have obeyed inverse principles. The gradual erosion of public aid and its revamping into workfare in 1996 has entailed restricting entry into the system, shortening 'stays' on the rolls and speeding up exit, resulting in a spectacular reduction of the stock of beneficiaries (it plummeted from nearly 5 million households in 1992 to under 2 million a decade later). Trends in penal policy have followed the exact opposite tack: admission into jail and prison has been greatly facilitated, sojourns behind bars lengthened and releases curtailed, which has yielded a spectacular ballooning of the population locked up (it jumped by over 1 million in the 1990s). The operant purpose of welfare shifted from passive 'people processing' to active 'people changing' after 1988 and especially after the abolition of Aid to Families with Dependent Children (AFDC) in 1996, while prison has travelled in the other direction, from aiming to reform inmates (under the philosophy of rehabilitation, hegemonic from the 1920s to the mid-1970s) to merely warehousing them (as the function of punishment was downgraded to retribution and neutralization).

The shared historical roots, organizational isomorphism and operational convergence of the assistential and penitential poles of the bureaucratic field in the United States are further fortified by the fact that the social profiles of their beneficiaries are virtually identical. AFDC recipients and jail inmates both live near or below 50% of the federal poverty line (for one-half and two-thirds of them, respectively); both are disproportionately black and Hispanic (37% and 18%, versus 41% and 19%); the majority did not finish high school and are saddled with serious physical and mental disabilities interfering with their participation in the workforce (44% of AFDC mothers as against 37% of jail inmates). They are closely bound to one another by extensive kin, marital and social ties, reside overwhelmingly in the same impoverished households and barren neighbourhoods, and face the same bleak life horizon at the bottom of the class and ethnic structure.

Punishing the Poor avers not only that the United States has shifted from the single (welfare) to the double (social-cum-penal) regulation of the poor, but also that 'the stunted development of American social policy' skilfully dissected by Piven and Cloward (1993: 409) stands in close causal and functional relation to America's uniquely overgrown and hyperactive penal policy. *The misery of American welfare and the grandeur of American prisonfare at the century's turn are two sides of the same political coin.* The generosity of the latter is in direct proportion to the stinginess of the former, and it expands to the degree that both are driven by moral behaviourism. The same structural features of the American State – its bureaucratic fragmentation and ethno-racial skew, the institutional bifurcation between universalist 'social insurance' and categorical 'welfare', and the market-buttressing cast of assistance programmes – that facilitated the organized atrophy of welfare in reaction to the racial crisis of the 1960s and the economic turmoil of the 1970s have also fostered the uncontrolled hypertrophy of punishment aimed at the same precarious population. Moreover, the 'tortured impact of slavery and institutionalized racism on the construction of the American polity' has been felt, not only on the 'underdevelopment' of public aid and the 'decentralized and fragmented government and party system' that distributes it to a select segment of the dispossessed (Piven and Cloward 1993: 424–25), but also on the overdevelopment and stupendous severity of its penal wing. Ethno-racial division and the (re)activation of the stigma of blackness as dangerousness are key to explaining the initial atrophy and accelerating decay of the

American social state in the post-Civil Rights era, on the one hand, and the astonishing ease and celerity with which the penal state arose on its ruins, on the other.[3]

Reversing the historical bifurcation of the labour and crime questions achieved in the late nineteenth century, *punitive containment* as a government technique for managing deepening urban marginality has effectively rejoined social and penal policy at the close of the twentieth century. It taps the diffuse social anxiety coursing through the middle and lower regions of social space in reaction to the splintering of wage work and the resurgence of inequality, and converts it into popular animus toward welfare recipients and street criminals cast as the twin detached and defamed categories that sap the social order by their dissolute morality and dissipated behaviour and must therefore be placed under severe tutelage. The new government of poverty invented by the United States to enforce the normalization of social insecurity thus gives a whole new meaning to the notion of 'poor relief': punitive containment offers relief not *to* the poor but *from* the poor, by forcibly 'disappearing' the most disruptive of them, from the shrinking welfare rolls on the one hand and into the swelling dungeons of the carceral castle on the other.

Michel Foucault has put forth the single most influential analysis of the rise and role of the prison in capitalist modernity, and it is useful to set my thesis against the rich tapestry of analyses he has stretched and stimulated. I concur with the author of *Discipline and Punish* (Foucault 1975) that penality is a protean force that is eminently fertile and must be given pride of place in the study of contemporary power. While its originary medium resides in the application of legal coercion to enforce the core strictures of the socio-moral order, punishment must be viewed not through the narrow and technical prism of repression but by recourse to the notion of production. The assertive rolling out of the penal state has indeed engendered new categories and discourses, novel administrative bodies and government policies, fresh social types and associated forms of knowledge across the criminal and social welfare domains. However, from here, my argument diverges sharply from Foucault's view of the emergence and functioning of the punitive society in at least four ways.

To start with, Foucault erred in spotting the retreat of the penitentiary. Disciplines may have diversified and metastasized to thrust sinewy webs of control across society, but the prison has not, for that, receded from the historical stage and 'lost its raison d'être' (Foucault 1975: 304–5 [1977: 297–98], all translations of Foucault are mine). On the contrary, penal confinement has made a stunning comeback and reaffirmed itself among the central missions of Leviathan just as Foucault and his followers were forecasting its demise. After the founding burst of the 1600s and the consolidation of the 1800s, the turn of the present century ranks as the third 'age of confinement' that penologist Thomas Mathiesen forewarned about in 1990 (Mathiesen 1990: 14).

Next, whatever their uses in the eighteenth century, disciplinary technologies have *not* been deployed inside the overgrown and voracious carceral

system of our *fin de siècle*. Hierarchical classification, elaborate time sche-
dules, non-idleness, close-up examination and the regimentation of the body:
these techniques of penal 'normalization' have been rendered impracticable by
the demographic chaos spawned by overpopulation, bureaucratic rigidity,
resource depletion and the studious indifference if not hostility of penal
authorities toward rehabilitation. In lieu of the *dressage* ('training' or
'taming') intended to fashion 'docile and productive bodies' postulated by
Foucault, the contemporary prison is geared toward brute neutralization, rote
retribution and simple warehousing – by default if not by design. If there
are 'engineers of consciousness' and 'orthopaedists of individuality' at work
in the mesh of disciplinary powers today, they surely are not employed by
departments of corrections (Foucault 1975: 301 [1977: 294]).

   In the third place, 'devices for normalization' anchored in the carceral
institution have *not* spread throughout society, in the manner of capillaries
irrigating the entire body social. Rather, the widening of the penal dragnet
under neoliberalism has been remarkably discriminating: in spite of con-
spicuous bursts of corporate crime (epitomized by the Savings and Loans
scandal of the late 1980s and the folding of Enron a decade later), it has
affected essentially the denizens of the lower regions of social and physical
space. Indeed, the fact that the social and ethno-racial selectivity of the prison
has been maintained, nay reinforced, as it vastly enlarged its intake demonstrates that penalization is not an all-encompassing master logic that blindly
traverses the social order to bend and bind its various constituents. On the
contrary, it is a skewed technique proceeding along sharp gradients of class,
ethnicity and place, and it operates to divide populations and to differentiate
categories according to established conceptions of moral worth. At the dawn
of the twenty-first century, America's urban (sub)proletariat lives in a 'punitive
society', but its middle and upper classes certainly do not. Similarly, efforts to
import and adapt US-style slogans and methods of law-enforcement – such as
zero-tolerance policing, mandatory minimum sentencing, or boot camps for
juveniles – in Europe have been trained on lower-class and immigrant offenders relegated in the defamed neighbourhoods at the centre of the panic over
'ghettoization' that has swept across the continent over the past decade.

   Lastly, the crystallization of *law-and-order pornography* – that is, the
accelerating inflection and inflation of penal activity conceived, represented
and implemented for the primary purpose of being displayed in ritualized
form by the authorities – the paradigm for which is the half-aborted reintro-
duction of chain gangs in striped uniforms – suggests that news of the death
of the 'spectacle of the scaffold' has been greatly exaggerated. The 'redistribution' of 'the whole economy of punishment' (Foucault 1975: 13 [1977: 7])
in the post-Fordist period has entailed not its disappearance from public view
as proposed by Foucault, but its institutional relocation, symbolic elaboration
and social proliferation beyond anything anyone envisioned when *Discipline
and Punish* was published. In the past quarter-century, a whole galaxy of
novel cultural and social forms, indeed a veritable industry trading on

representations of offenders and law-enforcement, has sprung forth and spread. The theatricalization of penality has migrated from the State to the commercial media and the political field *in toto*, and it has extended from the final ceremony of sanction to encompass the full penal chain, with a privileged place accorded to police operations in low-income districts and courtroom confrontations around celebrity defendants. The Place de Grève, where the regicide Damiens was famously quartered, has thus been supplanted not by the Panopticon but by Court TV and the profusion of crime-and-punishment 'reality shows' that have inundated television (Cops, 911, America's Most Wanted, American Detective, Bounty Hunters, Inside Cell Block F, etc.), not to mention the use of criminal justice as fodder for the daily news and dramatic series. So much to say that the prison did not 'replace' the 'social game of the signs of punishment and the garrulous feast that put them in motion' (Foucault 1975: 134 [1977: 131]). Rather, it now serves as its institutional canopy. Everywhere the law-and-order Guignol has become a core civic theatre onto whose stage elected officials prance to dramatize moral norms and display their professed capacity for decisive action, thereby reaffirming the political relevance of Leviathan at the very moment when they organize its powerlessness with respect to the market.

This brings us to the question of the political proceeds of penalization, a theme central to David Garland's book *The Culture of Control*, the most sweeping and stimulating account of the nexus of crime and social order put forth since Foucault. According to Garland, 'the distinctive social, economic, and cultural arrangements of late modernity' have fashioned a 'new collective experience of crime and insecurity', to which the authorities have given a reactionary interpretation and a bifurcated response combining practical adaptation via 'preventative partnerships' and hysterical denial through 'punitive segregation' (Garland 2001: 139–47 and passim). The ensuing reconfiguration of crime control bespeaks the inability of rulers to regiment individuals and normalize contemporary society, and its very disjointedness has made glaring all the 'limits of the sovereign state'. For Garland, the 'culture of control' coalescing around the 'new criminological predicament' pairing high crime rates with the acknowledged limitations of criminal justice both marks and masks a political failing. On the contrary, *Punishing the Poor* asserts that punitive containment has proven a remarkably successful political strategy: far from 'eroding one of the foundational myths of modern society' which holds that 'the sovereign state is capable of delivering law and order' (Garland 2001: 109), it has revitalized it.

By elevating criminal safety (*sécurité, Sicherheit, sicurezza*, etc.) to the front line of government priorities, state officials have condensed the diffuse class anxiety and simmering ethnic resentment generated by the unravelling of the Fordist-Keynesian compact and channelled them towards the (dark-skinned) street criminal, designated as guilty of sowing social and moral disorder in the city, alongside the profligate welfare recipient. Rolling out the penal state and coupling it with workfare has given the high State nobility an effective tool to both foster labour deregulation and contain the disorders that economic deregulation provokes in the lower rungs of the socio-spatial hierarchy. Most importantly, it has allowed politicians to make up for the deficit of legitimacy which besets them whenever they curtail the economic support and social protections traditionally granted by Leviathan. *Contra* Garland, then, I find that the penalization of urban poverty has served well as a vehicle for the *ritual reassertion of the sovereignty of the State* in the narrow, theatricalized domain of law enforcement that it has prioritized *for that very purpose*, just when the same State is conceding its incapacity to control flows of capital, bodies and signs across its borders. This divergence of diagnosis, in turn, points to three major differences between our respective dissections of the punitive drift in First World countries.

First, the fast and furious bend towards penalization observed at the *fin de siècle* is not a response to *criminal* insecurity but to *social* insecurity. To be more precise, the currents of social anxiety that roil advanced society are rooted in *objective* social insecurity among the post-industrial working class, whose material conditions have deteriorated with the diffusion of unstable and underpaid wage labour shorn of the usual social 'benefits', and *subjective* insecurity among the middle classes, whose prospects for smooth reproduction or upward mobility have dimmed as competition for valued social positions has intensified and the State has reduced its provision of public goods. Garland's notion that 'high rates of crime have become a normal social fact – a routine part of modern consciousness, an everyday risk to be assessed and managed' by 'the population at large', and especially by the middle class, is belied by both official crime statistics and victimization studies. Official statistics show that law breaking in the United States declined or stagnated for 20 years after the mid-1970s before falling precipitously in the 1990s, while exposure to violent offences varied widely by location in social and physical space. Relatedly, European countries sport crime rates similar to or higher than America (except for the two specific categories of assault and homicide, which compose but a tiny fraction of all offences), and yet have responded quite differently to criminal activity, with rates of incarceration one-fifth to one-tenth the American rate even as they have risen.

This takes us to the second difference: for Garland the reaction of the State to the predicament of high crime and low justice efficiency has been disjointed and even contradictory, whereas I have stressed its overall coherence. However, this coherence becomes visible only when the analytic compass is fully extended *beyond the crime-punishment box and across policy realms*, to link penal trends to the socioeconomic restructuring of the urban order, on the one hand, and to join workfare to prisonfare, on the other. What Garland characterizes as 'the structured ambivalence of the state's response' is not so much ambivalence as a predictable organizational division in the labour of management of the disruptive poor. Bourdieu's theory of the State is helpful here in enabling us to discern that the 'adaptive strategies' recognizing the State's limited capacity to stem crime by stressing prevention and devolution are pursued in the penal sector of the *bureaucratic* field, while what Garland calls the 'nonadaptive strategies' of 'denial and acting out' to reassert that very capacity operate in the *political* field, especially in its relation to the journalistic field.[4]

Third, like other leading analysts of contemporary punishment such as Jock Young (1999), Franklin Zimring *et al.* (2001) and Michael Tonry (2004), Garland sees the punitive turn as the reactionary spawn of right-wing politicians. However, *Punishing the Poor* finds, first, that the penalization of poverty is not a simple return to a past state of affairs but a genuine institutional innovation and, second, that it is by no means the exclusive creature of neoconservative politics. If politicians of the Right invented the formula, it was employed and refined by their centrist and even 'progressive' rivals. Indeed, the president who oversaw by far the biggest increase in incarceration in American history is not Ronald Reagan but William (Bill) Jefferson Clinton. Across the Atlantic, it was the Left of Blair in England, Schröder in Germany, Jospin in France, d'Alema in Italy and González in Spain that negotiated the shift to proactive penalization, not their conservative predecessors. This is because the root cause of the punitive turn is *not late modernity but neoliberalism*, a project that can be indifferently embraced by politicians of the Right or the Left.

The jumble of trends that Garland gathers under the umbrella term of late modernity – the 'modernizing dynamic of capitalist production and market exchange', shifts in households composition and kinship ties, changes in urban ecology and demography, the disenchanting impact of the electronic media, the 'democratization of social life and culture' – are not only exceedingly vague and loosely correlated. They are either not peculiar to the closing decades of the twentieth century, specific to the United States, or show up in their most pronounced form in the social-democratic countries of Northern Europe which have *not* been submerged by the international wave of penalization. Moreover, the onset of late modernity has been gradual and evolutionary, whereas the recent permutations of penality have been abrupt and revolutionary.

Punishing the Poor contends that it is not the generic 'risks and anxieties' of 'the open, porous, mobile society of strangers that is late modernity' (Garland 2001: 165) that have fostered retaliation against lower-class categories perceived as undeserving and deviant types seen as irrecuperable, but the specific *social* insecurity generated by the fragmentation of wage labour, the hardening of class divisions and the erosion of the established ethno-racial hierarchy guaranteeing an effective monopoly over collective honour to whites in the United States (and to nationals in the European Union). The sudden expansion and consensual exaltation of the penal state after the mid-1970s is not a culturally reactionary reading of 'late modernity', but a ruling-class response aiming to redefine the perimeter and missions of Leviathan, so as to establish a new economic regime based on capital hypermobility and labour flexibility, and to curb the social turmoil generated at the foot of the urban order by the public policies of market deregulation and social welfare retrenchment that are core building blocks of neoliberalism.

A sociological specification of neoliberalism

The invention of the double regulation of the insecure fractions of the post-industrial proletariat via the wedding of social and penal policy at the bottom of the polarized class structure is a major *structural innovation* that takes us beyond the model of the welfare-poverty nexus elaborated by Piven and Cloward just as the Fordist-Keynesian regime was coming unglued. The birth of this institutional contraption is also not captured by Michel Foucault's vision of the 'disciplinary society' or by David Garland's notion of the 'culture of control', neither of which can account for the unforeseen timing, socio-ethnic selectivity, and peculiar organizational path of the abrupt turnaround in penal trends in the closing decades of the twentieth century. For the punitive containment of urban marginality through the simultaneous rolling back of the social safety net and the rolling out of the police-and-prison dragnet and their knitting together into a carceral-assistential lattice is not the spawn of some broad societal trend – whether it be the ascent of 'biopower' or the advent of 'late modernity' – but, at bottom, an exercise in *State crafting*. It partakes of the correlative revamping of the perimeter, missions and capacities of public authority on the economic, social welfare and penal fronts. This revamping has been uniquely swift, broad and deep in the United States, but it is in progress – or in question – in all advanced societies submitted to the relentless pressure to conform to the American pattern.

Tracking the roots and modalities of America's stupendous drive to hyper-incarceration opens a unique route into the sanctum of the neoliberal Leviathan. It leads us to articulate two major theoretical claims. The first is that *the penal apparatus is a core organ of the State*, expressive of its sovereignty and instrumental in imposing categories, upholding material and symbolic divisions, and moulding relations and behaviours through the selective penetration of social and physical space. The police, the courts and the prison are not mere technical appendages for the enforcement of lawful order, but vehicles for the political production of reality and for the oversight of deprived and defamed social categories and their reserved territories. The second thesis is that the ongoing capitalist 'revolution from above' commonly called *neoliberalism entails the enlargement and exaltation of the penal sector* of the bureaucratic field, so that the State may check the social reverberations caused by the diffusion of social insecurity in the lower rungs of the class and ethnic hierarchy as well as assuage popular discontent over the dereliction of its traditional economic and social duties.

Neoliberalism readily resolves what for Garland's 'culture of control' remains an enigmatic paradox of late modernity, namely, the fact that 'control is now being re-emphasized in every area of social life – *with the singular and startling exception of the economy*, from whose deregulated domain most of today's major risks routinely emerge' (Garland 2001: 165, emphasis added). The neoliberal remaking of the State also explains the steep class, ethno-racial and spatial bias stamping the simultaneous retraction of its social bosom and expansion of its penal fist: the populations most directly and adversely impacted by the convergent revamping of the labour market and public aid turn out also to be the privileged 'beneficiaries' of the penal largesse of the authorities. Finally, neoliberalism correlates closely with the international diffusion of punitive policies in both the welfare and the criminal domains. It is not by accident that the advanced countries that have imported first workfare measures designed to buttress the discipline of desocialized wage work and then variants of US-style criminal justice measures, are the Commonwealth nations which also pursued aggressive policies of economic deregulation inspired by the 'free market' nostrums come from America, whereas the countries that remained committed to a strong regulatory State curbing social insecurity have best resisted the sirens of 'zero-tolerance' policing and 'prison works'. Similarly, societies of the Second World such as Brazil, South Africa and Turkey, which adopted superpunitive penal planks inspired by US developments in the 1990s and saw their prison populations soar as a result, did so not because they had at long last reached the stage of 'late modernity', but because they had taken the route of market deregulation and State retrenchment (Wacquant 1999). However, to discern these multilevel connections between the upsurge of the punitive Leviathan and the spread of neoliberalism, it is necessary to develop a precise and broad conception of the latter. Instead of discarding neoliberalism, as Garland does, on account of it being 'rather too specific' a phenomenon to account for penal escalation, we must expand our conception of it, and move from an economic to a fully sociological understanding.

Neoliberalism is an elusive and contested notion, a hybrid term awkwardly suspended between the lay idiom of political debate and the technical terminology of social science, which moreover is often invoked without clear referent. Whether singular or polymorphous, evolutionary or revolutionary, the prevalent conception of neoliberalism is essentially economic: it stresses an array of market-friendly policies such as labour deregulation, capital mobility, privatization, a monetarist agenda of deflation and financial autonomy, trade liberalization, interplace competition, and the reduction of taxation and public expenditures.[5] However, this conception is thin and incomplete, as well as too closely bound up with the sermonizing discourse of the advocates of neoliberalism. We need to reach beyond this economic nucleus and elaborate a thicker notion that identifies the institutional machinery and symbolic frames through which neoliberal tenets are being actualized.

A minimalist sociological characterization can now be essayed as follows. Neoliberalism is a *transnational political project* aiming to remake the nexus of market, State and citizenship from above. This project is carried by a new global ruling class in the making, composed of the heads and senior executives of transnational firms, high-ranking politicians, state managers and top officials of multinational organizations (the Organisation for Economic Co-operation and Development (OECD), World Trade Organization (WTO), International Monetary Fund (IMF), World Bank and the European Union), and cultural-technical experts in their employ (chief among them economists, lawyers and communications professionals with germane training and mental categories in the different countries). It entails not simply the reassertion of the prerogatives of capital and the promotion of the marketplace, but the articulation of four institutional logics:

- *Economic deregulation*, that is, re-regulation aimed at promoting 'the market' or market-like mechanisms as the optimal device, not only for guiding corporate strategies and economic transactions (under the aegis of the shareholder-value conception of the firm), but for organizing the gamut of human activities, including the private provision of core public goods, on putative grounds of efficiency (implying deliberate disregard for distributive issues of justice and equality).
- *Welfare state devolution, retraction and recomposition* designed to facilitate the expansion and support the intensification of commodification, and in particular to submit reticent individuals to the discipline of desocialized wage labour via variants of 'workfare', establishing a quasi-contractual relationship between the State and lower-class recipients treated not as citizens but as clients or subjects (stipulating their behavioural obligations as condition for continued public assistance).
- *An expansive, intrusive and proactive penal apparatus* which penetrates the nether regions of social and physical space to contain the disorders and disarray generated by diffusing social insecurity and deepening inequality, to unfurl disciplinary supervision over the precarious fractions of the post-industrial proletariat, and to reassert the authority of Leviathan so as to bolster the evaporating legitimacy of elected officials.
- *The cultural trope of individual responsibility*, which invades all spheres of life to provide a 'vocabulary of motive' – as C. Wright Mills would say – for the construction of the self (on the model of the entrepreneur), the spread of markets and legitimation for the widened competition it sub-tends, the counterpart of which is the evasion of corporate liability and the proclamation of State irresponsibility (or sharply reduced accountability in matters social and economic).

A central *ideological* tenet of neoliberalism is that it entails the coming of 'small government': the shrinking of the allegedly flaccid and overgrown Keynesian welfare state and its makeover into a lean and nimble workfare state, which 'invests' in human capital and 'activates' communal springs and individual appetites for work and civic participation through 'partnerships', stressing self-reliance, commitment to paid work, and managerialism. *Punishing the Poor* demonstrates that the neoliberal State turns out to be quite different *in actuality*: while it embraces laissez-faire at the top, releasing restraints on capital and expanding the life chances of the holders of economic and cultural capital, it is anything but laissez-faire at the bottom. Indeed, when it comes to handling the social turbulence generated by deregulation and to impressing the discipline of precarious labour, the new Leviathan reveals itself to be fiercely interventionist, bossy and pricey. The soft touch of libertarian proclivities favouring the upper class gives way to the hard edge of authoritarian oversight, as it endeavours to direct, nay dictate, the behaviour of the lower class. 'Small government' in the economic register thus begets 'big government' on the twofold frontage of workfare and criminal justice. The results are in on America's grand experiment in creating the first society of advanced insecurity in history: *the invasive, expansive and expensive penal state is not a deviation from neoliberalism but one of its constituent ingredients.*

Remarkably, this is a side of neoliberalism that has been obfuscated or overlooked by its apologists and detractors alike. This blind spot is glaring in Anthony Giddens's celebrated reformulation of neoliberal imperatives into the platform of New Labour. In his manifesto for *The Third Way*, Giddens highlights high rates of crime in deteriorating working-class districts as an indicator of 'civic decline' and curiously blames the Keynesian welfare state for it (not deindustrialization and social retrenchment): 'The egalitarianism of the old left was noble in intent, but as its rightist critics say has sometimes led to perverse consequences – visible, for instance, in the social engineering that has left a legacy of decaying, crime-ridden housing estates.' He makes 'preventing crime, and reducing fear of crime' through State-locality partnerships, central to 'community regeneration', and he embraces the law-and-order mythology of 'broken windows': 'One of the most significant innovations in criminology in recent years has been the discovery [sic] that the decay of day-to-day civility relates directly to criminality ... Disorderly behaviour unchecked signals to citizens that the area is unsafe' (Giddens 1999: 16, 78–79, 87–88). However, Giddens studiously omits the punishment side of the equation: *The Third Way* contains not a single mention of prison and glosses over the judicial hardening and carceral boom that have everywhere accompanied the kind of economic deregulation and welfare devolution it promotes. This omission is particularly startling in the case of Britain, since the incarceration rate of England and Wales jumped from 88 inmates per 100,000 residents in 1992 to 142 per 100,000 in 2004, even as crime was receding, with Anthony (Tony) Blair presiding over the single largest increase of the convict population in the country's history (matching the feat of Clinton, his co-sponsor of the 'Third Way', on the other side of the Atlantic).

A similar oversight of the centrality of the penal institution to the new government of social insecurity is found in the works of eminent critics of neoliberalism. David Harvey's extended characterization of 'the neoliberal State' in his *Brief History of Neoliberalism* is a case in point, which appositely spotlights the obdurate limitations of the traditional political economy of punishment which my book *Punishing the Poor* has sought to overcome. For

Harvey, neoliberalism aims at maximizing the reach of market transactions via 'deregulation, privatization, and withdrawal of the state from many areas of social provision'. As in previous eras of capitalism, the task of Leviathan is 'to facilitate conditions for profitable capital accumulation on the part of both domestic and foreign capital', but now this translates into penal expansion: 'The neoliberal state will resort to coercive legislation and policing tactics (anti-picketing rules, for instance) to disperse or repress collective forms of opposition to corporate power ... *The coercive arm of the state is augmented to protect corporate interests* and, if necessary, to *repress dissent*. None of this seems consistent with neoliberal theory' (Harvey 2005: 2–3, 77, emphasis added).

With barely a few passing mentions of prison and not a line on workfare, Harvey's account of the rise of neoliberalism is woefully incomplete. His conception of the neoliberal State turns out to be surprisingly restricted, first, because he remains wedded to the repressive conception of power, instead of construing the manifold missions of penality through the expansive category of production. Subsuming penal institutions under the rubric of coercion leads him to ignore the expressive function and ramifying material effects of the law and its enforcement, which are to generate controlling images and public categories, to stoke collective emotions and accentuate salient social boundaries, as well as to activate State bureaucracies so as to mould social ties and strategies. Next, Harvey portrays this repression as aimed at political opponents to corporate rule and 'dissident internal movements' which challenge the hegemony of private property and profit (such as the Branch Davidians at Waco, the participants in the Rodney King riots in Los Angeles in 1991, and the anti-globalization activists who rocked the G-8 meeting in Seattle in 1999; Harvey 2005: 83), when the primary targets of penalization in the post-Fordist era have been the precarious fractions of the proletariat concentrated in the tainted districts of dereliction of the dualizing metropolis who, being squeezed by the urgent press of day-to-day subsistence, have little capacity or care to contest corporate rule.

Third, for the author of *Social Justice and the City* the State 'intervenes' through coercion only when the neoliberal order breaks down, to repair economic transactions, ward off challenges to capital and resolve social crises. By contrast, *Punishing the Poor* argues that the present penal activism of the State – translating into carceral bulimia in the United States and policing frenzy throughout Western Europe – is an ongoing, routine feature of neoliberalism. Indeed, it is not economic failure but economic success that requires the aggressive deployment of the police, court and prison in the nether sectors of social and physical space. The rapid turnings of the law-and-order merry-go-round are an index of the reassertion of State sovereignty, not a sign of its weakness. Harvey does note that the retrenchment of the welfare state 'leaves larger and larger segments of the population exposed to impoverishment', and that 'the social safety net is reduced to a bare minimum in favour of a system that emphasizes individual responsibility and the victim is all too often blamed' (Harvey 2005: 76). However, he does not realize that it is precisely these normal disorders, inflicted by economic deregulation and welfare retrenchment, that are managed by the enlarged penal apparatus in conjunction with supervisory workfare. Instead, Harvey invokes the bogeyman of the 'prison-industrial complex', suggesting that incarceration is a major plank of capitalist profit-seeking and accumulation when it is a disciplinary device entailing a gross drain on the public coffers and a tremendous drag on the economy.

Fourth and last, Harvey views the neoconservative stress on coercion and order restoration as a temporary fix for the chronic instability and functional failings of neoliberalism, whereas I construe authoritarian moralism as an *integral constituent of the neoliberal State* when it turns its sights on the lower rungs of the polarizing class structure. Like Garland, Harvey must artificially dichotomize 'neoliberalism' and 'neoconservatism' to account for the reassertion of the supervisory authority of the State over the poor because his narrow economistic definition of neoliberalism replicates its ideology and truncates its sociology. To elucidate the paternalist transformation of penality at century's turn, then, we must imperatively escape the 'crime-and-punishment' box, but also exorcise once and for all the ghost of Louis Althusser, whose instrumentalist conception of Leviathan and crude duality of ideological and repressive apparatuses gravely hamstring the historical anthropology of the State in the neoliberal age. Following Bourdieu, we must fully attend to the internal complexity and dynamic recomposition of the bureaucratic field, as well as to the constitutive power of the symbolic structures of penality to trace the intricate meshing of market and moral discipline across the economic, welfare and criminal justice realms (Bourdieu 1994: 15–16; Wacquant 2005a).

In his meticulous comparison of eugenic measures in the 1920s, compulsory work camps in the 1930s, and workfare schemes in the 1990s in England and America, Desmond King has shown that 'illiberal social policies' that seek to direct citizens' conduct coercively are 'intrinsic to liberal democratic politics' and reflective of their internal contradictions (King 1999: 26). Even as they contravene standards of equality and personal liberty, such programmes are periodically pursued because they are ideally suited to highlighting and enforcing the boundaries of membership in times of turmoil; they are fleet vehicles for broadcasting the newfound resolve of State elites to tackle offensive conditions and assuage popular resentment towards derelict or deviant categories; and they diffuse conceptions of otherness that materialize the symbolic opposition anchoring the social order. With the advent of the neoliberal government of social insecurity mating restrictive workfare and expansive prisonfare, however, it is not just the policies of the State that are illiberal, but *its very architecture*. Tracking the coming and workings of America's punitive politics of poverty after the dissolution of the Fordist-Keynesian order and the implosion of the black ghetto reveals that neoliberalism brings about not the shrinking of government, but the erection of a *centaur State*, liberal at the top and paternalistic at the bottom, which presents radically different faces at the two ends of the social hierarchy: a comely and caring visage toward the middle and upper classes, and a fearsome and frowning mug toward the lower class.

Nor does it spring mechanically from the systemic necessities of some grand structure such as late capitalism, racism, or panopticism (as in various neo-Marxist and neo-Foucauldian approaches as well as in the activist demonology of the 'prison-industrial complex'). Rather, it arises from *struggles over and within the bureaucratic field*, aiming to redefine the perimeter, missions, priorities, and modalities of action of public authorities with respect to definite problem territories and categories. These struggles involve, crucially, not only battles pitting organizations stemming from civil society and state agencies, but also internecine contests between the various sectors of the bureaucratic field which vie to gain 'ownership' of the social problem at hand and thus valorize the specific forms of authority and expertise they anchor (medical, educational, social welfare, penal, economic, etc., and within the penal domain, the police, courts, and confinement institutions and post-custodial means of control). The overall fitness of punitive containment to regulating urban marginality at century's dawn is a rough *post-hoc functionality* born of a mix of initial policy intent, sequential bureaucratic adjustment, and political trial-and-error and electoral profit-seeking at the point of confluence of three relatively autonomous streams of public measures concerning the low-skill employment market, public aid and criminal justice. The complementarity and interlocking of state programs in these three realms is partly designed and partly an emergent property, fostered by the practical need to handle correlated contingencies, their common framing through the lens of moral behaviorism and the shared ethnoracial bias stamping their routine operations – with (sub)proletarian blacks from the hyperghetto figuring at the point of maximum impact where market deregulation, welfare retrenchment and penal penetration meet.

Whatever the modalities of their advent, it is indisputable that the linked stinginess of the welfare wing and munificence of the penal wing under the guidance of moralism have altered the make-up of the bureaucratic field in ways that are profoundly injurious to democratic ideals.[6] As their sights converge onto the same marginal populations and territories, deterrent workfare and the neutralizing prison foster vastly different profiles and experiences of citizenship across the class and ethnic spectrum. They not only contravene the fundamental principle of equality of treatment by the State and routinely abridge the individual freedoms of the dispossessed. They also undermine the consent of the governed through the aggressive deployment of involuntary programmes stipulating personal responsibilities just as the State is withdrawing the institutional supports necessary to shoulder these and shirking its own social and economic charges. They stamp the precarious fractions of the proletariat from which public aid recipients and convicts issue with the indelible seal of unworthiness. In short, the penalization of poverty splinters citizenship along class lines, saps civic trust at the bottom, and saws the degradation of republican tenets. The establishment of the new government of social insecurity discloses, *in fine*, that *neoliberalism is constitutively corrosive of democracy*.

By enabling us to break out of the crime-and-punishment box to relink welfare and justice while fully attending to both the material and symbolic dimensions of public policy, Bourdieu's concept of bureaucratic field offers a powerful tool for dissecting the anatomy and assembly of the neoliberal Leviathan. It suggests that some of the pivotal political struggles of this century's turn – if not the most visible or salient ones – involve, not the confrontation between the mobilized organizations representing subaltern categories and the state but battles internal to the hierarchical and dynamic ensemble of public bureaucracies that compete to socialize, medicalize or penalize urban marginality and its correlates. Elucidating the nexus of workfare, prisonfare and social insecurity, in turn, reveals that the study of incarceration is not a technical section in the criminogical catalogue but a key chapter in the sociology of the state and social inequality in the bloom of neoliberalism.

Notes

1 This article is an amended and abridged version of the 'theoretical coda' to my book *Punishing the Poor: The Neoliberal Government of Social Insecurity* (Wacquant 2009a). The book's overarching argument unfolds in four steps: part one maps out of the decline and misery of America's social state, climaxing with the replacement of protective welfare by punitive workfare in 1996; part two tracks the modalities of the growth and grandeur of the penal state from 1973 to the present; part three explains why penal activism has been aimed at two 'privileged targets', the collapsing black ghetto and the roaming sex offender; and part four follows recent declinations of the new politics of social insecurity in Western Europe to offer both a critique of the new law-and-order reason, prescriptions for escaping the punitive policy snare, and a characterization of the distinctive shape and missions of the neoliberal state.

2 Penal expansion and activism in the sixteenth century is acknowledged in passing by Piven and Cloward 1993: 20, n.32.

3 The catalytic role of ethno-racial division in the remaking of the state after the junking of the Fordist-Keynesian social compact and the collapse of the dark ghetto is analysed in depth in Wacquant 2009b.

4 On the analytic and historical differentiation of the political from the bureaucratic field, and their respective location inside the field of power, see Wacquant 2005b: esp. 6–7, 14–17 and 142–46.

5 From among a vast (and uneven) literature across the disciplines, see the pointed analyses of Fligstein 2001; Campbell and Pedersen 2001; Comaroff and Comaroff 2001; Brenner and Theodore 2002; and Duménil and Lévy 2004.

6 For a specification of republican and liberal conceptions of democracy at stake here, see Held 1996.

References

Bourdieu, P. 1994. 'Rethinking the State: On the Genesis and Structure of the Bureaucratic Field'. *Sociological Theory* 12, 1, 1–19.

——1999. 'The Abdication of the State'. In P. Bourdieu *et al.*, *The Weight of the World*. Cambridge: Polity Press, 181–88.

Brenner, N. and Theodore, N. (eds) 2002. *Spaces of Neoliberalism: Urban Restructuring in North America and Western Europe*. New York: Wiley/Blackwell.

Campbell, J. and Pedersen, O. (eds) 2001. *The Rise of Neoliberalism and Institutional Analysis*. Princeton: Princeton University Press.

Comaroff, J. and Comaroff, J.L. 2001. *Millennial Capitalism and the Culture of Neoliberalism*. Durham, NC and London: Duke University Press.

Duménil, G. and Lévy, D. 2004. *Capital Resurgent: Roots of the Neoliberal Revolution*. Cambridge, MA: Harvard University Press.

Fligstein, N. 2001. *The Architecture of Markets*. Princeton: Princeton University Press.

Foucault, M. 1975. *Surveiller et punir. Naissance de la prison*. Paris: Gallimard (trans. as *Discipline and Punish: The Birth of the Prison*. New York: Vintage, 1977).

Garland, D. 2001. *The Culture of Control: Crime and Social Order in Contemporary Society*. Chicago: University of Chicago Press.

Giddens, A. 1999. *The Third Way: The Renewal of Social Democracy*. Cambridge: Polity Press.

Harvey, D. 2005. *A Brief History of Neoliberalism*. New York: Oxford University Press.

——2008. *Social Justice and the City*, revised edn. Athens, GA: University of Georgia Press.

Hasenfeld, Y. 1972. 'People Processing Organizations: An Exchange Approach'. *American Sociological Review*, 37, 3.

Held, D. 1996. *Models of Democracy*. Stanford, CA: Stanford University Press.

King, D. 1999. *In the Name of Liberalism: Illiberal Social Policy in the United States and Britain*. New York: Oxford University Press.

Mathiesen, T. 1990. *Prison on Trial: A Critical Assessment*. London: Sage.

Piven, F.F. and Cloward, R.A. 1993 [1971]. *Regulating the Poor: The Functions of Public Welfare*. New expanded edn. New York: Vintage.

Tonry, M. 2004. *Thinking about Crime: Sense and Sensibility in American Penal Culture*. New York: Oxford University Press.

Wacquant, L.J.D. 1999. *Les Prisons de la misère*. Paris: Raisons d'agir Éditions (trans. *Prisons of Poverty*. Minneapolis: University of Minnesota Press, 2009).

——2005a. 'Symbolic Power and the Rule of the "State Nobility"'. In L.J.D. Wacquant (ed.) *The Mystery of Ministry*. Cambridge: Polity Press, 133–50.

——(ed.) 2005b. *The Mystery of Ministry: Pierre Bourdieu and Democratic Politics*. Cambridge: Polity Press.

——2009a. *Punishing the Poor: The Neoliberal Government of Social Insecurity*. Durham, NC and London: Duke University Press.

——2009b. *Deadly Symbiosis: Race and the Rise of the Penal State*. Cambridge: Polity Press.

Young, I.M. 2005. 'The Logic of Masculinist Protection: Reflections on the Current Security State'. In Marilyn Friedman (ed.) *Women and Citizenship*. New York: Oxford University Press.

Young, J. 1999. *Exclusive Society: Social Exclusion, Crime and Difference in Late Modernity*. London: Sage.

Zimring, F., Hawkins, G. and Kamin, S. 2001. *Punishment and Democracy: Three Strikes and You're Out in California*. New York: Oxford University Press.

Afterword

Theory of fields in the postcolonial age

Mathieu Hilgers and Eric Mangez

> I have attempted to show foreign publics the universal validity of models
> constructed in relation to the specific case of France.
>> (Pierre Bourdieu, opening lines of *Practical Reason:*
>> *On the Theory of Action*)

> A universal concept carries within it traces of what Gadamer would call 'pre-
> judice' – not a conscious bias but a sign that we think out of a particular
> accretion of histories that are not always transparent to us.
>> (Dipesh Chakrabarty, new Preface to *Provincializing Europe.*
>> *Postcolonial Thought and Historical Difference*)

These two juxtaposed quotations provide a perfect starting point for a consideration of some questions relating to the future life of Bourdieu's theory.
Maintaining a universalist ambition presupposes working through an objectivation which, despite all his efforts to promote a reflexive sociology and a
critique of the illusions of a certain kind of universalism, Bourdieu seems not
to have completed fully. The conquest of the scientific object is achieved, as
we know, against prejudice, but Gadamer's argument, which Chakrabarty
alludes to above, aims not to tend towards the impossible suspension of all
our prejudices to put forward a science or a hermeneutics devoid of any pre-
figuration, but rather to open up a dialogue with those who are capable of
spotting our prejudices and identifying their consequences. In this regard,
postcolonial approaches play a decisive role today. They invite us to rethink
hegemonic Western knowledges in global terms and the hermeneutic uncon-
scious of their tradition from a subaltern standpoint. Thinking postcolonially
means, in particular, determining 'how universalistic thought was always and
already modified by particular histories' (Chakrabarty 2008: xiv), controlling
the epistemic violence inherent within it, and seeking to move beyond it by
questioning the prejudgment 'rendered before all the elements that determine a
situation have been finally examined' (Gadamer 2013: 283).

Every concept and every judgement by concept is necessarily preceded
by a non-explicit pre-comprehension, a taken-for-granted prejudgement that

determines the judgement. At the heart of Pierre Bourdieu's theory of fields is an element that is never questioned, either by Bourdieu or by most of the authors who are concerned to take nothing for granted and who have developed a fruitful critical dialogue with his work: the distinction between differentiated and non-differentiated societies. This distinction, which is central in sociological thinking, appears to be taken for granted, and whose consequences need to be examined. This unquestioned certainty, a category of perception, hierarchization and discrimination that is constantly mobilized, is even sometimes used by the most stimulating heretical inheritors as a tool to distance themselves from the master.[1]

Every representation of the real, every ordering with a view to constructing intelligibility and, more generally, all knowledge, bears within it the seeds of an epistemic violence (Mudimbe and Hilgers 2013). The invention of the primitive, and with it of relatively or entirely undifferentiated societies, was part of the ambition, in mid-nineteenth-century Europe, to interpret and classify cultures along a scale according to their degrees of development (Kuper 1988). It served as the matrix for the history of the social sciences, which was partly constructed around couples of oppositions – Western and non-Western, close and remote, dynamic and static, heterogeneous and homogeneous, complex and simple, modern and archaic – which often took the form of a denial of otherness or a use of otherness as a leverage point for understanding our societies (Mudimbe 1988; Mbembe 2001, 2013). The violence of the categories of scientific understanding is all the greater when it is not made explicit. Works in postcolonial studies abound in attempts to deconstruct the hegemonic aspirations of this particular universalism.

Theory of fields and social differentiation

The distinction between weakly and strongly differentiated societies as conceived by Bourdieu is relatively simple. He draws, *inter alia*, on his experience of the precapitalist, agrarian society of Kabylia, in the colonial situation, where social practices unfold in a unified mythico-ritual universe, in order to define what constitutes the specificity of relatively undifferentiated societies. At the other extreme, he takes modern French society as the archetype of strongly differentiated societies, in particular because it contains fields, i.e. autonomized domains of activity.

How does he integrate this distinction into his theory? In his *Pascalian Meditations*, Bourdieu writes that 'precapitalist societies depend mainly on habitus for their reproduction whereas capitalist societies depend principally on objective mechanisms, such as those which tend to guarantee the reproduction of economic capital and cultural capital, to which should be added all the forms of organizational constraints … and codifications of practices' (Bourdieu 1997: 256; Bourdieu 2000b: 215–16). Bourdieu thus pursues reflection on a phenomenon which, as Lahire (2012) notes, enjoys a unanimity rarely found in sociology. The social differentiation of activities is found in Spencer, Marx, Durkheim, Simmel, Weber, Elias, Polanyi, Parsons and Luhmann to mention some but a few. For all their diversity, the sociologies of modernity are based on a minimum line of common interpretation which indicates 'how society progresses, evolving from the simple to the complex' (Martuccelli 1999). This shift from homogeneity to heterogeneity has consequences for social structures, psychic structures, behaviours, personalities and modes of domination.

A more detailed vision of his argument is developed in the first lines of his article on 'The Modes of Domination'. There, Bourdieu states that:

> in societies which have no 'self-regulating market' (in Karl Polanyi's sense), no educational system, no juridical apparatus and no State, relations of domination can be set up and maintained only at the cost of strategies which must be endlessly renewed, because the conditions required for a mediated, lasting appropriation of other agents' labour, services or homage have not been brought together. By contrast, domination no longer needs to be exerted in a direct, personal way when it is implied in the possession of the means (economic and cultural capital) of appropriating the mechanisms of the field of economic production and the field of cultural production, which tend to assure their own reproduction by their very functioning, independently of any deliberate intervention by the agents.
>
> (Bourdieu 1976: 122; Bourdieu 1977: 183–84)

The term 'field' should be taken here in the generic sense. It can be concluded from this statement that the sedimentation of the mechanisms of legitimacy and domination in relatively autonomous universes and institutions facilitates the reproduction and exercise of a domination that is more generally managed by institutions.

The distinction between differentiated and non-differentiated societies, however descriptive it may be, refers, as we have said, to a problematic lexical field which finds its most synthetic expression in the idea of the 'great divide', a formula that distinguishes modern societies from non-modern societies, i.e. archaic, exotic, non-differentiated societies whose mechanisms of reproduction are based not on institutions but on a kind of Cartesian continuous creation, a creation in every instant, of societies in which, as Mbembe puts it, 'the formulation of norms ... has nothing to do with reasoned public deliberation, since the setting of norms by a process of argument is a specific invention of modern Europe' (Mbembe 2001: 11), societies in which the individual must endlessly reaffirm all his characteristics because no social sedimentation, no institution takes charge of them, societies that are undifferentiated because they are precapitalist.

The lexicological discomfort revealed by the subaltern point of view stems from the hierarchical forms and the immanent teleology of the distinction made according to degree of differentiation. It is not a matter of denying a difference or the existence of variation in social differentiation, still less of calling its effects into question, but of examining the way they are perceived, ordered and analysed.

Provincializing Western differentiation

'Fields', Lahire tells us, 'only have a history and a meaning in the framework of differentiated societies' (Lahire 2012: 145 and see Chapter 2 of this volume). This is clearly what Bourdieu also seems to indicate, since he declares that 'to understand human practices in differentiated societies, one has to know about fields and, on the other hand, one has to take account of … habitus'. At the same time, the concepts of habitus and field seem so interlinked that one may wonder if there can be societies without fields. Moreover, he considers that 'Habitus is valid only in relation with field, capital is valid only in relation with field' (both quotations, Bourdieu 1989, quoted by Lahire in Chapter 2, this volume) or even that 'a capital does not exist and function except in relation to a field' (Bourdieu and Wacquant 1992: 101). Would 'traditional' and 'precapitalist' societies function without capital or without fields? In the case of Kabylia, is the relationship between habitus and field exclusively negative? In reality, the confusions stem rather from the semantic instability we referred to in the Introduction to this work. The term 'field' sometimes designates the social space, conceived as a structure of positions that must be understood relationally, and sometimes it refers to a relatively autonomized domain of activity. It is in the latter sense that 'traditional' and 'precapitalist' societies more or less lack fields. From the subaltern viewpoint, this assertion calls for an immediate reservation: do non-differentiated societies exist? What would such societies look like? If one follows Lahire, they are:

> traditional societies, with an oral tradition, … also … termed 'acephalous' societies, 'stateless' societies, 'lineage-based' or 'segmentary' societies … [To] account for the mythico-ritual phenomena of these social formations … one cannot speak of 'politics' in the sense of an autonomized practice of power separate from other social practices … The situation has nothing in common with that of societies in which separate institutions of power have emerged.
>
> (Lahire 2012: 145)

The remark is significant but too general, and does not take into account the advances of anthropology over at least the last 30 years, no doubt for Lahire because it is essentially read through Bourdieu and for Bourdieu, and – as the references he mobilizes suggest – because he has not followed the developments of the discipline. What does this anthropology say? First, at a reflexive level, it has underlined that despite the paradigmatic succession that structures its history (evolutionism, diffusionism, functionalism, structural functionalism, structuralism, etc.), the idea of 'primitive society' has remained abnormally stable within the discipline (Kuper 1988: 1). It has shown that classic anthropology constructed its object through constant recourse to allo-chrony, postulating that undifferentiated societies belonged to an earlier tem-porality, although they were generally contemporary with the analyst (Fabian 1983), or by emphasizing that societies which underwent Western annexation could be understood, even in their symbolic structures, independently of the colonial 'situation' (Balandier 1951, and in another way the Manchester school). This 'denial of coevalness' (Fabian 1983) – i.e. the assignment to our contemporaries of another position in the temporal structure of humanity by converting a cultural distance, presumed to separate the West from the non-Western world, into linear historical time, on the basis of which hierarchies and distinct places are assigned (Friedman 1994; Chakrabarty 2008; Boa-ventura de Sousa 2014) – has analytic consequences that are hard to accept today – complex societies have actors with complex psychology, plural actors and plural worlds, undifferentiated societies have actors with undifferentiated psychology, singular worlds and singular people acting, paradoxically, almost without singularity.

In parallel with its self-critique, anthropology has shown, without necessarily falling into orientalism, that where primitive societies are described, there have also been societies with an elaborate oral tradition (Vansina 1985), with a State (Terray 1995), profoundly varied societies (Vidal 1995), some of which have had a complex administrative apparatus, a bureaucracy and domains with a specific language (Izard 2003; Hilgers 2012). Even in acephalous societies one finds autonomized practices of power and even fields, if this term is taken to mean domains of autonomized activities, i.e. activities requiring the learning of a specific language known to certain initiates, the transmission of a knowledge and a history specific to an activity, associated rituals, condi-tions of entry, the development of beliefs, a specific *illusio*, a specific capital, a structure of relational positions within which differences and forms of dom-ination come into play. One only has to think of secret societies or the hier-archies linked to earth altars in precolonial African societies to measure their complexity.

If precolonial African societies are not 'undifferentiated societies', what human groups would count as such? No doubt some 'primitive hordes', 'bands' of hunters, gatherers or fishers that existed beyond the imagination of anthro-pologists but the heuristic necessity of which for constructing the model of differentiation is not clear, not only because they no longer exist, not only because they belong to too remote a past, but also because behind these labels lies an immense variation and heterogeneity and it seems problematic on the one hand to valorize a sociology of complexity and on the other to totalize and classify extremely different societies on the basis of such a rudimentary category.

To calm the debate we could more simply say that there are no non-differentiated societies, first, because sexual difference in itself constitutes a biological distinction that leads to a minimum social differentiation, but above all because many of these so-called primitive societies are much more complex than they seem. Suffice it to say that we can read the classic authors generously, skipping over the occasional careless use of language, and agree that they are dealing with weakly or strongly differentiated rather than differentiated and undifferentiated societies.

However, this remains insufficient to avoid the risk of perceiving the process of social differentiation solely through the prism of the West, of the expansion of capitalism, with, in addition, the return of the Great Divide and the naturalized ontological distinctions that accompany it.[2] The ethnocentric deployment of this difference, albeit tempered by levels and forms, brings the risk of not perceiving the richness that results from the variation of the degree and type of differentiation. The critical intervention of postcolonial epistemology makes it possible to avoid the teleological pitfall and the danger of presenting the West and capitalism as the paradigmatic framework for the realization of social differentiation. Clearly, the obligation of vigilance does not imply the denial of difference and differentiation. Rather, it is a tactic to avoid the prejudices latent in the distinction.

If it appears necessary to reconsider the opposition between differentiated and non-differentiated societies and replace it, as we have suggested, with a continuum of more or less differentiated societies, it can also be useful to introduce some complementary distinctions depending on the types of differentiation with which one is dealing. The differentiation with which field theory is concerned is in fact a particular form of functional differentiation. However, as has been said, it does not imply that societies that are presumed to be little or non-differentiated in this respect are not differentiated in other respects – religion, language, ethnicity, local particularity and territory. In these other respects, moreover, France would have to be regarded as a relatively undifferentiated society compared to many others. There is much to be gained from considering alternative differentiations instead of considering all societies deviating from the Western model as necessarily poorly differentiated.

Extending field theory

Reconsidering differentiation in a less exclusive way makes it possible to enrich the contextualist and dispositionalist perspectives in empirical and theoretical terms. What happens when one tries to implement this theory in spaces that are less differentiated or imagined to be so (i.e. the countries of the South)? What questions arise from this transposition? What do they illuminate? It is a complex issue, and to introduce it we shall limit ourselves to three preliminary considerations that lead to a decentring of the conventional use of field theory. The first concerns the unification of the cultural market; the second, the unification of the economic market; and the third, globalization.

The unification of the cultural market

One characteristic of many societies of the South is that there is no unification of the market in cultural capital. In contrast to French republican society, where the educational hierarchy is always a decisive element in the evaluation and profitability of this capital, where the educational system establishes what Bourdieu calls 'a unified market for all cultural capacities' and guarantees 'the convertibility into money of cultural capital acquired at a determinate cost in time and labour' (Bourdieu 1976: 125), in most African countries it seems difficult to identify absolute cultural reference points within the local horizon. The overlapping of different sets of norms means that several hierarchies coexist and appear as more or less legitimate depending on the context. Aside from extreme cases, where individuals accumulate – or are totally deprived of – all the legitimate facets of cultural capital, it is difficult, but not impossible, to identify precisely the value of the specific components of an individual's overall cultural capital (including its incorporated and therefore dispositional form). It is even more complex to determine a uniform hierarchy based on this capital. That would presuppose establishing what constitutes the legitimate culture, which in some social universes is highly problematic, as shown by the work of the Euro-African Association for the Anthropology of Social Change and Development (APAD) school analysing the 'superimposition', 'overlapping' and 'intertwining' of a 'plurality of norms' in a sub-Saharan Africa marked by the multiple belonging of social agents to several hierarchies (Bierschenk and Olivier de Sardan 1998; Chauveau *et al.* 2001; Hilgers 2009; Blundo 2012; Lund 2013). The great variety of the legitimacies that shape the hierarchies makes it difficult to establish an overall hierarchy spanning the whole of the social space.

In contrast to economic capital, which draws very clear dividing lines and is almost always determinant in the structuring of social positions, cultural capital here relates to different forms of legitimacies, often competing and generally hybrid.[3] The legitimacy of the facets of cultural capital varies profoundly according to the context. It is less subordinate to a hegemonic, uniform, totalizing hierarchy than in Jacobin French society. The hierarchies are not fixed but situational. This does not mean that they are constantly reinvented or that there are no institutions stabilizing them in an idiosyncratic, or even idiosyncretic way, but simply that they are not unified. Is this the sign of weak differentiation? If so, it has to be acknowledged that weakly differentiated societies can produce individuals who have an extremely plural register of dispositions.[4] Is it the sign of strong differentiation? It is then clear that it is not identical to the type of differentiation considered by Bourdieu. The multiplicity of these legitimacies seems, indeed, to be the product of a social differentiation, while at the same time resulting from the difficulty of establishing a State institution which could, as in the French case, constitute a 'meta-field', a 'meta-power', a 'meta-capital' that irradiates the other fields (Bourdieu 2012: 488–89). If one considers a good number of southern countries, it seems difficult to agree

that 'in the modern world state actors alone have the formal authority to intervene in, set rules for and generally pronounce on the legitimacy and viability of
most nonstate fields' (Fligstein and McAdam 2012: 19). The theory of fields has
to take into consideration the configurations in which it is deployed, the impact
of the variation of the state configurations (i.e. authoritarian, semi-authoritarian,
weak or failed) and the historical trajectory of societies.

How is the hierarchy of these multiple legitimacies organized? How do
fields relate to one another when the State does not constitute a meta-field?
How does the variety of orders of legitimacies affect dispositions? More generally, 'Does the concept of the field still function in the same way (and as
effectively) when translated into a context other than that of French society?'
Mangez and Liénard ask in this volume (Chapter 7). These authors examine
the question, taking the example of a country neighbouring France – Belgium –
and show the importance of understanding the differentiation into fields by
cross-comparing it with other types of differentiations based on religious,
philosophical, ethno-linguistic and territorial affiliations. These overlappings
generate specific mechanisms, neutralize certain intra-field struggles and stimulate inter-field solidarities. The State in Belgium is not as centralized as in
France, the cultural hierarchy is less unified, the linguistic hierarchies remain
subject to controversy, the federal, community and regional institutions compete in many areas. If such differences are already observable between neighbouring countries, it is clear how important it is to undertake a serious
historical and geographical comparison between the countries of the North
and of the South(s).

The colonial situation, for example, established a form of differentiation
probably much more violent and radical than the differentiation generally
associated with the dynamics of capitalism in Western societies. Nonetheless,
and without minimizing its violence or the fact that this debate is never
entirely closed, numerous works by historians, political scientists and anthro-
pologists have shown that in many regions colonization did not take the form
of a break but rather constituted a radical moment of composition or
recomposition of hegemonic alliances (Bayart 1994). Colonization should not
necessarily be conceived as the collision and coexistence of two societies
(undifferentiated and differentiated). It can also be seen as the recomposition
of a social assemblage, or of a society marked by radical levels of autonomy
and internal differentiation, extreme forms of exclusion and strong logics of
ambivalence, heteronomy and encounter.

With the works on the colonial experience, we now have a vast and
particularly fertile corpus for understanding intra- and inter-individual dispositional differences. At the empirical and theoretical levels, many studies
provide excellent resources for advances in relational and dispositionalist
sociology, for example, the works of Jean Comaroff and John Comaroff on
the body, the historical transformation of culture, the colonization of consciousness and the consciousness of colonization (1985, 1991, 1992, 1997), or
Serge Gruzinski (1988) on the 'colonization of the imagination', or life

trajectories that directly question dispositional plurality, such as that Valentin Mudimbe (1988), the equivalent of Edward Said in African Studies. Mudimbe grew up in a village in Zaire and received a Jesuit schooling in that country before studying in Europe, living in the Latin Quarter in Paris, and writing a thesis in classical philology at the Catholic University of Louvain, becoming a Marxist, and spending another ten years in his country of origin before finally being expelled from it and being appointed to a chair of literature at Duke University in the United States. A whole aspect of his work can be reread as one of the highest forms of reflexivity on the dispositional plurality induced by this individual and collective trajectory, which can be condensed in the term 'postcolonial' in the historical, theoretical and epistemological sense (see for example his novel *L'Écart*, translated as *The Rift*). Who am I, what am I, when my identity and my relation to myself are constituted through contexts and learning experiences inducing such radically opposed readings and rereadings of myself?

Practices that the academic observer considers dissonant or out of phase are not always perceived or conceived as illegitimate from an emic point of view. The existence of great variations within societies probably allows other modes of conversion of capital. It may be supposed that there are some forms of cultural capital that transcend local spaces and others that play a sometimes auxiliary, sometimes dominant role but have only a regional efficacy. These observations invite us to nuance a point of view in which practices that anthropologists designate as those of fusion, *bricolage*, hybridity – or, in some cases, breaks that constitute not a total rupture but an outlet facilitating the management of existential tensions – through the prism of dissonance relative to a cultural space presented as a homogeneous reference. Many variations do not appear to the agents as discordant, not only because they result from a 'practical sense' but also because they are not understood in terms of a totalization of a lifetime's experience of the world that might seek to define an aesthetic of homogeneous existence.

Some societies are marked by tendencies valorizing ambivalence, playing on multiple registers, living with ruse or conscious but non-problematic contradictory associations. Practices are not necessarily evaluated in terms of a lifestyle that ostentatiously manifests its coherence. The conscious heterogeneity of practices generates less guilt than that produced by dissonance in postmodern Western societies, tolerant of contradiction though they are. The explanation probably lies not in a weak differentiation that would produce a less complex psychological structure, but perhaps, over the long term, in a different relation to the moral ideal of coherence in societies long untouched by Christianity and, above all, structured with a less unified market in cultural capital. These considerations are important for refining our understanding of cultural capital outside and perhaps for seeing how particular the French context is.

The unification of the economic market

Therefore, there are highly differentiated societies in which, in contrast to the French case, there is no unified market in cultural capital. Given that Bourdieu's analysis of cultural capital is in many respects a transposition of the analysis of economic capital as worked out by Marx, it might be wondered whether the critique should not be extended to the sources of inspiration themselves, i.e. to the process of unification of the economic market.

In sociological thought, as is shown by the recurrent use of the term 'precapitalist' to designate relatively non-differentiated societies, functional speciation is generally posited in relation with capitalism. The main societies in which Bourdieu grounds the empirical underpinning of his reflection are, moreover, 'traditional', 'precapitalist' Algeria – where he analyses in part the forms of social violence linked to economic transformations, and especially their impact on the temporal and affective structures of perception (Bourdieu 1979 – and a broadly 'capitalist' French society. Bourdieu does not present these configurations as specific but seems to regard them as the expression of a universal. While one can legitimately examine Algeria and France as forms of practical embodiments of a universal, it is essential to question the universal character of the association between 'precapitalism' and 'weakly differentiated' on the one hand, and 'capitalist' and 'strongly differentiated' on the other.

These associations seem to be so assimilated by Bourdieu that they efface themselves, disappear, become quasi-invisible in his work. Apart from some of his early texts on Algeria or the polemical texts of Bourdieu the 'public intellectual' against neoliberalism, in his major texts – *Outline of a Theory of Practice, The Logic of Practice, Distinction, Pascalian Meditations* – capitalism is a background, incorporated into the logic of differentiation without being made fully explicit, so that it ends up constituting a presupposition and even an implicit motor of the process of differentiation. However, it may be questioned if the dynamics of demographic growth, which mechanically engenders a competition leading to differentiation, is exclusively articulated with the logic of capitalism. Historically, given the variety of forms of social organization, the answer can only be negative. It is not a question of claiming that capitalist societies are not differentiated but rather of pointing out that not all differentiated societies have necessarily been capitalist. In other words, a questioning of the forms and degrees of differentiation invites one to consider the potentially idiosyncratic character of the differentiations that develop in capitalist spaces. This requires one to shed the retrospective illusion whereby any non-capitalist space is necessarily seen as 'precapitalist'.

Making this assumption explicit raises several questions: what happens in autonomized domains of activities in non-unified economic spaces, in frameworks where the capitalist and non-capitalist economy are hybrid? How do fields function there? How do conversions take place between the forms of capital possessed by the agents (cultural, economic, symbolic, specific) when there is no homogeneous hierarchy and unified market in cultural and/or economic terms? Are the modes of conversion of capital as Bourdieu theorizes them really pertinent in non-capitalist but differentiated societies? Are these not questions that arise and are necessary both for grasping the social dynamics of relatively autonomous activities at a general and comparative level and identifying the historical particularity on the basis of which Bourdieu built up his model?

Notwithstanding the arguments put forward in the Introduction to this work, which indicate how to use the theory of fields to understand social change, it seems that Bourdieu neglected the extent of historical variations. His strange relationship to Kabyle society is the most perfect expression of this. On the one hand, the texts from his youth are political and analyse the impact of colonization on the transformation of economic and social dispositions. On the other hand, his best-known and most decisive texts based on Algeria are theoretical works which present and analyse a Kabyle society that exists outside time and the colonial experience. Beyond the fieldwork, the work of theoretical investigation and powerful interdisciplinary discussions, one cannot fail to be surprised by this situation. One of the most stimulating and innovative analytical models of the twentieth century is based on the difficult transposition to 'highly differentiated' societies of a 'anthropological mythology',[5] established in relation to 'weakly differentiated societies'.[6]

It is all the more disconcerting since it was by means of this detour that Bourdieu was able to shed a revealing, pertinent and innovative light on many aspects of the organization and functioning of the social world. At the level of conceptual productivity, Bourdieu's binary comparisons have proven extremely fertile. At the level of their descriptive value, some of them nonetheless remain profoundly problematic – all the more so since Bourdieu presents them not as tactics devised to construct an analytical apparatus but as analyses in their own right.

Without falling into naïve realism, it seems, however, that a rigorous study of the social world based on his concepts can be conducted by moving beyond some analytical fictions that were necessary for their construction. This presupposes that one take account of the historical particularities in all their complexity. Analysing the logic of fields in their historical movement requires taking seriously the profound variations that distinguish the trajectories of societies. However, Bourdieu's ambition of developing a general theory led him sometimes to neglect the specificity of epochs, societies and cultures, sometimes to reify and naturalize differences. The structural opposition between weakly and strongly differentiated societies was a resource for initiating the modelling; nothing now prevents us from nuancing and enlarging the field of investigation. In questioning the distinction between weakly and strongly differentiated societies, in seeking to implement the theory of fields in the countries of the South, not in order to destroy it or highlight its limits but to refine it and extend its efficacy, the postcolonial approach expands the analysis of social differentiation. It explores alternative differentiations and introduces nuances.

Globalization

Expanding the field of investigation also means considering one final point which, contrary to what many people think, appears marginal in Bourdieu's work and yet decisive for pursuing decentring without limiting it to the study of the past. His polemical essays against neoliberalism and several late articles discuss globalization, and even associate it with the theory of fields (Bourdieu 1998a; Bourdieu and Wacquant 1999; Bourdieu 2000a, 2001). Bourdieu shows, for example, how the field of the neoliberal economy progressively establishes itself on a world scale and reduces the autonomy of the other fields. However, and even if he sometimes appears as a standard bearer of the anti-globalization movements, beyond his polemical interventions, Bourdieu died too soon really to become a theorist of globalization. The theme is not the preoccupation of any of his major works and the main lines of force of his theoretical approach were worked out without taking this dynamic into consideration. On the contrary, in many ways he gives the impression of having studied relatively isolated societies, circumscribed on one territory. This observation is not insignificant. It suggests that rather than limiting oneself to the relatively contextual sketches that Bourdieu devoted to globalization, it seems more fruitful to confront his model seriously with the questions that emerge when it is deployed in the global framework.

The growing interconnectedness of societies, the emergence of a global consciousness, and technological transformations should be handled with care, especially when one is studying isolated regions, but they are having a decisive impact on social structuring and historical, institutional and bodily dynamics (Hilgers 2009). As Duval's Chapter 6 in this volume shows, internationalization is having a profound effect on relatively autonomized domains of activity. A number of these domains have experienced an intensification of their global dimensions in recent decades: sport, religion, power, science, politics, the economy, art, fashion, journalism, literature, the media, law, education, to limit ourselves to those that Bourdieu studied. The deployment of relatively autonomized domains of activity must henceforward be considered in local, national, regional and international contexts defined by legalities, institutional frameworks, reforms, modes of regulation, struggles and historicities that engender strong variations in their structuring. How are these variations organized? Consideration of the systemic logics in specific domains, the efficacy of the modes of refraction, the modification of rules and strategies according to the scale, the impact of the trajectories of connections and disconnections with global flows, and the transformation of the forms of autonomy are some of the many questions that arise.

Our own research on the Programme for International Student Assessment (PISA) has documented the transformation of the field of education, describing its evolution towards heteronomy following the introduction of new actors and the growing submission of those richest in cultural capital to economic and political interests. The diffusion of standardized modes of evaluation and a culture of accountability has reduced the autonomy of national fields of education (Mangez and Hilgers 2012). Researchers are increasingly drawing on Bourdieu to analyse the most varied domains in relation to the dynamics linked to globalization. These major advances cannot be detailed here, but it should be noted, given the small place of this theme in the Bourdieusian corpus – a place which, in the 47 books published to date, becomes even smaller when one omits the occasional essays and polemical texts – that these developments always constitute original extensions of his work rather than the academic, standardized duplication of his theoretical model.

This fertility derives, *inter alia*, from the fact that the implementation of this theory in the context of globalization raises many questions – that of whether the growth of connections and the strengthening of external forces leads to a shortening of the cycle of transformation of fields; or the question of establishing the impact of the contraction of space and time on their functioning; or that of clarifying the relationship between deterritorialization, the structuring of a domain of activity, and individual dispositions.

International institutions are playing an historically unprecedented role. Often, they construct and disseminate international evaluations or standards which, in many fields, increasingly function as principles of ranking, imposing a specific form of capital and so unifying cultural hierarchies beyond regional or national frontiers.[7] As a corollary, the role and function of the State are being transformed. The objective structures that constitute relatively autonomized domains of activity are no longer limited to the local level. The principles of classification and judgement mobilized within them are becoming globalized (Fenwick *et al.* 2014, Andre and Hilgers 2015). How are the effects and the relations between fields, the intersections, the interrelations and the inter-fields articulated? Are there trans-field effects? If so, on what scale do they occur? How do we articulate the variations of scale between the local, regional, national and global with the theory of fields? What can this teach us? Does the theory of fields constitute an adequate structural framework to deal with the multiple variations, experiments and contingencies included in the historical dynamics specific to each level of articulation? There are countless questions and they seem to be extremely fertile.

Conclusion

Despite its aspirations, in many of its aspects Bourdieu's theory of fields is a regional theory. It is built up from a local history in order to grasp a specific part of the social space. If we understand it restrictively, this theory therefore seems useful, first and foremost, in societies where a relatively strong State guarantees the existence of a unified market in cultural and economic capital and has the power to preserve certain domains of activity from subordination to external hierarchies such as that of the economic market. However, if one thinks that Bourdieu was right to claim that his theory goes far beyond loc-alism, there is no reason to limit oneself to this standard interpretation. There is a choice to be made in methodological, theoretical and interpretative terms. If the theory is regarded as a general theory capable of being developed to shed light on the emergence and organization of any relatively autonomized domain of activity, then its implementation in alternative spaces and discussion with the most recent advances of the social sciences open a horizon of empirical and theoretical inquiries that has a promising future before it.

Notes

1 In his argument with Bourdieu, Lahire takes up the distinction between non-differentiated and differentiated societies and makes it so much his own that he considers that Bourdieu's main error was to have imported a model dispositionalist conceived in the observation of traditional societies (whether Kabylia or Béarn) into modern societies, where, as Martuccelli notes, economic capital is of much greater importance, where symbolic domination is codified by the mediation of the State, and where mismatches between subjective representations and objective reality increase (Martuccelli 1999). 'The paradox', Lahire declares, 'lies in having … retained the model of the habitus, appropriate for the study of weakly differentiated societies (preindustrial, precapitalist) in order to study strongly differentiated societies, which, by definition, necessarily produce actors who are more differentiated from one another, but also internally' (Lahire 2012: 31).

2 In addition to a postcolonial perspective, for a stimulating way of moving beyond this dichotomy, see the now classic works of Descola (2013) and Latour (1993).

3 Beyond economic capital and cultural capital, autochtony seems to play the role of capital that can be invested, valued and profited from in many societies in Africa; see Hilgers 2011.

4 For one of the most stimulating developments of Bourdieu's dispositionalist theory, which precisely considers dispositional plurality in highly differentiated societies, see Bernard Lahire's *The Plural Actor* (2010).

5 We borrow the term from Burawoy and van Holdt 2012.

6 This is even more surprising given that in these early works Bourdieu analyses the relations of cultural domination imposed by colonization (Bourdieu 1958, 1962). He shows, for example, that modern activities presuppose the dissociation of the symbolic and the economic, and consequently 'the knowledge and recognition of imported models' (Bourdieu 1963: 302). Some agents, incapable of adapting to this system, abandon the effort and cling by default to a 'traditionalism of despair' (Bourdieu 1964: 201), generating obsolete attitudes, while others oscillate between the modern and the traditional modes of functioning and develop a structure of hybrid conducts. Hence young people brought up within the administrative and educational system imposed by colonization find it easier to internalize the rules of colonial society and to produce appropriate practices. The peasants' hybrid systems of representations, classifications and actions lead to a disjunction between their subjective intentions and their objective chances because they are less able to grasp the functioning of a changing world. At the same time, the massive and rapid changes in the conditions of existence and the transformations of norms and behaviours facilitate conscious awareness of models that were previously taken for granted. Bourdieu stresses the complexity of this social structure. According to him, all behaviour can be read in two ways, since it bears within it reference to the two logics. 'It follows that each of the one-sided descriptions of the reality suffices to account for the whole of the reality, except for what constitutes its essence, namely contradiction' (Bourdieu 1964: 164). Indeed, these logics very often interpenetrate each other and give rise to complex

behaviours. Bourdieu even refers to 'a double inner life' (Bourdieu 1958: 123; Bourdieu 1962: 144), oscillating between uncertain identification with the dominant model and the urge to revolt that arises from the dominated model. He shows to what extent 'the abandonment of the traditionalist attitude does not coincide with adoption of the ethos historically associated with the capitalist attitude' (Bourdieu 1963: 374). However, although these empirical works describe this complex interpenetration, a dual theoretical representation of the world is progressively set up, and the traditional mode of thought and the modern mode of thought come to constitute quasi-antinomic forms of theoretical objectivation.

7 For a reflection on these questions see for example a recent study on the process of dissemination of a standardized conception of childhood, the simultaneous emergence of the field of worldwide child protection and its impact in Africa (Andre and Hilgers 2015).

References

Andre, G. and Hilgers, M. 2015. 'Childhood in Africa between Local Powers and Global Hierarchies' B. Mayall, L. Alanen and L. Brooker, *Studying Childhood with Bourdieu*. Palgrave McMillan: London, 179–209.

Balandier, G. 1951. 'La situation coloniale: approche théorique'. *Cahiers internationaux de sociologie*, IX, 44–79.

Bayart, J-F. 1994 *The State in Africa: the Politics of the Belly*. London and New York: Longman.

Bierschenk, T. and Olivier de Sardan, J.-P. (eds) 1998. *Les pouvoirs au village: le Bénin rural entre démocratisation et decentralisation*. Paris: Karthala.

Blundo, G. 2012. 'Le roi n'est pas un parent. Les multiples redevabilités de l'Etat postcolonial en Afrique. In P. Haag and C. Lemieux, *Faire des sciences sociales*. Vol. I *Critiquer*. Paris: Ed. de l'EHESS, 59–86.

Boaventura de Sousa, S. 2014. *Epistemologies of the South: Justce against Epistemicide*. Boulder London: Paradigm Publishers.

Bourdieu, P. 1958. *Sociologie de l'Algérie*. Paris: Presses Universitaires de France (translated as Bourdieu 1962).

——1962. *The Algerians*. Boston: Beacon Press.

——, with Darbel, A., Rivet, J.-P. and Seibel, C. 1963. *Travail et travailleurs en Algérie*. The Hague: Mouton.

——, with Sayad, A. 1964. *Le déracinement: La crise de l'agriculture traditionelle en Algérie*. Paris: Éditions de Minuit (translation forthcoming, *Uprooting*. Cambridge: Polity Press, 2014).

——1976. 'Les modes de domination'. *Actes de la Recherche en Science Sociales*, 2(2–3), 122–32 (translated in 1977, 183–97).

——1977. *Outline of a Theory of Practice*. Cambridge: Cambridge University Press.

——1979. *Algeria 1960. The Disenchantment of the World; the Sense of Honour; the Kabyle House or the World Reversed; essays*. Cambridge: Cambridge University Press.

——1989. *Intérêt et désintéressement*. Cours du Collège de France, Cahiers de recherche du GRS, no. 7, Lyon.

——1994. *Raisons pratiques. Sur la théorie de l'action*. Paris: Seuil (translated as 1998c).

——1997. *Méditations pascaliennes*. Paris: Seuil (translated as 2000b).

——1998a. *Contre-feux*. Paris: Éditions Raison d'agir (translated as 1998b).

——1998b. *Acts of Resistance: Against the New Myths of Our Time*. Cambridge: Polity.

——1998c. *Practical Reason: On the Theory of Action*. Cambridge: Polity; Stanford, CA: Stanford University Press.

——2000a. *Les Structures sociales de l'économie*. Paris: Seuil (translated as 2003a).

——2000b. *Pascalian Meditations*. Cambridge: Polity; Stanford, CA: Stanford University Press.

——2001. *Contre-feux 2: pour un mouvement social européen*. Paris: Raisons d'agir.

——2003a. *The Social Structures of the Economy*. Cambridge: Polity Press.

——2003b. *Firing Back: Against the Tyranny of the Market 2*. London: Verso.

——2012. *Sur l'Etat*. Paris: Seuil.

Bourdieu, P. and Wacquant, L.J.D. 1992. *An Invitation to Reflexive Sociology*. Chicago: University of Chicago Press; Cambridge: Polity Press.

——1999. 'On the Cunning of Imperialist Reason'. *Theory, Culture and Society*, 16(1), 41–58.

Burawoy, M. and van Holdt, K. 2012. *Conversations with Bourdieu: The Johannesburg Moment*. Johannesburg: Witwatersrand University Press.

Chakrabarty, D. 2008. *Provincializing Europe: Postcolonial Thought and Historical Difference*. Reissue, with new Preface. Princeton: Princeton University Press.

Chauveau, J.-P., Le Pape, M. and Olivier de Sardan, J.-P. 2001. 'La pluralité des normes et leurs dynamiques en Afrique. Implications pour les politiques'. In G. Winter (ed.) *Inégalités et politiques publiques en Afrique: pluralité des normes et jeux d'acteurs*. Paris: Karthala, 145–62.

Comaroff, J. 1985. *Body of Power, Spirit of Resistance: The Culture and History of a South African People*. Chicago and London: University of Chicago Press.

Comaroff, J. and Comaroff, J. 1991, *Of Revelation and Revolution* Vol. 1. Chicago: University of Chicago Press

——1992. *Ethnography and the Historical Imagination*. Boulder: Westview Press.

——1997. *Of Revelation and Revolution* Vol. 2. Chicago: University of Chicago Press

Descola, P. 2013. *Beyond Nature and Culture*. Chicago: University of Chicago Press.

Fabian, J. 1983. *Time and the Other: How Anthropology Makes its Object*. New York: Columbia University Press.

Fenwick, T., Mangez, E. and Ozga, J. 2014. 'Introduction'. In T. Fenwick, E. Mangez and J. Ozga (eds) *Governing Knowledge: Comparison, Knowledge-Based Technologies and Expertise in the Regulation of Education*. London: Routledge, 3–10.

Fligstein, N. and McAdam, D. 2012. *A Theory of Fields*. Oxford: Oxford University Press.

Friedman, J. 1994. *Cultural Identity and Global Process*. London: Sage.

Gadamer, H.G. 2013. *Truth and Method*. London and New York: Bloomsbury Academic.

Gruzinski, S. 1988. *La colonisation de l'imaginaire, Sociétés indigènes et occidentalisation dans le Mexique espagnol, XVIe–XVIIIe siècle*. Paris: Gallimard (translated as *The Conquest of Mexico: The Incorporation of Indian Societies into the Western World, 16th–18th Centuries*. Cambridge: Polity Press, 1993).

Hilgers, M. 2009. *Une ethnographie à l'échelle de la ville*. Karthala: Paris.

——2011. 'Autochtony as Capital in a Global Age'. *Theory, Culture and Society*, 28 (1), 34–54.

——2012. 'Réflexivité du pouvoir et pouvoir de la réflexivité'. In D. Casajus and F. Viti, *La terre et le pouvoir. Textes offerts en hommage à Michel Izard*. Paris: CNRS, 49–65.

Izard, M. 2003. *Moogo: L'émergence d'un espace étatique ouest-africain au XVIe siècle*. Paris: Karthala.

Kuper, A. 1988. *The Invention of Primitive Society: Transformations of an Illusion*. London: Routledge.

Lahire, B. 2010. *The Plural Actor*. Cambridge: Polity Press.

——2012. *Monde pluriel: Penser l'unité des sciences sociales*. Paris: Seuil.

Latour, B. 1993. *We Have Never Been Modern*. Cambridge, MA: Harvard University Press.

Lund, C. (ed.) 2013. *Development and Rights: Negotiating Justice in Changing Societies*. London: Routledge.

Mangez, E. and Hilgers, M. 2012. 'The Field of Knowledge and the Policy Field in Education: PISA and the Production of Knowledge for Policy'. *European Education Research Journal*, 11(2), 189–205.

Martuccelli, D. 1999. *Sociologies de la modernité: l'itinéraire du XXe siècle*. Paris: Gallimard.

Mbembe, A. 2001. *On the Postcolony*. Berkeley: University of California Press.

——2013. *Critique de la raison nègre*. Paris: La Découverte.

Mudimbe, V. 1988. *The Invention of Africa: Philosophy and the Order of Knowledge*. Bloomington: Indiana University Press.

——1993. *The Rift*. Minneapolis: University of Minnesota Press.

Mudimbe, V. and Hilgers, M. 2013. 'Réflexions sur l'interdisciplinarité et le pouvoir de l'épistémologie'. *Anthropologie et Sociétés*, 37(1), 137–60.

Terray, E. 1995, *Une histoire du royaume Abron du Gyaman des origines à la conquête colonial*. Paris: Karthala.

Vansina, J. 1985. *Oral Tradition as History*. Madison: University of Wisconsin Press.

Vidal, C. 1995. 'Le royaume abron du Gyaman vu du royaume tutsi du Rwanda. Essai d'histoire africaine comparée'. *L'Homme*, 35, 51–71.

Index

corporate interests, coercive arm of state
and 252
Courtade, Pierre 145
Courtin, E. 211
creativity, support for 157–59
Crime Omnibus Act (1993) 241
critical reflection on concept of field 62,
63
criticism and cultural journalism 154–56
cross-comparison of differentiation
263–64
Crozier, M. and Friedberg, E. 201
Crozier, Michel 201, 217n4
cultural capital 8, 10, 14, 27–28, 89–90,
108, 111, 185, 186, 194–95, 240, 250;
collective agents in school field 122,
124, 128, 130–31, 132, 134–35;
postcolonial age, theory of fields in
258, 262–63, 265, 268
cultural fragmentation, process of 186
cultural journalism, role of 154–56
cultural market, unification of 262–65
cultural policy 156–59; analysis of
210–11
cultural production: fields of 170;
specificity of 80–81
cultural sciences 41
The Culture of Control (Garland, D.)
245, 246–47, 248

Daccache, M. 209
d'Alema, Massimo 247
Darnton, R. 149
Darré, Yann 172, 174, 178n1
de Munck, J. 183, 188
Defrance, J. 59n18, 215
del Toso, J. 174, 177
Delporte, C. 144
Delvaux, B. and Joseph, M. 123, 137n7
Democratic Leadership Council (DLC)
226
Denord, F. 209
Derouet, J.-L. 121
Desage, F. and Godard, J. 202
Descola, P. 270n3
Descombes, Vincent 96n10
Desmond, M. 54
d'Estaing, Valéry Giscard 159, 205
Détienne, M. 98n27
Détienne, M. and Camassa, G. 98n27
Deventer, Jasmine van 160n1
Devineau, S. 136n3
Devos, Raymond 155
Dewey, John 95, 99n36

Dickson, P. 231, 234n2, 235n13
Diderot, D. 174
differentiation: differentiated and
non-differentiated societies,
distinction between 258, 259–60,
261–62; differentiation-autonomization
of spheres of activity 95–96; of fields
and limits of the field 72; process of
64, 67–72
Digby, J. 235n13
Dilthey, W. 41
DiNardo, J. 225
disciplinary society, Foucault's vision
239, 243, 248
Discipline and Punish (Foucault, M.)
243, 244–45
discourse production without discourse
89–91
Discovery Institute 233
discretion between pillars 191–94
distinction, concept of 114–15
Distinction (Bourdieu, P.) 266
division of labour: Durkheim's thesis of
progress of 202; limits of the field 70
Dobbelaere, K and Voyé, L. 188
Domhoff, G.W. 235n9
dominant position 125–26
Dostoyevsky, Fyodor 174
Dragomir, L. 144
Dreyfus, Captain 148
duality or 'twofold truth': in economic
journalism 169; in Hollywood films
173
Dubet, F. 121
Dubois, J. 29, 89
Dubois, V, and Dulong, D. 208
Dubois, Vincent xiv, 156, 158, 199–218
Duffy, M.M. *et al.* 217n2
Duménil, G. and Lévy, D. 255n5
Dupont, F. 98n27
Dupuy, F. and Th?nig, J.-C. 201
Durand, G. 30n1, 31n13
Duranty, Louis Edmond 85
Duras, Marguerite 155
Durkheim, Émile 5, 27, 45, 62, 65, 67,
68, 69, 70, 71, 78, 97n18, 103, 104,
114, 117n18, 202, 238, 259
Dury, M. 142
Duval, Julien xiv, 28, 30n1, 165–78, 268
Dye, T.R. 235n9
dynamics of social fields 4

Eastwood, Clint 177
economic capital 228

278   *Index*

economic deregulation, neoliberalism
and 250
economic journalism and revelatory
aspects of the field: analyses in terms
of the field 168–69; *L'Argent* (Zola,
E.) 168; business scandals 168;
Charlie Hebdo 167; duality or
'twofold truth' in economic
journalism 169; economic world,
dependence on 168–69; field, concept
of 166–69; *Le Figaro* 167; *L'Humanité*
167; information, corporate influences
on 169; journalistic training 167;
media analysis, 'reflection theories' in
167; *Le Monde diplomatique* 167;
money and press, debates about 168;
'la pensée unique', uniform adherence
to 167; 'reflection,' analyses in terms
of 168; rigour, lack of 168; tautologies
167–68; world vision 169
economic market, unification of 265–67
Economic Policy Institute (EPI) 224–25
economic world, dependence on
168–69
economism, cinema as model against
170–73
economy, principle of 106
Éditions du Seuil 1
L'Éducation sentimentale (Flaubert, G.)
88–89
educational research, discretionary
demarcation within 193
Ehrenfels, Christian 41
Einstein, Albert 40, 46
electro-magnetism 40
Elias, Norbert 67, 72, 78, 259
Ellis, R.J. 235n10
Éluard, Paul 84, 145, 147
empirical tasks, imposition of 65–66
Encrevé, Pierre 205
entrepreneurialism and social fields 14
epistemic communities 200–201
epistemic violence 257, 258
esprit de corps, policy production and
question of 208
ethno-racial division 242–43
eugenic measures 253
Euro-African Association for the
Anthropology of Social Change and
Development (APAD) 263
European Union (EU): policy
production, construction of space of
207; workfare and prisonfare in
bureaucratic field 250

excluded 'off-field' individuals 74–75
Eyal, Gil 227, 230, 232

Fabian, J. 260
family as field 73, 77–78
Faraday, Michael 43, 56, 57n5
Fascist National Institute of Culture 143
Faucheux, C. 3
Fenwick, T. *et al* 269
Ferenczi, T. 173, 174
field, concept of: action in relation to
field 109–12; cinema and empirical
implementation of the field 170–73;
commoditization of cultural industries
177–78; distinction, concept of
114–15; economic journalism and
revelatory aspects of the field 166–69;
economy, principle of 106; field of
forces, metaphor of 77–78; fields in
perspective 112–14; general theory of
fields, tasks of 113–14; genesis of
fields, historical analysis of 214–15;
ideas, Bourdieu's perspective on uses
of 102–3; inter-expression, relations of
107–8; Leibnizian perspective in
sociology 102–15; limits of the field
62–63; literary field, model of 173–77;
Le Métier de sociologue (Bourdieu, P.
Chamboredon, J.-C. and Passeron,
J.-C.) 166; monadological status of
105–6; opposing paths, ethic
treatment of 104–5; original relative
indistinction of fields 69; rationalist
empiricism 104; relational thinking 3,
27, 115; as research instrument
165–66; scientific posture 102; sensible
and intelligible, relationship between
103–5; social force of forced choice
105; social space, analysis of 106–7;
socio-occupational categories, status
given to 108; spatial coexistence of
positions, fields as 112–13; statistical
sociology 165; variety and order,
compatibility between 105–9; vision,
theory as instrument of 165
field theory: Bourdieu's work in terms of
47–57; brain processes 44; causality in
social sciences 40; characteristics of
39–41; cultural sciences 41;
development of 41–47; dualities in
Bourdieu's approach 45–46;
Durkheim and beginnings of 68–71;
electro-magnetism 40; epistemological
basis of 2–5; essences of 39–41; field

empirical tasks, imposition of 65–66; excluded 'off-field' individuals 74–75; family as field 77–78; family framework 73; field, concept of 62–63; field of forces, metaphor of 77–78; field theory, Durkheim and beginnings of 68–71; fields, original relative indistinction of 69; fleshless field 86–93; focal distance, problem of 88; game, inside and outside of 83–86; individual stocks *(patrimoines)* of dispositions 82–83; interdependence, Elias' notion of configuration of relations of 78; intra-individual variations of behaviours 82–83; literary field without literature 87–89; literary game vs literary field 78–86; literary interludes, Flaubert's double life of 81–83; literary universe, specificity of functioning of 83; literary writing, social universe of 79–81; non-field areas of activity 63, 64; power, Bourdieu and emergence of field of 67–68; problematic homology 91–93; professional participation 74; reductionist explanations, slippage towards 63–64; regional theory claiming universality 76–77; religious beliefs and practices 69; secondary fields 64; social action, Weber and spheres of activity and 71–72; social configurations and fields 63; social differentiation, phenomena of 72–73; social differentiation of activities 67–72; social discourses, quarantining of 90–91; social microcosms, multiplicity of 64; social relations, analysis in terms of field 77–78; social universes 63; social world, differentiation in 69–70; social worlds, plurality of 74–75; socially mixed interaction sites 63; sociological imagination, expansion of 65–66; space of producers and space of consumers, homology between 93; specificity of fields 63, 64; temporary engagement 74
Lindon, Jérôme 159
Lingard, B. *et al.* 217n2
Lingard, B and Rawolle, S. 217n2
linguistic-cultural divide in Belgium 187
literary field, model of 173–77; autonomy, degrees of 177; cinema and

literature, relationship between 174–75, 176–77; cinematography, artistry of 175; *Comédie française* 174; field, concept of 173–77; independence, value of 176; journalism and literature, relationship between 173–74, 175–76, 177; *Le Monde* 174, 176; *Nouvelle Vague* 174; posterity, judgement of 176; scientific prestige 176; symbolic recognition 176–77
literary field between state and market 140–60; authoritarian socio-political configurations 140, 141, 143, 144, 145, 147, 148, 159; autonomization, process of 140–41; book market, industrialization of 150; book market, liberalization of 142; *Cahier noir* (Mauriac, F.) 147; censorship, repression and 141–43; Centre National des Lettres (CNL) 158–59; communist regimes 144; copyright law 156–57; creativity, support for 157–59; criticism and cultural journalism as intermediaries 154–56; cultural journalism, role of 154–56; cultural policy 156–59; Fascist National Institute of Culture 143; freedom of publishing, principle of 142–43; *L'Honneur des poètes* (Éditions de Minuit) 147, 160n4; ideological control, economic regulation and 141–48; ideological control, professional organization as instrument of 143–44; industrial literature 149; liberal-democratic configurations 160; literary prizes 150; literary property, principle of 157; market, law of 148–56; names and naming, value of 152–54; national literary fields 140–41; Nazi regime 143–44; *La Peste* (Camus, A.) 147; professional deontology, writing practices and 146–48; professional organization as instrument of ideological control 143–44; profit (short-term) vs investment (long-term) 149–52; proper name, value of 152–54; *Le Puits des miracles* (Chamson, A.) 147; resistance to political constraint, strategies of 145–46; revolutionary romanticism 144; *The Silence of the Sea* (Vercors) 147; socialist realism 144; ultra-liberal

position: effects on teachers' judgement
123; homologies of 13, 14–15, 16;
position-taking and 10–16, 128–35,
135–36
positions: reconstitution of structure of
21
possibility, social conditions of 183
postcolonial age, theory of fields in
257–69; ambivalence, valorization of
265; anthropological perspective
260–61; capital, modes of conversion
of 266; coevalness, denial of 260;
colonial situation 264; cross-
comparison of differentiation 263–64;
cultural capital 263; cultural market,
unification of 262–65; differentiated
and non-differentiated societies,
distinction between 258, 259–60,
261–62; *Distinction* (Bourdieu, P.)
266; economic market, unification of
265–67; epistemic violence 257, 258;
Euro-African Association for the
Anthropology of Social Change and
Development (APAD) 263; extension
of field theory 262–69; globalization
267–69; international institutions, role
of 268–69; intra- and inter-individual
dispositional differences 264; localism,
Bourdieu's theory of fields and 269;
The Logic of Practice (Bourdieu, P.)
266; 'The Modes of Domination'
(Bourdieu, P.) 259; *Outline of a
Theory of Practice* (Bourdieu, P.) 266;
Pascalian Meditations (Bourdieu, P.)
258–59, 266; *Practical Reason: On the
Theory of Action* (Bourdieu, P.) 257;
pre-comprehension, judgement and
257–58; precapitalist societies 265–66;
precolonial African societies 261;
Programme for International Student
Assessment (PISA) 268;
provincialization of Western
differentiation 260–62; *Provincializing
Europe. Postcolonial Thought and
Historical Difference* (Chakrabarty,
D.) 257; *The Rift* (Mudimbe, V.) 264;
social differentiation, perception of
261; social differentiation, theory of
fields and 258–60; social world,
organization and functioning of
266–67; societies, interconnectedness
of 268; societies, variations within
264–65; sub-Saharan Africa 263;
traditional societies, non-

differentiation in 260; traditional
societies, oral traditions in 261
posterity, judgement of 176
Poulantzas, N. 207
Pourtois, J.-P. *et al.* 136n1
poverty: punitive politics of 253–54;
regulation via public assistance 239
power: Bourdieu and emergence of field
of 67–68; dimensions of field of
power, relative autonomy and 195;
dynamics of transformation on field
of 123, 135; field of, functional
differentiation and cultural
fragmentation in 186–87; field of
power and relation to specific fields
8–10; field of power as site of
struggles between holders of powers
185, 194–95; influence and, accrual
within organizations 221;
organizational power, forms of
223–33, 234; separation of powers in
contemporary liberal democracies
214; social and symbolic power,
sharing within fields 191–92
power, relative autonomy of social fields
and field of 183–96; alliances for
consolidation of autonomy 195–96;
autonomy of the field as central
theoretical issue 183–84; dimensions
of field of power, relative autonomy
and 195; field of power as site of
struggles between holders of powers
185, 194–95; functional differentiation
and cultural fragmentation in
Belgium 186–94; multi-dimensionality
of power and field theory 194–96;
plurality of lines of division within
field of power 195; possibility, social
conditions of 183; power field as site
of struggles between holders of
powers 185, 194–95; relative
autonomy 183, 184, 185, 186, 189,
194–95; *see also* Belgium, functional
differentiation and cultural
fragmentation in
*Practical Reason: On the Theory of
Action* (Bourdieu, P.) 257
pre-comprehension, judgement and
257–58
precapitalist societies 265–66
precolonial African societies 261
Prévert, Jacques 131
primate behaviour, phenomenology of
45